Ancient Egypt

Art & Magic

Dr Bob Bianchi

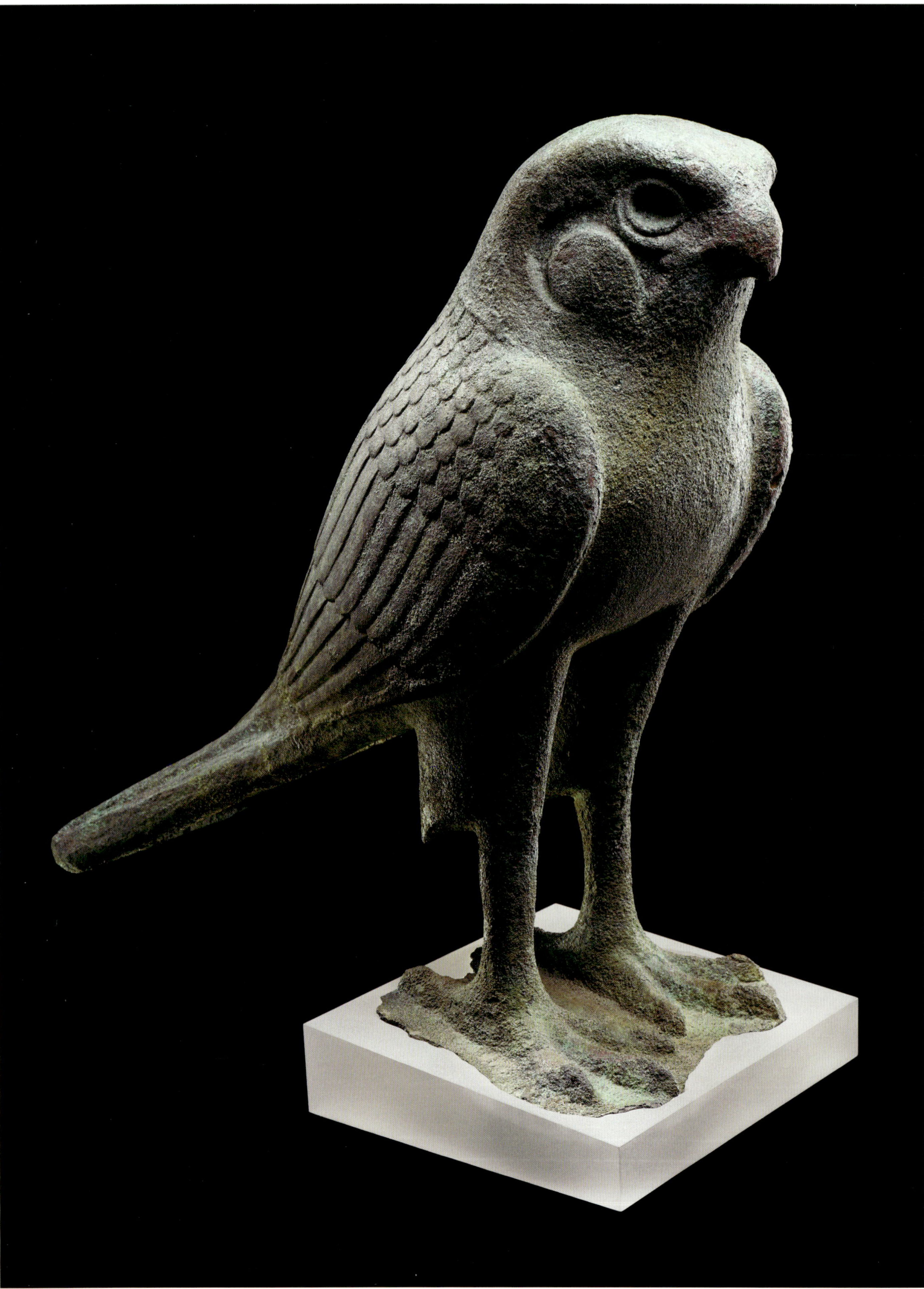

Ancient Egypt

Art & Magic

Treasures from the Fondation Gandur pour l'Art

Robert Steven Bianchi

Museum of Fine Arts
St. Petersburg, Florida

Published on the occasion of the exhibition
Ancient Egypt – Art and Magic: Treasures from the Fondation Gandur pour l'Art

Organized by the
Museum of Fine Arts, St. Petersburg, Florida
17 December, 2011, to 29 April, 2012

Printed in the United States of America

Museum of Fine Arts
255 Beach Drive N.E.
St. Petersburg, Florida 33701

ISBN: 1-878390-10-4

Coordination for the catalogue: Jennifer Hardin
Design and production: Voshardt/Humphrey, New York
Editor: Judith Hanson, New York
Printing: Shapco, Minneapolis

Front Cover:
Lid of an Anthropoid Sarcophagus Inscribed for Hor-em-akhet
Dynasty XXI–XXV, 1080–655 BC
Wood with inlays of white stone (alabaster or limestone) and blue glass

Frontispiece:
The God Horus as a Falcon
Dynasty XXI–XXV, 1080–655 BC
Bronze, originally with inlaid eyes

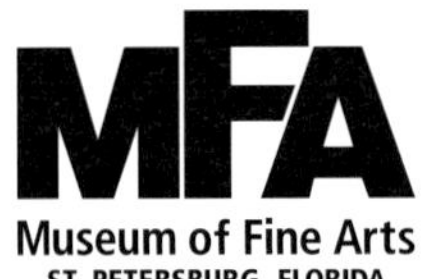

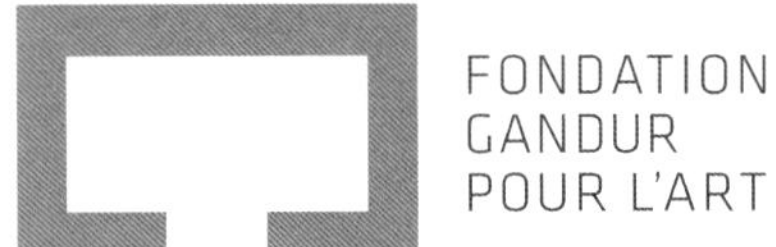

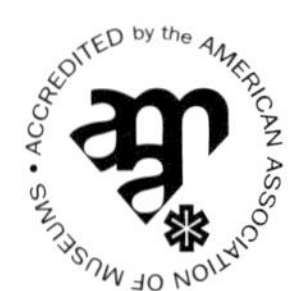

The Museum of Fine Arts, St. Petersburg, Florida, is fully accredited by the American Association of Museums.
The Museum of Fine Arts, St. Petersburg receives funding from the State of Florida, Department of State, Division of Cultural Affairs, and the Florida Council on Arts and Culture and the City of St. Petersburg.

Table of Contents

Foreword & Acknowledgements

Ancient Egypt has unrivaled power to stir the imagination. The Great Pyramids—architectural triumph of the early pharaohs—are as astonishing now as when first created; artistic works in every media inspire and instruct as they did in ancient times; and the amazing continuity of ancient Egypt's cultural achievement over three millennia is as immutable as the ever-flowing Nile. This exhibition, *Ancient Egypt—Art and Magic: Treasures from the Fondation Gandur pour l'Art*, explores an important theme in this grand civilization's art—the links between materials, artistic skill, and belief that informed Egyptian practice. Magic is indeed a key evocative term, because for the Egyptians art transformed and ordered the cosmos so as to assure the ordered continuity of the natural and human worlds.

Ancient Egypt—Art and Magic is the first major exhibition of ancient Egyptian art held at the Museum of Fine Arts in St. Petersburg, Florida. With 101 artworks dating from the pre-Dynastic era to the Ptolemaic periods, the essential media in which the Egyptians worked are represented—stone, bronze, gold, wood, papyrus, pigment, and encaustic. As the exhibition's curator Robert Steven Bianchi thoughtfully explains, each material conveys a variety of meanings associated with life and the afterlife of Egypt's elite, as well as with their cosmology. These objects were thought to possess transformative powers.

We would like to express our most sincere thanks and gratitude to the collector Monsieur Jean Claude Gandur, founder and President of the Fondation Gandur pour l'Art, Geneva, Switzerland, for agreeing to share these compelling treasures from his world-class collection. We would also like to thank the whole team of the Fondation Gandur pour l'Art for their assistance. The majority of objects in this striking exhibition have never been exhibited in the United States, so their presentation is a landmark event.

We also wish to thank the exhibition's curator and the catalogue's author, renowned Egyptologist Dr. Robert Steven Bianchi, who insightfully illuminates the exhibition's themes in the subsequent essay and diligently addresses each artwork in the catalogue entries that follow. Based in the Tampa Bay area, Dr. Bianchi has had a long-term collegial relationship with the Museum and has been an invaluable advisor to the Museum's own ancient collection. We are deeply indebted to him for helping us to bring the most important works from the Fondation's collection to our community. We also thank the Museum's Chief Curator Jennifer Hardin, who initially discussed with Dr. Bianchi such an exhibition, and the Museum's Director Emeritus Dr. John E. Schloder, who supported the project in its early stages and visited the Fondation's Collection in Geneva with Jennifer Hardin.

The exhibition would not have been possible without our major sponsors, Progress Energy and The Margaret Acheson Stuart Society of the Museum of Fine Arts, as well as the many corporate and individual donors who made this project possible: The Focardi Family, Hennessy Construction Services, the State of Florida, *St. Petersburg Times*, Bright House Networks, Renaissance Vinoy Resort & Golf Club, the Damkoehler Family Foundation, Mr. Donald and Mrs. Ruth Campagna, Mr. Eugene and Mrs. Julia Sorbo, Mrs. Jean Giles Wittner, Mrs. Diane H. Fair, Franklin Templeton Investments, Maurice A. and Thelma P. Rothman Family Foundation, SunTrust, Bank of America, Mr. William R. and Mrs. Hazel Hough, and Mrs. Barbara Godfrey Smith. This handsome catalogue, which remains with us long after the exhibition is completed, has been produced in part through the generosity of the following individuals: Arlene Fillinger Rothman, Mrs. Mary L. Shuh, Mrs. Carol A. Upham, Director Emeritus Dr. John E. Schloder, and Ms. Aila Erman/McEwen Trust.

We are also grateful to all the Trustees and volunteers at the Museum of Fine Arts, and members of the Museum's staff, especially Jennifer Hardin and former Curatorial Assistant Robin O'Dell. Jordana Weiss, Timothy Welsh, and Heather Rush contributed substantively to the process of producing the exhibition's catalogue. This publication was industriously edited by Judith Hanson and superbly designed by Voshardt /Humphrey, both of New York. Staff members Thaddeus Root, Louise Reeves, Thomas U. Gessler, David Connelly, Sabrina Hughes, Anna Glenn, Judy Whitney, Roger Zeh, Mary Szaroleta, Allison Canfield, and Vicki Sofranko labored intensely to make this exhibition, its educational programs, and special events a success in every way.

It is a great privilege to be the only North American venue for this exhibition of ancient Egyptian artifacts from the Fondation Gandur pour l'Art. The residents and visitors to St. Petersburg and every community in the Tampa Bay area will benefit from this important project, which contributes so much to scholarly and popular knowledge of Egyptian antiquity and its enduring magic.

KENT LYDECKER
DIRECTOR
MUSEUM OF FINE ARTS
ST. PETERSBURG, FLORIDA

Preface

From my earliest childhood, I have always been fascinated by the allure of Egypt. It is an enchanted land, anciently animated by the pulsating rhythms of the rising and setting sun, the waxing and waning of the moon, and the annual inundation of the River Nile.

These recurring cosmic cycles played on the imagination of anonymous theologians of the remote past and formed the unmovable foundations of a religion that was to last for millennia. The beasts of the farm and wilderness, the plants of the garden and marsh, the minerals of the desert and mountain were also incorporated into that elaborate theological system from which the deities of the land were to emerge. Those deities, whose number is infinite, were each associated with an animal, a plant, a mineral, and each were possessed of symbolic characteristics and represented almost invariably on walls of tombs and temples from Aswan to Alexandria for over four millennia.

All foreign conquerers from the Assyrian kings to Roman Emperors who came into contact with this civilization of the Nile were overwhelmed by what they found there. So powerful was the attraction of this civilization that even after its fall when the last hieroglyphs were carved into a wall on the Temple of Philae the land of the pharaohs continued and continues to inspire painters, sculptors, architects, poets, playwrights, novelists, composers, choreographers, actors and actresses.

I share their passion for ancient Egypt, and like those individuals desire to share my passion with a wider audience. I do so by collecting, continuing the example set by my grandfather and father. I do, however, insist that my collection represents aesthetically and technically accomplished works of art, which present ancient Egypt in its best light so that these works may become outstanding ambassadors in public programs aimed at students and adults alike. It gives me great personal pleasure, therefore, to present a part of my collection as a special loan exhibition to the Museum of Fine Arts in St. Petersburg, Florida, with its insistence on promoting fine art in all of its manifestations and its track record for outstanding public programming. I thank Kent Lydecker, the Museum's Director, and his staff and recognize how they have worked in a spirit of friendly academic cooperation the Foundation. A very special thank you goes to Professor Doctor Bianchi. This exhibition would not have been possible without his dedication and his personal involvement contributing to this great success.

JEAN CLAUDE GANDUR
PRESIDENT
GANDUR FONDATION POUR L'ART

Author's Preface

As one involved in Egyptology, I am constantly bombarded with questions from family, friends, and neighbors about the mysteries of ancient Egypt, born of a popularization of the subject that has spawned schools of mysticism. I have attempted to refute such ideas by maintaining that ancient Egyptian culture was indeed permeated by magic, but it was magic of a particular kind. An examination of ancient Egyptian magic demonstrates that the truth of the matter is stranger and more wonderful than the fictions presented to the general public by those proponents. It is that subject that is the focus of both this exhibition and its accompanying catalogue. Both are attempts to come to grips with the essence of ancient Egyptian culture, a culture that respected nature and regarded human beings as part of a larger environment, in which people, animals, and plants were of equal value. I think that the ancient Egyptians would wholeheartedly embrace Green initiatives aimed at protecting the ecosystem and the delicate balance of flora and fauna within it.

Because of my narrow focus, I have avoided jargon and art historical exegesis in which the dating of an object becomes the primary objective. I am of the firm conviction that currently applied methods aimed at placing objects in a timeline by the application of stylistic criteria developed for Western art history and criticism are woefully inadequate when it comes to ancient Egyptian art. It is for this reason that I pay little attention to dating for its own sake. I should also point out that there is a crisis of chronology in the field of Egyptology, because the discipline as a whole, while embracing a relative chronology, disagrees on its details. The majority of dates found in this catalogue are, therefore, only approximate, but they are internally consistent. Recourse to other academic works will doubtless result in slightly different dates because there is, currently, no *consensus omnium*. It is only with the inauguration in 664 BC of Dynasty XXVI, the Saite Period, that dating become more absolute because of synchronisms with contemporary cultures. Earlier dates are, therefore, relative and in dispute.

I have proceeded from two assumptions to which I strictly adhered. The first is that ancient Egyptian art is hieroglyphic. By understanding the nature of the hieroglyphs and how they were designed, one gains an enhanced appreciation of ancient Egyptian art. The second premise is that ancient Egyptian art was created in institutionally affiliated craft ateliers under the direction of literate, elite foremen in concert with the pharaoh, so that the non-elite craftsmen actually manipulating their chosen medium were not given artistic license. These works of art were created by and for an elite whose number was never more than ten percent of the total population. Within this strict adherence, I purposefully avoid reference to the remaining ninety percent of the population.

My chosen approach has two advantages. It replaces the Western, Eurocentric method applied to the art history and appreciation of ancient Egyptian art with a system that is hieroglyphically based. I attempt to demonstrate the religious basis underlying the procurement of raw material and in so doing suggest how these materials and their colors were anciently possessed of a polyvalent, multifaceted significance, both magical and symbolic, which extended and reinforced the function to which any given object was put. The symbolism of color and material is profound and possessed of nuanced, often antithetical meanings. These are so skillfully integrated into a religious-philosophical system that easily accepts seeming contradictions and inconsistencies.

I am, understandably, indebted to several individuals. I acknowledge Monsieur F. Antonovich for having introduced me to Monsieur Jean Claude Gandur, with whom I have been associated for over a decade. Madame Isabelle Borel has unfailingly been of enormous administrative support. Jean-Luc Chappaz has steadfastly and generously offered his opinions about the inscriptions on several of the objects in this exhibition. Discussion with Susanne Moser has proved most beneficial with regard to catalogue no. 101 (Lid of an Anthropoid Sarcophagus Inscribed for Hor-em-akhet). I appreciate the understanding of my wife, Anna, who has had to deal with my extended absences abroad. The visit of the Museum of Fine Arts' Chief Curator, Jennifer Hardin, to our home when we first moved to the Tampa Bay area fostered our commitment to the Museum of Fine Arts, an association that continues to grow, as the premiere of this exhibition at that institution reveals.

The exhibition and this catalogue were labor-intensive efforts. The ability to work long-distance was vital; the February 2011 Revolution in Egypt, which saw me confined to my flat in Alexandria and eventually airlifted to Greece, may have resulted in a delay if not for the willingness of my colleagues in Geneva to assist in every way. I wish, therefore, to thank in particular Véronique Pittori and Rebecca Lubicz for scanning and transmitting documents to me. I recognize the efforts of Jacques Besson who, whenever I was in Geneva, served as an able preparator, making objects available for study, and cheerfully shuttling me back and forth between venues and appointments. I wish to thank Sandra Pointet for her photographs of the objects in the exhibition; Janet Jarret for her line drawings of the situla (cat. 16); and Darwin Media Ltd. for the photograph of Rameses II (cat. 28).

Kent Lydecker, the Director of the Museum of Fine Arts, and his staff were no less cooperative. I recognize former staff member Robin O'Dell's support as well as that of Interim Curatorial Assistant Timothy Welsh. I also appreciate the friendly assistance and cooperation of Louise Reeves, Jordana Weiss, Thaddeus Root, and Thomas Gessler. I wish to thank Judith Hanson for her copyediting of the manuscript, which improved its readability.

I acknowledge Thierry Benderitter, both Edward Bleiberg and Ruth Jansen of the Brooklyn Museum, Tadashi Kikugawa of the Ancient Egyptian Museum/Shibuya; both Katja Lembke and Barbara Magen of the Pelizaeus Museum/Hildesheim; Barbara and Jack Mansfield; Christopher Naunton of Egypt Exploration Society/London; David Pierce, and Roxanne Sanders Wilson for their invaluable assistance in providing many of the illustrations that appear in this catalogue. Last, but not least, I must express my indebtedness to Linda Feinstone of Archaeological Tours, New York, who has extended to me the unprecedented opportunity of visiting Egypt time and again. The resulting familiarity gained about that land, its monuments, museums, and people informs this essay in a myriad of ways.

Robert Steven Bianchi

For my parents,

Robert and Bessie Bianchi,

who instilled in me a love of learning

and nurtured my passion for art

Art & Magic in Ancient Egypt

Treasures from the Fondation Gandur pour l'Art

By Robert Steven Bianchi

There is something magically attractive and mysterious about ancient Egyptian art. One of the principal objectives of this exhibition is, naturally enough, an exploration of that magic and mystery. Ancient Egyptian art was created by and for an elite, one that represented but a fraction of the entire population. That art was created in institutionally affiliated ateliers, or workshops, attached either to royal palaces or located in major temple complexes. The non-elite artisans in those ateliers were under the immediate control of elite foremen who were responsible for designing the works of art and guiding the processes by which that art was fashioned. Those foremen were ultimately accountable to the pharaoh. Working under the direction of foremen, the artisans, those individuals actually manipulating their chosen medium, were denied artistic license. They were obliged to follow a prescribed program from which they could not deviate. It is for this reason that Egyptian art presents a seemingly uniform appearance for the entire four millennia of its existence.

This is the story of that art, with an emphasis on its magical, symbolic characteristics. But it is also about how to look at Egyptian art with a view toward understanding the design principles that contribute to its meaning and significance. The wonderful works of art on view in this exhibition, as beautiful and aesthetically pleasing as indeed they are, were intended to function in a specific manner in order to be placed into the service of the elite members of society for whom they were created.

The story is introduced by this Egyptian elite, of whom the pharaoh was a member. Within the social structure of ancient Egypt, a distinction is maintained between the pharaoh and the rest of the elite. At no time during the history of pharaonic Egypt, according to reliable estimates, did that elite number more than ten percent of the population. In order to gain an appreciation of that statistic, consider for a moment that there are approximately one thousand known, numbered tombs inscribed for members of the elite who lived during Dynasties IV–VI of the Old Kingdom, when pyramid-building was at its height. The period during which these inscribed, private tombs were erected spans approximately 430 years. By means of simple division, one calculates that approximately ten tombs per year were built. Taking into account an average lifespan of thirty to forty-five years for an individual living at that time, one suggests that the total tomb-owning population at any one time numbered about 150 individuals.

There is a further dimension to these statistics. Studies in ancient Egyptian literacy suggest that only one percent of the entire population at that time was literate. Put into perspective, that number translates into one scribe, defined as an individual who could both read and write, for every twenty to thirty active male members of the elite. A ratio, we repeat, of a maximum of 1:30. Thus, during the Old Kingdom, one would encounter ten literate individuals for every mile-stretch of the Nile River from Aswan in the south to the shores of the Mediterranean Sea in the north. Viewed in contemporary terms, one would encounter approximately twenty-five literate individuals along the route linking Tropicana Field in St. Petersburg with Raymond James Stadium in Tampa. Although the population of ancient Egypt increased from an estimated total of about one million subjects during the Old Kingdom to about 4.5 million subjects around the time of Cleopatra the Great through the reign of the Caesars of the Roman Empire, the literacy rate did not increase exponentially. A generous estimate during this later period places the number of literate individuals at under 50,000.

We assume that the foremen were drawn from this small literate pool of one percent of the population. The artisans under their direction likely were not literate. Knowledge was, therefore, restricted, and its possession conveyed both power and authority. Pharaoh could be referred to as "the all-knowing." The literate foremen serving him simultaneously held other secular and clerical offices. They were scions of established families in which positions were inherited and passed on from one generation to the next, as ancient texts inform us:

> *[the one] who knows the secret which one does not see and*
> *which one does not hear which a father passes on to a son.*

Clearly, ancient Egyptian art, which we all admire, was not created for the non-elite members of ancient Egyptian society; it was created for a very small percentage of the population.

At some point near the end of the Neolithic Period, this emerging elite established a unique notational system now known as hieroglyphs, a modern English word derived from the ancient Greek phrase for "sacred carvings," so called because many of the inscriptions in hieroglyphs are found in tombs and temples. The name or names of the inventor of this writing system is not recorded, but ancient Egyptian tradition maintains that it was introduced by Thoth, god of writing and patron of scribes. His hypostasis, or alternate form, might be a baboon or an ibis. The divine origin of the hieroglyphs imbued them from their very first appearance with magical qualities.

Hieroglyphs are one of the most important foundations of ancient Egyptian civilization. An understanding of the nature of the hieroglyphs is, therefore, essential for a more complete understanding of ancient Egyptian art, because ancient Egyptian art is hieroglyphic.

Hieroglyphs, in the earlier periods numbering approximately one thousand of which only two to three hundred were commonly employed, are pictograms representing real objects encountered by the Egyptians in their environment. These include plants and animals, men and women, buildings and boats, often including their individual component parts, as well as celestial bodies such as the sun, the moon, and stars, and objects of daily life such as vessels, crowns, and staves. Each of these real, tangible objects is designed with the specific intention of representing it by the view that provides the greatest amount of visual information, so that even with a single fleeting glance the identification of the object depicted is crystal clear and not ambiguous. Accordingly, fish are represented in a side, or profile, view, because a fish regarded from the front, back, top, or bottom would appear as an indistinct sliver. Similarly, a turtle would be represented from the top, a view that includes its head, tail, and four legs all protruding from its shell.

Within this system, complex objects, such as the human figure, had to be deconstructed, so that each of its component parts might be designed to provide the most visual information necessary for its immediate and unambiguous comprehension. As a result, the human head was represented in profile, because the profile provides the most visual information about the appearance of an individual with regard to the shape of one's nose and mouth and still includes the eye. It is for this reason that images of rulers depicted on coins habitually rely upon the profile view. But the ancient Egyptian design tenets modified this view so that the eye was depicted frontally, in order that that element might be represented to fullest advantage. The human torso was shown

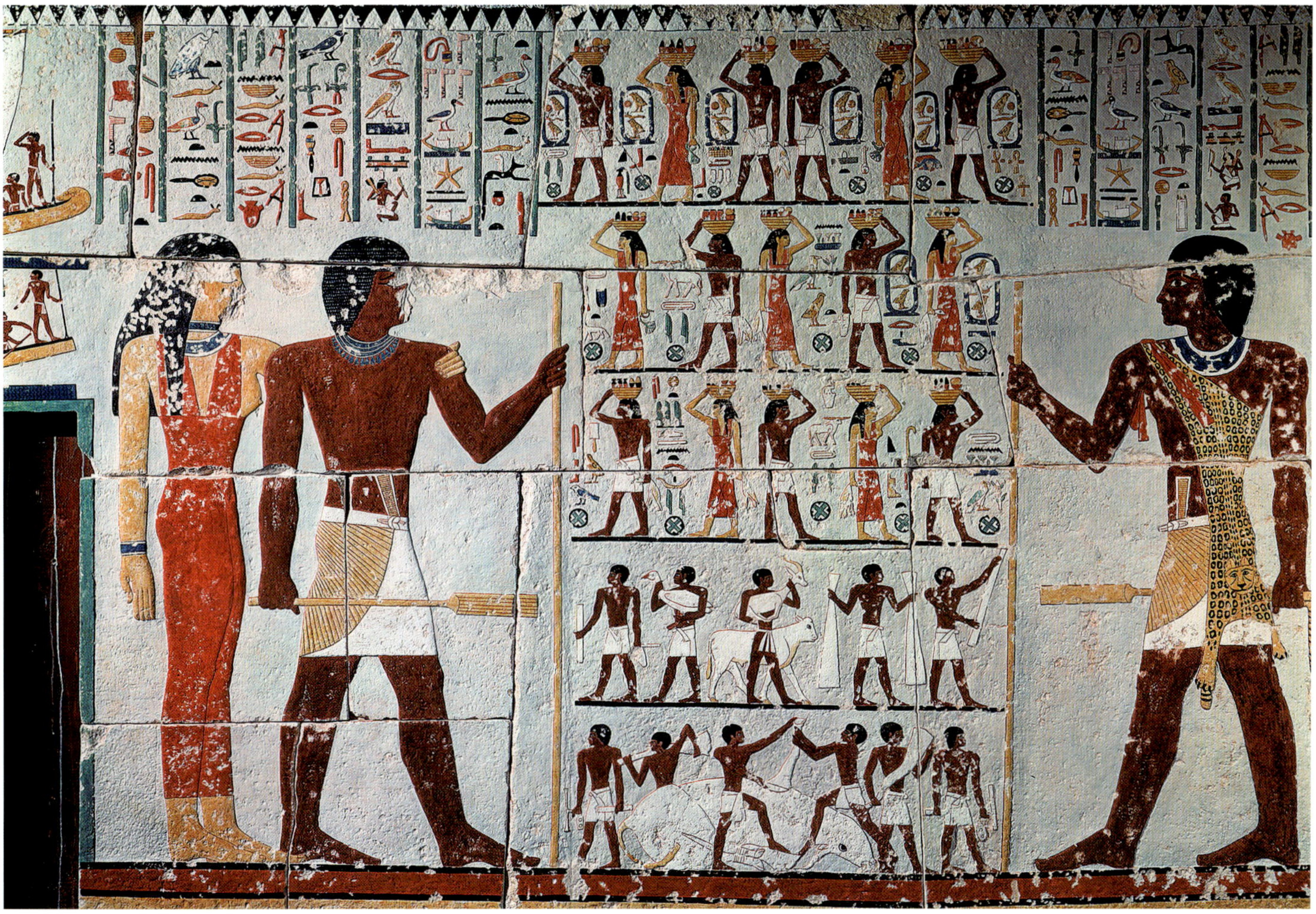

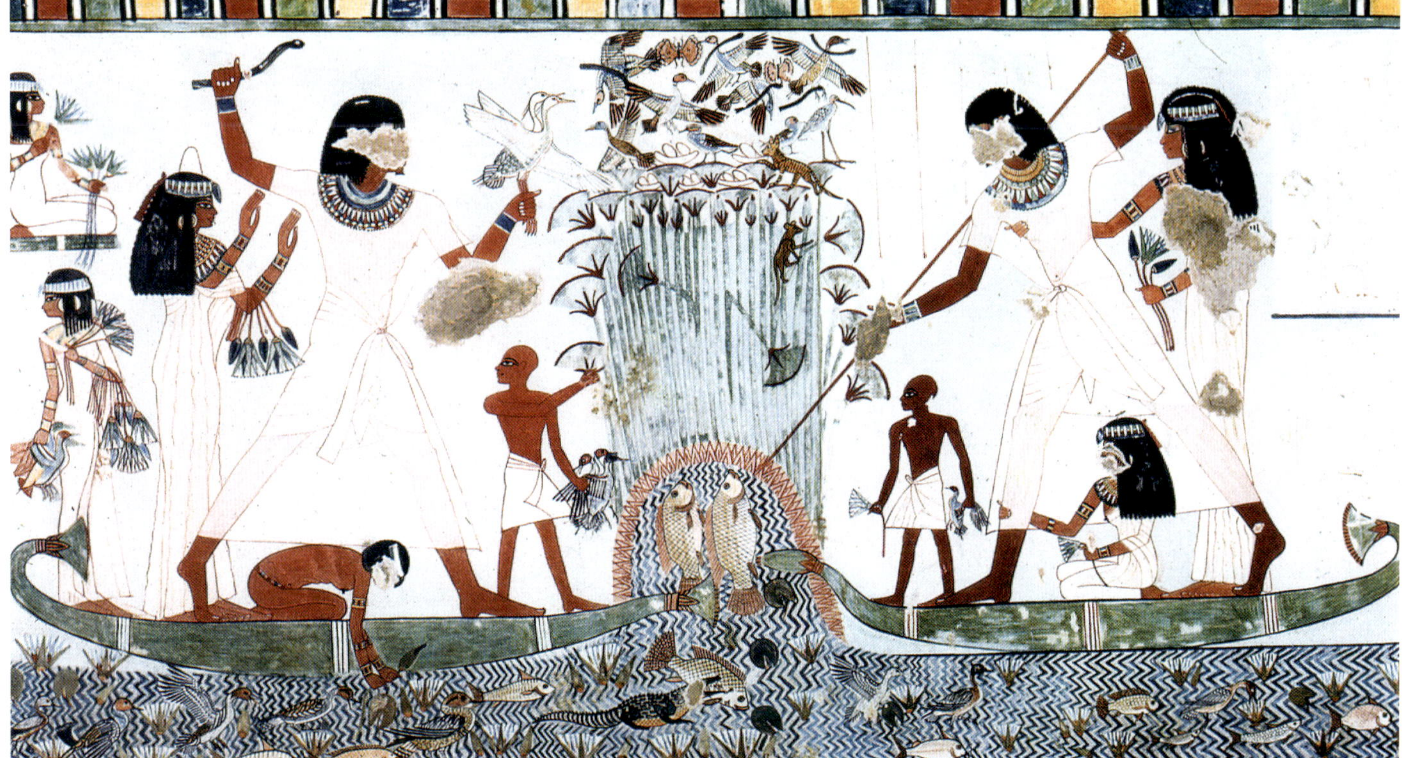

Figure 1 (above)
Detail of the West Wall of the Offering Chamber from the Tomb of Mer-ib (Egyptian Museum and Papyrus Collection, Berlin; 1107)

Figure 2 (below)
Detail of a scene of fishing and fowling in the marshes of the Nile River (Thebes, Tomb of Menna; Theban Tomb 69)

frontally, but the breast, both male and female, was depicted in profile. The arms were likewise in profile, with the five fingers of each hand clearly delineated. The legs, feet, and toes were depicted in profile view (fig. 1).

These component parts of the human body were then recombined to form the figure in such a way as to be parodied in the West by the "walk like an Egyptian" poses (fig. 3).

These figures, based on the very same artistic tenets used for the design of hieroglyphs, were created prior to the introduction and acceptance of those Western conventions of representation, and often with different goals. Attempts to interpret ancient Egyptian art by the application of Western art historical criteria are doomed to fail.

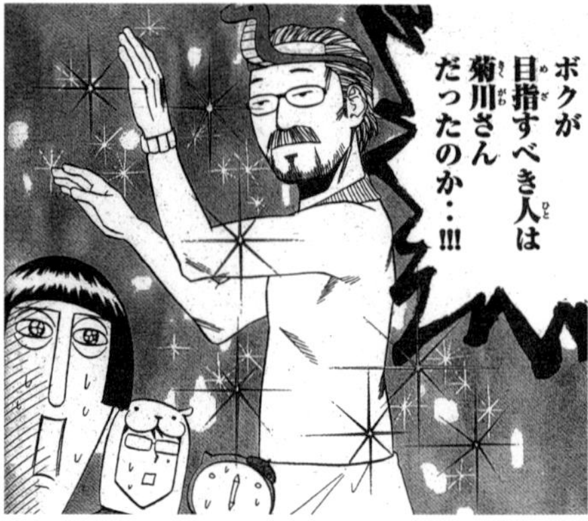

Figure 3
"Walking like an Egyptian,"
by the Japanese cartoonist Yuki Okada

The principal objective of the designers of hieroglyphs was visual clarity, not an illusion of reality. There is virtually no interest in generating illusions of the third dimension in the decoration of flat, two-dimensional surfaces in ancient Egyptian art. The design of each of these figures—fish, turtle, human being—was intentionally flat (fig. 2).

As flat representations designed with an emphasis upon visual clarity, these images are generic, not specific, and capture the essence of the object. This hieroglyphic insistence upon an object's essence is in part responsible for the general idealizing tendencies which most examples of the human figure in Egyptian art exhibit. In some ways, then, these hieroglyphs may be compared to the subject of one of Plato's dialogues, particularly that of shadows cast on the wall of a cave, in which he defines the purest form of any object as an abstract that cannot be cloned or replicated in the real world.

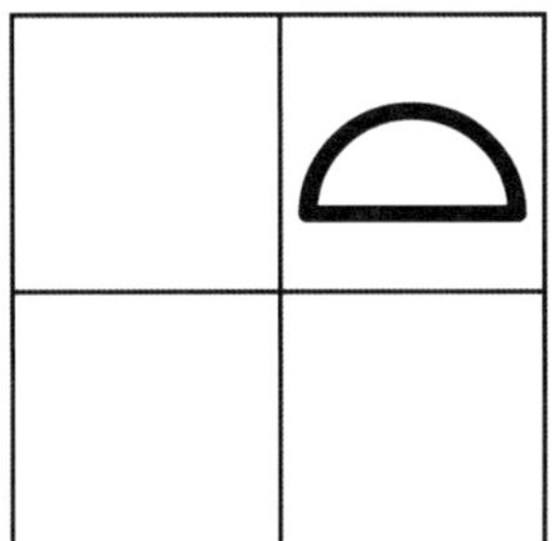
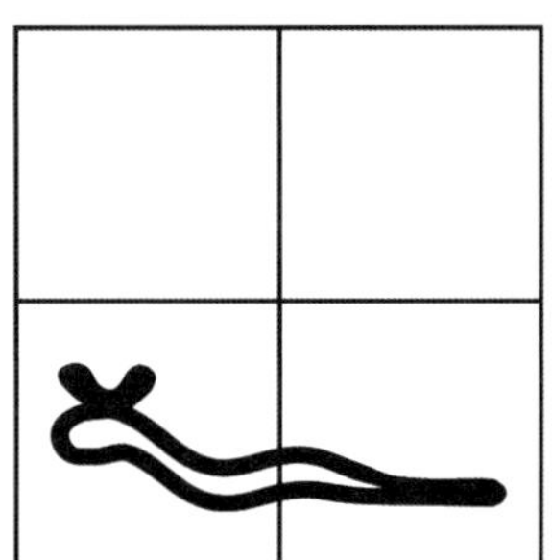
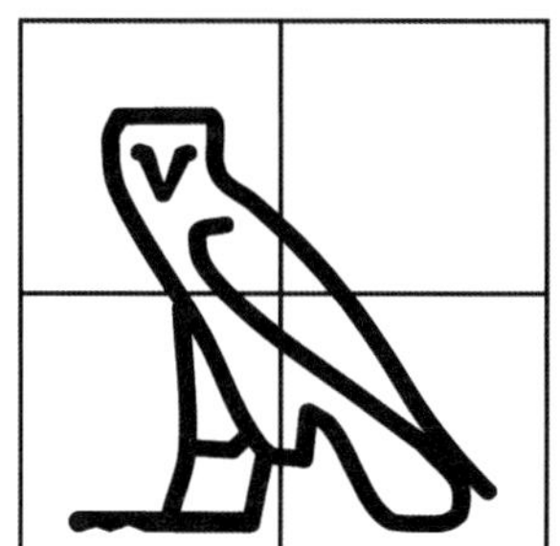

Figure 4
The design of three hieroglyphs according to a grid of four squares

The design of each of these hieroglyphs corresponds to its relation to a square divided into four quadrants. So, for example, a loaf of bread occupies only one quadrant. A horned viper, one of the most venomous serpents in the Egyptian environment, occupies two horizontal quadrants, whereas an owl occupies all four quadrants of the square (fig. 4).

Within such a system, the relative scale of one object to another is inconsequential, because the actual height of objects in the real world is ignored. The Egyptians employed this principle of scalar indifference to advantage by creating compositions in which larger and smaller figures could be combined in one and the same scene. Larger figures are symbolically imbued with greater significance than smaller figures, thus establishing a visual hierarchy. The bigger an object is, the more important it becomes.

The hieroglyphs so designed are then arranged in either rows or columns against neutral backgrounds. These generic, nonspecific representations of real objects encountered in the Egyptian environment, designed with an emphasis on visual clarity rather than as illusions of reality, are placed in atemporal, aspatial settings. The same principles of design governing the hieroglyphs are thus applied to the creation of ancient Egyptian art, as an examination of any two-dimensional work of art in this exhibition reveals.

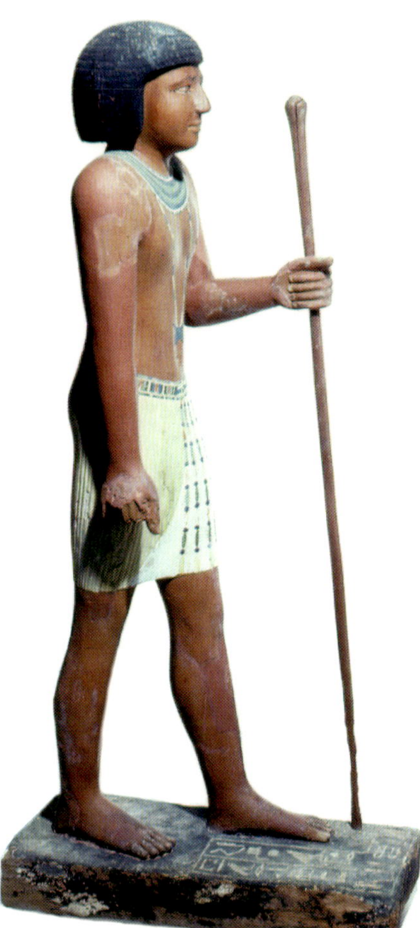

Figure 5
A statue of Methety
The Brooklyn Museum; 50.77

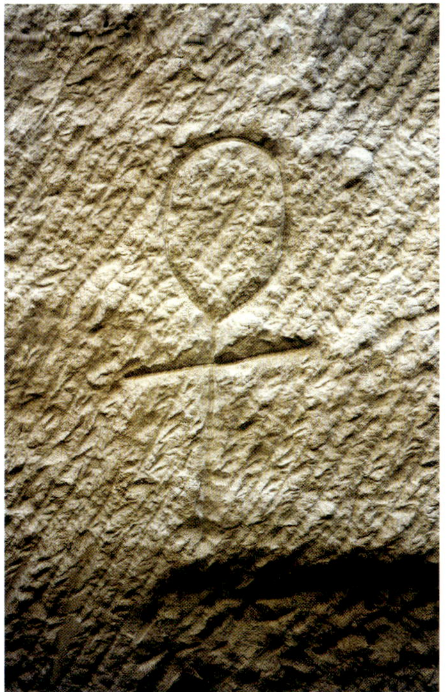

Figure 6
An ankh-sign carved into one of the faces of the sandstone quarry at Gebel el-Silsileh

Within this system, primacy of place was reserved for the left-hand side of any two-dimensional surface when viewed by a spectator. A human figure in that part of the composition, generally larger in scale than the rest, was regarded as the most significant. Such a figure, in the Old Kingdom for example, is usually the tomb owner, who is represented in a striding attitude, with the left leg advanced. When designing three-dimensional sculpture, therefore, these same design tenets were strictly observed, so that statues, as three-dimensional transformations of these hieroglyphic principles, generally exhibit an advanced left leg as well (fig. 5).

Hieroglyphs are generic representations of real, one might say concrete, tangible objects familiar to the ancient Egyptians. Assuredly, the members of the elite who designed this system were well aware of the fact that there are more, many more, abstract concepts in the minds of human beings than there are concrete objects in the world. As a result, they developed a very ingenious and sophisticated system of pressing representations of concrete objects into the service of expressing abstract concepts. One example will suffice. The ankh, or sign of life, is perhaps one of the most familiar of all hieroglyphs (fig. 6).

In reality, the ankh-sign is a sandal strap. It served double duty, conveying the meaning of the concrete object and that of a completely different abstraction. Within this system, puns and homonyms abound.

One marvels at the mental agility of these anonymous members of society who developed a notational system rooted in reality that nonetheless enabled them to express the most profound concepts of life and death. In so doing, these sophisticated intellectuals developed a philosophical exegesis in which natural phenomena might be substituted with one another in order to provide real-world parallels for those abstract ideas.

Annually, in August, the Nile River would flood, depositing a rich layer of silt from which the agricultural bounty of ancient Egypt would grow. The grains planted would sprout and, after harvesting, their seeds would become dormant until replanted the following season. The sun would rise at dawn and set at dusk. The moon would wax and wane. Women would become pregnant and, after term, deliver. Each of these readily observable, recurrent natural phenomena formed the basis of an interlocking network of explanations that might be extended to represent either concepts of cosmic creation or rebirth after death. Within such a system, any one phenomenon became imbued with polyvalence, or multiple meanings, in the same way a sandal strap was both a concrete object and an abstract idea. Such polyvalence is rooted in the hieroglyphs and embraces contradictions in a philosophical system that eschews Aristotelian categorization. The ancient Egyptian elite understood and accepted that Ptah at Memphis could be the supreme deity of the land, whereas simultaneously at Dendera she could be Hathor and, while at Thebes, Amun. On occasion the same deity might be invoked on the same monument in two different forms, as seen on catalogue no.16, where one encounters

> *Amun-re, the lord of the thrones of the Two Lands, the one who is foremost in Ipet-sut, the lord of heaven and earth*

> *Amun-re, who is foremost among his harem.*

The first depiction represents Amun-re as one might expect, wearing the two tall plumes that traditionally serve as his attribute. In the second, Amun-re, foremost among his harem, is ithyphallic and holds a flail, iconographic markers that suggest his association with Min, a fertility deity. Such associations are appropriate within the

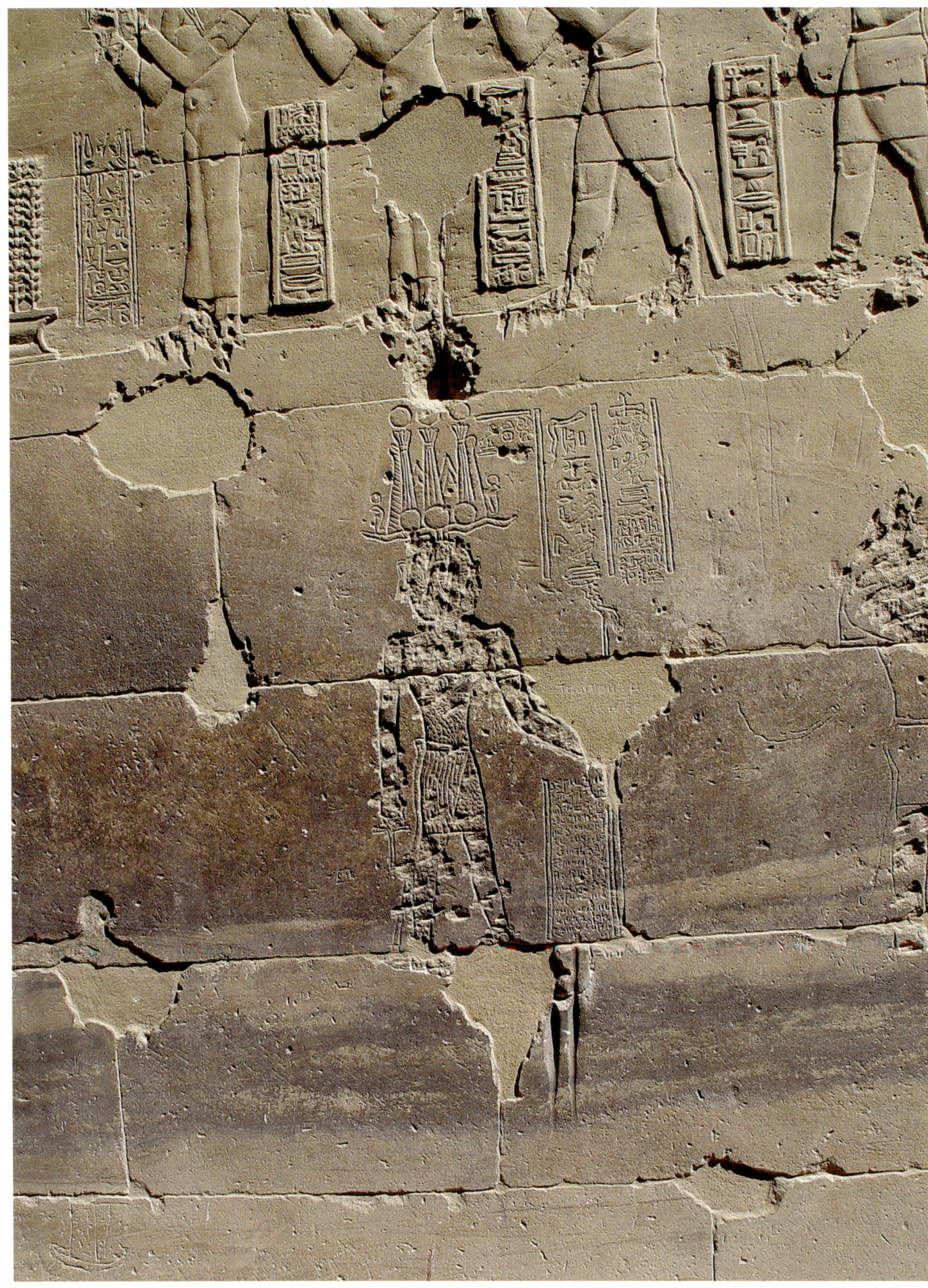

Figure 7
The last known dated hieroglyphic inscription from the Gateway of the Roman Emperor Hadrian at Philae

context of his harem. The ancient Egyptians routinely accepted such multiple associations, which might appear to be contradictory and, perhaps, utterly confusing.

The elite members of ancient Egyptian society who pioneered the development of the hieroglyphs were intellectuals, philosophers, theologians. Their system survived for millennia, until the last datable inscription, carved in the Gateway of the Roman Emperor Hadrian on the island of Philae some time afterward in AD 394 by a priest of Isis, perhaps to be identified as Esmet-akhom. Esmet-akhom is suggested to have been the last Egyptian individual who was conversant with that system (fig. 7).

With his death, the secret of the hieroglyphs also died, but not their memory, which was kept alive in the West by descriptions found in the works of authors writing in Greek, Latin, and Arabic. Those sources often allude to the magical aspect of Egyptian civilization. Although often garbled, they contain a kernel of truth, because the hieroglyphs themselves were magical, imbued by their creators with the potential to become animate. The individual hieroglyphs, and the objects created in accordance with their design tenets, could come to life by virtue of simply being represented (compare cat. 42) or by being pronounced. Ancient Egyptian tombs were habitually provided with a funerary prayer bestowing upon the deceased:

> *a thousand loaves of bread [and] a thousand jars of beer*

representing provisions necessary for sustaining life in the hereafter (compare cat. 1). The very depiction of these commodities was sufficient to ensure their availability. On those rare occasions in which the living could not provide additional supplies of bread and beer, the deceased, in inscriptions found within some tombs, would implore the living to recite the offering formula, termed *The Appeal to the Living* (compare cat. 4), in which these commodities were specified. This formula would be followed with the observation that no effort was required, because the recitation was simply one's breath. Used to pronounce these commodities, one's breath was sufficient for animating them. In like manner, one often finds this poignant imploration in tombs addressed to the living:

> *to pronounce my name so that I might live.*

One's name, written, and the pronunciation of that name were anciently regarded as means by which eternal life might be secured (compare cat. 12 and cat. 18).

There is another side to this potential animation, because some concrete objects in the real world, if animated, could harm or kill. A singular example of an attempt to nullify the potential danger posed by the animation of malevolent animals, whose appearance was necessary to write some words properly, is found in certain spells of The Pyramid Texts. These texts appeared during the late Old Kingdom within the pyramids of certain pharaohs and were related to their aspired resurrection. The spells containing individual hieroglyphs representing potentially dangerous creatures were purposely truncated or incomplete, so that when brought to life they would be incapacitated and rendered harmless. In like manner, the ears of the composite deity Seth (cat. 61) were intentionally mutilated in antiquity in order to nullify his malevolent aspects.

The suggested animation of a cippus (cat. 17) is perhaps one of the best examples of just how this process worked in the minds of the ancient Egyptians. The object is decorated with a relief of a nude youth in the midst of dangerous predators, but he remains unharmed. The back of the cippus is covered with magical spells in hieroglyphs. In order to activate the object, one could recite the prayers; one could pour a liquid, generally water, over the cippus, which would then be collected and drunk, with the belief that the water had become infused with the power inherent in the image and inscriptions; one could apply the cippus directly to a wound in order to effect the physical transference of curative powers of the cippus to the body; or one could simply kiss it. All of these methods harnessed the powers inherent in image and word for the benefit of its owner, and each method was judged just as efficacious as the other.

The members of the ancient Egyptian elite, that one percent of the population who were literate, were well aware of the hieroglyphic nature of ancient Egyptian art and of its magical potential to become animate. They worked in concert with the pharaoh to decide which materials were to be used for the creation of which object. These deliberations also specified the object's appearance, function, and meaning, which once established, became canonical, to be repeated with seemingly little or no variation. This process was not static, and over time successive generations of the elite and their pharaohs introduce new types of objects with their own appearances, functions, and meanings. Having thus decided upon the nature of any given object, the elite and the pharaoh created the cultural and societal norms that gave rise to the enlistment of a workforce for the procurement of raw materials and their transport, manufacture, and ultimate functioning as actual objects for their exclusive use. It is to these subjects that one now turns.

Until the Aswan High Dam became operative in 1971, Egypt was anciently a land renewed by the annual fructifying flood of the Nile River, which occurred in August and deposited a rich layer of silt on what was to become arable land. It was an environment characterized by a long and narrow fertile belt conforming to the flood plain of that river, bounded in the south, or Upper Egypt, by the steep hills into which the Nile had laboriously cut its channel over the course of millennia. The channel then spread out, fanlike, to form the Delta, or Lower Egypt, north of modern Cairo, through which the Nile's seven branches emptied into the Mediterranean Sea. The terms Upper and Lower Egypt orient one to the direction of the Nile's current, which flows from south to north, so that sailing upstream, against the current, brought one to destinations in Upper Egypt, while floating downstream enabled one to reach those in Lower Egypt.

This flood plain was the Black Land, so named because of the color of that rich layer of silt, still moist, when freshly deposited by the Nile River. It is here that the ancient Egyptians lived and worked. They regarded the Black Land as their universe, over which the pharaoh and the elite were expected to maintain cosmic, harmonious order.

This same ancient Egyptian worldview considered the desert, bordering the Black Land, as a place of chaos and disorder, teeming with demons and monsters, a place harboring every conceivable force of evil. To the Egyptians, the desert was the Red Land, so designated from its perceived color, a color, one might add, that in some contexts was imbued with malevolent connotations. As a result, they developed an inherent fear of what might lurk in the desert, and avoided it at all costs. This polarity between the Black Land of order and harmony and the Red Land of chaos and confusion was to inform the ancient Egyptian approach to the natural resources abounding in the Red Land.

In theory, at least, no ancient Egyptian could unilaterally travel to the Red Land to obtain stone and create a statue. Expeditions to quarry stone were ordered by the pharaoh. Members of these expeditions included priests who performed specific ceremonies before the quarries were opened and as they were being closed. Within this context, the procurement of stone, any stone, whether for architectural or sculptural use, was a religiously sanctioned activity, initiated by the pharaoh who was simultaneously the religious and secular head of state. The stone extracted was thought to be possessed of power, a numen, which could be controlled. A chunk of green feldspar in the Brooklyn Museum is inscribed with the name of the Kushite pharaoh Taharqa of Dynasty XXV and is tied with cords of wax, the knots of which are gilded (fig. 8).

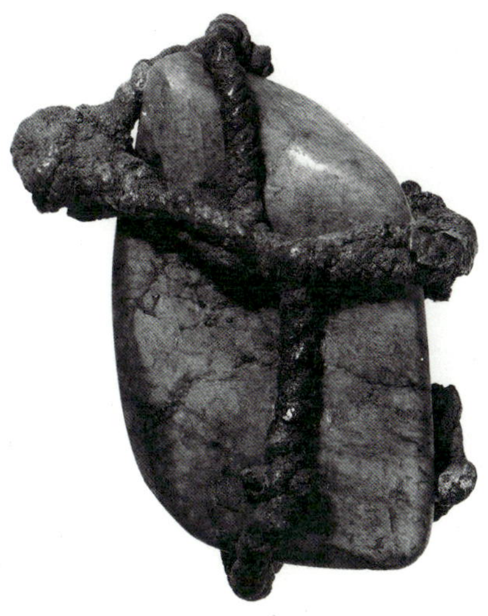

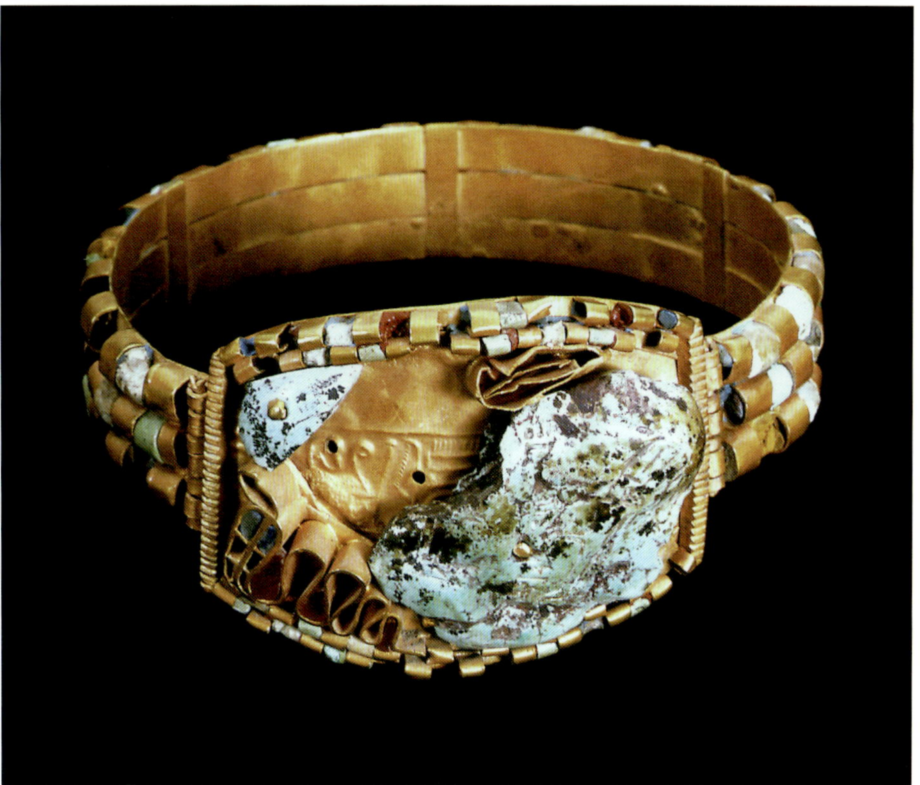

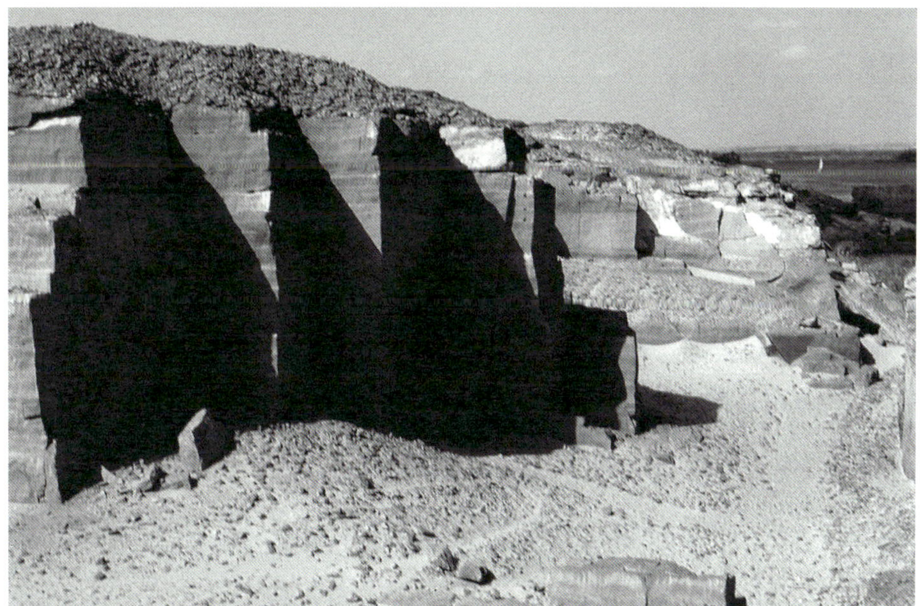

Shown clockwise:

Figure 8
A shackled piece of feldspar inscribed for pharaoh Taharqa
The Brooklyn Museum; 51.134

Figure 9
A bracelet incorporating into its design a piece of raw turquoise.
The Roemer- und Pelizaeus-Museum, Hildesheim, Germany; Leihgabe der Niedersächsischen Sparkassenstiftung

Figure 10
One of the quarry faces at Gebel el-Silsileh

The intention is clear—to shackle and, in so doing, harness the energy inherent in that stone. A bracelet in Hildesheim, Germany, incorporates into its design a piece of raw turquoise inscribed with the name of its owner and decorated with an image of the Amun-Min, an ithyphallic, syncretistic deity charged with cosmic creative powers which, it was thought, might be placed at the disposal of the bracelet's owner (fig. 9).

The rock-cut faces of the sandstone quarries at Gebel el-Silsileh, situated on the east bank of the Nile River on the route linking Thebes and Aswan, were apparently randomly incised with ankhs, or signs of life, underscoring the belief that the stone quarried there was animate (fig. 6 and fig. 10).

Those graffiti in turn relate to the most ancient architectural practice, first attested in Nubia and later adopted and modified by the Egyptians, of selecting specific cavelike

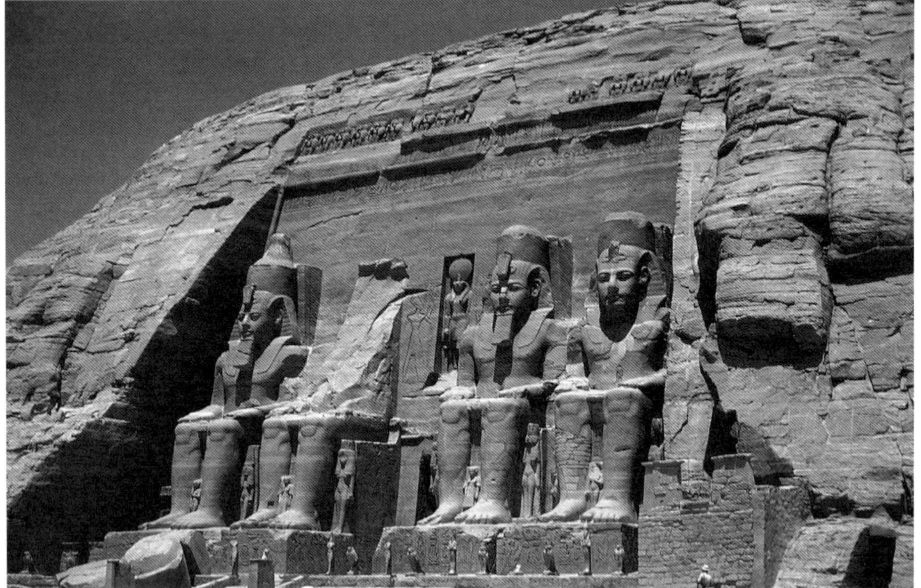

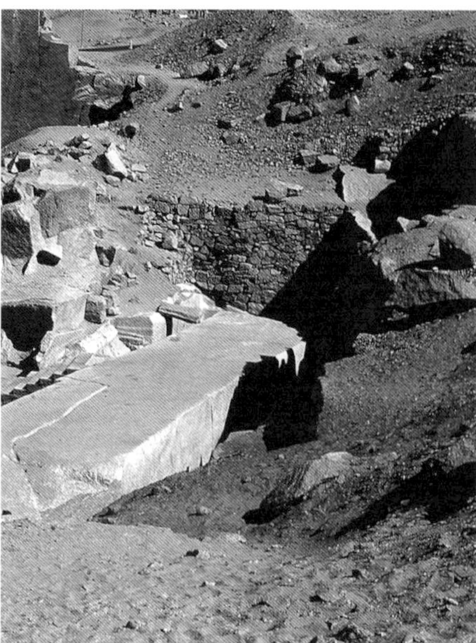

Figure 11
The Southern or Greater Temple at Abu Simbel

Figure 12
The top and one side of the unfinished obelisk still married to the bedrock in a quarry at Aswan

crevices as the site of the earliest documented shrines in the northeastern quadrant of the African continent. This development reached its culmination during the reign of Rameses II, who commissioned the two monumental, awe-inspiring rock-cut sanctuaries at Abu Simbel (fig. 11).

Here, according to some, the rays of the dawning sun would metaphorically strike his cult statue, sculpted in the living rock in the deepest part of this manmade, cavernlike edifice, triggering symbolic rebirth and the replication of divine creation.

The extraction of stone from these quarries appears to have been methodical and well planned. Some were exploited as open operations in which the stone was removed from the surface of the earth. One example of this method can be seen at the granite quarry at Aswan, where an unfinished obelisk lies still married to the bedrock from which it was never divorced (fig. 12).

In other quarries, the stone was extracted by following suitable veins or strata deep into the mountain side. During these quarrying operations the ancient Egyptians seem to have developed a certain respect for Mother Nature, as one realizes by examining the source quarry of the worked blocks for The Temple of Dendur (fig. 13).

That temple, originally erected in Lower Nubia to the south of Aswan during the reign of the Roman Emperor Augustus in the late first century BC, is now reerected in a splendid environment, complete with reflecting pool evocative of its original setting on the banks of the Nile, in the Sackler Wing of The Metropolitan Museum of Art in New York. It was given as a gift of gratitude by the people of Egypt to the citizens of the United States for their generous financial contributions toward the salvage operations that rescued the material culture of ancient Egypt and Nubia, which the waters rising behind the Aswan High Dam to form Lake Nasser might otherwise have obliterated.

The Temple of Dendur was erected from approximately 630 blocks of Aeolian, or wind-blown, sandstone extracted from a quarry not too far distant from the Temple's construction site. These worked blocks vary in color from rusty red to a mustard yellow, each color once clearly visible as separate layered strata in the quarry, now under the waters of Lake Nasser. On the basis of color, one can determine that the courses of stone in the Temple of Dendur respected the order in which those blocks had been found in nature. The lower courses of those worked blocks came from the lower strata of the Aeolian sandstone deposits in the quarry, the higher from the upper strata. In

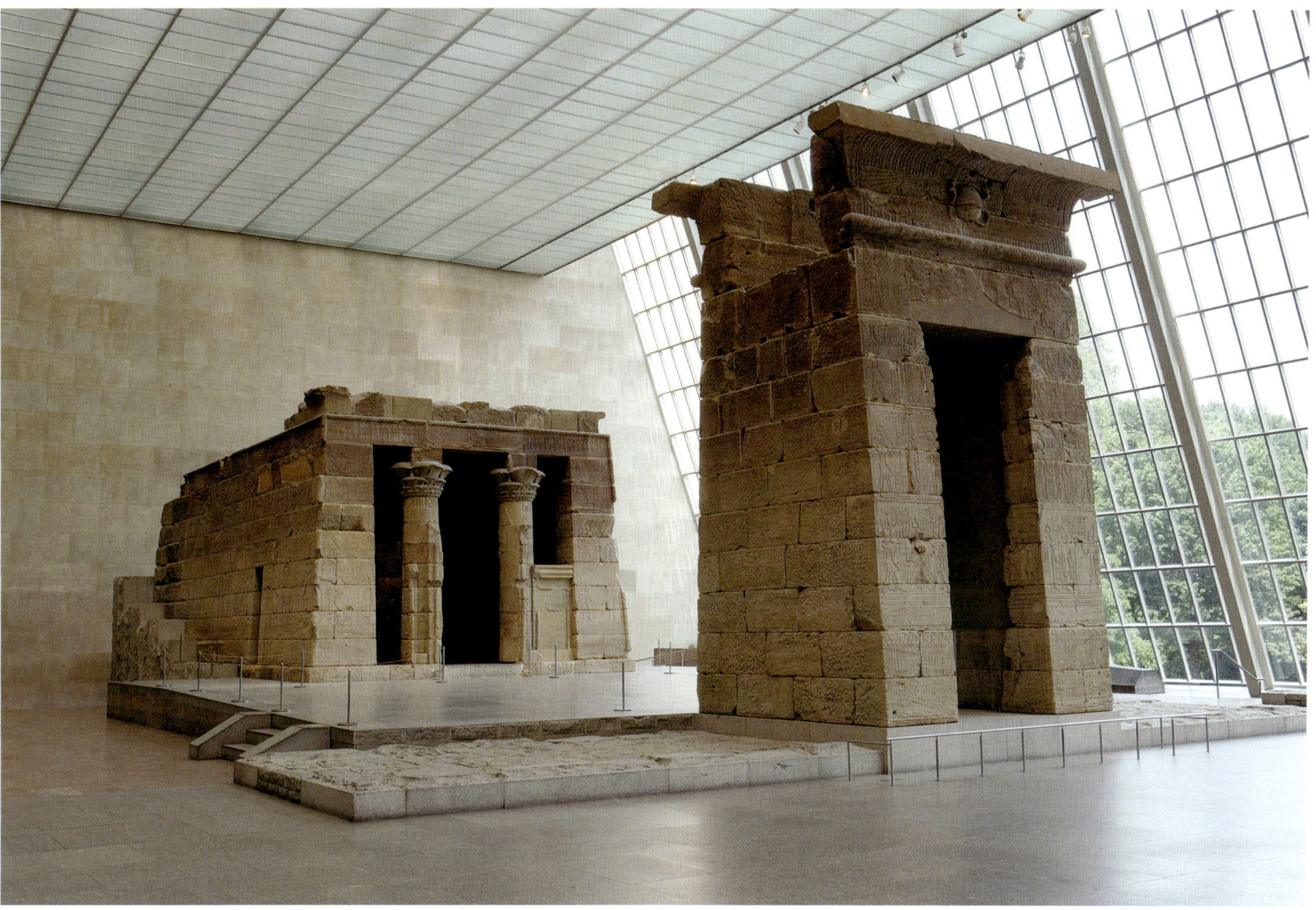

Figure 13
The Temple of Dendur reerected at the Metropolitan Museum of Art, New York.
Egyptian, Roman Period, 15 B.C.
Aeolian sandstone
Given to the United States by Egypt in 1965 and awarded to the Metropolitan Museum of Art in 1967; 68.154

other words, the worked blocks of stone used for the construction of the temple were laid in approximately the same order, bottom to top, as the strata had been laid by nature. This example is but one of many that can be adduced to demonstrate just how intricately connected the ancient Egyptians were to their environment, for which they exhibited great respect.

For the ancient Egyptians, stone was considered a privileged material that symbolized eternity, permanence, immutability, and incorruptibility. Its use imparted an independence from any temporal state. Any object created in stone or any text inscribed into stone remained intact and immune to the agents of time. Possessed of a vital energy, it was alive. All of these properties could be magically conveyed to the owner of monuments created in the material, so much so that in *The Book of Going Forth by Day* (more popularly called *The Book of the Dead*), the deceased aspired to be transformed into a type of stone that would not sink. It was magically thought to float, in a conceit that linked the immaterial nature of the deceased's spirit, one's most immaterial manifestation, with the vital eternal qualities inherent in stone. So central was stone in the creative processes of the ancient Egyptians that the drill used for hollowing out the interiors of stone vessels served as the hieroglyph for *hemit*, representing the concept of "craft" in general.

The natural formation of geological deposits favored the ancient Egyptians. Many of the semiprecious gemstones—carnelian, feldspar, jasper, amethyst, agate—utilized by their artisans were obtained from the Eastern Desert, that region lying between the Nile River and the Red Sea. Over the course of time, that part of the landscape was uplifted, with the result that deposits of these minerals were relatively closer to the surface than they would ordinarily have been. The operations ordered by the pharaoh to obtain these stones were religiously sanctioned and were intricately linked to

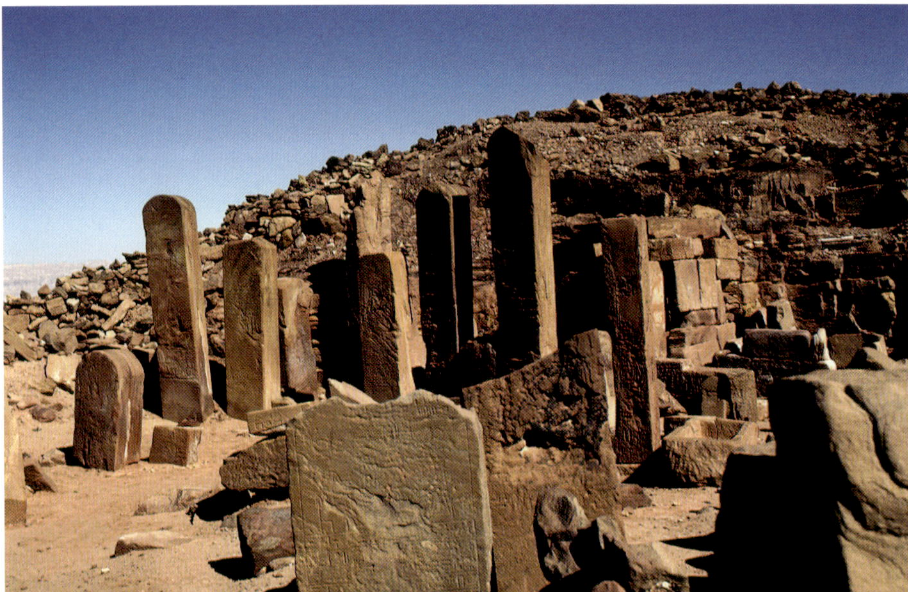

Figure 14
A view of the turquoise-rich region of Serabeit el-Khadim in the Sinai

the deities of the land. Their extraction from the landscape was regarded as part of a complex mythology. The religious dimension in the procurement of some of these raw materials is further emphasized by the observation that many of these semiprecious stones were mined by expeditions scheduled so that their importation into Egypt would coincide with the arrival of the New Year, celebrated in August, when the annual inundation of the Nile River began. The complexities of these associations are profound and are linked by connotative significances revolving around themes of cosmic renewal and containment of nefarious forces.

The example of the mining of turquoise in the Sinai reveals yet another aspect of these religious associations. Here, at the remote site of Serabeit el-Khadim (fig. 14), the dominant deity appears to be the goddess Hathor, among whose epithets is "The Mistress of Turquoise." Despite her seeming dominance, her cultic role here is that of an expediter, because turquoise belongs to the realm of Geb, an earth god who, as the first mythological sovereign on earth, was regarded as the incarnation of legitimacy. The exploitation of the mineral wealth was linked to the pharaoh's own legitimacy as the beneficiary of the mineral largess of Geb. As the recipient of that mineral wealth, the pharaoh was considered the successor of Geb.

A similar mythology developed around the mining of ores, particularly copper. In these operations, the principal deity was Sokar, himself a chthonic, or underworld, deity, associated at times with death and resurrection. As early as the Old Kingdom, Sokar was connected with metalsmiths. His festivals were linked to the processes of smelting ores, the individual episodes of which clearly parallel the stages of smelting metal, as seen in their depictions and accompanying inscriptions in the temple of Medinet Habu. One of that god's attributes was designed as a reed pipe, which served much like bellows. The participants might also wear garlands of onions worn around the neck as protective talismans and would sacrifice swine in the performance of the rituals.

Because of the polyvalent nature of ancient Egyptian philosophical discourse, the properties of mineral resources of the land could be equated with those of species of the floral kingdom. Marsh plants and stones might, accordingly, be periodically renewed according to the regenerative qualities of the annual flooding of the Nile River. In a sense, then, the mineral world of the desert became the analogue of the floral kingdoms of the Nile Valley. The ancient Egyptian version of the modern Periodic Table of Elements contained twenty-four absolute minerals. These were linked not only to their analogues in the floral kingdom but also to the dismembered body parts of Osiris. Re-membered by Isis, he became "mineralized," because his body parts, equated with the twenty-four elements, represented the sum total of the earth's mineral wealth. Thus, all of their powers were transferred to and harnessed by the resurrected Osiris.

All of these natural resources were themselves imbued with specific characteristics, characteristics that articulated and placed into sharper focus their underlying animate propensity, as an examination of faience reveals. Faience is a manmade material mainly composed of crushed quartz or sand with small amounts of lime into which either natron or plant ash is added. The copper component contributes to its predominant blue-green color. Its name, faience, is derived from the Italian city of Faenza, famed at one time as a principal center for the manufacture of a type of majolica, mostly turquoise blue-green in color. When Europeans first encountered this particular ancient Egyptian material, principally in the form of beads and amulets, they immediately associated it with that Italian ware and modified the name Faenza to refer to this ancient Egyptian material, by which it continues to be known.

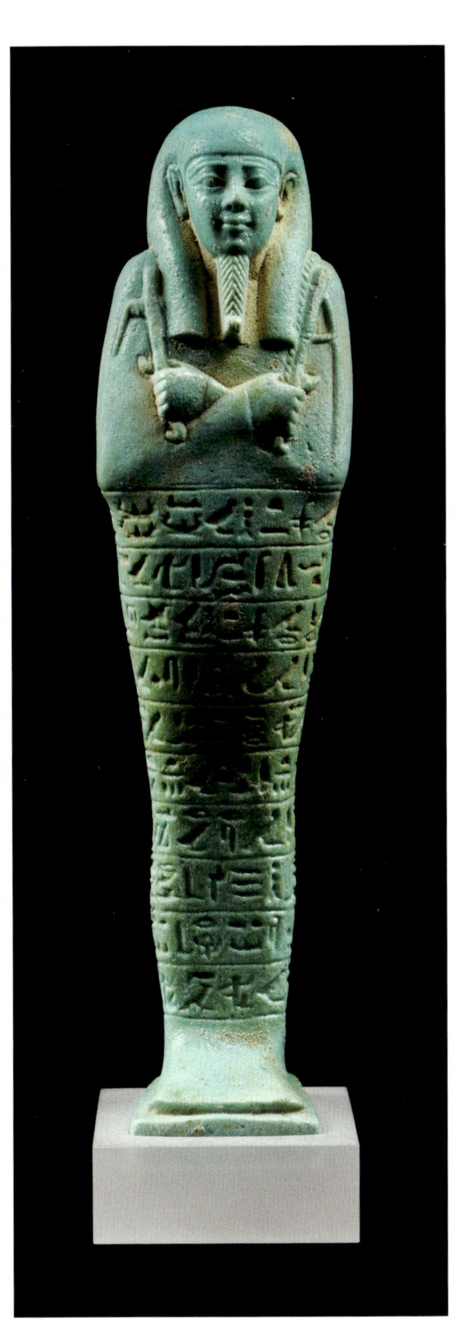

Cat. 97, page 237

In the ancient Egyptian language, faience was called *techenet*, etymologically related to verbs meaning "to glisten, shine, sparkle." This ancient Egyptian noun adequately articulates the shimmering quality inherent in faience. The same root provides the ancient Egyptian vocabulary for the descriptives of the sun's rays. Through a complex conceit, driven by both puns and homonyms, the elite members of Egyptian society established a tight relationship between the sun and faience. As a result, shabtis, or small funerary figurines, were often created in faience and were inscribed for the deceased whose name was introduced by the ancient Egyptian word *sehedj*, literally, "that which causes something to become illuminated" (compare cat. 97). The word *sehedj* was consequently translated into English as "the inspector," the one who throws light onto a subject. A recent re-examination of the role of faience within the material culture of ancient Egypt, together with a deeper understanding of the function of the shabti, has resulted in a revisionist approach. One now translates the word *sehedj* as "the illuminated one," namely, "the one who shines like the sun," because in death all Egyptians aspired to become resurrected so that they might ride in the divine boat of the sun god eternally and become one with him (compare cat. 98). Accordingly, the use of faience for the manufacture of shabtis reinforces the function of these funerary figures.

One can also place silver and gold within this same framework of religious associations that the ancient Egyptian elite attributed to media utilized for the creation of art. During certain periods of ancient Egyptian history, silver was the more valuable of these two precious metals. That conclusion is drawn from commodity lists in which products were traditionally compiled in order of importance. Commodities placed at the beginning assumed greater value than those at or near the end of such lists. In the ancient Egyptian commodities lists under discussion, the placement of silver before gold indicates their hierarchical relationship, and the primacy accorded silver.

The ancient Egyptians envisioned their deities as divine beings with skin of gold and bones of silver. Consequently, objects made of gold were imbued with divine flesh, as those of silver were imbued with divine skeletal associations. These theological associations of gold and silver as the very flesh and bones of the deities rendered the thought of using gold and silver coins for mundane commercial transactions sacrilegious. It is for this reason that a barter economy, in which commercial transactions were conducted exclusively by the exchange of goods without recourse to coinage, so dominated the ancient Egyptian economy even into the Ptolemaic Period. The coins minted in Egypt during that epoch were primarily for use by the immigrant Greeks and were, for the most part, eschewed by the native Egyptians, who still relied upon the system of barter for their commercial transactions.

The color of the material employed for the creation of any given object also imbued that object with symbolic properties. Before the subject of color symbolism can be addressed, one must understand that the ancient Egyptian lexicon is not a rich one, and contains only five certain terms for colors. These five divide the Western spectrum of colors—red, orange, yellow, green, blue, indigo, violet—into two parts, not seven. The term red, used to describe the color of the desert, encompassed the European hues of red, orange, and yellow; the term for green encompassed green, blue, indigo, and violet. Black and white were two additional color terms, and the fifth, variegated, or multicolored, was applied to objects such as the plumage of certain birds. These ancient Egyptian terms for colors—red, green, black, white, variegated—appear to have been very limited. The multicolored palette used to decorate the painted tombs at Thebes during the New Kingdom, for example, leave scholars wondering about how those different colors were described by the ancient Egyptians. Color differentiation may have been indicated by the use of either adjectives or adverbs in conjunction with these five color words, but evidence in support of this suggestion is so far lacking. The names of minerals might have served to enrich the palette of such designations, which would additionally add a metaphorical dimension to the object described. Within this system, colors might also become surrogates for minerals and stones, reflecting the persistent interchangeability inherent in ancient Egyptian polyvalent philosophical discourse. This is evident from the ancient description of colors used for a statue of Rameses VI, which replaces stones such as red jasper and lapis lazuli with color words.

As a result of this limited lexicon, the five terms for color were also polyvalent. Red, encompassing red, orange, and yellow, might be regarded as the color of the sun and imbued with positive characteristics. But red was also the color of blood and of the desert, and thus simultaneously had negative characteristics. Green was associated with the floral kingdom, but since the color term "green" applied equally to blue, indigo, and violet, objects exhibiting those hues were regarded as the equivalent of green and might possess similar connotations, perhaps representing aspects of the floral kingdom.

The color black was possessed of nuanced polyvalence in ancient Egyptian thought. The mass of the twenty-four elements was visualized for its "blackness," and this characteristic is reflected in the bitumen used in mummification. It was a color associated with rebirth and eternal preservation. As the color of the moist silt deposited by the Nile River, it also possessed qualities of a rejuvenating nature and became the preferred color for the flooring of temples because of this association. All of these qualities were transferred to dark gray stones such as granodiorite. Such black images were also thought to be bathed in the secret unguent of the god Min, himself associated with cosmic creation. Black also imbued the object so hued with characteristics of protection and renewed vigor and strength. And yet the color was itself its own antonym signifying "nothingness." It is for this reason that the negative stone, appearing between the legs or the arms and torso, on statues, particularly during the Old Kingdom, was painted black, suggesting to the viewer that that part of those statues should be "ignored" as nonexistent.

White was often considered to be possessed of the most beautiful of qualities, exhibiting a festive character, appropriate for ritual performance and valued for its associations with ritual purity, joy, and innocence. These characteristics were also inherent in both silver and electrum, a naturally occurring alloy of gold and silver. The color might also connote dominance and offensive positioning against an adversary, which may explain its association with onions and their smell. Onions supposedly possessed magical properties for use against hostile powers.

It is within this context of color that different types of stones play a symbolic role in ancient Egyptian art, particularly as stone was considered the most durable material in their landscape. Objects created with stone were, therefore, imbued with characteris-

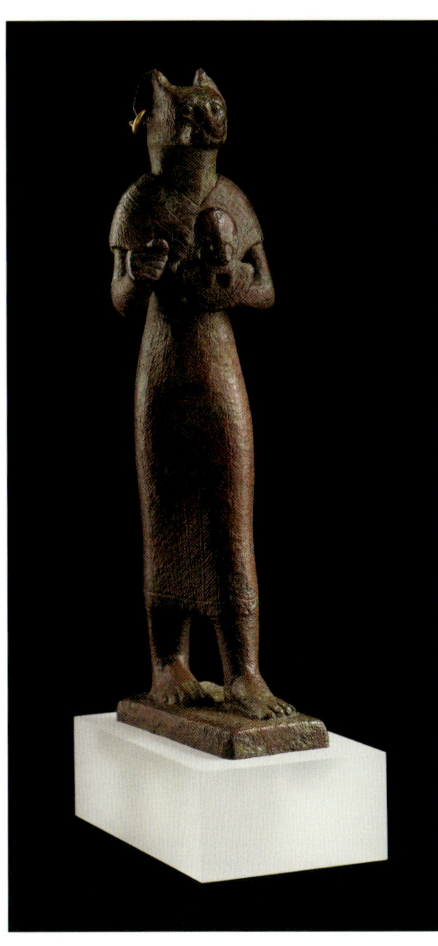

Cat. 73, page 191

tics connoting permanence and everlastingness. Their colors furthered such concepts. Red granites and quartzite were thought to possess solar characteristics, while black granites and dark stones embodied the regenerative aspects of the black silt annually deposited by the Nile River, which suggested rebirth, regeneration, and the like.

Alabaster is particularly interesting in this regard. As stone, it connoted permanence, while its white color also suggested purity and cleanliness. It is one of the six commodities habitually mentioned in the funerary offering prayer, literally,

> *a thousand of bread and beer, a thousand of oxen and*
> *fowl, and a thousand of alabaster and linen.*

It is a stone inextricably associated with the goddess Bastet (compare cat. 73). Its name, in modified form, became the designation of a particular form of vase. And it was the material of preference for the majority of vessels, of a bewildering number of shapes, created during the course of the New Kingdom. These, as the inscribed examples reveal, were containers for balms and unguents, whose function was likewise polyvalent, because one and the same balm or unguent might be used in funerary rituals, temple cults, and in festivals involving the pharaoh.

Almost all media utilized for the creation of these ancient Egyptian works of art were possessed of symbolic value, even materials such as wax. Its ability to melt, ostensibly causing it to disappear and then congeal in order to reshape itself was considered a metaphorical transformation that might symbolically indicate any seemingly altered state of creation, be it rebirth, resurrection, or the initiation of divine cosmic cycles. These characteristics were related to the ancient Egyptian view of the bee, which was regarded as a spontaneously regenerating creature emerging from either dung or a corpse. The resulting unstable equilibrium between life and death was central to the meanings anciently attached to wax. It could afford defensive powers of protection, which were extended to guardian deities in the panoply of mummies. Wax is featured as a principal ingredient in prophylactic charms. All of these positive associations are brought to bear on the encaustic technique, in which pigments suspended in molten wax were then used to paint objects created in both alabaster and linen. Nevertheless, in keeping with ancient Egyptian polyvalence, wax could be employed in destructive rituals:

> *A spell to be recited over a statuette of the god Seth*
> *created in red wax as that statuette is hurled into the fire...*

These stones, ores, semiprecious gems, and similar raw materials were obtained by expeditions ordered by the pharaoh and acquired by religiously sanctioned operations often inextricably linked to the deities with whom they were mythologically associated. They were then transported to the institutionally affiliated ateliers for transformation into finished products. The ancient Egyptians developed a delivery system that was both efficient and exacting. For example, ateliers using copper, such as metalsmithing foundries and faience workshops, were located in proximity to one another, so that one drop-off could service two industries and inventory could be better controlled.

The primacy of the pharaoh in these endeavors is clearly indicated during the course of the Old Kingdom, as seen in numerous inscriptions in which the members of the elite record how their sarcophagus, for example, was obtained through the agency of the pharaoh. His role in all aspects of ancient Egyptian life is often overlooked, but remained so pervasive that as late as the Roman Imperial Period, the millennia-old funerary offering formula still began with the time-honored phrase,

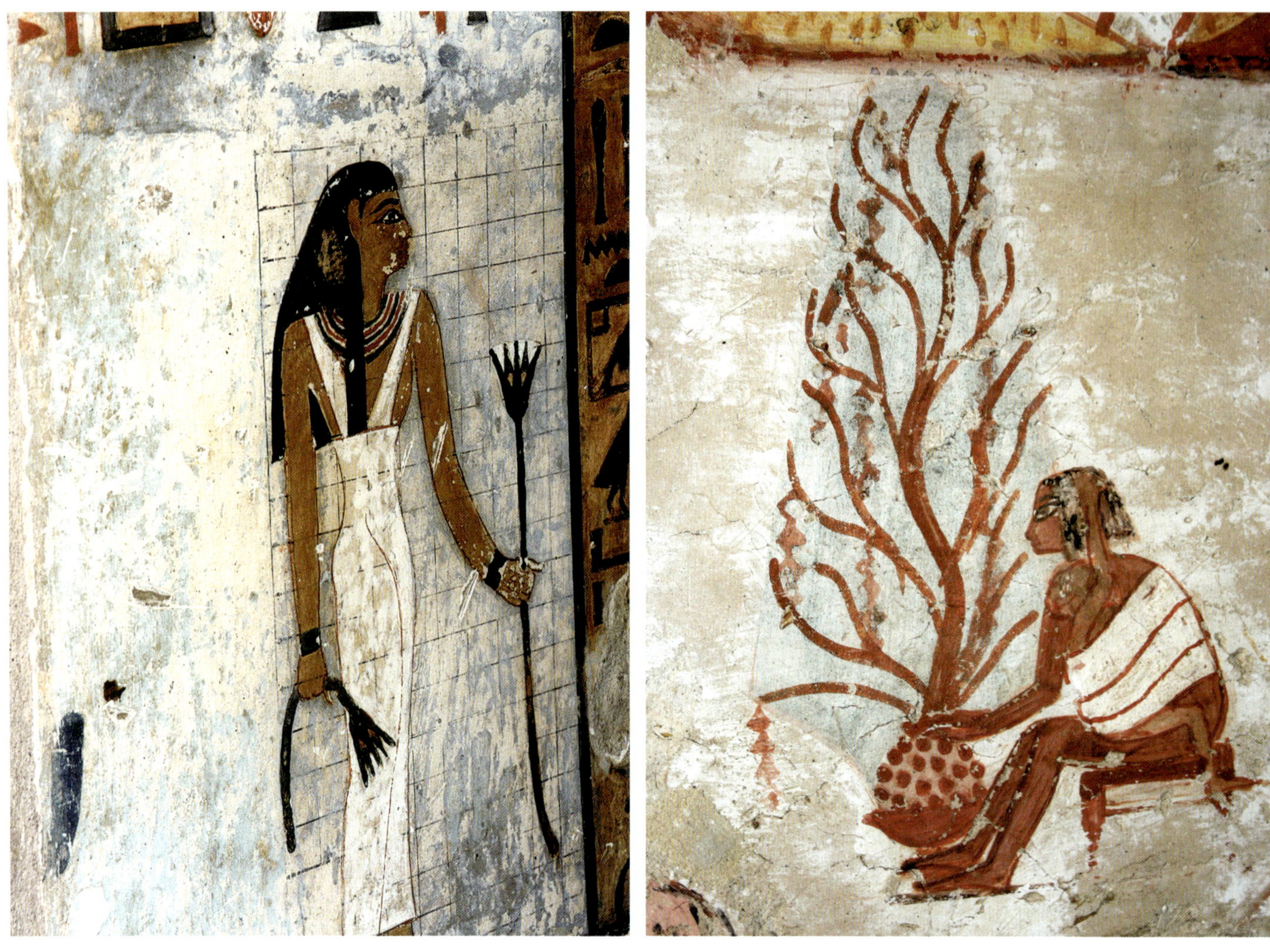

Figure 16 (left)
The grid still in place on one of the figures in the Tomb of Sarenput II at Qubbet el-Hawa

Figure 17 (right)
A vignette from the Tomb of Menna (Theban Tomb 69), Dynasty XVIII

A gift which Pharaoh grants to any number of deities so that those deities in turn may bestow upon the deceased a thousand of bread and beer, a thousand of oxen and fowl, a thousand of alabaster and linen.

The deceased, even in the twilight of ancient Egypt's civilization, were in theory dependent upon the pharaoh's largess in order for their spirits to receive the bare necessities so vital to their use in the hereafter.

Controlled by the pharaoh and dependent upon his initiative, these institutionally affiliated craft ateliers then were placed under the control of members drawn from the literate coterie of the elite. Some of these individuals are known to us because monuments occasionally contain their name and titles. So, for example, one learns that Imhotep, discharging his duties for the pharaoh Djoser of Dynasty III of the Old Kingdom, is styled a carpenter, a sculptor, and a creator of (stone) vessels. His name, together with those of a handful of other elite members serving in similar capacities, has come down to us. In general, however, the names of these foremen or overseers were not recorded because the governance of ancient Egypt can be characterized as totalitarian, rule by a single individual in the person of a pharaoh, in a social system in which the collective good was stressed at the expense of an individual's.

In examining the decoration of tombs and temples, one finds that the decoration assigned to any given wall or section is perfectly accommodated to the two-dimensional surface. There is never any crowding of individual elements that gives rise to the contemporary aphorism depicted at left (fig. 15).

The overseers and foremen were methodical in the designing of these works of art. A telling example of how these scenes were planned may be seen in the way in which a grid was applied to either a two- or three-dimensional surface to guide the artisans whose hands were actually manipulating the medium (fig. 16).

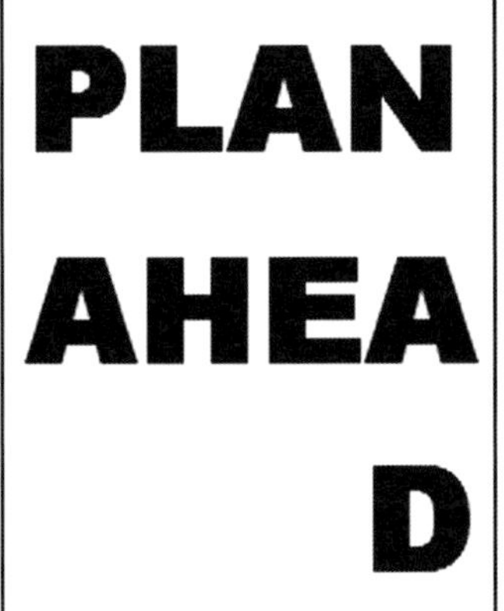

Figure 15

This grid provided a convenient guide on which the composition was superimposed in black. There are occasions when, in the judgment of the overseer, the craftsmen had made a mistake, and these are indicated by going over the design and correcting it in red. One can see such an error in the misspelling of the name of the god Path (compare cat. 2), which was subsequently corrected by recutting the correct signs over the mistake.

The use of such a grid and the apparent repetition of certain motifs has led some to suggest that these elite overseers had access to models, presumably in the form of pattern books or similar resources, in which recurrent images were stored for present and future retrieval. The congruent design in different scale and occasionally in different media of the shapes of some vessels (compare cat. 47 with cat. 48; see also cat. 41) and statuettes (cat. 86 and cat. 87) in this exhibition would certainly suggest the existence of patterns or model on which the overseers might draw.

That the ancient Egyptians were capable of researching their own past for models that might serve their present, immediate needs is clear. Selected scenes in the tombs of the elite of Dynasty XXV and XXVI, for example, copy vignettes found in the tombs of both the Old and New Kingdoms. The principle is termed archaizing, defined as a characteristic of ancient Egyptian design whereby an element, be it a motif or a technical innovation, once introduced into the artistic repertoire, might be reintroduced at any subsequent time. Literary accounts, composed around the personality of Prince Kha-em-waset, fourth son of Pharaoh Rameses II, portray characters in quest of scrolls containing information vital to the progress of the plot. They travel great distances to find it, in a process not unlike that of a contemporary genealogist traveling to a remote, rural city hall to consult official records. The Shabaka Stone in the British Museum, dated to the Kushite Dynasty, claims to be a copy of an older religious document found on papyri that was so worn that the lacunae, or missing parts, of the alleged original were reproduced in the copied text. Aba, a member of the Theban aristocracy, refers to a like-named official of the Old Kingdom in certain scenes that he had copied almost verbatim in his own tomb. His near-contemporary, Montuemhat, witnessed the inclusion into the decorative program of his tomb of small vignettes found on the walls of early tombs of the New Kingdom, which were within a reasonable walking distance from the site of his tomb (fig. 17 and fig. 18).

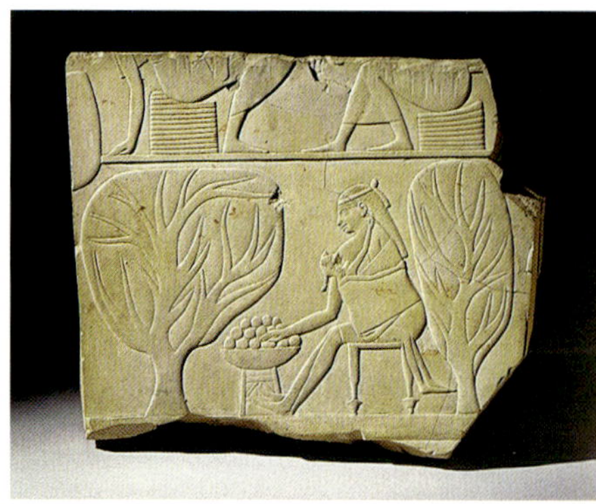

Figure 18
A relief from the Tomb of Montuemhat (Theban Tomb 34), Dynasty XXV–XXVI
The Brooklyn Museum; 48.74

The King's Lists, such as that at Abydos, compiled with the propagandistic intent of denying the existence of the kings of the Amarna Period, nevertheless demonstrate the historical, corporate memory of the ancient Egyptians that informed the principle of archaizing. This same archaizing is also operative in the transmission of texts, thought to be housed in the *per ankh*, "the house of life," thought to be a scriptorium found in all major temples.

> *O ye pure priests, who are conversant with divine writ and*
> *have access to the house of life, and enter the archives.*

In summary, ancient Egyptian art is hieroglyphic. As such, it is imbued with a potential to become animated. It was created by and for an elite, estimated to be less than ten percent of the population, in concert with the pharaoh. The design tenets governing its creation had their own logic, which is not that of Renaissance representation. It is an art, firmly rooted in religious praxis, destined from the beginning to fulfill a function, both symbolic and magical. Its materials enhance and further that function.

Whether the ancient Egyptian elite considered these creations to be art is moot, because the concepts of what a modern might term art history and connoisseurship were pioneered by the ancient Greeks and furthered by the Romans. These issues were apparently of little or no concern to the ancient Egyptians. Nevertheless, one gains the distinct impression, gleaned from a very small sample of preserved inscriptions, that the ancient Egyptians were aware of, and recognized, quality. There is evidence from a few texts that indicate that skilled administrators, but not those toiling under their oversight, were richly remunerated for the creation of works deemed technically accomplished. This situation obtained despite the ancient Egyptian proverb,

> *There never existed a craftsman who reached the limit of his craft.*

To which at least one individual retorted,

> *I am a craftsman successful in my craft through that which I know.*

Here again, knowledge, the domain of the elite, enables one to excel. Clearly, then, the ancient Egyptians were not concerned with such issues as aesthetics and beauty when judging their craft productions; their criterion was rather one of technical accomplishment and achievement.

If remuneration for services rendered may be taken as an index of worth, then the payments in kind and other perks enjoyed by these overseers in relation to those allocated to the laborers in their employ is telling. Indeed, in all ancient Egyptian elite, institutionally affiliated crafts, the preparatory, planning stages were more highly regarded than was the physical execution. Texts describing the remuneration of individuals involved in all stages of such craft production are explicit in this regard. Those performing the actual work, who were in direct physical contact with the material—be it stone, metal, faience, or other medium—received smaller quantities of daily rations as payment than the overseers in charge of the operation. One telling example is the record of activities of 18,741 individuals dispatched by royal decree to the Wadi Hammamat in the Eastern Desert, to quarry stone for sixty sphinxes and 150 statues. The

Opposite page, shown clockwise:

Figure 19
The Doryphoros by Polykleitos

Figure 20
Hermes with the Infant Dionysos by Praxiteles

Figure 21
A group of pedimental figures from the Parthenon in Athens

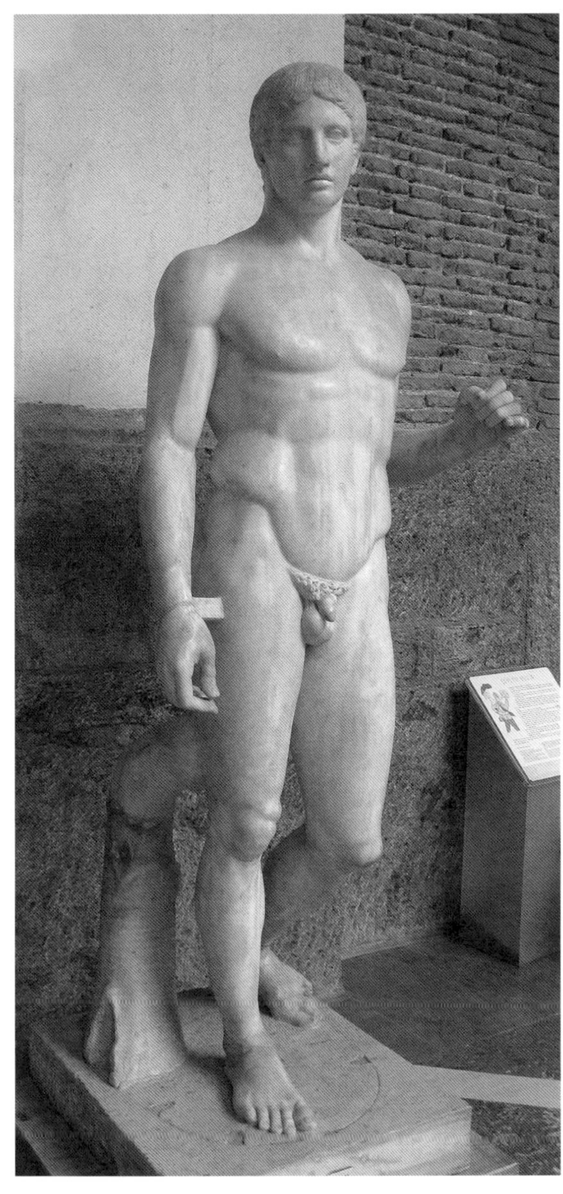
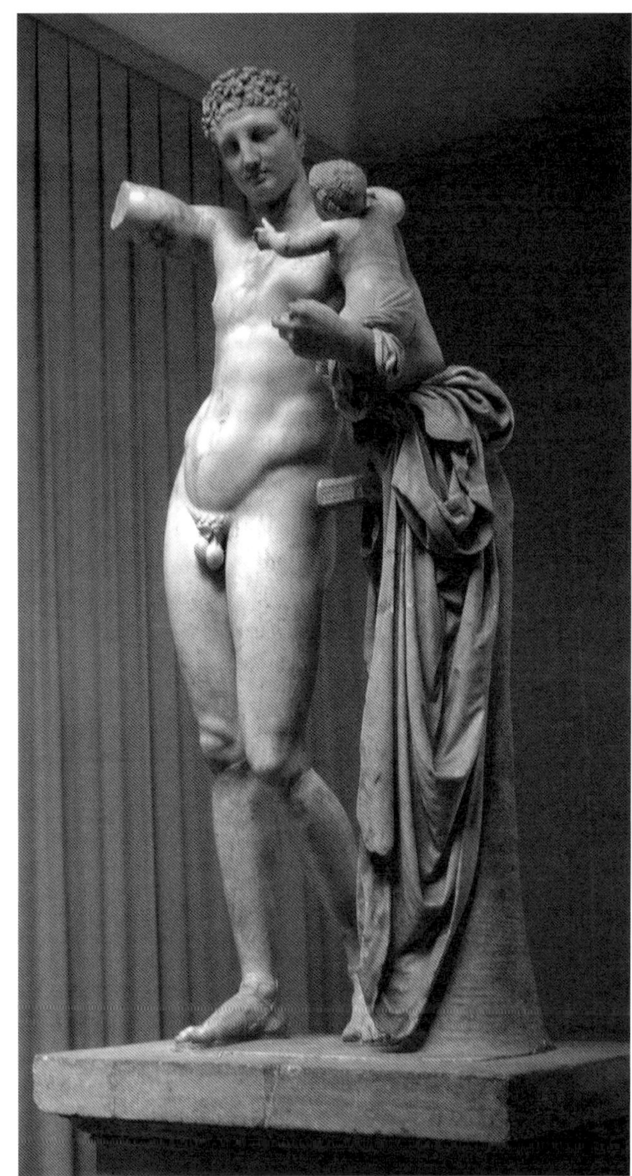
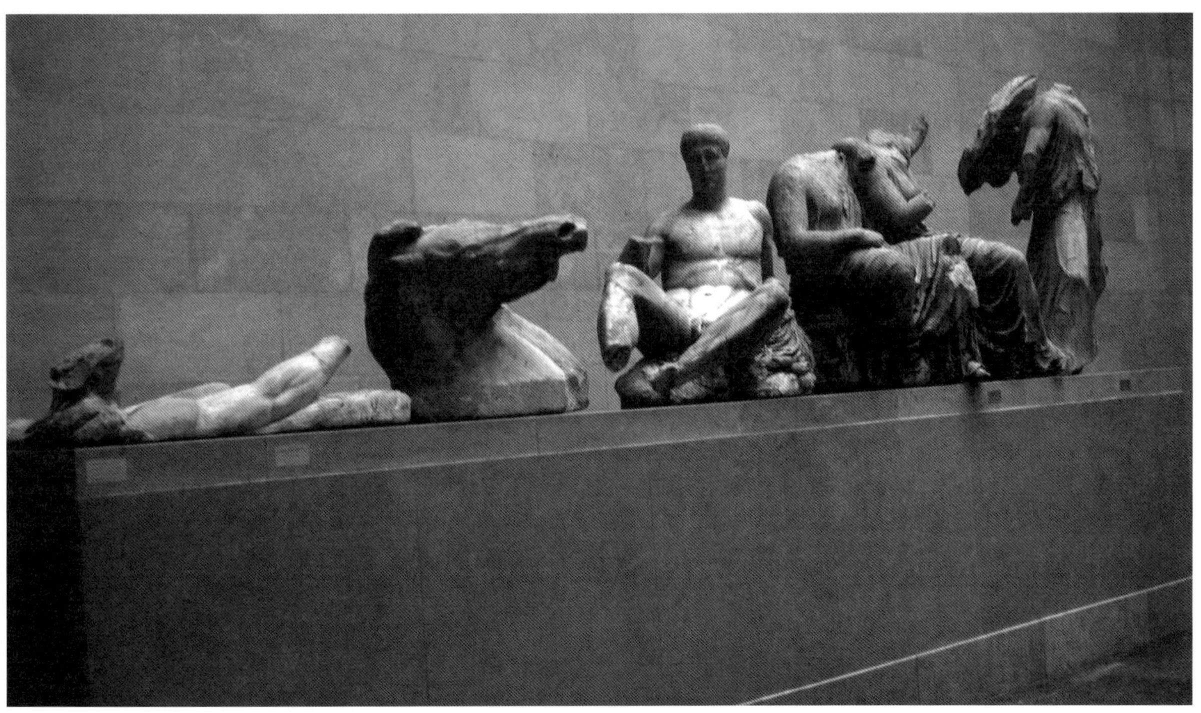

individual responsible for overseeing this operation received a wage of twenty loaves of bread and five measures of beer daily. The craftsmen received the same twenty loaves of bread but only half a measure of beer, and each of the 17,000 laborers received just five loaves of bread and two-fifths of a measure of beer. In terms of the beer allocation alone, then, the administrator's wage was almost 1,200 percent greater than that of the stone cutters working under his direction.

Such differentials between the overseers and the artisans under their direction appear to have continued unchanged into the Roman Imperial Period of the first century AD, when coinage appears to have gradually replaced barter. A preliminary study of a fragmentary inscription dealing with the transport of stone from a quarry in Upper Egypt to the Nile River records the sums paid to about twenty workmen and their apparent foreman, who personally received one-third of the total amount of the payroll.

Although the names of a handful of overseers and other individuals associated with those creative processes do exist from ancient Egypt, their occurrences are the exception and not the rule, because ancient Egyptian society promoted the collective and at the expense of the individual. The concept of an artist as a clearly identifiable individual of creative genius was pioneered by the ancient Greeks as was the discipline of art history and connoisseurship. That discipline was furthered by the Romans, many of whom are remembered as zealous, perhaps aggressive, patrons and collectors of art. These traditions were bequeathed to the philhellenes of the West, who laid the foundations in the West for the study of art as a recognized division of the humanities. The academic methods introduced and refined for that study were specifically geared to Greek art. Accordingly, concepts of development—a beginning, a climax, a decline—were used to trace the evolution of the male figure from the kouros of the sixth century BC to the canon of Polykleitos of the fifth century BC (fig. 19) and the Praxitelian mannerisms of the fourth century BC (fig. 20).

Notions of finished and unfinished were based on the perceived perfection of the Parthenon's pedimental sculptures created in Athens in the fifth century BC (fig. 21).

The increased awareness of the material culture of ancient Egypt following the Napoleonic mission at the end of the eighteenth century led to a flood of pharaonic works in Western collections. The aesthetic standards of the time regarded these works as inferior to and unworthy of exhibition alongside ancient Greek art, as the derisive comments of Sir John Bankes, *a propos* of the colossal bust of Rameses II known as the Younger Memnon (compare cat. 28), reveals:

> *We have not placed that statue among the works of Fine Arts...whether any statue that has been found in Egypt can be brought into competition with the grand works of the Townley Gallery remains to be proved.*

Indeed, the study of ancient Egypt was driven by the twin engines of archaeological excavation and philology, the study of texts and inscriptions. The social science of art history and connoisseurship lagged woefully behind, and was often regarded as an embarrassment, because its chosen scientific method could not be independently quantified. It was, therefore, only in 1987 that the association of German-speaking Egyptologists sanctioned a session on art history during the course of their annual meeting. The prejudice against art historians of Egyptian material has to some degree remained, and the discipline of Egyptology continues to be characterized as one in which the edition of primary sources, meaning texts and inscriptions, ranks as the first priority.

The prejudice persists in no small part because the principles of art history and appreciation, originating in ancient Greece, have been indiscriminately applied to the study of ancient Egyptian art without the recognition that ancient Egypt's material culture was created neither for the West nor by Europeans. The premise that art should be

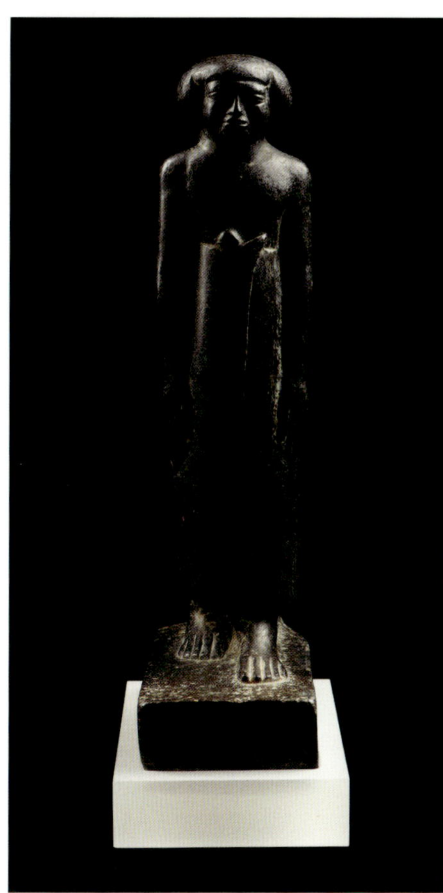

Cat. 25, page 101

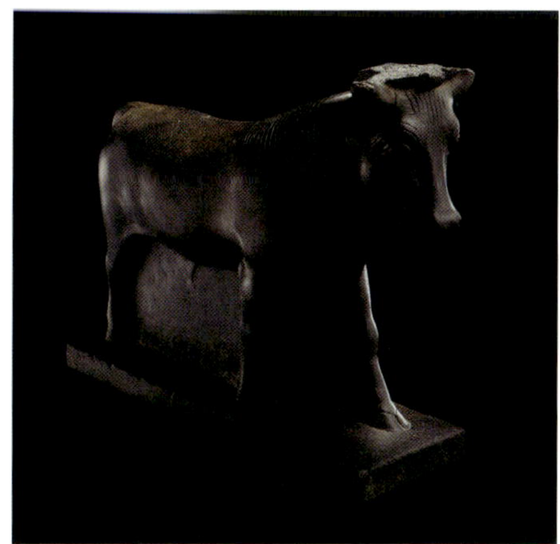

Cat. 31, page 112

regarded as developmental, with a beginning and a decline, is inappropriate when applied to Egyptian material culture. The hieroglyphic notational system seems to have appeared fully developed, without a perceptible gestation period. Western concepts of finished or unfinished do not obtain (cat. 86 and cat. 87). Finished images were intentionally damaged in order to continue to function in their altered state (cat. 61). Nevertheless, the principles of Western art history have become so wholeheartedly embraced by some members of the Egyptological community that the loose application of varying interpretations of stylistic analysis by two different scholars to one and the same work of art does not lead to consensus. Indeed, the application of these Hellenocentric principles might suggest that the striding male figure cast in a cupreous alloy (cat. 60) is contemporary in date with a faience amulet of a composite, ram-headed deity (cat. 89), because both exhibit seemingly identical stylistic features in the design of the torso with its navel, the disproportionately long limbs, and the manner in which the kilt rides low on the hips.

Representations in the round created in ancient Egypt rely on the frontal view as the principal one; they were not intended to be regarded from other vantage points. There is no attempt to integrate the frontal with the profile views, because such an integration, first pioneered by Greek artists in the fourth century BC, was at variance with the principle of visual clarity. Three-dimensional images in stone, and some in metal (cat. 60), created in ancient Egypt do not cantilever limbs into space and often leave negative stone, which classical sculptors would have removed, between arms and torsos or between feet (cat. 25 and cat. 31). The negative stone on statues, particularly during the Old Kingdom, was painted black as a visual clue suggesting that the spectator ignore it.

Designed frontally, these images in the round, in various materials, exhibit a back pillar (cat. 22 and cat. 26), an integral, vertical element, flush with the back of a statue, often running from the soles of the feet to the area of the neck and head. Often inscribed in hieroglyphs and on occasion with figural decoration, the purpose and significance of this characteristic feature of most ancient Egyptian sculpture remains enigmatic. Incorporated into the design of some of the earliest sculpture, this back pillar is regarded by some as a deity's perch, perhaps the seat of the statue's life force, metaphorically present to endow the statue, as the surrogate for the individual represented, with divine power. Attempts to explain its function in purely technical terms, as a support to keep the statue upright, appear too prosaic. The back pillar remained an integral component of Egyptian-designed statues into the first century BC and beyond.

These observations about sculpture in the round must be understood against an emerging background regarding the symbolism inherent in the body of literature conveniently termed *The Vision of a Statue in Stone*, a corpus of inscriptions whose meaning and interpretation remain disputed. According to one view, a sem-priest, whose ministrations animated both mummies and statues and who was associated with *The Ritual of Opening the Mouth*, by which both statues and mummies were metaphorically animated, was completely enveloped in a costume from which his face alone emerged and was visible. So clothed, he sat on either a stool or a bed, entered a dreamlike state or trance, and by his actions mimicked, and thereby contributed to, the spiritual rebirth of the deceased. Others suggest that the sem-priest, during his trancelike state, envisioned the statue within the block of stone (cat. 22 and cat. 25) and actualized it spiritually as a craftsman simultaneously worked the block so that the statue, when completed, would become animate and reinforce the deceased's transition into the hereafter. Despite the lack of consensus, both arguments agree about the sem-priest's powers, which result in enabling the statue of the deceased, identified with its mummy, to become animated. This ultimate sculptural animation is consistent with observations that the stones from which statues were sculpted were already possessed of a numen.

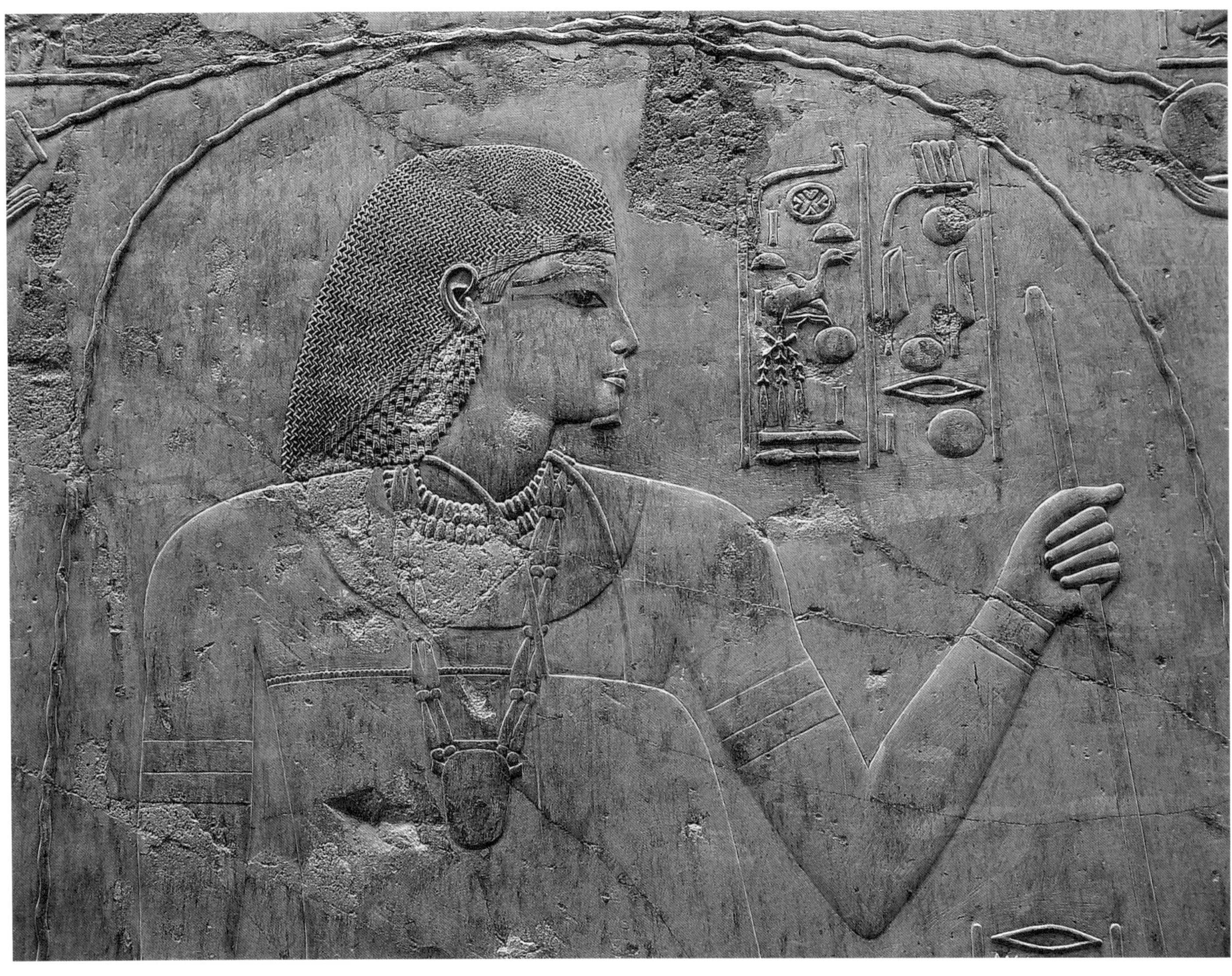

Figure 22
A detail from the sculpted relief decorating the Tomb of Ramose (Theban Tomb 132)

Such animation was not limited to statues in stone. Three documents from the Third Intermediate Period dealing with shabtis, or funerary figurines (cat. 92), reinforce the performance described in *The Vision of a Statue in Stone*. The first of these documents is a contract between the commissioner of a set of shabtis and the overseer of the craftsmen manufacturing them within the precinct of the god Amun at Thebes. This document specifies the manner in which these gangs of shabtis (cat. 92) could be animated. The overseer, as a literate member of the elite, also served as a ritualist. The contract contains clauses obliging the overseer to recite a specific spell in a designated sacred place in the presence of several deities. The ceremony had to be witnessed by a scribe. Then, and only then, after the performance of this actualizing ritual, could the shabtis be placed into the service of the deceased.

Two other documents dated to the same period are more nuanced in their description of the animation process. Relatives of the deceased, after her death, had commissioned two identical sets of shabtis and had made partial payment. For reasons that remain opaque, the final payment was not made, but the relatives insisted that the shabtis be animated. On the fiftieth day of the traditional period of seventy days intervening between death and burial, the relatives participated in an oracular ceremony in which they put the question of the actualization of the shabtis in a form requiring either a "yes" (they are actualized) or "no" (they are not actualized) response to the state god Amun. The answer was delivered by a motion oracle determined by the direction in which Amun's sacred barque moved (cat. 67). The oracle affirmed that the shabtis were animated. This episode reveals, perhaps more than any other, the various levels by which objects were anciently believed to be animated. In this case, the agent of animation was the will of a god responding oracularly to a petition of relatives.

One final point must be stressed. The overseer in this document exercises his authority, according to a strict reading of the text, over the makers of amulets. The context clearly indicates that the contract is for shabtis. One may, therefore, surmise that these foremen-ritualists performed similar ceremonies for the animation of other objects created under their direction.

Corpulence is not linked to physical appearance, but serves rather as an index of rank and status (cat. 14). Nonidealizing images are not portraits as defined by Western tenets (cat. 23, cat. 27, cat. 68, and cat. 98). They are, rather, ideological statements by individuals distancing themselves from those adhering to the status quo, depicted in idealizing idioms, as a means of self-presentation that signal a differing political, religious, or ethnic message. Indeed, code and its understanding by the viewer permeate ancient Egyptian imagery and contribute to its meaning. A uraeus adorns the head of a deity and a pharaoh, but not of a member of the elite. The apron of a kilt and the way it is formed connotes a pharaoh. Deities may present the sign of life to the nose; the elite sniff a lotus. Both gestures visually express the presentation of the breath of life to one's nostrils, but in different ways, to maintain the distinction between the pharaoh and the elite.

Western art historical tenets suggest that wealthier, more advantaged patrons could commission accomplished artists whose creations were aesthetically superior to those created for less economically advantaged patrons. An examination of the material culture of ancient Egypt, particularly during the apogee of its wealth and international prestige during Dynasty XVIII of the New Kingdom, reveals just the opposite. Stone vases inscribed with the names of several pharaohs of that period appear to be maladroitly fashioned (cat. 37). Vignettes from two virtually contemporary tombs from the same Memphite necropolis, seemingly near clones of one another, reveal differences, so that the vignette from the tomb of Nefer-hotep (cat. 9) appears more accomplished than that from the tomb of Horemheb, who is presumably of a higher social status. The decoration of the tomb of the sun king, Amenhotep III, in the Valley of the Kings appears to be perfunctorily executed in paint (fig. 22) in comparison with the lavish skill by which the tomb of his courtier, Ramose, is sculpted in delicate relief (fig. 23). The above value judgments are both subjective.

Clearly such scientific methods employed for the art historical criticism and connoisseurship of the material culture of ancient Egypt require revisiting the subject with a view toward revision.

In revisiting the subject of ancient Egyptian art, one must stress that it was created by the elite, less than ten percent of the entire population. Designs were based on the same principles that governed the appearance of the hieroglyphs. They were representations of real objects seen and used by the ancient Egyptians, depicted from their most characteristic view, stressing visual clarity. Ancient Egyptian art appears eternal and unchanging because designs, once introduced, became standardized and were repeated, with little modification, for millennia. Like hieroglyphs, art could be symbolically animated, so that it might magically come alive to serve the needs of the elite for whom it was created.

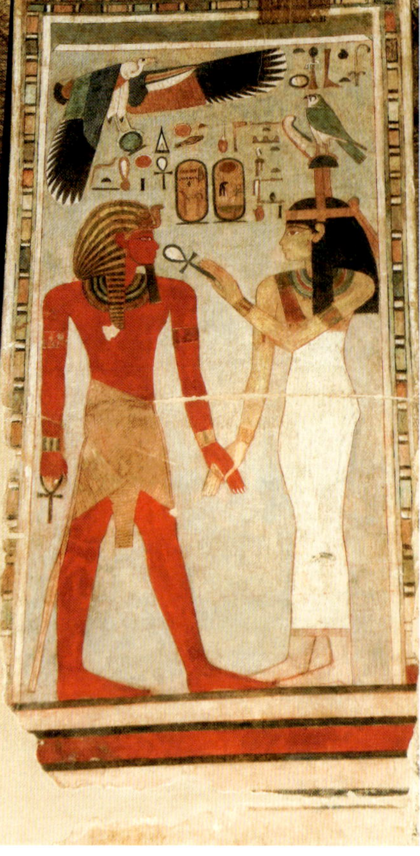

Figure 23
A painted scene from the royal tomb of Pharaoh Amenhotep III (Valley of the Kings 22)

Indeed, it is this magical characteristic of ancient Egyptian art that is often overlooked. The raw materials used by the craftsmen were obtained by religiously sanctioned expeditions ordered by the pharaoh. Those expeditions traveled to the Red Land of the desert, the realm of chaos and anarchy, in which forces of evil were lurking. The procurement of raw materials, their transport back to institutionally affiliated ateliers in the Black Land, and their crafting into finished objects, were transformational acts, linked to religious ceremonies. Stones used were considered by the ancient Egyptians to be the most durable of materials. Any object created in stone was, therefore, associated with permanence (cat. 26). Those objects created in alabaster, a white stone, were associated with ritual purity and cleanliness as well (cat. 24). These types of connections extended to other colors. Blues and greens might be associated with the annual flooding of the Nile River and the floral kingdom (cat. 56). Reds were associated with the sun (cat. 29) and its positive attributes but, as the color of blood, could also have malevolent associations (cat. 61). This polarity, in which a color could have both positive and negative characteristics, is typical of the nuanced, often antithetical, meanings that the ancient Egyptians were so skilled at weaving into their religious-philosophical system.

One's name and person were considered the same. A name sculpted in hieroglyphs in stone, the most durable of materials, would survive forever. Pronouncing the name of the deceased by a relative or friend would ensure their survival in the hereafter. The recitation of the offerings depicted in tombs would likewise magically ensure that those representations would become animate, to satisfy the needs of the deceased (cat. 12 and cat. 18).

This exhibition explores that fascinating magical characteristic of ancient Egyptian art.

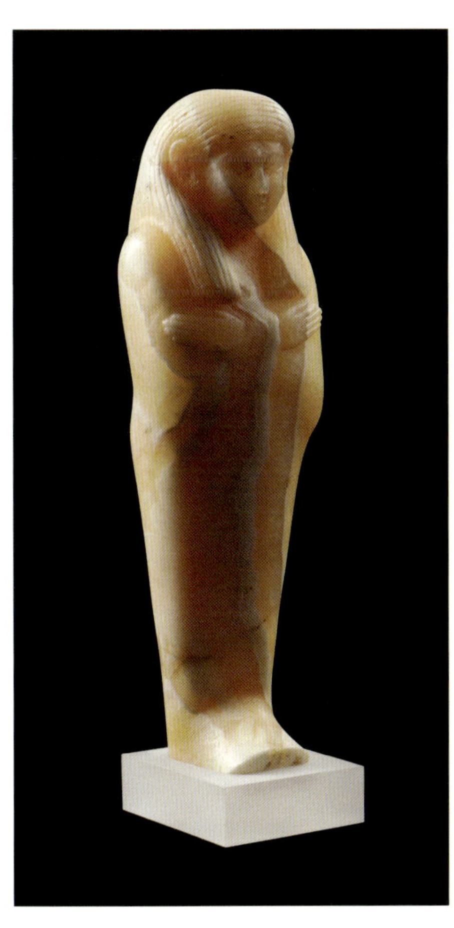

Cat. 92, page 226

An Historical Synopsis of Ancient Egypt

For reckoning the passage of time, the ancient Egyptians devised several systems, one of which divided the year into three seasons, keyed to the annual agricultural rhythms driven by the rise and fall of the Nile River. Within this system, the three seasons were termed *Akhet*, or inundation; *Peret*, or growing; and *Shemu*, or drought. These three seasons uniformly consisted of four months, each of thirty days. Those months were subdivided into three weeks, each of ten days. Five epagomenal, or additional, days were added, so that the traditional year contained 365 days (cat. 92). The five epagomenal days were each dedicated to the birth of a single child—namely, Osiris, Horus the elder, Seth, Isis, and Nephthys—whose parents were Geb, lord of the earth, and Nut, mistress of the heavens.

The ancient Egyptians possessed an historic sense and were aware of their past. The survival of King's Lists, most notably in the Temple of Sety I at Abydos, demonstrates that they knew their ancestors and could place them in a seemingly reliable, relative chronological order. Manetho, a learned scribe, was said to have composed a history of his country in Greek which, although it has not survived, is quoted by later ancient historians. That system, which placed pharaohs into dynasties that were then grouped into kingdoms still forms the basis for chronologies of ancient Egypt used to this day. These ancient records enable one to establish a working chronological framework for ancient Egypt, in which dynasties are grouped into kingdoms and kingdoms are separated from one another by periods of instability termed Intermediate Periods. The following historical synopsis is necessarily brief and does not claim to be comprehensive. It is intended to provide the reader with an initial point of reference.

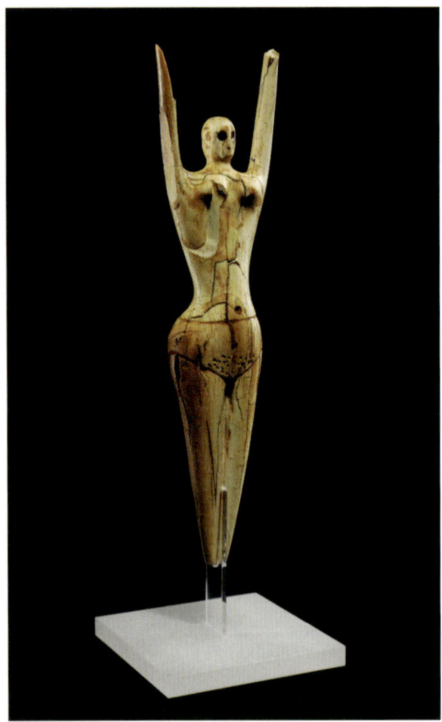

Cat. 19, page 89

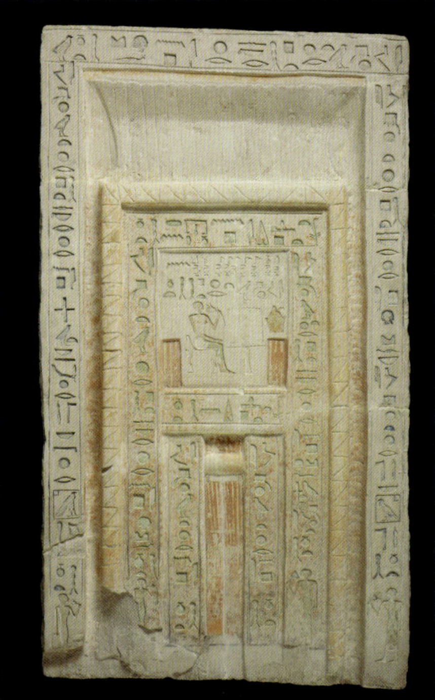

Cat. 1, page 49

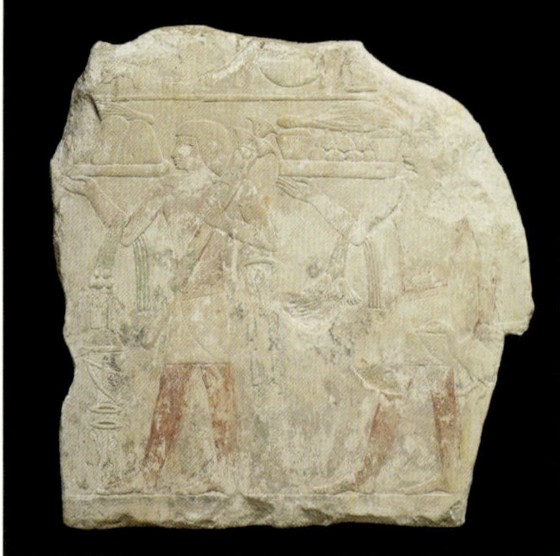

Cat. 2, page 55

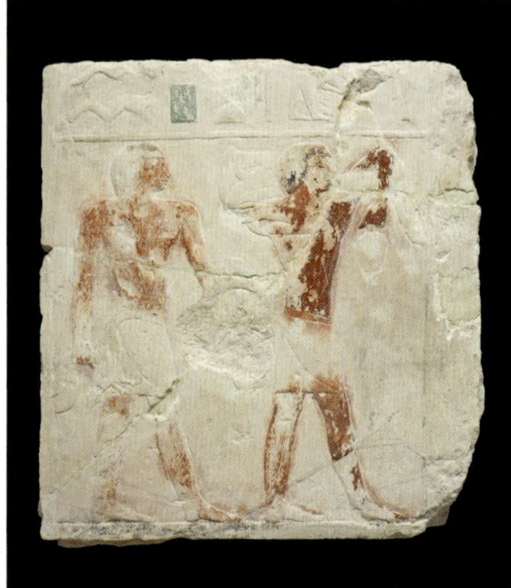

Cat. 3, page 54

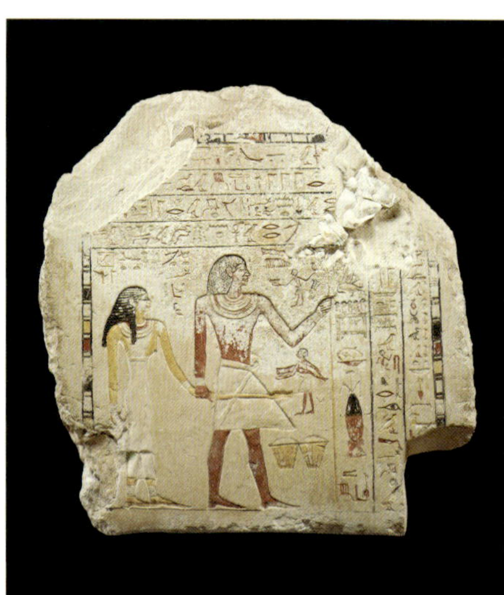

Cat. 4, page 56

One is not concerned with the more remote periods of ancient Egypt prior to the arrival of the Neolithic Period, in about 4000 BC (cat. 19 and cat. 20). From that point on, for approximately a millennium, archaeologists have been able to suggest the development of ancient Egyptian society based on graves and their contents. Over time, large graves developed. These were located in discrete areas of cemeteries, often removed from the clusters of smaller graves. Increased quantities of grave goods, often of a deluxe nature, are characteristic of the finds within these larger graves. Such evidence suggests the emergence of an elite within a stratified community. In time, competing elites vied with one another for control of larger geographic areas until the period termed Dynasty 0, an artificial designation suggested by scholars to represent a time of critical transition from political instability, in which communities were ruled by competing elites, to unification and the formation of a nation state led by a pharaoh. With the nation state came a concomitant bureaucratic administration and the introduction of hieroglyphs.

The Archaic Period witnessed further refinements to the established social systems, a consolidation of power into the hands of a central government, craft specializations, the introduction of leisure activities, and a gradual codification of religious practices. These trends culminated in the Old Kingdom, best represented perhaps in the popular imagination by the majestic pyramids on the Giza Plateau and its guardian the Great Sphinx (cat. 1). This was a period of an absolute monarchy, in which the pharaoh controlled all of the resources of the land. Trading expeditions with foreign lands became commonplace. As the Old Kingdom drew to a close, elite members of society became more advantaged and gradually challenged the position of the pharaoh (cat. 2 and cat. 3). Competing local elites consolidated economic and political power and began to openly challenge others for supremacy, effectively destroying the centralized administration and plunging Egypt into the First Intermediate Period (cat. 4).

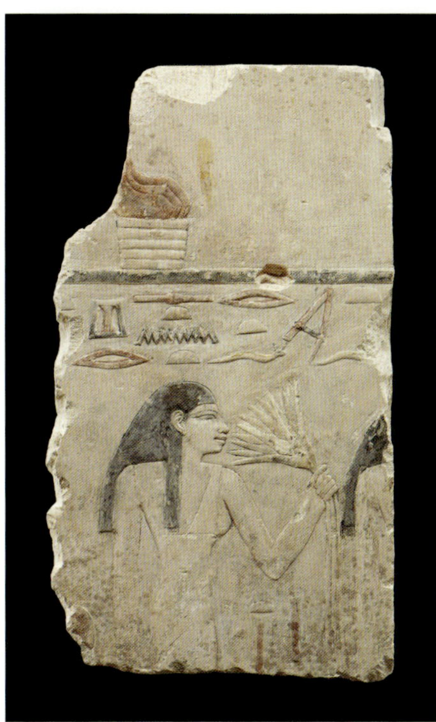

Cat. 5, page 59

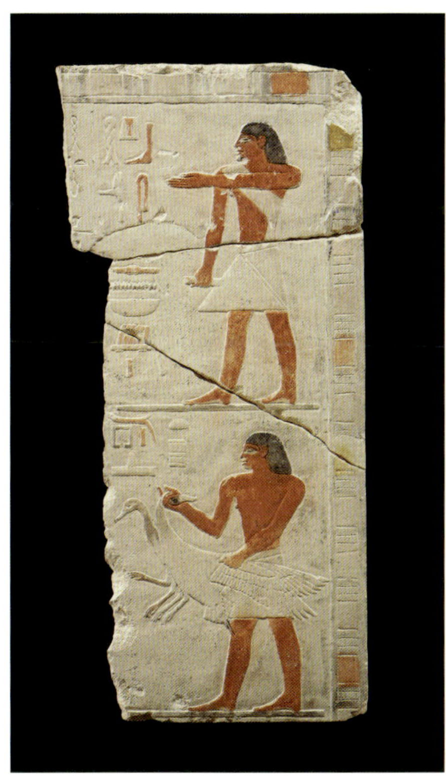

Cat. 6, page 60

This situation of internal instability continued until the Theban elite, rallying around the banner of one of several individuals, reestablished the order that was to bring about the stability of the Middle Kingdom (cat. 5). Despite this seeming veneer of stability, the competition between ruling factions was never completely resolved. Sumptuary laws were imposed, limiting the overt display of wealth by the members of the elite so as not to overshadow their occasionally less advantaged pharaohs against whom assassination plots were not uncommon (cat. 6). Internecine struggles brought the Middle Kingdom to an end.

The lack of a strong central government that characterized the Second Intermediate Period led to the first of several foreign attempts to take over Egypt. The Eastern Delta became home to Western Asiatics, peoples from the Syria-Palestine region, generally termed the Hyksos. Whether these individuals entered Egypt en masse as the result of a planned migration, or gradually trickled in as smaller groups only to unite when they realized the superiority of their numbers, is debated. As the Hyksos were establishing their stronghold on Egyptian soil, the Nubians to the south stormed Egyptian forts along the cataracts and settled in the vicinity of Aswan, the southern frontier of Egypt. Tradition maintains that the Egyptian elite, sequestered in the region of Thebes, found itself the object of an alleged two-pronged attack, in which the Hyksos planned to move south in concert with the northern movement of the Nubians, the objective of which was to engage the Egyptian military on two fronts.

The Wars of Liberation followed, in which the Egyptians successfully defeated both foreign elements. It has been suggested that, while the male members of Egyptian society were engaged in these military campaigns, the female members of elite families maintained the home fires, a set of circumstances that is theorized to explain the prominent role of elite women in the religion and politics of the ensuing period. Their combined efforts established the New Kingdom, with its capital at Thebes. Warring pharaohs led campaigns into the Syria-Palestine region and punitive campaigns into Nubia. The wealth of the known world poured into Egypt, the superpower of the day, whose presence so dominated foreign affairs that some historians have referred to the period as the Pax Aegyptiaca on the model of the Pax Romana of a later date.

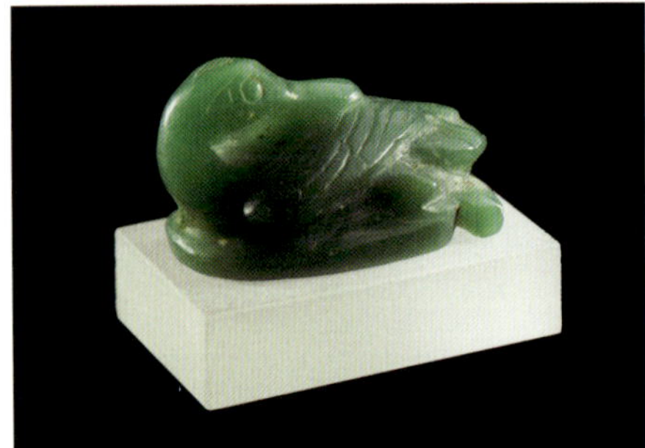

Cat. 56, page 156

This was a period of unsurpassed material wealth. Works of art that qualify as masterpieces by the application of Western standards were created. This was the period in which many of the sumptuously decorated and appointed tombs in Thebes and the Valley of the Kings date, and many of the temples at Luxor and Karnak were erected. Women played active roles, and one, Hatshepsut by name, was elevated to the throne as pharaoh (cat. 56).

One of her successors, Amenhotep III, called the Sun King by many, ruled over a land both prosperous and secure, in which his wife, Tiye, played a leading role. The opulence of his court should not blind one from potential dangers lurking in the background, particularly with regard to religious matters. An initial shift is evident during his reign, in which the Aton, or sun disk, divorced of all anthropological associations, inveigles its way into the pantheon, which it will later dominate.

Akhenaten, their son and successor, is perhaps the most enigmatic of all ancient Egyptian pharaohs. Represented in art as what has been described as a grotesque caricature, he and his wife, Nefertiti, promoted the cult of the Aton to the exclusion of other deities in official worship (cat. 10). They moved their capital from Thebes to Amarna and dismissed established elite members from their administration, replacing them with others in an attempt to curry the favor of those newly appointed. Their agents attempted to remove

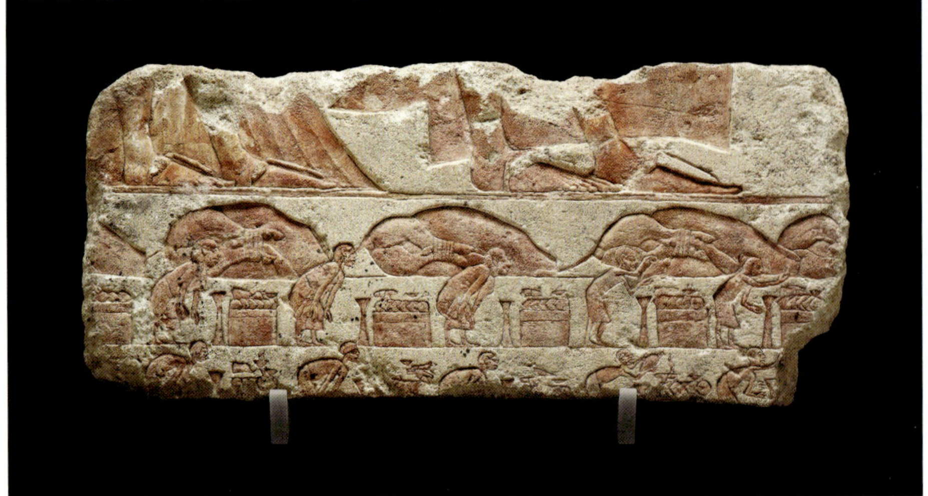

Cat. 10, page 69

the name and symbols of other deities, the god Amun being particularly targeted, from all monuments throughout the land. Tiye appears to have continued to play a dominant role in the life and administration of her son until her death. The origins and fate of Nefertiti remain speculative, although she appears to have been estranged from her husband late in his reign. The identification and sequence of the immediate successors of Akhenaten are hotly debated issues, in part because later pharaohs so proscribed his memory that the historical record became purposefully lacunose. In the end, the boy-king, Tutankhamun, emerged as the successor, returned the capital to Thebes, and restored the ancient orthodoxy.

The Amarna epoch, as this period of late Dynasty XVIII is known, also witnessed dislocation in the Ancient Near East, as the smaller principalities in the Syria-Palestine region were torn between allegiance to Egypt or to the Hittites, an Indo-European people who had established their homeland in the central part of what is now the modern nation state of Turkey. It has been suggested that a woman in the court of Egypt was poised to marry a Hittite prince in an effort to unite both realms, but his assassination en route to Egypt may have contributed to the resulting bellicosity between the two realms.

War soon broke out during the Ramesside Period of the New Kingdom. The period is so termed because the overwhelming number of pharaohs were named Rameses (cat. 95). Of these, perhaps the best known is Rameses II of Dynasty XIX, who warred against, and eventually signed, a peace treaty with a series

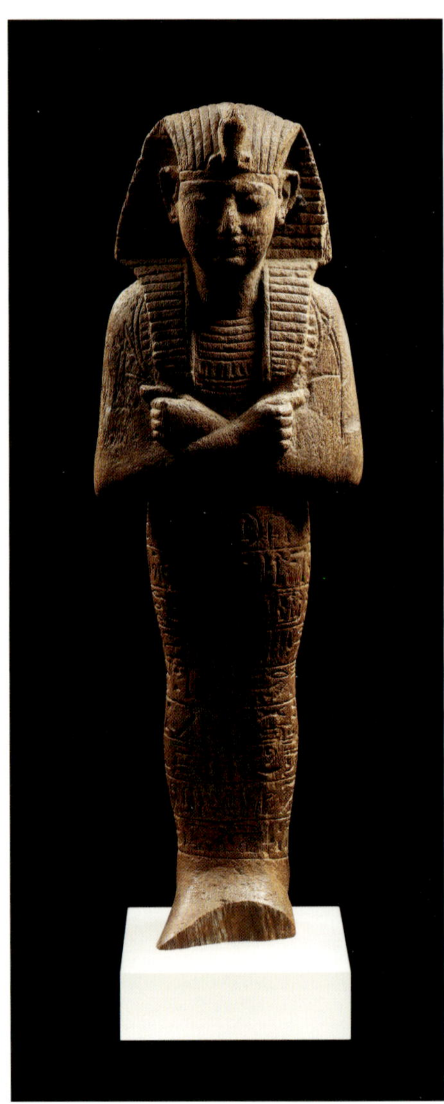

Cat. 95, page 233

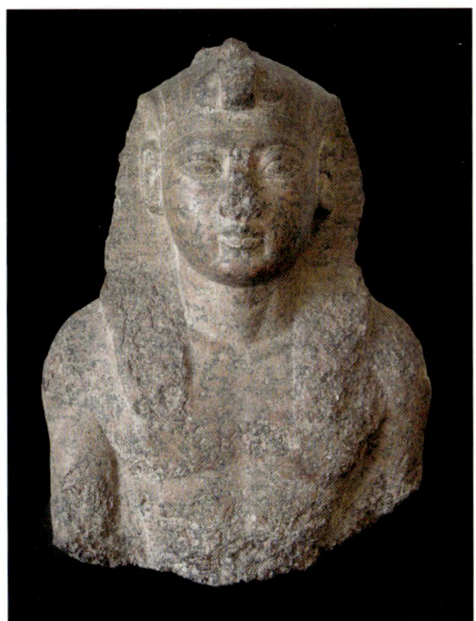

Cat. 28, 107

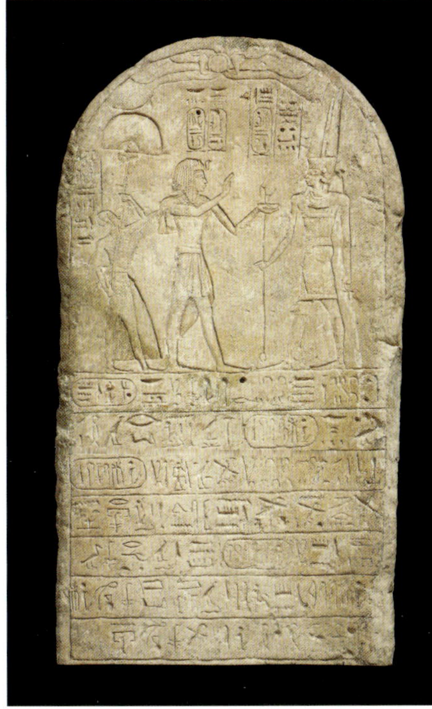

Cat. 13, page 77

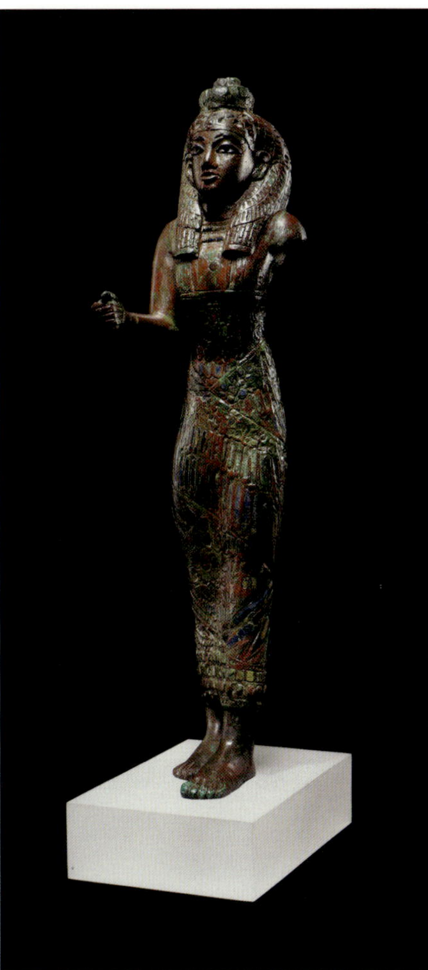

Cat. 62, page 169

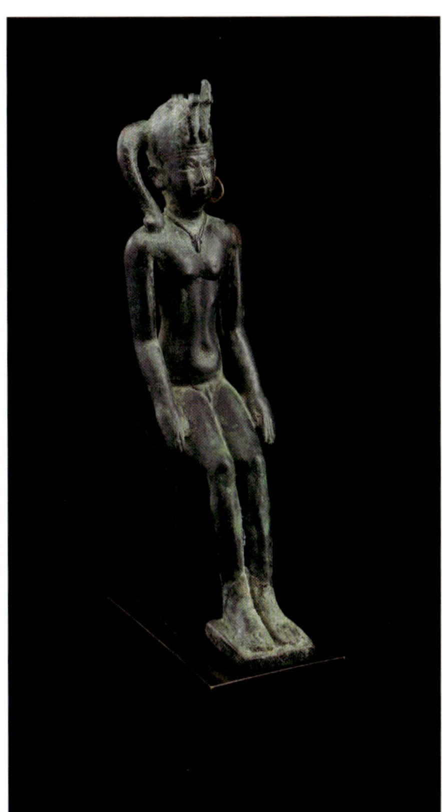

Cat. 68, page 180

of his Hittite counterparts (cat. 28). Although he proclaimed his triumphal victory over the Hittites in monuments throughout the land, the most famous of which is, arguably, at Abu Simbel, the Hittites made a similar claim, indicating that the military campaign was a draw. The megalomania which characterizes the monumentality of the architectural and sculptural programs initiated by Rameses II may be regarded as attempts to polish the ancient glory of Egypt, which present circumstances had tarnished.

The invasion of the Sea Peoples that brought the Bronze Age to a close affected Egypt as well, but their assault upon Egypt was successfully repelled by Rameses III of Dynasty XX, as recounted in the reliefs and inscriptions on the walls of his temple at Medinet Habu in Western Thebes (cat. 13).

A series of weaker pharaohs, loss of empire, and the rise of competing elites, many with ties to regions now lying within the modern nation state of Libya, gave rise to the Third Intermediate Period, in which a bewildering array of kinglets and counter-kinglets struggled with each other for control of the land (cat. 62). In the process, the Nubians marched north and through a series of astute diplomatic and religious negotiations successfully gained control of Egypt and established themselves as the legitimate pharaohs of Dynasty XXV (cat. 68). Their rule however, was short-lived because of the imperialistic policies of the Assyrian Empire, whose kings targeted the Kushites as enemies but relied upon elite Egyptian families in the Delta for administrative support. The Assyrians successfully expelled the Nubians from Egypt, who returned to their homelands in the modern nation state of the Republic of the Sudan, where their culture and way of life was continued during the Napatan Period (cat. 98). Dislocations at home eventually toppled the Assyrian empire, with the result that the Delta elite found themselves in control of the country. They established their capital at Sais, in the Delta, and, through a series of negotiations similar to those that had earlier established the Nubians, eventually gained control of the entire land (cat. 70).

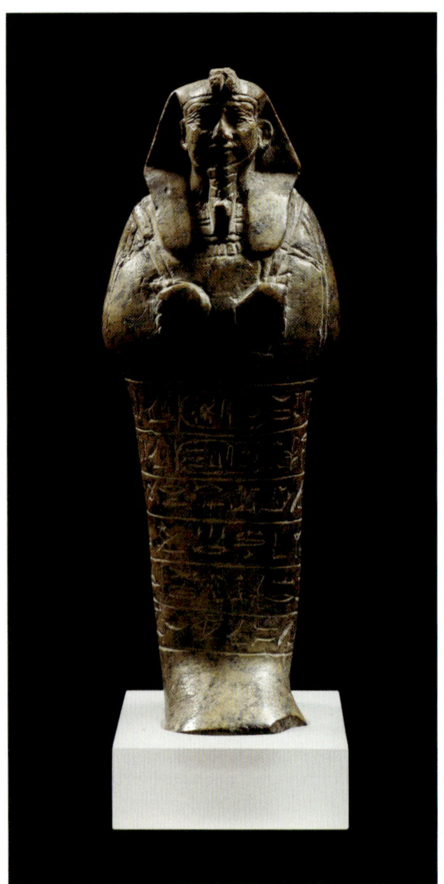

Cat. 98, page 238

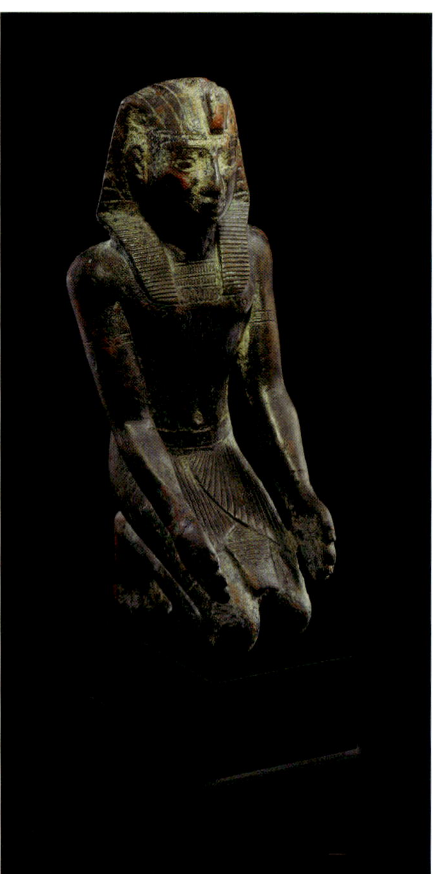

Cat. 70, page 184

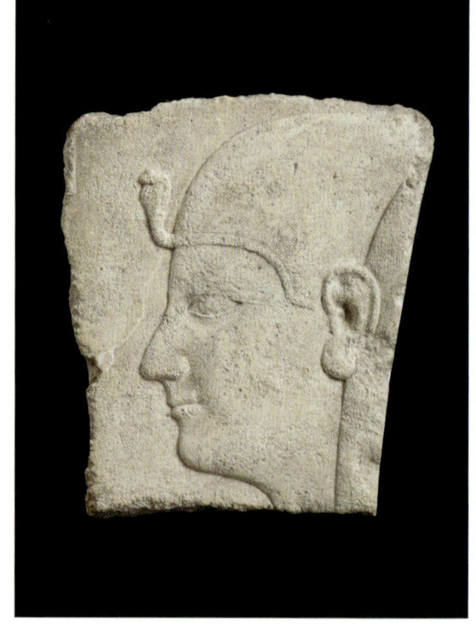

Cat. 14, page 79

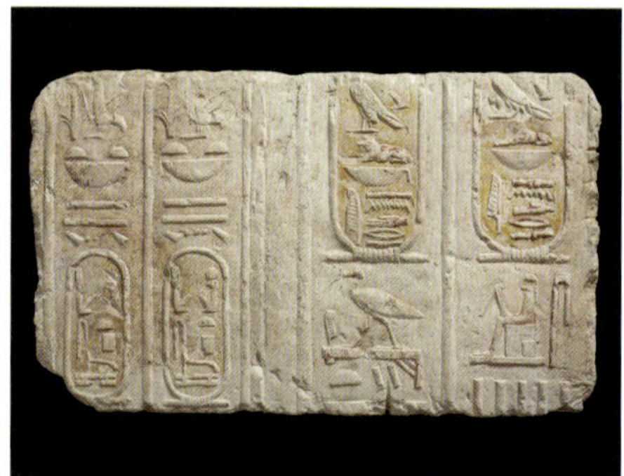

Cat. 15, page 81

The Saite pharaohs of Dynasty XXVI were eventually conquered by the Persians who ruled Egypt as a satrapy, or province, through a governor (cat. 51). They were in turn ousted by the native Egyptians, who regained control of their nation and established a series of short-lived dynasties, each of which became progressively more integrated into the changing world of the Eastern Mediterranean, dominated by Greek interests. The last native pharaoh of Dynasty XXX was forced into exile by the Persians who had returned (cat. 14) and successfully recaptured the land. Their tenure was brief and ended with the arrival of Alexander the Great (cat. 15), whose Macedonian Greek general Ptolemy ruled the land first in Alexander's name and then in the names of Alexander's successors until he proclaimed himself pharaoh in his own right in 305 BC. That act inaugurated the Ptolemaic Dynasty (cat. 32), named in his honor, whose Macedonian Greek descendants were to rule Egypt until the suicide of his distant relative, Cleopatra VII, in 30 BC. With her death, Egypt was incorporated into the political fabric of the Roman Empire, but that story lies beyond the scope of this exhibition and catalogue.

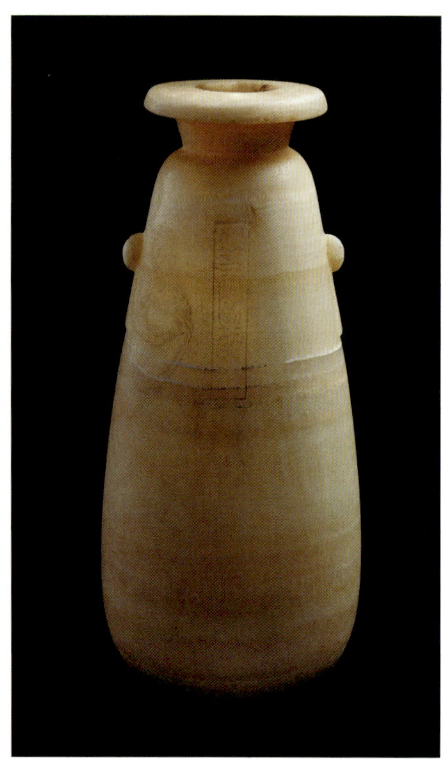

Cat. 51, page 146

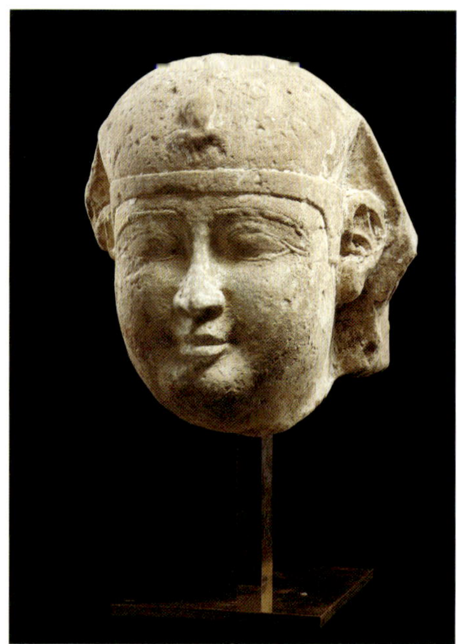

Cat. 32, page 115

Ancient Egypt — A Brief Chronology

Most of the following dates are approximate but all are to be understood as BC.

4000–3200	The Predynastic Period
3000–2955	Dynasty 0
2955–2635	The Archaic Period Dynasty I–II
2635–2155	The Old Kingdom Dynasty III–VI
2155–2134	The First Intermediate Period Dynasty VII–XI
2134–1785	The Middle Kingdom Dynasty XI–XII
1785–1554	The Second Intermediate Period Dynasty XIII–XVII
1554–1305	The New Kingdom Dynasty XVIII
1305–1080	The New Kingdom The Ramesside Period Dynasty XIX–XX
1080–656	The Third Intermediate Period Dynasty XXI–XXV
664–342	The Late Period Dynasty XXVI–XXX
342–332	The Second Persian Period
332–305	The Macedonian Period
305–30	The Ptolemaic Period
30	The Roman Imperial Period Begins

Selected Bibliography

Abd-alla, Aly. "Graeco-Roman Statues Found in the Sebbakh at Dendera." In *The Broken Reed. Studies in the Culture and Heritage of Ancient Egypt in Honour of A .F. Shore*, ed. Christopher Eyre, Anthony Leahy, and Lisa Montagno Leahy. London, 1994, pp. 1–24.

Altenmüller, Hartwig. "Totenliturgie und Mundöffnungsritual. Bermerkungen zur Vermuteten 'Vision von der Statue im Stein.'" In *Honi sont qui mal y pense. Studien zum pharaonischen, griechisch-römischen und spätantiken Ägypten zu Ehren von Heinz-Josef Thissen*, ed. Hermann Knuf, Christian Leitz, and Daniel von Reckoinghausen. Orientalia Lovaniensia Analecta 194. Leuven/Paris/Walpole, Mass., 2010, pp. 3–14.

Andrews, Carol. *Amulets of Ancient Egypt*. Austin, 1994.

Arnold, Dorothea. *The Royal Women of Amarna. Images of Beauty from Ancient Egypt*. New York, 1996.

Aubert, Jacques-F., and Liliane Aubert, *Statuettes égyptiennes. Chaouabtis—Ouchebtis*. Paris, 1974.

Aufrère, Sydney H. "Evolution des idées concernant l'emploi des couleurs dans le mobilier et les scènes funéraires en Egypte jusqu'à l'époque tardive." In *La couleur dans la peinture et l'émaillage de d'Egypte ancienne*, ed. Sylvie Colinart et Michel Menu. Autour de l'universe mineral XII. Bari, 1998, pp. 31–42.

Aufrère, Sydney H. "L'origine de l'albâtre à la Ire dynastie d'après les inscriptions des vases provenant des galeries de la pyramide à degrés," *Bulletin de l'Institut français d'Archéologie orientale* 103 (2003), pp. 1–15.

Aufrère, Sydney H. *Thot Hermès L'Egyptien. De l'infiniment grand à l'infiniment petit*. Paris, 2007.

Baines, John R. "Color Terminology and Color Classification: Ancient Egyptian Color Terminology and Polychromy." *American Anthropologist* 87 (1985), pp. 282–97.

Baines, John R. "Restricted Knowledge, Hierarchy, and Decorum: Modern Perceptions and Ancient Institutions," *The Journal of the American Research Center in Egypt* 27 (1990), pp. 1–24.

Baines, John R. *Visual and Written Culture in Ancient Egypt*. Oxford, 2007.

Barbotin, Christophe. *Les statues égyptienne du Nouvel Empire. Statues royales et divines* I. Paris, 2007

Bianchi, Robert Steven. "An Elite Image." In *Chief of Seers. Egyptian Studies in Memory of Cyril Aldred*, ed. E. Goring, London, 1992, pp. 34–48.

Bianchi, Robert Steven. "Ancient Egyptian Reliefs, Statuary, and Monumental Paintings." In *Civilizations of the Ancient Near East* IV, ed. Jack M. Sasson. New York, 1995, pp. 253–54.

Bianchi, Robert Steven. "Symbols and Meaning." In *Gifts of the Nile. Ancient Egyptian Faience*, ed. Florence Dunn Friedman. Providence/London, 1998, pp. 22–31.

Bianchi, Robert Steven. "Egypt, Ancient: First Intermediate Period-Middle Kingdom (ca. 2150–1650 BCE);" "Second Intermediate Period—New Kingdom Pre-Amarna (ca. 1715–1554 BCE;" "New Kingdom—Amarna (ca. 1554–1347 BCE);" "New Kingdom—Post-Amarna—Third Intermediate Period (ca. 1347–720 BCE);" "Late Period—Roman Period (ca. 720 BCE - CE 395." In *The Encyclopedia of Sculpture*, vol. 1, ed. Antonia Boström. New York, 2003, pp. 490–99.

Bianchi, Robert Steven. *Daily Life of the Nubians*. Westport/London, 2004.

Broekman, G. P. F., R. J. Demarée, and O. E. Kaper, eds. *The Libyan Period in Egypt*. Leiden, 2009.

Castiglione, Baldessare. *The Book of the Courtier*. Trans. G. Bull. London, 1976.

Davis, Whitney. *The Canonical Tradition in Ancient Egyptian Art*. Cambridge/New York/Port Chester/Melbourne/Sydney, 1989.

Derchain-Urtel, Marie-Theresia. *Priester im Tempel*. Wiesbaden, 1989.

der Manuelian, Peter. "Prolegomena zur Untersuchung saitischer 'Kopien'." *Studien zur altägyptischen Kultur* 10 (1983), pp. 221–45.

der Manuelian, Peter. "An Essay in Document Transmission: Nj-k3-'nh and the Earliest hrjw-rnpt." *The Journal of Near Eastern Studies* 45 (1986), pp. 1–18.

Eaton-Krauss, Marianne, and Erhardt Graefe, eds. *Studien zur ägyptischen Kunstgeschichte*. Hildesheimer ägyptologische Beiträge 29. Hildesheim, 1990.

Fischer, Henry George. *L'écriture et l'art de l'Egypte ancienne*. Paris, 1986.

Freed, Rita E., Yvonne J. Markowitz, and Sue H. D'Auria, eds. *Pharaohs of the Sun. Akhenaten, Nefertiti, Tutankhamun*. Boston/New York/London, 1999.

Gardiner, Sir Alan Henderson. *Egyptian Grammar*. Oxford/London, 1969.

Goyon, Jean-Claude. *Le papyrus d'Imouthès fils de Psintaes*. New York, 1999.

Grimnal, Nicholas. *A History of Egypt*. Trans. Ian Shaw. Oxford/Cambridge, 1992.

Hardin, C. L. *Color for Philosophers. Unweaving the Rainbow*. Indianapolis/Cambridge,1988.

Helck, Wolfgang. "Zu Ptah und Sokar." In *Religion und Philosophie im Alten Ägypten. Festgabe für Philippe Derchain zu seinem 65. Geburtstag am 24. Juli 1991*, eds. Ursula Verhoeven and Erhart Graefe. Orientalia Lovaniensia Analecta 39. Leuven, 1991, pp. 159–64.

Hill, Lana. "Their Heads to Keep: The Iconography of Ancient Egyptian Headrests." In American Research Center in Egypt, *The 60th Annual Meeting of the American Research Center in Egypt, April 24–26, 2009. The Adolphus Hotel, Dallas, Texas*. San Antonio, 2009, p. 53.

Hornung, Eric. *The Valley of the Kings. Horizon of Eternity*. Trans. David Warburton. New York, 1990.

Kitchen, Kenneth A. *Pharaoh Triumphant. The Life and Times of Rameses II*. Cairo, 1982.

Kuhlmann, K[laus P.], and W. Schenel. *Das Grab des Ibi. Theben Nr. 36*. Vol. I, text and plates. Mainz, 1983.

Lauer, Jean-Philippe. "Remarques concernant l'inscription d'Imhotep gravée sur le socle de statue de l'Horus Neteri-Khet (roi Djoser)." In *Studies in Honor of William Kelly Simpson II*, ed. Peter Der Manuelian. Boston, 1996, pp. 493–98.

Lichtheim, Miriam. *Ancient Egyptian Literature III. The Late Period*. Berkeley/Los Angeles/London, 1980, p. 138.

Mairs, Rachel. "A Bilingual Account from the Aswan Quarries (*O. Brookl.Dem.180 / P.Brookl.81*)." *Proceedings of the Twenty-Fifth International Congress of Papyrology*. Ann Arbor 2007. American Studies in Papyrology. Ann Arbor, 2010, pp. 463–70.

Málek, Jaromir. *The Cat in Ancient Egypt*. London, 1993.

Manniche, Lise. *Sacred Luxuries. Fragrance, Aromatherapy, and Cosmetics in Ancient Egypt*. Ithaca, 1999.

Mathieu, Bernard. "Les couleurs dans les Textes des Pyramides: Approache des systèmes chromatique (Enquêtes dans les Textes des Pyramides, 2)." *Egypte Nilotique et Méditerranéenne* 2 (2009), pp. 25–52.

Meeks, Dimitri. "Le nom du dieu Bes et ses implications mythologiques." In *The Intellectual Heritage of Egypt*, ed. Ulrich Luft. Studia Aegyptiaca 14. Budapest, 14ff.

Menu, Bernadette. "Les ouchebtis de Neskhons, entre droit et croyances." *Egypte Nilotique et Méditerranéenne* 4 (2011), pp. 39–49.

Müller, Hans Wolfgang. "Der Kanon in der ägyptischen Kunst." In *Der "vermessene" Mensch. Anthropometrie in Kunst und Wissenschaft* (Munich, 1973), pp. 9–31.

Neureiter, Sabine. "Schamanismus im Alten Ägypten." *Studien zur altägyptischen Kultur* 33 (2005), pp. 281–330.

Niwinski, Andrzej. "The Origin of the Two Sacred White Attributes of the Early Egyptian King: Crown and Mace." In *Les civilisations du bassin méditerranéen. Hommages à Joachim Sliwa*, eds. K. M. Cialowicz and J. A. Ostrowski. Cracow, 2000, pp. 25–52.

Ogdon Aquino, Jorge R. "Some Reflections on the Meaning of the Megalithic Cultural Expressions in Ancient Egypt." *Varia Aegyptiaca* 6 (1990), pp. 17–22.

Plato. *The Republic*, Book VII.

Raven, Maarten J. "Magic and Symbolic Aspects of Certain Materials in Ancient Egypt." *Varia Aegyptiaca* 4 (1988), pp. 237–42.

Redford, Donald B. *Akhenaten. The Heretic King*. Princeton, 1984.

Redford, Donald B. *Pharaonic King-Lists, Annals, and Day-Books*. Mississauga, Canada, 1986.

Redford, Donald B. *Egypt, Canaan, and Israel in Ancient Times*. Princeton, 1992.

Reeves, Nicholas. *The Complete Tutankhamun. The King, The Tomb, The Royal Treasure*. London, 1990.

Romano, James R. "The Origin of the Bes-Image." *The Bulletin of the Egyptological Seminar* 2 (1980), pp. 39–56.

Romer, John. *The Valley of the Kings*. New York, 1981.

Romer, John. *The Great Pyramid. Ancient Egypt Revisited*. Cambridge/New York, 2007.

Schäfer, Heinrich. *Principles of Egyptian Art*. Ed. Emma Brunner-Traut; trans. and ed. by John Baines, with a foreword by E. H. Gombrich. Oxford, 1986.

Staehelin, Elisabeth. *Von der Farbigkeit Agyptens*. Leipzig, 2000.

Tallet, Pierre. "Amenemhat III et la chapelle des rois à propos d'une stèle rupestre redécouverte à Sérabit al-Khadim." *Bulletin de l'Institut français d'Archéologie orientale* 109 (2009), pp. 473–95.

Tiradritti, Francesco. "Meaning and Use of Colors in Ancient Egypt: Proposal for a New Paradigm." In American Research Center in Egypt, *The 60th Annual Meeting of the American Research Center in Egypt, April 24–26, 2009. The Adolphus Hotel, Dallas, Texas*. San Antonio, 2009, pp. 108–9.

Valbelle, Dominique. "Craftsmen." In *The Egyptians*, ed. Sergio Donadoni; trans. Robert Steven Bianchi. Chicago, 1997, pp. 31–60.

von Beckerath, Jürgen. *Abriss der Geschichte des Alten Ägypten*. Munich/Vienna, 1971.

Winckelmann, Johann Joachim. *Gedanken über die Nachahmung der griechischen Werke in der Malerei und Bildhauerkunst*. 1755; 2nd ed. 1756.

Winckelmann, Johann Joachim. *Geschichte der Kunst des Alterthums*. 1764.

Catalogue of the Exhibition

1.

An Architectural False Door

Dynasty VI, 2290–2155 BC
Painted limestone
Height 43 ½ in.
Inv. no. EG-254

In ancient Egyptian art, the false door is related to stelae that commemorate the deceased. In its classic form, the false door was simply a rectangular stela. These early rectangular stelae were then set into niches. Over the course of time, the sides and tops of these niches were gradually ornamented until a decorative scheme was achieved in which the false door itself was framed by a series of receding elements, each representing a niche. These niche-evocative framing elements, here four in number, were successively shorter and ended with the depiction of that door.

During the course of the Old Kingdom, the false door became the primary focus of the funerary cult of the deceased. These doors are so named because they do not physically function. Their purpose was to permit the symbolic passage of the spirit of the deceased through the chambers and corridors of the tomb so that it might exit to partake of offerings and then return. In classically designed false doors, such as this one, the false door proper is represented as having two leaves; these are closed by means of a bolt, one of which is depicted on each of the leaves of this door.

The act of partaking offerings may have taken several forms, one of which required the living to place actual offerings on a specially offering table for the benefit of the deceased's spirit (compare cat. 18). In the event that practice could not be fulfilled, the offerings might still be made available to the spirit through the act of pronouncing the offering formula contained within this false door's inscriptions, or simply by the inherent potential for those spells and objects to become animated by virtue of their representation in the stone in which they were sculpted.

This false door is inscribed for an elite woman named Henat, the equivalent perhaps of the British "Lady." Her only title is Priestess of the goddess Hathor. Her accompanying funerary inscriptions repeatedly name both the gods Ptah Sokar and Anubis as her protecting deities. There is no other autobiographical information contained in the inscriptions and there is no mention of any members of her family. Henat is presented as an elite woman who appears to have been both independent and relatively affluent. Her status is indicative of that of other elite women during most periods of ancient Egypt's history, who were more liberated than their counterparts in other cultures. Certain details of this false door suggest it was created during Dynasty VI of the Old Kingdom.

The false door contains a square funerary stela, featuring an image of Henat and inscribed across the top with two rows of hieroglyphs. Henat is depicted barefoot, wearing a tightly fitting linen sheath and a bobbed wig exhibiting small, tight curls. She holds a lotus flower to her nose (compare cat. 5) and is seated upon an elaborate chair with a curved, bolsterlike back and legs terminating in lion's feet, set on cylindrically formed casters. In front of her is a table, on top of which appears a now-empty rectangular panel. That panel originally depicted a series of long loaves of bread, resembling baguettes, cut transversely down the middle and placed on the table. They were probably painted yellow. To the left of the offering table is a ewer, which provided Lady Henat with ritually pure water. At the lower left and right of the funerary stela are two rectangular recesses painted in alternating stripes of color. These are to be understood as braces used to hold the funerary stela in place.

Beneath a drum-shaped element, suggested to represent an ancient Egyptian equivalent of a window shade, is the false door through which the deceased was magically

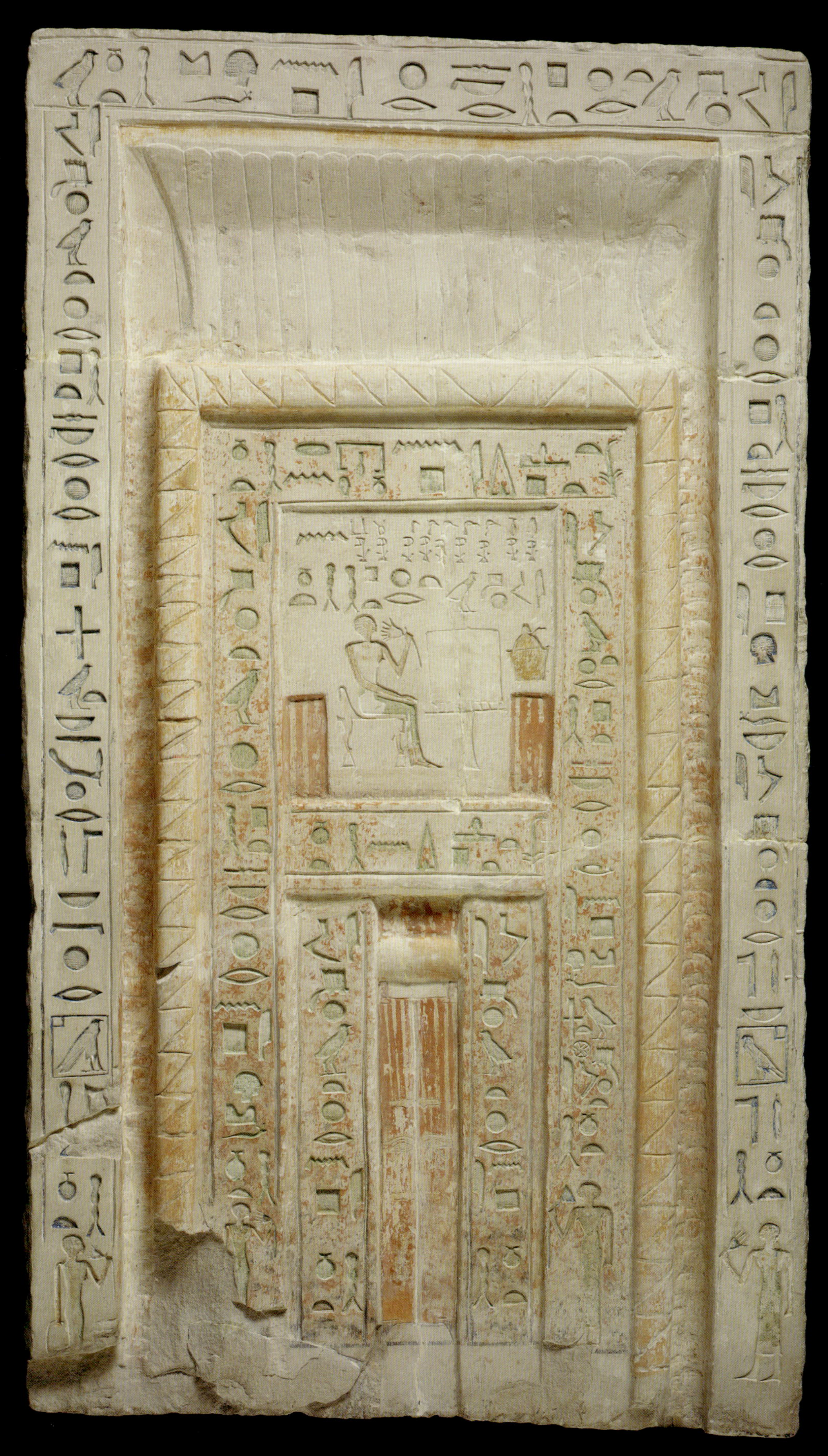

able to pass. The upper and lower edges of both leaves are designed as triangular projections. These are hinges which enabled the leaves to swing open and closed. Each leaf of the door is decorated with a wadjet-eye, an emblem of protection to ensure that evil is diverted from the entry to the tomb. The leaves are locked by two sets of door bolts, one above and one below each wadjet-eye. It is interesting to note that the door bolt is actually the ancient Egyptian hieroglyph for the letter "s."

The amount of color preserved on the false door is remarkable, but that color is not decorative. It serves a symbolic function. The yellow color of the torus moulding decorated with Z-shaped motifs is intended to suggest that this element is constructed of dried reeds or the like. The second framing element as well as the lintel and jambs of the door itself are painted in a stippled red in imitation of granite. The leaves of the door itself as well as the braces of the funerary stela are decorated with distinctive red stripes meant to imitate cedar. The ancient Egyptians pioneered the use of faux finishes, and this tradition ultimately contributed to the development of Roman wall painting. The color used for the ewer suggests it is made of copper. In keeping with ancient Egyptian traditions, the flesh of Lady Henat is yellow, as are the skin tones of most depictions of women of the Old Kingdom. This is to distinguish them from men, whose flesh is generally painted red. The reason for this gender-based color distinction is societal. Egyptian women generally spent their time within their homes or palaces while men worked outdoors. As a result, women's skin was not tanned from exposure to the rays of the sun. The false door of Lady Henat is designed and painted to convey an impression of great wealth in the form of deluxe copper implements, the use of Aswan red granite, and imported cedar of Lebanon.

There are four virtually identical images of Lady Henat on the bottom of each of the vertical framing elements. In each case she is depicted in a standing position and wears the tightly fitting sheath with the same bobbed wig as in her funerary stela. In three of these four representations she is shown holding a lotus flower to her nose while her free arm hangs down along the side of her body. In keeping with ancient Egyptian design tenets that dictate that primacy of place is to the far left of the viewer looking at the work of art, the image of Henat in that position must be regarded as the principal image of the composition. Here she appears to be holding the stem of a second flower, which hangs down alongside her legs. The addition of this second flower reinforces the importance attached to this particular representation.

The significance and symbolic value of the lotus flower in this context cannot be overlooked. Lady Henat does not smell the lotus simply because she enjoys its fragrance. In ancient Egyptian civilization, only deities could grant the breath of life to pharaohs. It is common, therefore, to encounter images in which a god or goddess extends an ankh-sign to the nose of a pharaoh. Such a ritual presentation could not be appropriated by members of the elite because they would thereby be committing *lèse-majesté*. In order to enjoy the benefits of receiving the breath of life, the members of the Egyptian elite developed an artistic conceit by which the lotus served as both the equivalent of, and substitute for, the ankh-sign. As a result of this artistic convention, Lady Henat is able to present the breath of life to her own nose. The appearance of a second lotus flower in her hand in the left-most image serves to reinforce this conceit as well as to emphasize the importance of that particular image.

One is reminded that ancient Egyptian nouns are generally followed by a determinative, that is, a hieroglyphic sign that provides a visual clue to the meaning of the signs that precede it. So, for example, words meaning to eat or to speak are determined by a hieroglyph representing an individual with his hand raised to his mouth. In the case of this false door of Henat, each of the four images at the bottom of the false door serves as its own determinative because these images are found immediately after the hieroglyphs used to spell her name. She is, therefore, represented multiple times in both name and image.

The inscriptions may be translated as follows:

(The top of the outer frame, from right to left)

> *The one who is venerated under the god Ptah-Sokar and the one who is venerated under the god Anubis who is upon his mountain is the Lady Henat.*

(The left-hand column of the outer frame)

> *The one who is venerated under the god Ptah-Sokar and the one who is venerated under the god Anubis, who is in the place of embalming, who is the lord of the necropolis, who is the great god, and who is the lord of heaven, is the Lady Henat who is the priestess of the goddess Hathor.*

(The right-hand column of the outer frame)

> *The one who is venerated under the god Ptah-Sokar and the one who is venerated under the god Anubis, who is upon his mountain, is the one who is venerated under the great god, the lord of [heaven?]; she is the Lady Henat, the priestess of the goddess Hathor.*

(The top of the second frame)

> *A funerary offering which pharaoh grants to Anubis consisting of an invocation offering of bread and beer on behalf of the Lady Henat.*

(The left-hand column of the second frame)

> *The one who is venerated under the god Ptah-Sokar and the one who is venerated under the god Anubis who is upon his mountain is the Lady Henat.*

(The right-hand column of the second frame)

> *The one who is venerated under the god Ptah-Sokar and the one who is venerated under the god Anubis who is in the place of embalming is the Lady Henat, the [possessor of] veneration.*

(The two lines at the top of the funerary stela)

> *One thousand loaves of bread, one thousand jugs of beer, one thousand geese, one thousand geese, one thousand geese, one thousand geese, one thousand geese, one thousand vases of alabaster, and one thousand bolts of linen cloth for the one who is venerated under the god Ptah, namely the Lady Henat.*

The mention of "one thousand geese" five times is not necessarily an error and may be regarded as a desire to provide Lady Henat with an abundance of geese, duck, foie gras, and the like in the hereafter, perhaps suggesting that she was fond of such food.

(The lintel over the door)

> *An invocation offering which pharaoh bestows upon the Lady Henat.*

(The left and right lintel, which bear identical inscriptions)

> *The one who is venerated under the god Anubis is the Lady Henat.*

Anonymous, "La porte du rêve," 2007, pp. 38–39.

2.

A Procession of Bearers of Funerary Offerings (Suggested to have come from the Tomb of Ny-ankh-nesut)

Late Dynasty V or early Dynasty VI, 2450–2155 BC
Three painted limestone panels
Lengths: 37 ¼ in.; 20 ⅞ in.; 18 ½ in.
Inv. no. EG-125

3.

A Procession of Bearers of Funerary Offerings (Suggested to have come from the Tomb of Ny-ankh-nesut)

Late Dynasty V or early Dynasty VI, 2450–2155 BC
Painted limestone
Length: 17 in.
Inv. no. EG-337

These four panels are sculpted in wafer-thin relief. Taken together, the images provide a textbook illustration of the way in which ancient Egyptian principles governing the design of the hieroglyphs are equally applied to two-dimensional presentations. Accordingly, each object is depicted from the view that provides the most visual information required for immediate and unmistakable identification. More complex objects, the male figures in particular, are designed with their component parts so viewed, reassembled for the same reasons of visual clarity. All of the figures, objects, and hieroglyphs may be profitably compared to cut-out paper dolls affixed to a background that is both timeless and spaceless. There are no Western conventions for light and shadow that might indicate the time of the day in which this procession takes place. In like manner, there are no suggestions of any landscape that could site the figures in a definable environment. The avoidance of overlapping and of other spatial-generating devices denies the third dimension.

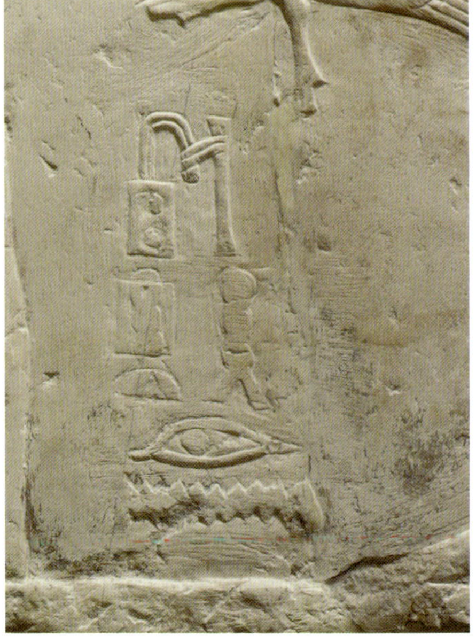

Cat. 2, Detail

At right:
Cat. 2, Two of the panels

The entire decoration of such a tomb was laid out by elite overseers called outline scribes, whose task it was to design the composition so that it accommodated itself perfectly to the wall. The actual sculpting was presumably entrusted to a crew of illiterate workmen who then executed the predetermined design. One notes with particular interest that errors could be, and in fact were, introduced as a consequence of this practice. In this particular relief, the hieroglyphs forming the name of the god Ptah were incorrectly sculpted.

The error was subsequently discovered in what may have been a practice akin to proofreading a manuscript. The misspelling was corrected by re-sculpting some of the signs (detail).

These sculpted and painted panels once decorated a tomb. Their function was to perpetuate the supply of myriad offerings, held and carried, for the benefit of the deceased whose tomb these relief blocks adorned. Some of these offering-bearers are identified as

> *the son of Onas-sanakh*

> *his son, the lector-priest, Onas-soneb.*

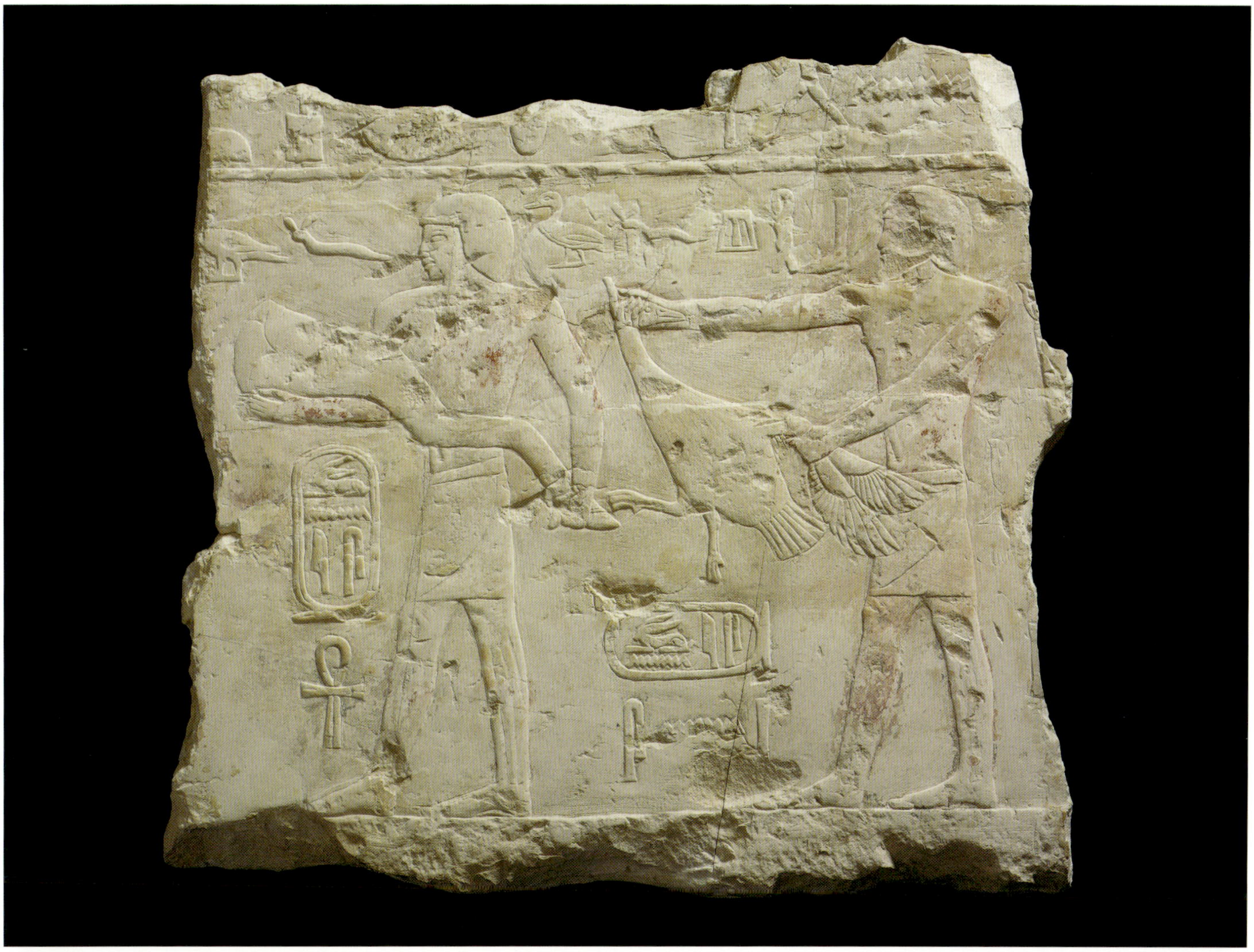

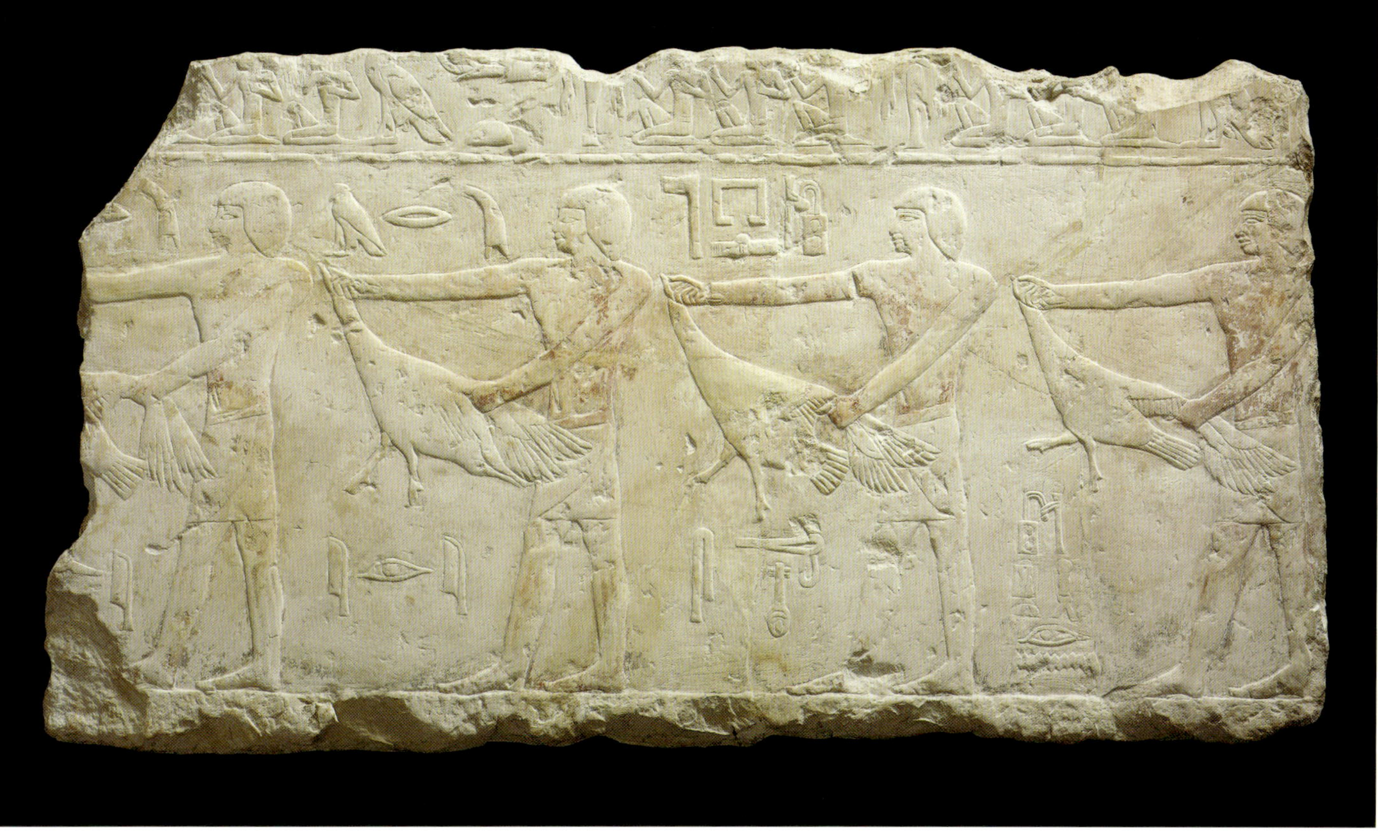

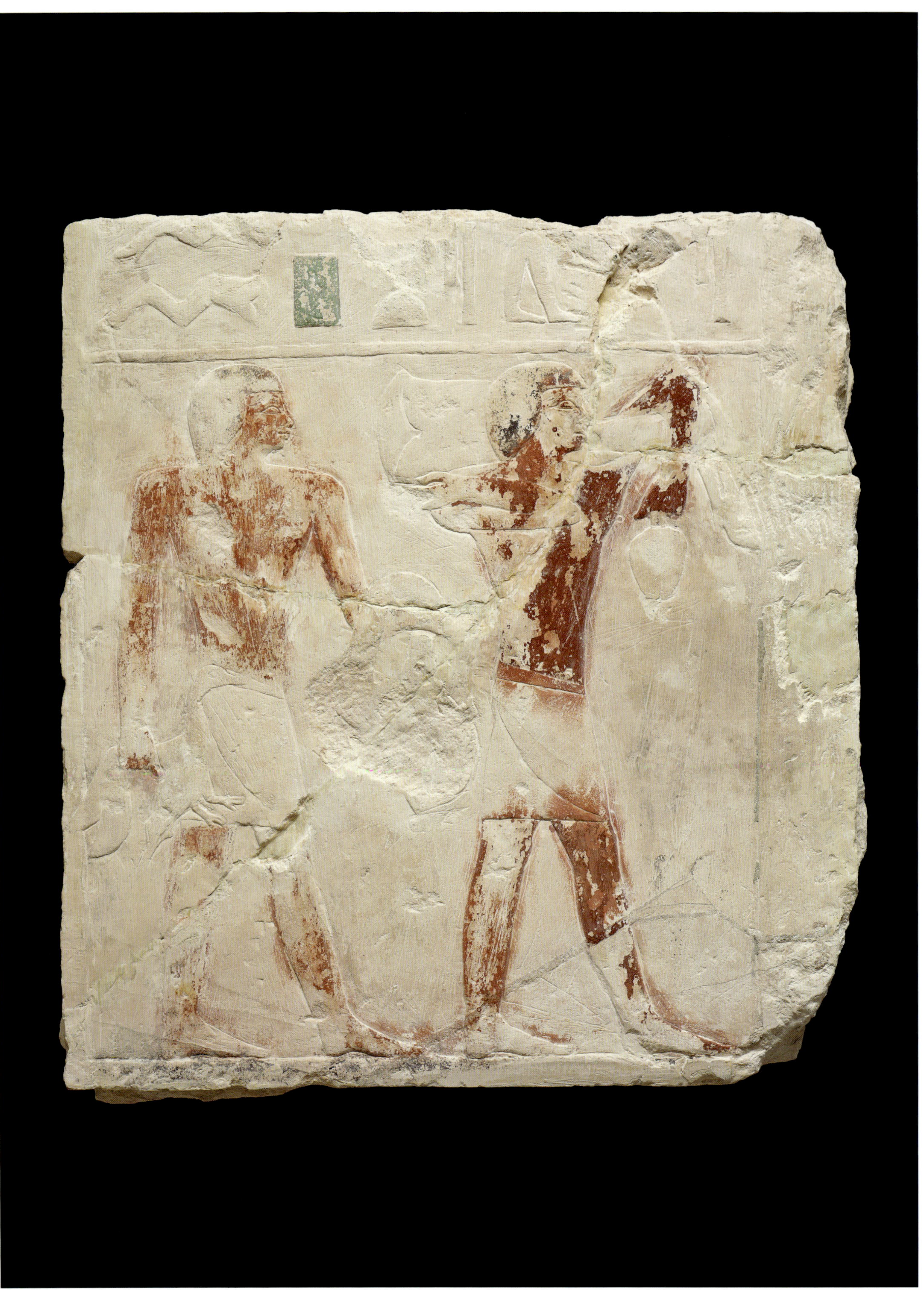

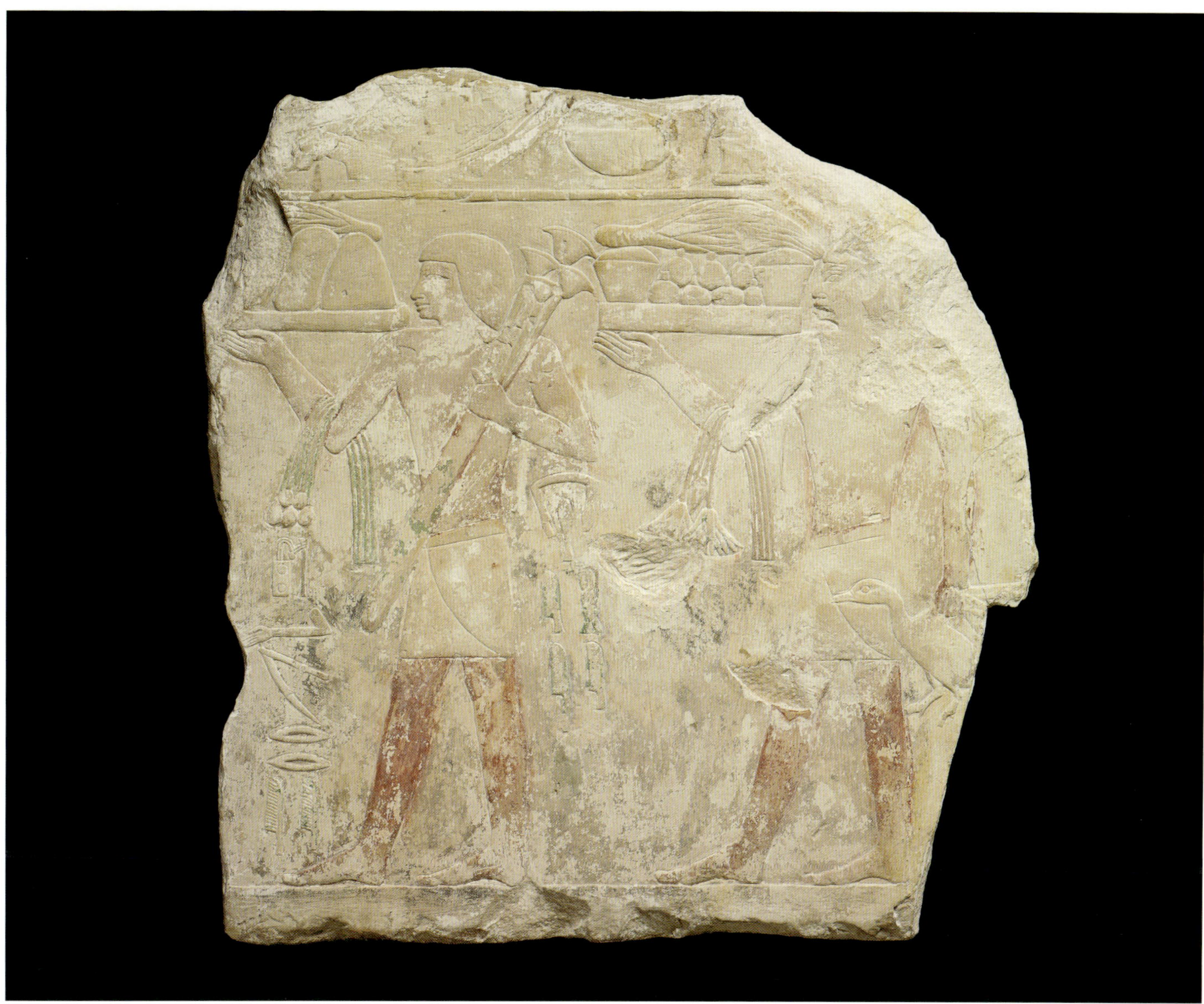

Above:
Cat. 2, A third panel

At left:
Cat. 3

Although these four panels may not originally have fitted together edge to edge, particularly since one panel depicts the offering bearers moving in an opposite direction, they are, nevertheless, being exhibited as a unit because they possess the same characteristics and are suggested to have come from the same tomb. This observation is confirmed by recent research. The tomb belongs to a high official named Ny-ankhnesut, discovered in or about 1917, at which time its ruinous state had already been noted. This led to the recovery of approximately sixty or so worked blocks that have been so widely scattered among museums and private collections worldwide that it now appears to hold a "dispersion record among ancient Egyptian tombs." One hastens to emphasize that the conditions governing such acquisitions in 1917 were far, far different than they are today; as recently as the 1950s the Egyptian government authorized the sale of works of art found in the collections of the Egyptian Museum in Cairo. The exact location of this tomb was lost and remained unknown until its rediscovery in January 2000, when its position close to the northwest corner of the enclosure wall of pharaoh Sehemkhet at Saqqara was re-established (compare cat. 7).

References for Cat. 2:
Berman, *Catalogue*, 1999, p. 135; Leahy and Mathieson, "Tomb of Nyankhnesut," 2001, pp. 33–42, pls. IV–V; Mahmoud, "Preliminary Report," 2002, pp. 75–88; Málek, "Provenance," 1980, pp. 201–06; van Dijk, *Objects*, 2006, p. 39.

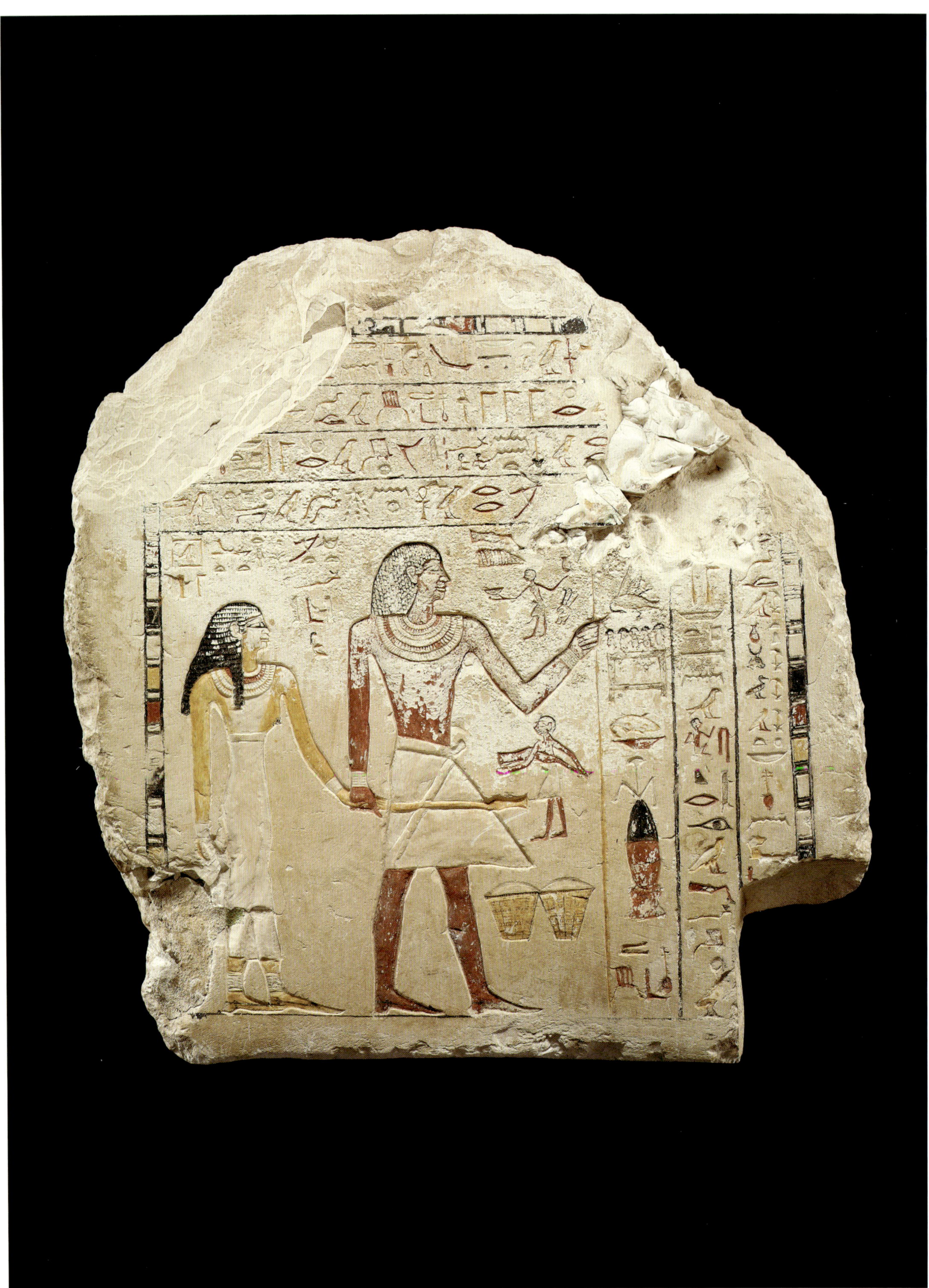

4.

Stela of Nefer-tchebau and his wife, Ibi

Dynasty X, 2134–2040 BC
Painted limestone
Height 32 ½ in.
Inv. no. EG-359

The top and both sides of this stela are bordered by a rectangular ornamental band of alternating colored squares (blue-black, red, yellow, and white) framing four lines of hieroglyphic text at the top and three columns at the right. The principal figural scene depicts the deceased, Nefer-tchebau, facing right with his left leg advanced. He is shown wearing a plain, wrap-around kilt, belted at the waist, and a curled wig that leaves his ear exposed. His accessories include a broad collar and bracelets. He holds a staff in his raised near hand and a baton in his lowered far hand, which his wife, standing behind him, clasps. She is identified as Ibi and is painted yellow, in contrast to her husband, who is painted red. She wears a white, tightly fitting sheath, a broad collar, bracelets, and anklets. Her tripartite wig, like her husband's, is characterized by curls. The hieroglyphs over her head and in front of her face translate as

> *His beloved wife, the sole ornament of the king, the priestess of the goddess Hathor, [named] Ibi.*

Two attendants, in smaller scale and somewhat more summarily rendered, are placed in the field in front of Nefer-tchebau but do not stand on ground lines. The figure before his face offers a bowl held in the hand of his extended arm. Two offerings, in larger scale, appear above the bowl while the heads of a fowl and an ox appear behind him. These are hieroglyphs for fowl and oxen. The offering bearer below presents a haunch of beef. Below the wrap-around kilt of Nefer-tchebau are two baskets containing foodstuffs, presumably bread. The column of hieroglyphs closest to the image of Nefer-tchebau contains offerings in the form of trussed geese, an offering table, a loaf, and his name,

> *The [possessor of] veneration, [named] Nefer-tchebau*

The four columns of inscription, partially damaged across the top of the stela, which contain *The Appeal of the Living*, may be translated as

> *[An offering that the king gives to the god Anubis, who is upon his mountain], who is in the place of embalming, who is the lord of the necropolis in order that he might give an invocation offering consisting of bread and beer for the [count named Nefer-tchebau]...the one venerated under all the deities, Nefer-tchebau. He says, [I was one beloved of my father, blessed by my mother], one beloved by his brothers and sisters, one honored by the great god who is the lord of heaven . . . all you who are living upon this earth, who love life and despise death, may you say, a thousand loaves of bread and a thousand jugs of beer, a thousand head of cattle and a thousand fowl, a thousand of every thing [good and pure] for the count . . . the great god, the lord of heaven, for the prosperous commoner, who acted with his strong arm, the possessor of veneration, named Nefer-tchebau.*

The two fragmentary columns of hieroglyphs to the far right contain an additional list of thousands of various types of offerings together with an invocation to the great god, the lord of heaven, on behalf of the count Nefer-tchebau.

The stela may be assigned to a series of similar reliefs from Naga ed-Deir, created during the Heracleopolitan era of the First Intermediate Period. This period was characterized by competing elites vying with one another for supremacy. Because there was no central authority to promote adherence to canonical models upon which designs were to be based, certain principles were relaxed, contributing to local variations of established norms. The oversized baskets in the field beneath the owner's kilt and other anomalies in the some of the hieroglyphs are representative of this trend, as is the presence of several flint nodules, clearly evident in the break on the right-hand side of the stela, suggesting that access to better-quality limestone was unavailable.

The Appeal to the Living contained within the inscriptions of this stela is ample demonstration of the magical characteristics of ancient Egyptian art in which hieroglyphs and images, represented in stone, were symbolically thought to become animate for the everlasting benefit of the deceased.

References: Dunham, *Naga el-Der*, 1937.

5.

Two Registers from an Elite Tomb

Dynasty XI, 2134–1991 BC
Painted limestone
Height 18 ⅛ in.
Inv. no. EG-352

Consummately sculpted in wafer-thin raised relief with extensive traces of its black and red polychromy still preserved, this worked block features two partially preserved registers. At the top is the forefoot of what appears to be a lion resting on a profiled bolster, doubtless representing a lion-footed chair on which the deceased was presumably seated. This detail rests on a thin black ground line that separates it from the better-preserved vignette below.

In this lower vignette, one finds a train of three women, the center being the best preserved. She is shown wearing a tightly fitting linen sheath with a V-shaped bodice that exposes one breast. This V-shaped bodice is a well-established dating criteria because it represents a fashion current during the Middle Kingdom. The figure is coiffed in a tripartite wig, painted black, and holds a large lotus to her nose, symbolically presenting herself with the breath of life (compare cat. 1). Her facial features are sculpted with care and attention to detail and include a hieroglyphic eye with its pupil and thin brow painted black, a nose with fleshy wing, and thick lips. Her ear is likewise detailed. There is a column of hieroglyphs in front of her, too incomplete to translate, and by a single line of hieroglyphs over her head, which can be translated as

> *his female relative, whom he loves, [whose name is] Setnetkher...*

One cannot determine whether Setnetkher was his wife or his daughter because of the signs missing at the beginning of the line and because that personal name does not appear to be attested elsewhere.

The sculpting of the relief is of the highest quality and compares favorably with the royal relief representations associated with the pharaoh Mentuhotep Nebhetepre and members of his immediate family, created at Thebes during his reign in Dynasty XI, when he unified the country after the First Intermediate Period.

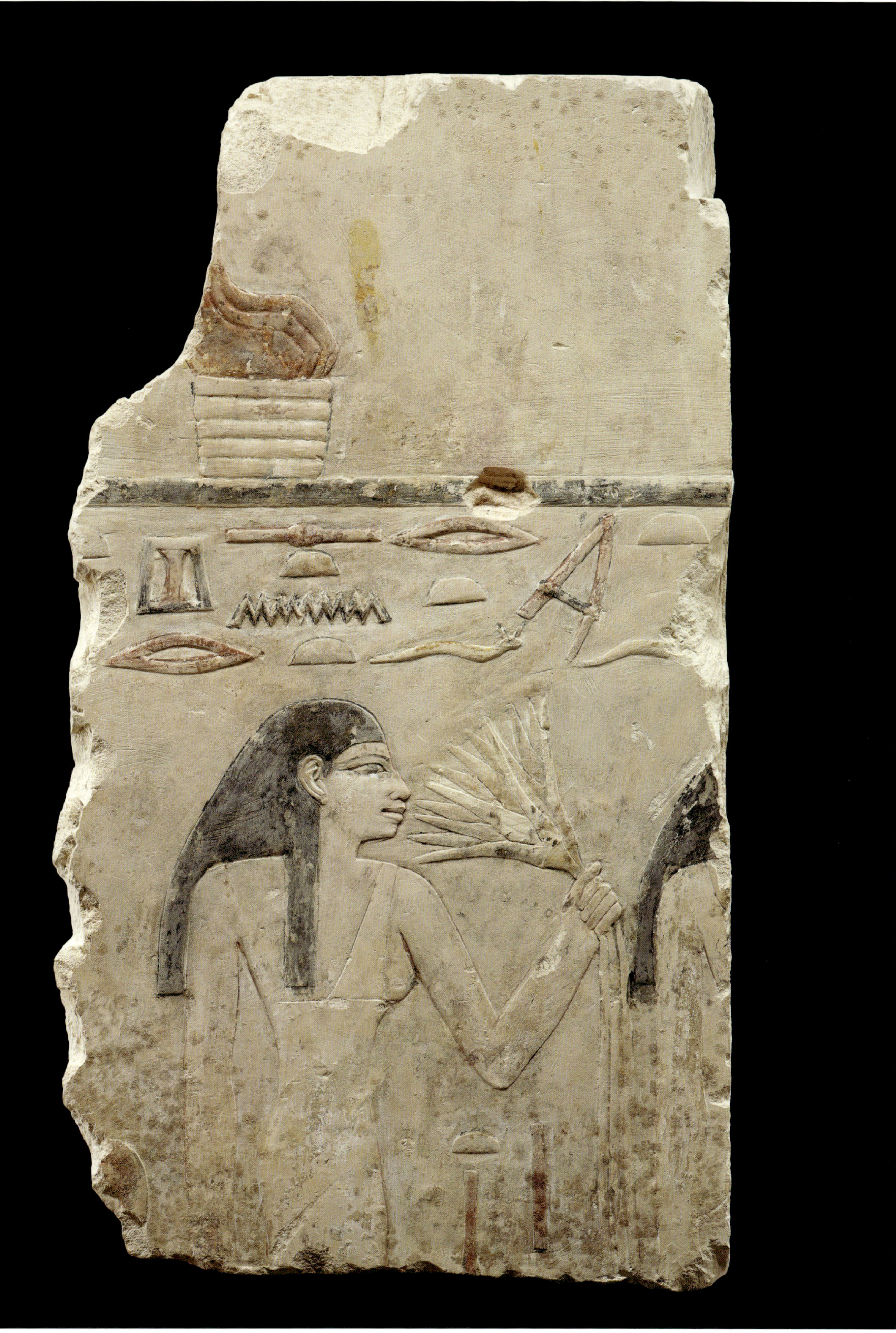

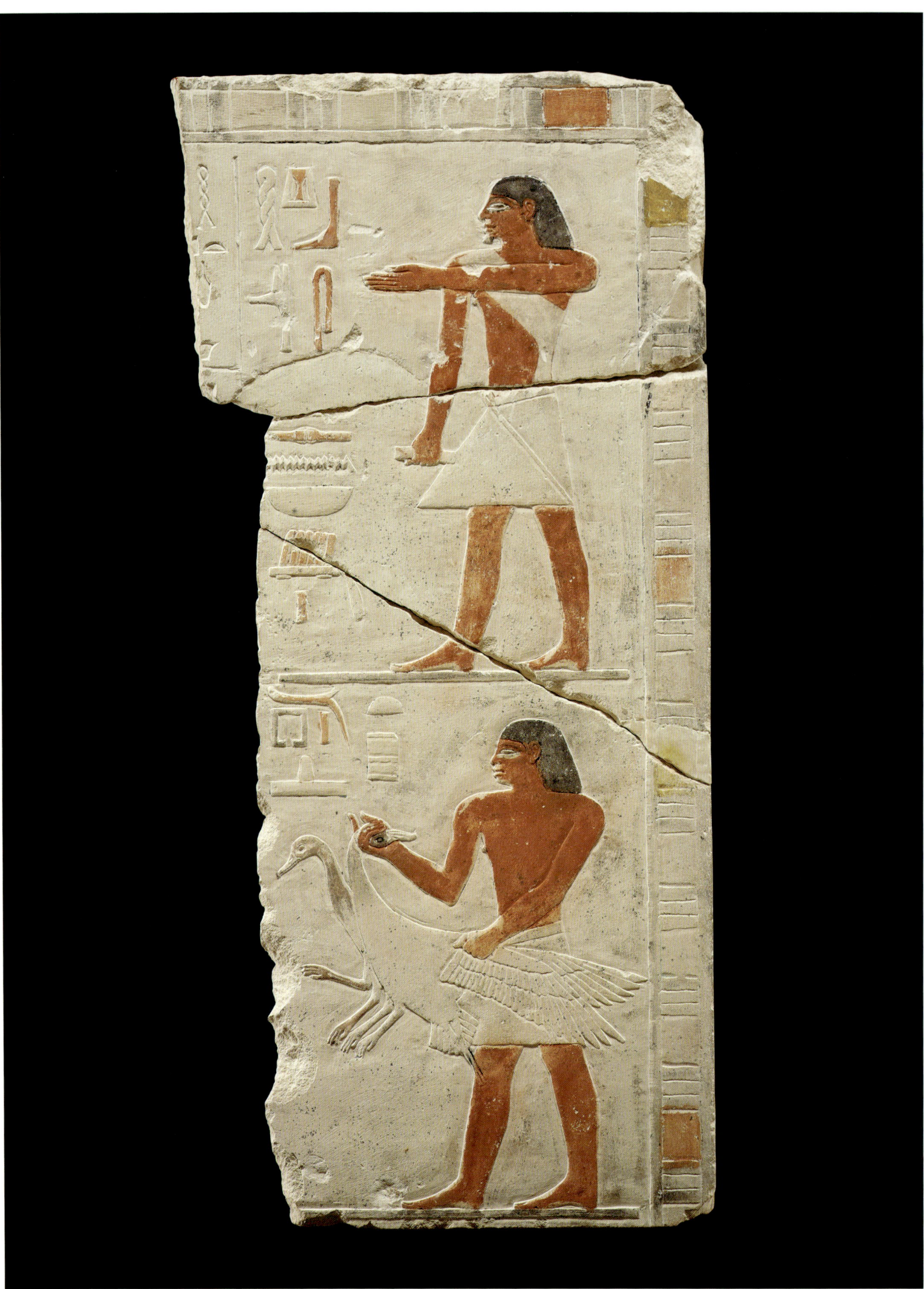

6.

Two Registers from an Elite Tomb

Dynasty XII, 1991–1785 BC
Painted limestone
Height 22 ¾ in.
Inv. no. EG-351

The worked block, sculpted in wafer-thin relief and then painted, comes from the upper right-hand corner of a tomb wall, to judge from the ornamented, painted border of squares and triglyphs that frame the composition at the top and right-hand side. The preserved portion depicts two offering bearers, facing left, standing on a thin ground line, and painted in the traditional orange-red color for male figures, suggesting that their spheres of activities are in the outdoors. Both wear wigs and undecorated wrap-around kilts secured at the waist with knotted belts. The figure at the top additionally has a goatee and sports a bandolier placed asymmetrically over his chest. The fisted hand of his lowered arm holds a papyrus scroll, and his raised arm is held straight and horizontal in front of his body in a gesture of recitation. He is identified by the single column of unframed hieroglyphs accompanying his image as

> *the lector-priest, possessed of veneration, [named] Senwesret.*

The bandolier and papyrus scroll are emblems of this particular office, because one of the duties of a lector-priest was to recite prayers and spells on behalf of the deceased. A column of imperfectly preserved hieroglyphs, whose translation is therefore impeded, appears in sunk relief to the left of this inscription, separated from the hieroglyphs by an incised vertical line. His companion below presents two geese by holding them up by their wings. The row of hieroglyphs accompanying his image identify him as

> *the superintendent [named] Hetep.*

The appearance of both figures sculpted into the limestone of the tomb was intended to perpetuate the recitation of appropriate spells and prayers for the benefit of the deceased and to provide him with the provisions necessary for continued existence in the hereafter.

The relief is stylistically dated to the Middle Kingdom, a dating that is confirmed by the presence of the name of the lector-priest, Senwesret, which is that of several pharaohs of Dynasty XII, after whom this cleric was doubtless named.

7.

A Relief from the Tomb of Djuhty-nefer

Dynasty XVIII, 1554–1305 BC
Limestone
Length 35 7/8 in.
Inv. no. EG-196

This relief, from the wall of an elite tomb, is designed as two horizontal vignettes, sculpted in shallow, sunk relief and separated by a thinly incised vertical line, each with its own accompanying hieroglyphic captions. The shallow relief has been filled with a golden yellow pigment, which, if ancient, extends the divine nature of the deities depicted to the tomb owner and his wife.

The vignette to the left features an image of the mummiform Osiris standing on a small base, identified by two columns of text in the field above his face:

> *Osiris, the great god.*

Before him to the left stands the deceased with arms raised in adoration wearing a broad collar and belted kilt reaching to just below his knees. His wig features a series of small, rectangularly arranged curls. The five columns of hieroglyphs identify him as

> *The scribe and counter of the cattle and fowl of the temple of the god Amun, the overseer of the fowlers, whose name is Djuhty-nefer, also called Seshu.*

Behind him at the far left is a female figure accompanied by three columns of hieroglyphs identifying her as

> *His beloved wife, the mistress of the house, Bembu, the justified.*

The vignette to the right, only partially preserved, depicts the jackal-headed god, Anubis, so labeled in the accompanying hieroglyphs, and a second image of the deceased tomb owner, Djuhty-nefer, called Seshu.

All of the figures are arranged on a thin horizontal ground line and are designed in accordance with the principle of combining characteristic views of each component part of the human body into one in which every element is immediately and unmistakably comprehended. Djuhty-nefer's skirt, belted at the waist and reaching a level just above the ankles, is woven of very fine linen, which is so transparent that his legs are clearly visible beneath it. This artistic interest in transparency first appears in certain representations of Old Kingdom date but gains wider currency during the course of Dynasty XVIII and XIX of the New Kingdom (compare cat. 13).

The function of the tomb, its decoration, and its appointment was to ensure the resurrection of the deceased. To that end, Djuhty-nefer and Bembu are represented in stone in perpetual adoration before two of the more important funerary deities, Osiris, god of the hereafter, and Anubis, lord of embalming.

The tomb from which this relief came was discovered by legendary German Egyptologist R. Lepsius in the nineteenth century, when the antiquities market was open and relatively unregulated. Its location, subsequently forgotten and lost, was only rediscovered in the second half of the twentieth century (compare cat. 2 and cat. 3).

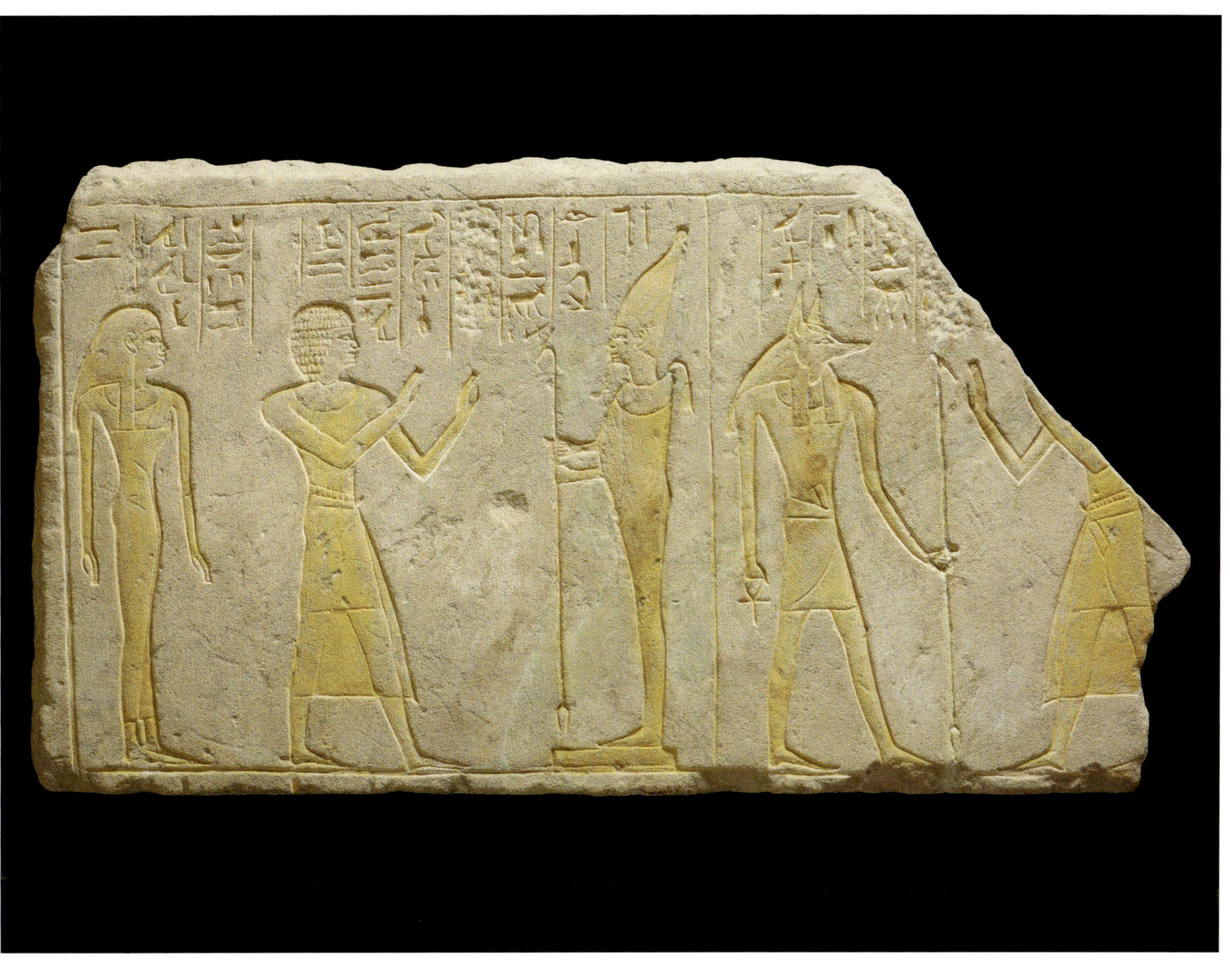

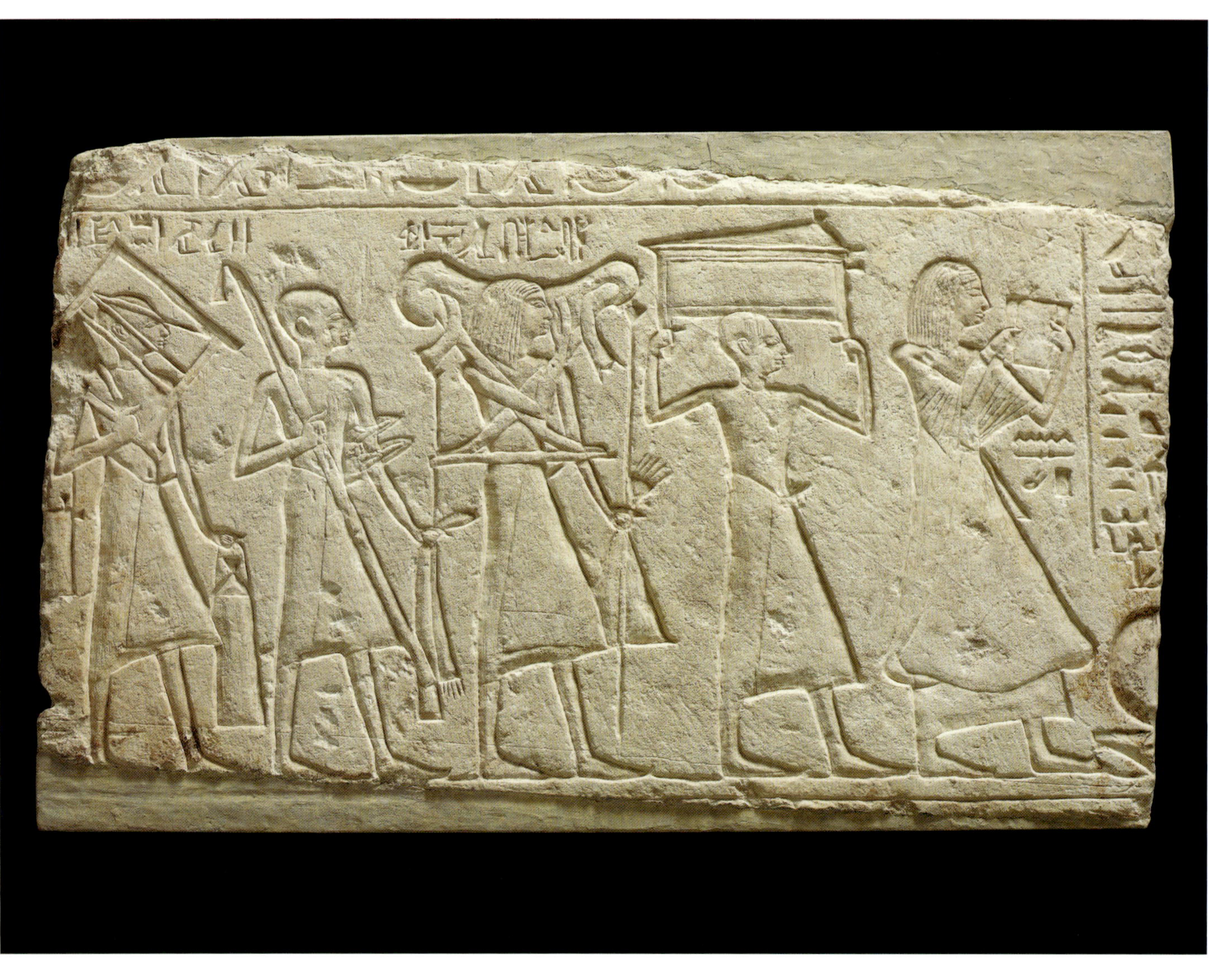

8.

A Procession of Offering Bearers from an Elite Tomb

Dynasty XVIII, 1554–1305 BC
Limestone
Length 29 ½ in.
Inv. no. EG-213

This vignette, once decorating the wall of an elite tomb, is inscribed with a single horizontal row of hieroglyphs across the top, so damaged as to preclude a translation. The signs in the vertical column at the right, also damaged, appear to contain traces of the now illegible name of the tomb owner followed by a reference to the god Osiris in his role as lord of the dead. The figural scene features a funerary procession in which objects beneficial for the deceased's use in the hereafter are being symbolically delivered to the tomb for the perpetual use of its owner.

The traces of a rounded object placed upon a sledge that appears at the very far right of the scene, although very fragmentary, is unmistakably a *tekenou*, an enigmatic object habitually depicted immediately behind the catafalque and box containing the jars in which the organs removed during mummification were preserved. Some suggest that the *tekenou* contains the detritus of the embalming processes, which could not be discarded as refuse, but had to be gathered up, preserved, and interred with the deceased.

The procession as preserved is led by a barefoot male wearing a striated wig and an elaborate costume featuring a skirt with a voluminous apron and short, pleated bolero-type sleeves. He holds an unrolled papyrus in his capacity of lector-priest, responsible for the recitation of the requisite prayers. Behind him follows a figure with shaven head, clothed only in a long skirt, knotted at the waist, who carries a chest on his head, the legs of which he holds in his hands. He is followed by an individual, identified as *his* [the pharaoh's] *companion and scribe* [named] *Hormin*, with one hand, palm open, held to his face. Hormin carries an upholstered (folding?) chair on his shoulders and a bag and staff in his lowered hand. The individual behind Hormin, wearing only a long, belted skirt, also has a shaved head. He has slipped a pair of sandals over the biceps of his lower arm, the hand of which holds linen bandages. The hand of his other arm carries a long, unidentifiable tubelike object. The fifth offering bearer, *Yau-amon, true of voice*, whose head is likewise shaved and who wears a long skirt, apparently not belted, carries an object identified as either a sack or a vessel in his lowered hand, a table in his raised hand, and a basket with its strap suspended over his elbow. All of these offerings were symbolically intended for the use of the deceased in the hereafter.

Published: Chappaz and Chamay, *Reflets du divin*, 2001, p. 84, no. 69.

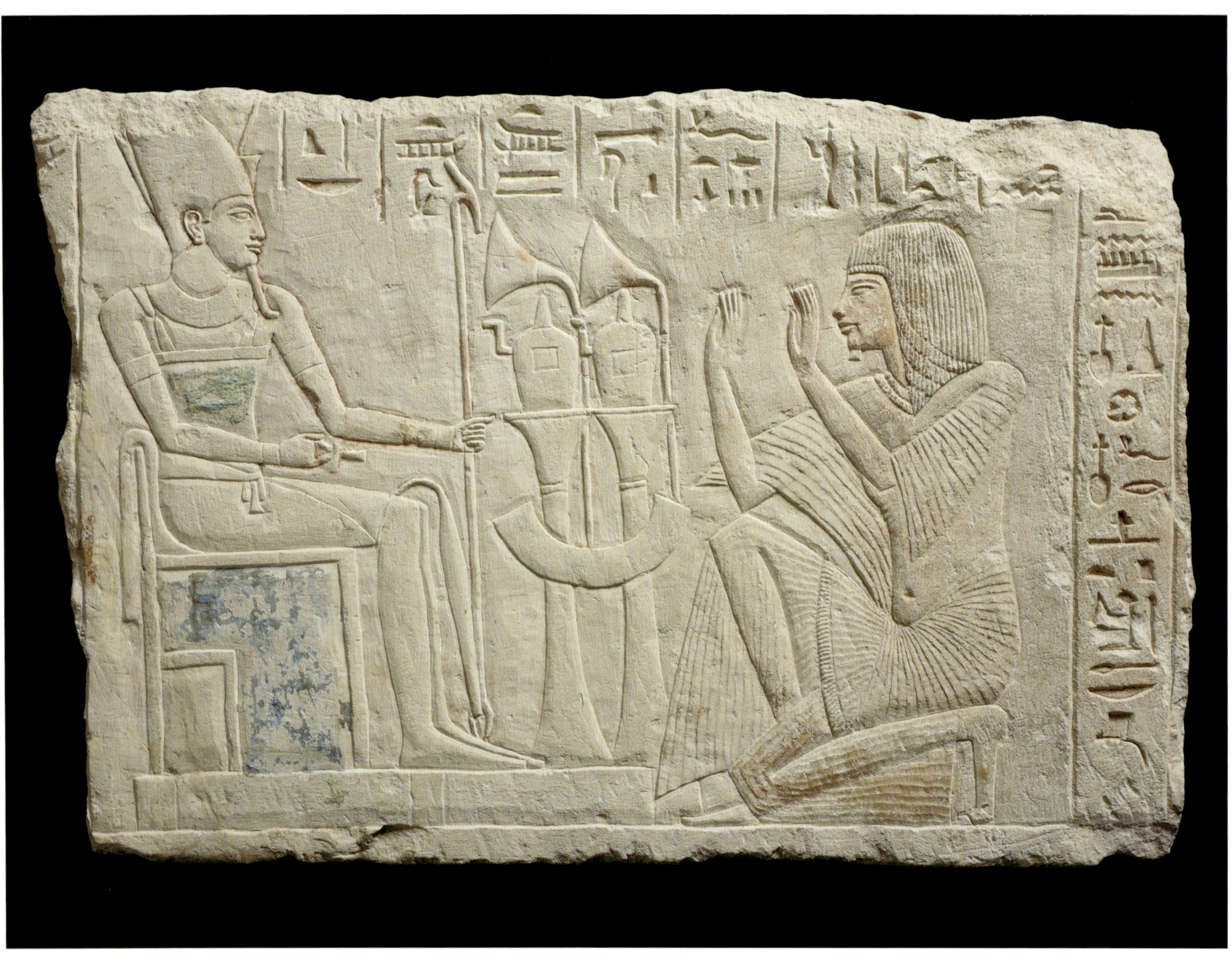

9

A Relief from the Tomb of Nefer-hotep

Late Dynasty XVIII, 1403–1305 BC
Painted limestone
Length 22 ⅛ in.
Inv. no. EG-271

This vignette from his tomb represents Nefer-hotep, sporting a goatee, in a kneeling pose, with his hands, palms open, raised in a gesture of adoration. He wears a double-echeloned wig (compare cat. 27) and an elaborately pleated costume, woven of gossamer linen that reveals the forms of his body. The god Atum wears a corslet as well as a belted kilt, to which is attached the tail of a bull, conferring upon him that animal's strength. In accordance with Egyptian design principles that stress visual clarity, that tail is depicted emerging from and rising up between the god's knees before it trails down in front of his lower legs. His accessories include the Double Crown, armlets on his biceps, and a broad collar. Atum holds an ankh-sign in one hand and a was-scepter in the other. He shares a dais with two cylindrically shaped offering stands, their tables shaped like papyrus umbels, upon which are placed a ewer and a lotus blossom, with a U-shape floral garland suspended between them. Atum was a creator god and solar deity associated with the site of Heliopolis. The extensive use of green reinforces his generative powers. Traces of perhaps as many as eight columns of imperfectly preserved hieroglyphic inscriptions across the top of this vignette name Atum, while the single column behind Nefer-hotep contains both his name and the toponym, *Mennefer*, the Egyptian proper noun for the city of Memphis.

This vignette assumes a central role in any discussion regarding the means by which scenes were designed and transmitted, with particular attention to pattern books, because it is a mirror image of a virtually identical vignette found in tomb of Horemheb at Memphis (fig. 24). Horemheb's tomb was created while he was still commander-in-chief of the army under Tutankhamun, before he himself became pharaoh after Tutankhamun's death.

There are differences between the two vignettes that indicate there was a great deal more attention paid to the detail in the relief created for Nefer-hotep than in that for Horemheb. The costume of Nefer-hotep is pleated, whereas that of Horemheb, which represents the same style and fashion, is plain. Nefer-hotep does not wear sandals; Horemheb does. In both vignettes, Atum shares his dais with two offering stands, but there is only one stand before Atum in Horemheb's relief, and this is placed in front of, rather than on, the dais. That single offering stand displays a similar ewer but its lotus flower is accompanied by two lotus blossoms. There are other differences as well, including the degree of detail to be found in the depiction of the costume of the god Atum. In the vignette from the tomb of Nefer-hotep, this god wears a belt, to which is attached what is called the "knot of Isis," the *tyt* amulet (compare cat. 61). This is not found in the costume of Atum in the vignette in the tomb of Horemheb.

Because of the astonishing similarities that these vignettes share, the designers of both are suggested to have used the same template, perhaps in the form of suggested pattern books (compare cat. 48). It is even conceivable that both tombs were designed by the same overseers employing craftsmen from the same atelier. What remains perplexing, however, is the quantifiable difference in execution. The details found in the relief of Nefer-hotep, judged from Western standards, appear to be fuller and more complete than those found in that of Horemheb, who, one assumes, enjoyed a slightly higher social status than Nefer-hotep. This same quantifiable difference is discernible when comparing the decoration of the Theban tomb of Ramose (Theban Tomb 55) with that of his sovereign Amenhotep III in the Valley of the Kings. One cannot, therefore, automatically conclude that objects created for the pharaoh were in any way aesthetically superior or technically more accomplished than those created for the elite in their service. The reverse appears to be true, and this situation, which runs counter to Western expectations, deserves further inquiry (compare cat. 37).

Figure 24
Detail from the Memphite Tomb of Horemheb, Dynasty XVIII

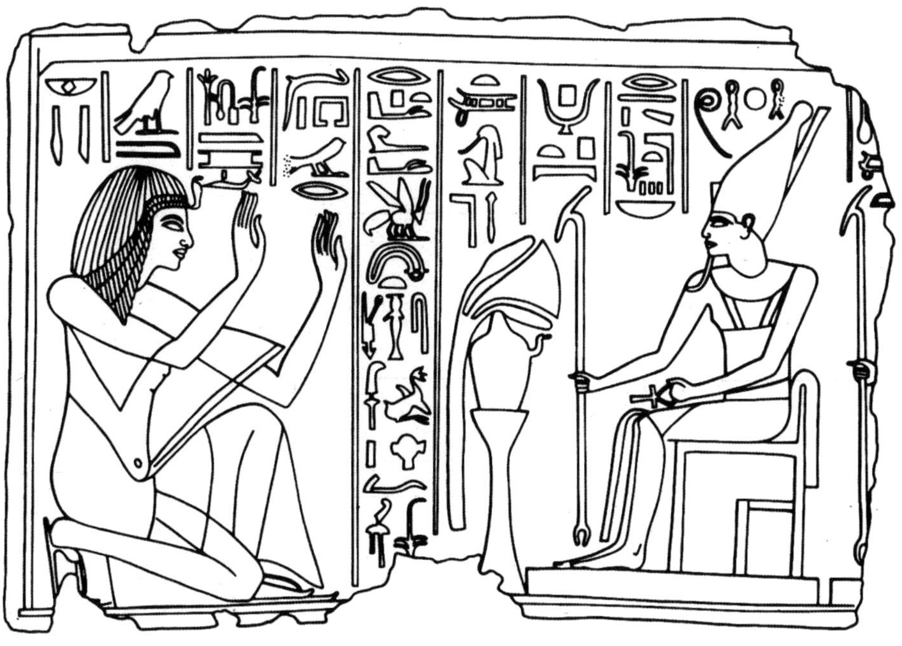

References:
Andrews, *Amulets*, 1994, pp. 44–45, and 98, fig. 100. This amulet is closely related to the legend of Osiris. It appears to represent an open loop of material, from which two folded loops hang down. They are commonly encountered among the funerary amulets of the period in which Neferhotep lived. Martin, *Tomb of Horemheb*, 1989, p. 47, plate 38, fig. 36. This vignette served as one of the panels decorating one of the columns in the first court. In the recent restoration of this tomb at Saqqara, this panel has been positioned above the drums of Column D.

10.

Offerings to the Aton

Dynasty XVIII, The Amarna Period, reign of Pharaoh Akhenaten, 1365–1349 BC
Limestone
Length 21 in.
Inv. no. EG-322

This worked block is designed in two registers, the bottom of which is divided into three. At the top are the ankles and feet of two individuals, both of whom are wearing sandals. Research has demonstrated that Nefertiti, when shown with her husband, Akhenaten, generally wears a pleated ensemble that covers her feet and trails on the ground. Her husband's ensemble is generally shorter, unpleated, and reaches only to his ankles. Accordingly, Nefertiti is to be identified here as the figure to the left, whereas the figure to the right is Akhenaten. Both figures are depicted with the left leg advanced. It is significant that, in this instance, the toes of the right foot are clearly shown. This attention to detail is consistent with other advances in art pioneered by the elite foremen in consultation with the pharaoh during this period.

Below the ground line on which the royal couple stands are the remains of three shorter registers. At the top are representations of five bulls, each with three of their legs tied together, bound so that their one foreleg and head might be severed in the ritual act of sacrifice.

The next register depicts all or part of six altars, each attended by an official. These altars are to be regarded as being set in an open court, because the worship of the Aton occurred out-of-doors under the sky overhead. Each of the altars is piled high with offerings and is preceded by an hourglass-shaped incense burner, one of which is being ignited by the attendant at the far right. The attendant behind him appears to be making a libation, perhaps of oil. The three remaining attendants are all bent forward at the waist in an attitude of reverence, and are to be understood as either having completed their service or waiting patiently for their turn to do so. The partially preserved lowest register depicts five attendants, again bowing at the waist, in various acts of ritual practice.

The series to which this work belongs was discovered in the spring of 1939, perhaps even earlier, by Professor Günther Roeder, who was excavating at Hermopolis Magna (modern Ashmunein), near Mellawi in Middle Egypt. The reliefs had originally been erected at Tell el-Amarna, across the river from Hermopolis Magna, in buildings commissioned by Akhenaten. Later, Pharaoh Rameses II dismantled the buildings and used these reliefs as filler in the foundations of his new structures, which were being erected at Hermopolis Magna.

In keeping with the practices at the time of their discovery, most of these reliefs were modernly enhanced with the application of a water-soluble red pigment, the application of which was intended to increase the visual appeal of their sculpted scenes.

Published: Chappaz, *Akhénaton et Neféfertiti*, 2008.

References: Redford, *Akhenaten*, 1984.

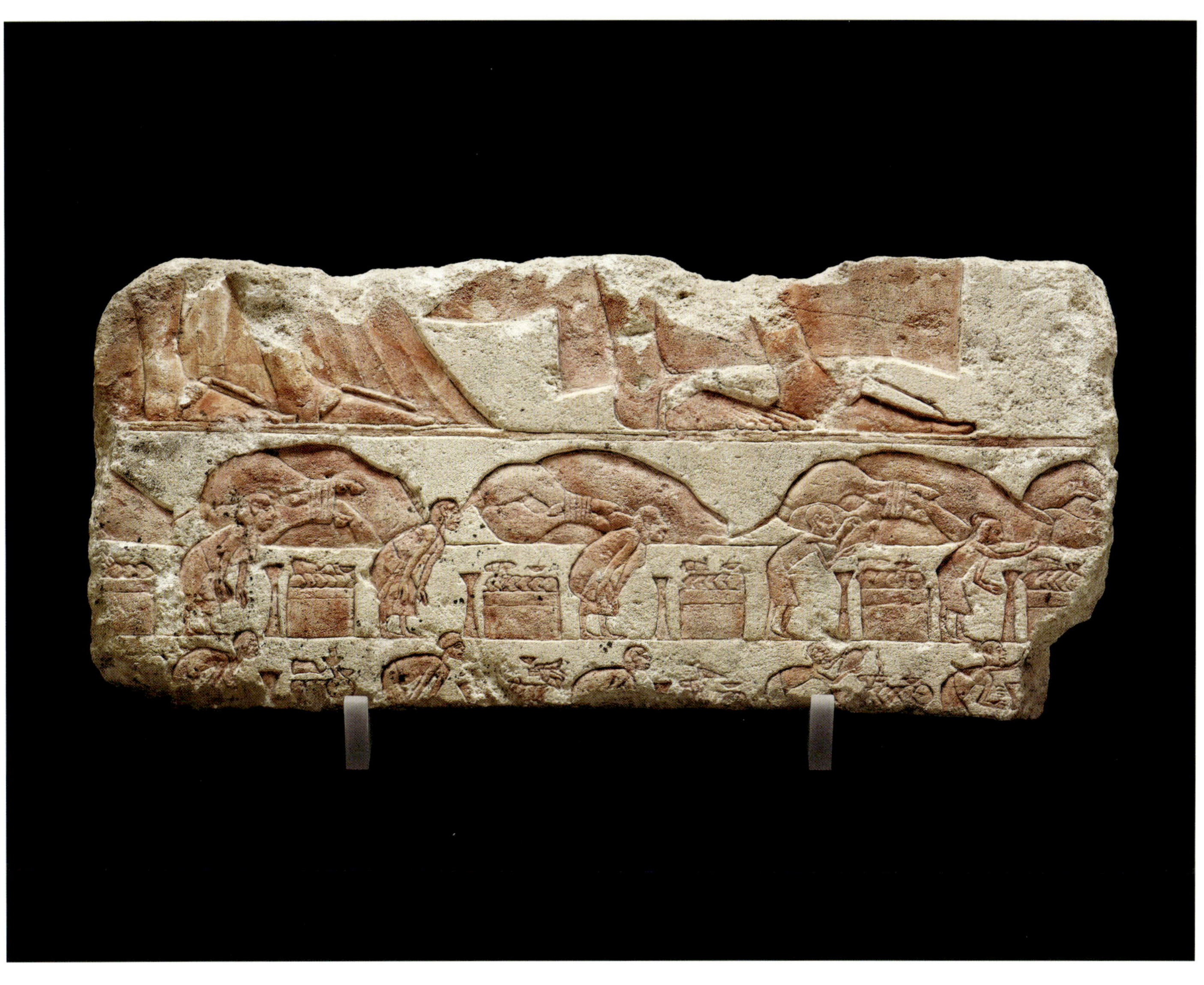

11.

A Round-Topped Funerary Stela Inscribed for Neheh

Late Dynasty XVIII, 1554–1305 BC
Limestone
Height 36 ½ in.
Inv. no. EG-360

This monumental, round-topped stela is significant because it reflects the style of the Amarna Period as perpetuated in private dedications of the post-Amarna Period of late Dynasty XVIII. Neheh, the owner of this stela, is depicted with the typical shaved, egg-shaped head characteristically employed for representations of the royal family during the Amarna Period. One of his titles, "a member of the corps bearing the sacred, processional barque [christened] Itentehen [the resplendent Aton, or sun disk]," associates him with the sun disk of the Amarna Period. The style of this stela should be considered in association with a second (cat. 12) which, although somewhat later in date, likewise reflects the style of the Amarna Period in the presence of a similarly designed egg-shaped head.

The stela itself is composed in four principal registers, framed at the top by a sun disk with only one wing, the space to the left occupied by a lightly-incised wadjet, or sacred, eye. Single-winged sun disks in the lunettes of round-topped stelae of Dynasty XVIII are well attested.

The principal, upper figural register depicts the deceased to the left wearing a long, pleated festive kilt and broad collar, offering incense in his upraised hand and cool water (compare cat. 12) in his lowered hand. Before him is a table piled high with offerings to a larger, seated image of the god Osiris, depicted mummiform on a throne with footrest. Osiris's accessories include an atef-crown, a curled, false beard, and a broad collar with a menat-counterpoise behind. He holds a large heka-scepter and flail in his fisted hands. A large attribute, suggested to be either a fan or floral element, protects his back.

The seven columns of inscription associated with the owner may be translated as

> *I have offered libations and incense to [the god] Osiris-Wenenefer, the lord of the city of Busiris, the ruler of the necropolis so that he might afford me a burial in the west, like that enjoyed by the praised ones who follow in peace and join the others so praised. May you enable me to go forth and to receive water offered by the hands of the living. I worship Re when he rises and appease him when he sets, being an exceptional individual, beloved of the god, great in the praise of Osiris-Wenenefer, a member of the corps bearing the sacred, processional barque [christened] Itentehen, [whose name is] Nehen.*

The four columns of hieroglyphs, two in the field above and two behind the figure of Osiris, reads

> *Osiris, the great god, the lord of heh-eternity, the master of djet–everlastingness.*

> *May all protection, may all life, may all stability, may all power, may all health together with all joy surround you as they do for Re, eternally.*

The nouns *heh* and *djet* were used for slightly different concepts of eternity in ancient Egyptian theological thought. Taken together, they may be considered as the equivalent of "forever and ever."

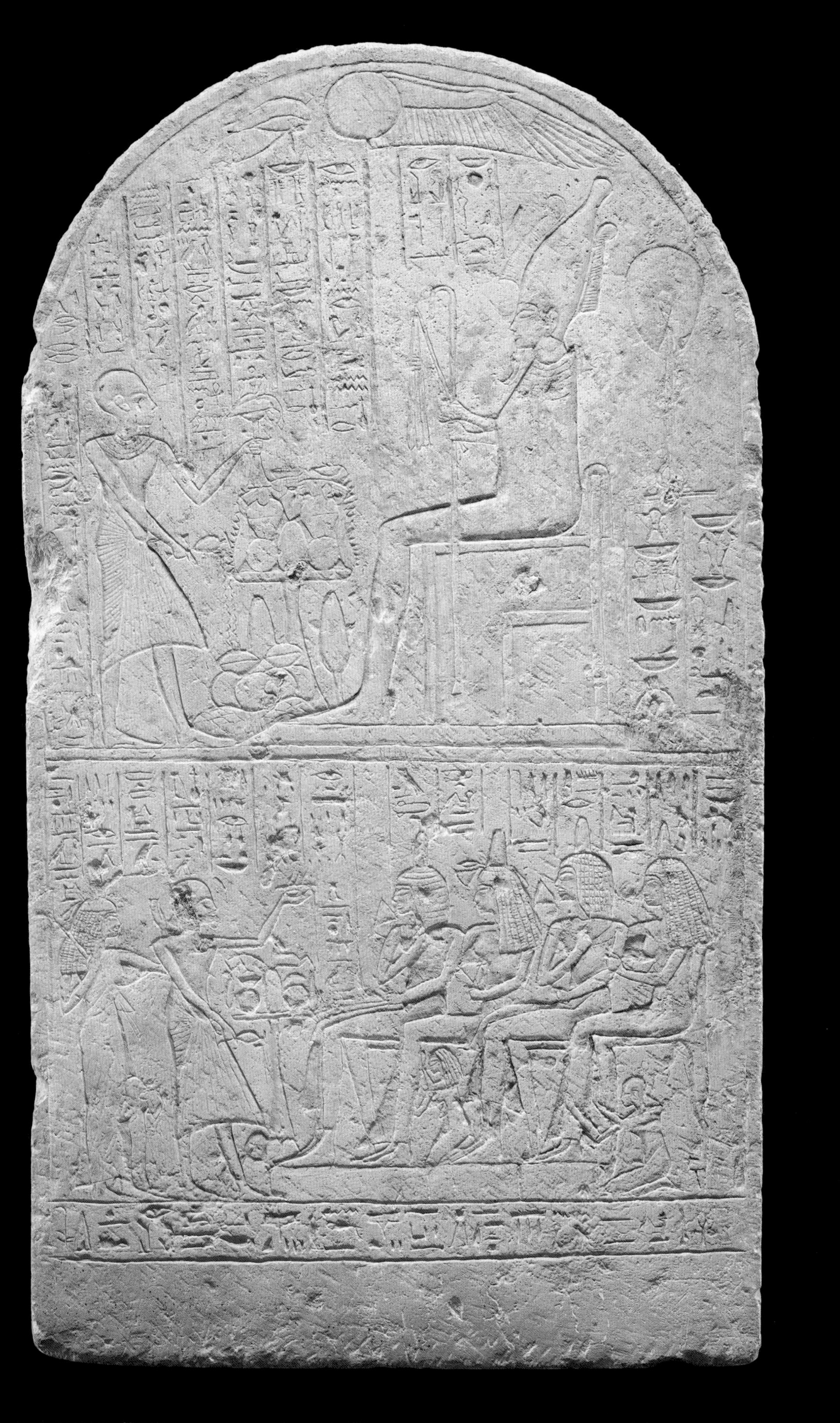

The lower figural register contains a scene in which Neheh's wife, Tiye, stands at the far left. She is dressed in a pleated garment and wears a wide wig, topped with a so-called ointment cone, representing her aura in an altered state in the hereafter (compare cat. 12). She holds one arm over her chest, its hand holding a long stem of a lotus flower, while her other arm is raised with its hand in a gesture of adoration behind the head of her husband. Their (presumably) daughter, not named, stands by her side in a smaller scale. Nehen is represented, as above, offering incense and cool water before a table piled high with offerings. Behind him is a row of four family members, one male and three female, all seated on chairs. A smaller male and female figure, unnamed and with arms raised in adoration, kneel at the feet of the second and fourth figure.

The hieroglyphs associated with Neheh and Tiye may be translated as

> *Making [an offering] of bread and beer, oxen and fowl, alabaster and linen, wine and milk, all things good and pure on which a spirit lives for the spirit of his father [named] Tatjetetet, the one true of voice, as well as for his mother named Tiy. This was done by the a member of the corps bearing the sacred, processional barque [christened] Itentehen, [whose name is] Nehen.*

With the last phrase repeated,

> *a member of the corps bearing the sacred, processional barque [christened] Itentehen, [whose name is] Nehen.*

The columns of hieroglyphs over the seated figures to the right may be read as

> *Tatjetjet, true of voice, together with Tiy, true of voice*
>
> *Imenerhatef, true of voice*
>
> *Tiye, true of voice and the possessor of veneration.*

The stela ends with a single line of hieroglyphs along the bottom:

> *An offering which pharaoh presents to the god Osiris-Wenenefer in order that he may bestow the sweet breeze of the north wind to the spirit of the member of the corps bearing the sacred barque, Nehen, repeating life.*

The stela commemorates members of an extended family and reinforces their hope for continued benefactions in the hereafter.

12.

A Round-Topped Funerary Stela

Late Dynasty XVIII to early Dynasty XIX, 1350–1250 BC
Limestone
Height 21 ⅞ in.
Inv. no. EG-186

Recalling the shape of some modern headstones, this funerary stela, or upright stone monument, features an offering scene and nine columns of hieroglyphs. The top of the lunette is adorned on the left with a wadjet, representing the injured left eye of Horus, which was eventually healed. A shen-sign, the circular form of which symbolizes "all that which the sun encompasses," occupies the center, below which are three horizontal lines and a cup.

According to ancient Egyptian design tenets, the male and female figures to the left are to be understood as sitting next to one another in a row, not one in front of the other, as Western compositional principles would seem to suggest. They sit on high-backed chairs, the legs of which terminate in stylized lion paws, placed upon a rectangular dais. The woman wears a tightly fitting sheath, woven of fine linen, which is repeatedly represented in ancient Egyptian art as if it were the staple of every woman's wardrobe. She is identified as "his beloved sister named Tai." During the New Kingdom, "sister" was commonly used as a term of affection and endearment applied to one's wife. In such contexts, the use of this noun is not to be taken literally as an expression of a specific sororial relationship. She wears a wide wig, its locks indicated by incisions.

Her husband is identified as

> *Kay, the divine father [i.e., a priestly title] of the god Sobek [generally associated with the crocodile] of Chedet [a district in the Faiyum, a rich agricultural region located to the southwest of modern Cairo].*

His hair is closely cropped, as the incised hairline clearly reveals. He is bare-chested but wears a broad collar, armlets, sandals, and a belted, long skirt. His lowered hand holds a folded handkerchief, apparently appropriated from the repertoire of royal regalia to enhance his status. He holds a lotus to his face (compare cat. 1 and cat. 5). This detail must be understood as a rebus or visual pun, because the lotus is often a motif substituted for the ankh, or sign of life. In traditional Egyptian iconography deities offer the sign of life to the nose of the pharaoh. Elite members of society appropriated this royal prerogative by replacing the ankh with the lotus, thereby presenting the breath of life to their own noses without employing imagery reserved for the exclusive use of the pharaoh. A cone is placed on the top of each head of the couple, the wife's ornamented with a flower. Once regarded as ointment cones intended to perfume the air around the wearer, these cones have recently been reinterpreted as symbols for one's aura, suggesting that those so represented are spirits in the hereafter (compare cat. 11).

The large figure on the right is the couple's elder son, "Mahu, the pure priest of the god Sobek." Mahu was a common name in ancient Egypt, and individuals so named are not necessarily one and the same person. This Mahu is bareheaded and barefoot and wears a short, belted kilt. He offers to his parents incense from a censor held in one hand and cool water from a ewer held in the other. This act is performed in front of a table laden with stylized images of loaves of bread, various vegetables, and the head of an ox. The curved ends of this tabletop suggest the shape of the sacred boat in which the sun god travels. These offerings, designed in accordance with Egyptian conventions, are placed one above the other as if floating to avoid overlapping. So designed, they

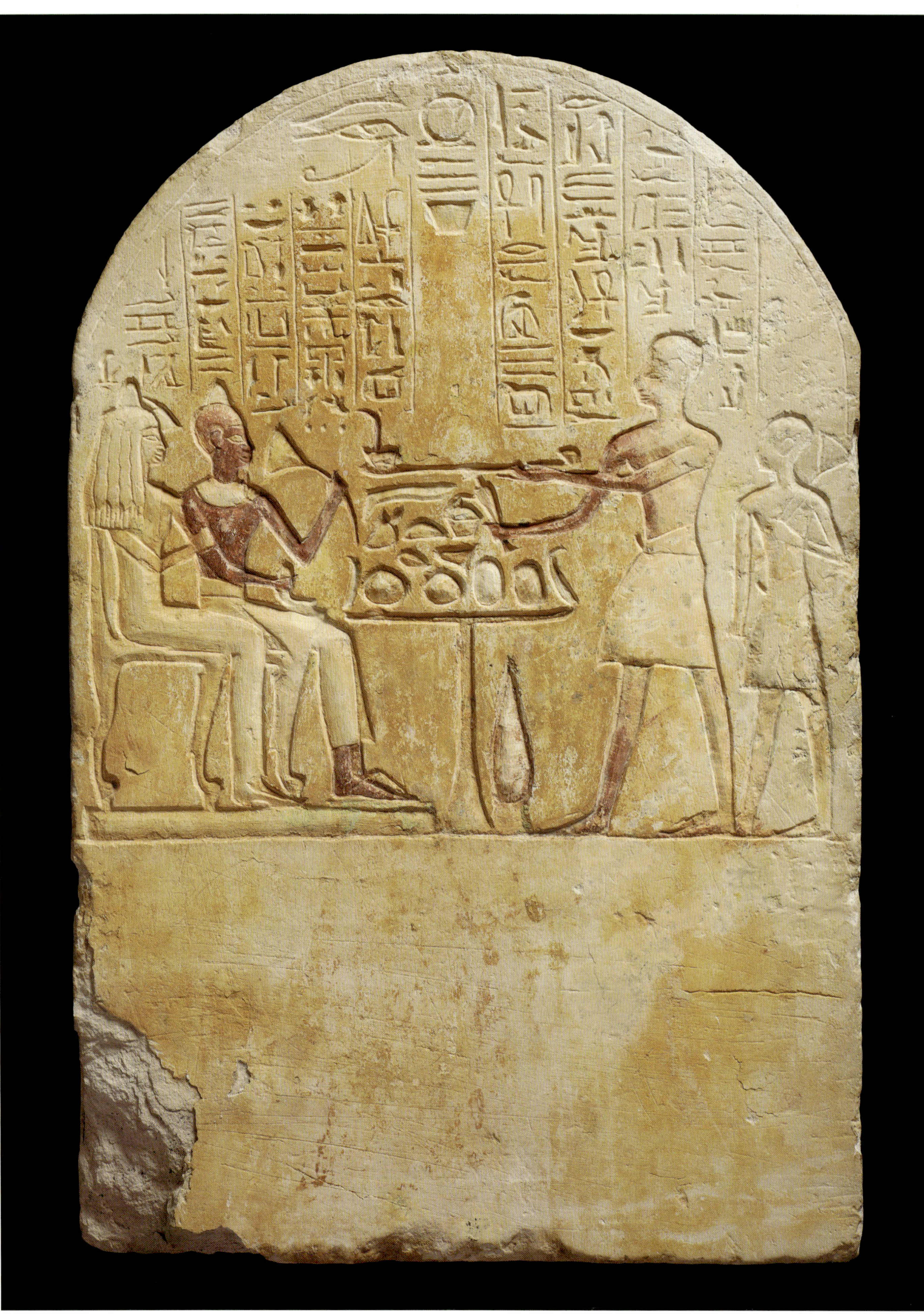

reaffirm the principle of the visual clarity of the commodities shown, composed in conformity with the tenet that "above is behind." One is therefore to understand that these offerings have been spread out over the tabletop.

The smaller figure to the right is Mahu's younger brother, "the pure priest, Teti," who is similarly represented but holds a lotus by its long stem in his raised hand.

The scene is described as

> *An offering which pharaoh grants to Osiris and to Sobek who dwells in the Faiyum to that they in turn may offer bread and beer as well as oxen and fowl together with all things good and pure to the ka of the divine father of Sobek of Chedet, Kay, and to that of his beloved sister, Tai.*

The design of the scene is interesting in the extreme because Egyptian design tenets hold that primacy of place in a two-dimensional composition is accorded to the area on the spectator's left. According, this place should be reserved for the couple being honored. That convention is here modified because the largest figure, and hence the most important by means of the status implied by his scale, is the elder son, Mahu. His importance is clearly indicated because he dedicated this stela to his father so that Kay's "name might live."

The blank area occupying almost one third of the surface of the stela suggests to some that the stela was not finished. This theory gains support from the fact that the inscription mentions a third individual, *his beloved sister, Sitamun*, who is not represented (compare cat. 13) and whose familial relationship to the couple and their two sons remains moot. Others suggest that the empty space is intentional, because it was intended to be covered and not seen when the stela was erected, set either into the ground or another element.

The four individuals are designed with the so-called egg-shaped head, which one associates with depictions of members of the Amarna family at the end of Dynasty XVIII. The convention of depicting elite members of society with this particular head shape persisted into the Third Intermediate Period and does not serve as a critical chronological index (compare cat. 11). Consequently one can only suggest that this monument is to be dated to late Dynasty XVIII or early Dynasty XIX.

Published: Chappaz and Chamay, *Reflets du divin*, 2001, p. 85, no. 70.

13.

A Stela Commemorating a Land Grant for the Maintenance of a Cult Statue in the Name of Pharaoh Rameses III

Dynasty XX, reign of Pharaoh Rameses III, 1193–1162 BC
Limestone
Height 32 ⅝ in.
Inv. no. EG-224

The lunette of this round-topped stela is crowned with a winged sun disk, flanked left and right by a uraeus, each facing away from the disk. The field beneath contains three figures, each with a corresponding caption in hieroglyphs. The largest, to the right, is identified as a cult statue of the god Amun, further designated by the inclusion of its cultic name

> *[a statue of the god] Amun [whose cultic name is] "The powers of Rameses are great."*

The statue is depicted wearing a plain, knee-length kilt, secured to the waist by an undecorated belt, and a corslet, resembling a modern tank-top, with a wide strap over each shoulder. The accessories of this cult statue include armlets on the biceps, a broad collar, and a thin, curving false beard. Two tall plumes comprise its headdress, the streamer of which is visible at the back of the neck. These plumes suggest one of the main epithets of this god, "the-one-whose-two-plumes-are-tall."

The figure in the center, Pharaoh Rameses III, is identified by the caption above his head, which contains his prenomen and nomen, each introduced by its traditional prefatory epithets

> *The Lord of the Two Lands, Wesir-maat-re-mery-amun*

> *The Lord of Appearances in Glory, Ra-mes-su [Rameses III], ruler of the city of On [Heliopolis].*

This pharaoh is barefoot and wears a pleated kilt, bound at the waist by an uninscribed belt that trails off between his two legs before stopping just under the knee of his far leg. He wears the so-called Nubian wig, popular during the preceding Amarna Period, its two streamers cascading over his shoulders. The wig is fronted by a uraeus. The king also wears an armlet on his biceps. He offers incense in a shallow bowl designed in the shape of the neb-hieroglyph, representing the adjective *many*, from which smoke rises as he fumigates the cult statue of the god Amun. It is interesting to note how the was-scepter intersects the incense bowl and how the smoke of the incense imitates the animal-headed terminal of the was-scepter.

The smallest figure occupies the leftmost side of the lunette, a position generally commanding primacy. He is identified as

> *the son of the king, [named] Rameses-mery-amun.*

He carries a fan, and is shown wearing a long, transparent tunic, suggesting finely woven, gossamer linen, with flaring sleeves reaching the elbow (compare cat. 7). He, too, is barefoot, with a shaven head, to which is attached the so-called sidelock of youth.

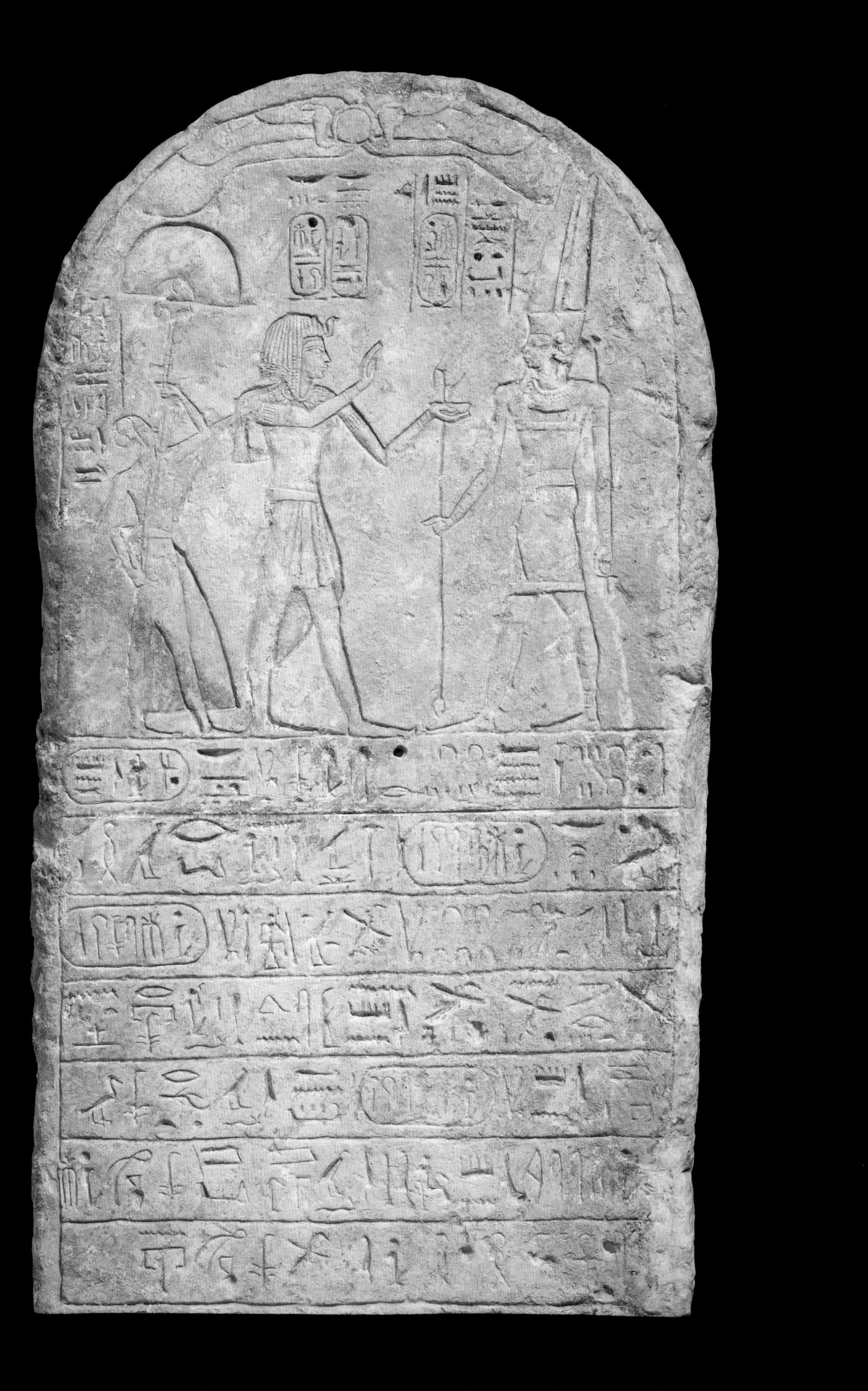

The main body of the stela is inscribed with seven lines of hieroglyphs below, here oriented from right to left

> *Regnal Year 25, on the 26th day of the month of Shemu, under the majesty of the king of Upper and Lower Egypt, the lord of the Two Lands, Wesir-maat-re-mery-amun, the son of Re, the lord of appearances in glory, Rameses III, sovereign of Heliopolis: his majesty ordered that a donation of land measuring fifty aroras be granted to the great statue of Rameses-sovereign-of-Heliopolis, for the love of Re and the favor [?] of Amun. His majesty proceeded to the palace which is found in the Mansion of Amun, named Rameses-lord-of-Heliopolis-great-of-victories, in the company of the son of the king (i.e., his son), Prince Rameses-mery-amun, true of voice. This is a divine statue [?] executed under the direction of the royal cup-bearer [whose name is] Rameses-ankh-nekh, true of voice...the royal cup-bearer of the treasury.*

The stela is important for several reasons. First, it is only the fifth such donation stela known. Second, the text names, but does not represent, the elite overseer, Rameses-ankh-nekh, whose title, royal cup-bearer of the treasury, seems initially to mask his role as the individual under whom the cult statue was created (compare cat. 12). Third, the cult statue, like all such statues in ancient Egypt, is named. Fourth, the land grant provided an income-generating endowment, so that the statue and its cult could be maintained. That maintenance was intended to ensure that the proper rituals were duly performed so that the cult statue, when animated, as surely it was, might symbolically perpetuate the might of Rameses III.

In addition to this significant art-historical information, those seven lines also contain biographical information of primary historical importance. Prince Rameses-mery-amon is mentioned in only one other source, a list of names of royal children inscribed on the wall of the Theban mortuary temple of his father, Rameses III, at Medinet Habu. The present stela contains the epithet, *true of voice* (compare cat. 53), which may be evidence of his death and posthumous commemoration. If this interpretation obtains, Prince Rameses-mery-amun would have already been deceased before his father's twenty-fifth regnal year, the year in which this stela was erected.

Published: Chappaz, "Une stèle," 2005–07, pp. 5–19; Künzi et al., *Les trésors*, n.d., fig. 188, pp. 154–55.

14.

A Relief Depicting a Pharaoh

Dynasty XXX, 380–342 BC
Limestone
Height 6 ¼ in.
Inv. no. EG-366

This extraordinary object was initially inventoried as a sculptor's model or votive object (compare cat. 86 and cat. 87). On closer inspection, however, it appears to have been part of a relief rather than a model, as it lacks both the expected framing elements and the incised grid lines that one would normally associate with such objects.

Corpulence in ancient Egyptian art is generally not an indicator of one's physical appearance; it is a polyvalent sign of decorum. It may signify rank and status as some statues of high-ranking members of society, dated from the Old Kingdom through

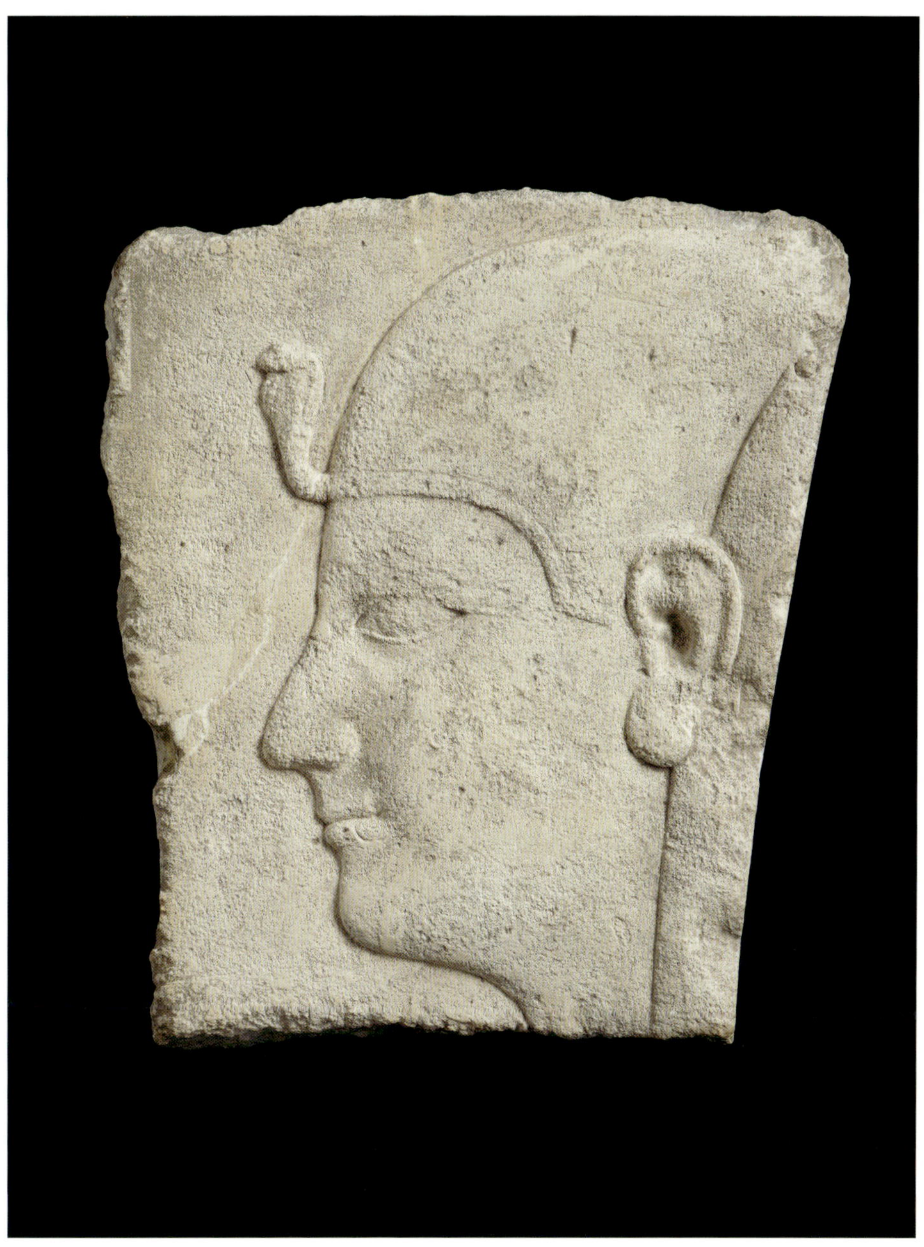

the Late Period, reveal. During the course of the New Kingdom, pharaohs such as Amenhotep III and his son and successor, Akhenaten, might likewise be represented as obese, but such representations are imbued with overtones of fecundity because the pharaoh was regarded as the guarantor of the prosperity of the land over which he ruled.

The subject of the present work of art is a very rare example in two-dimensional relief of a nonidealizing representation of a corpulent pharaoh, so identified by the presence of the nemes-headdress fronted by a uraeus. There is a tendency to regard such images as influenced by the presence of the Ptolemies, the Macedonian Greeks who ruled Egypt as pharaohs after the death of Alexander the Great. Several of the Ptolemies, but in particular Ptolemy VIII Euergetes II, were notoriously overweight and were anciently nicknamed *physkon*, that is, "fatso." Corpulent images of Egyptian pharaohs in two-dimensional representations, although rare, are occasionally documented from Dynasty XXVI onward. On the basis of certain details one can suggest a dating within Dynasty XXX for this particular image.

References: Tomoum, *Sculptors' Models*, 2005, p. 215, no. 42.

15.

Fragment of a Temple Relief with the Names and Titles of Alexander the Great

Macedonian Period, 323–305 BC
Painted limestone
Length 27 ½ in.
Inv. no. EG-162

This raised relief, from the wall of a temple, contains four vertical columns of hieroglyphs in which the names of Alexander the Great, preceded by their titles, are recorded. The two columns on the left are identical may be translated as

> *the king of Upper and Lower Egypt, Setepenre [the one selected by the god Re] Meryamun [the one beloved by the god Amun].*

These are Alexander's prenomen, one of five names specifically composed for every pharaoh.

The two columns on the right introduce Alexander's relationship to the deities of the temple to which this block belonged. They may be translated as

> *Alexander...of Thoth, the lord of...Alexander...of Shepsi, the one of Hermopolis.*

The mention of these two deities is significant. Thoth, the god of wisdom and patron of scribes, was traditionally credited with inventing hieroglyphs. He is here associated with Shepsi, a solar and creator deity often depicted as a mummy. The principal cult of Thoth associated with that of Shepsi was centered at the site of Hermopolis in Middle Egypt, near the modern town of Mellawi. Travelers and scholars visiting Hermopolis in the nineteenth century have left accounts of a now-destroyed temple to Thoth inscribed in part with cartouches of Alexander the Great. One can, therefore, confidently suggest that this block came from that temple.

A careful examination of the worked surfaces of this block reveals a change of plane, with the narrower area featuring the prenomen on the left at a higher position than the wider area to the right containing the names of Thoth and Shepsi. This change of plane is significant, because it demonstrates that this relief formed part of the left-hand jamb of a door of an interior room of the temple.

The block is, therefore, doubly important. It is one of the only surviving architectural elements from that temple. But, more significantly, it is the only architectural example with the names and titles of Alexander the Great in ancient Egyptian hieroglyphs within cartouches to be found anywhere outside of Egypt. Here, Alexander's name in hieroglyphs is enclosed in cartouches, or royal rings, that surround the signs spelling royal names. This device was used because hieroglyphs exhibit neither capitalization nor punctuation.

Alexander the Great acquired Egypt without a battle when the country was surrendered to him by Mazaces, the Persian satrap, or governor. Despite received wisdom, he was never formally crowned pharaoh of Egypt, although he was the undisputed ruler of the land. He was, however, portrayed as a pharaoh by his representatives, who depicted him in pharaonic guise and formulated his name and titulary in hieroglyphs, as this inscription demonstrates.

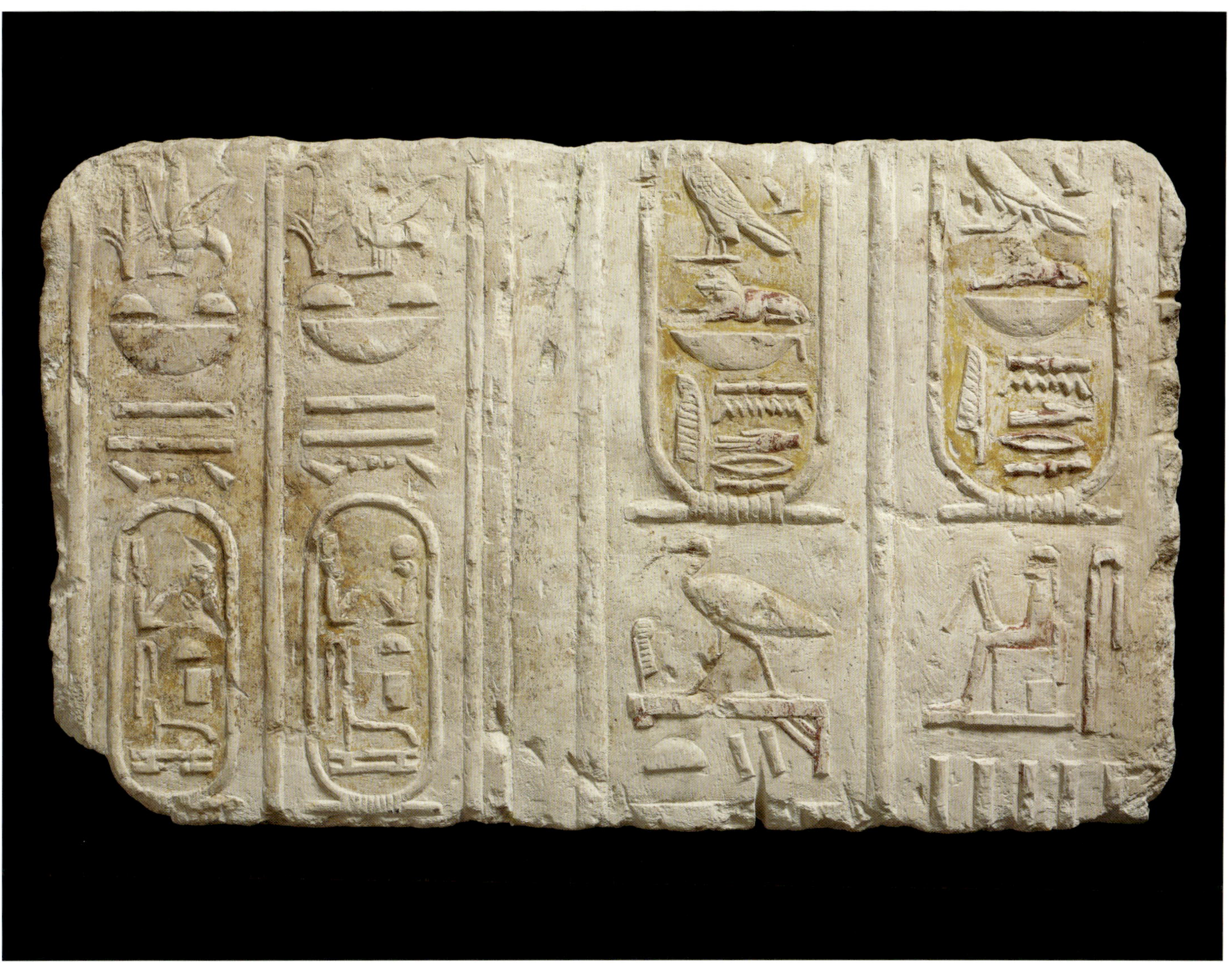

The four columns of inscription afford a very clear example of how hieroglyphs, as generic representations of objects in the real world, had been designed with an emphasis on visual clarity without regard for actual scale. The vulture and lion at the top of the third cartouche from the left are dwarfed by the striding ibis below, and that ibis towers over the face-to-face representations of the seated deities in the two cartouches in the left-hand columns. All of these hieroglyphs were then arranged on a neutral atemporal and aspatial environment. Traces of both red and yellow pigment enable one to visualize just how colorfully painted these reliefs were in antiquity, but, more importantly, the colors selected imparted symbolic value to the worked block. The cartouches to the right in which the name "Alexander" is spelled have been painted yellow, the color of gold, from which the ancient Egyptians believed the skin of their deities was made. Because one's name was interchangeable with one's person, painting the hieroglyphs that spell the name "Alexander" yellow in imitation of gold associates him with Thoth and Shepsi and suggests his divine status.

Published: Chappaz and Chamay, *Reflets du divin*, 2001, p. 52, no. 39; Winter, "Alexander der Grosse," 2005, pp. 204–15.

16.

A Situla, or Ritual Pail

Dynasty XXVI–XXX, 664–342 BC
Bronze
Height with handle extended: 9 ⅜ in.
Inv. no. EG-232

The situla, or ritual pail, is of tapering form with a rolled rim and rounded bottom, its original handle round in cross section. That handle is affixed to two rings, placed opposite one another on the rim. The body of the vessel is engraved with a principal scene consisting of a train of five deities to the left and two worshippers to the right. Beneath this figural register is a single line of hieroglyphic text. The bottom of the situla is decorated with an incised floral motif (fig. 25).

The inscriptions name the deities depicted, from right to left, as Amun-re, Lord of the Thrones of the Two Lands; Amun-re, who is foremost among his harem; Mut, the great goddess; Khonsu in Thebes Neferhotep; and Ptah. The fact that Amun is twice mentioned should cause no surprise, because different aspects of the same deity are often indicated by the repetition of its name followed by a different epithet (compare cat. 53).

The two figures to the right are very similar in their design, differing only in scale and in the details of their costumes. Both are depicted with shaved heads, wear broad collars, are barefoot, raise their arms in a gesture of adoration, and wear pleated, belted kilts. The taller of the two is perhaps to be identified as the pail's owner, of uncertain name, followed by Nakht, presumably his son. Both are the subject of the single line of inscription below that contains a prayer granting them an enjoyably long life.

Such situlae were employed in making liquid libations, particularly offerings of milk, to the deities. The gods named and their epithets associate this vessel with Thebes where Amun-re, in both of his manifestations, formed a triad with Mut, his consort, and their son, here identified as Khonsu-neferhotep. The dating of the vessel is suggested by parallels.

References: London, The British Museum 38212: Morigi Govi et al, *Il sense*, 1990, pp. 173–75, no. 120, inscribed for Pa-di-amun-neb-nesu-tawy, who lived under pharaoh Nectanebo II of Dynasty XXX, as the presence of the cartouche of that pharaoh on this vessel suggests.

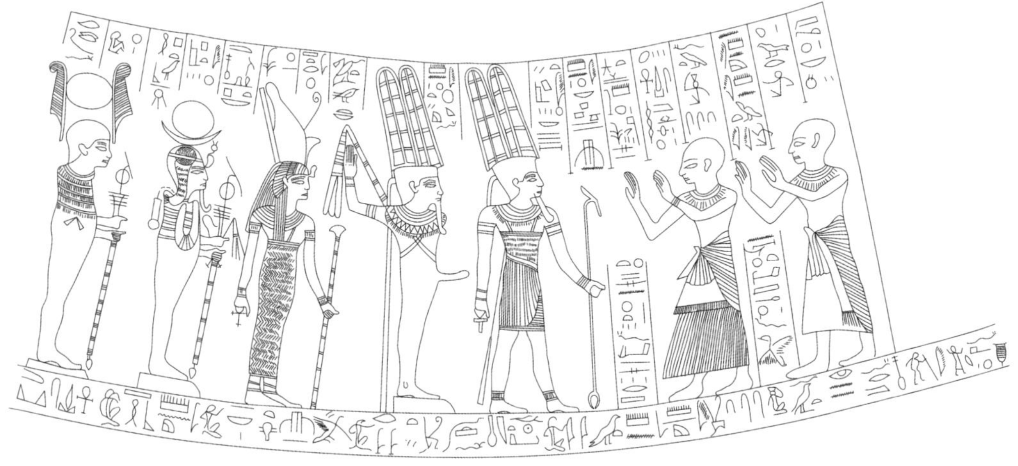

Figure 25
Line drawing of the scene and inscriptions depicted on the situla by Julia Jarrett

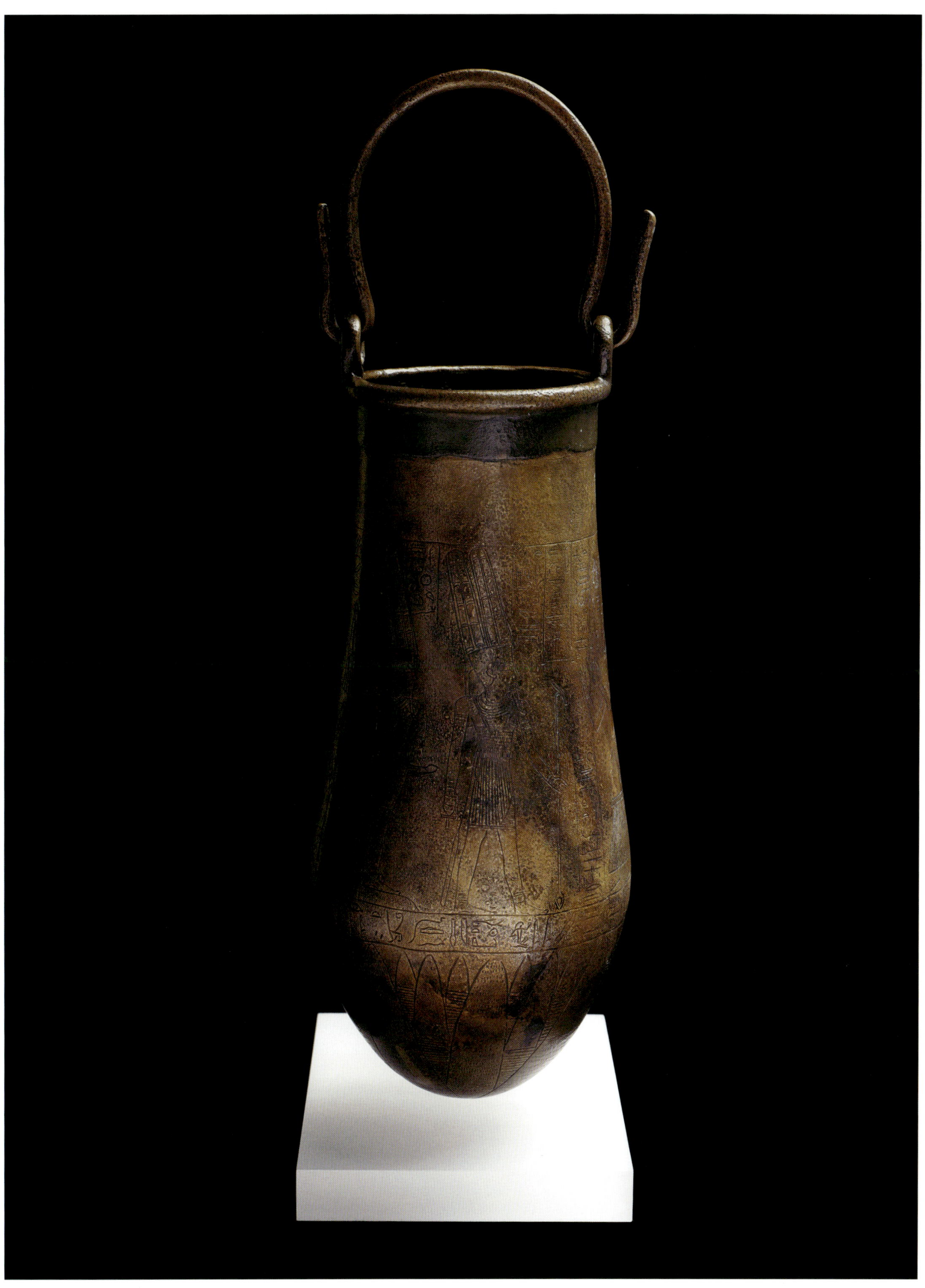

17.

A Cippus, or Magical Stela, Representing Horus on the Crocodiles

Early Ptolemaic Period, 305–200 BC
Crystalline alabaster
Height 7 in.
Inv. no. EG-77

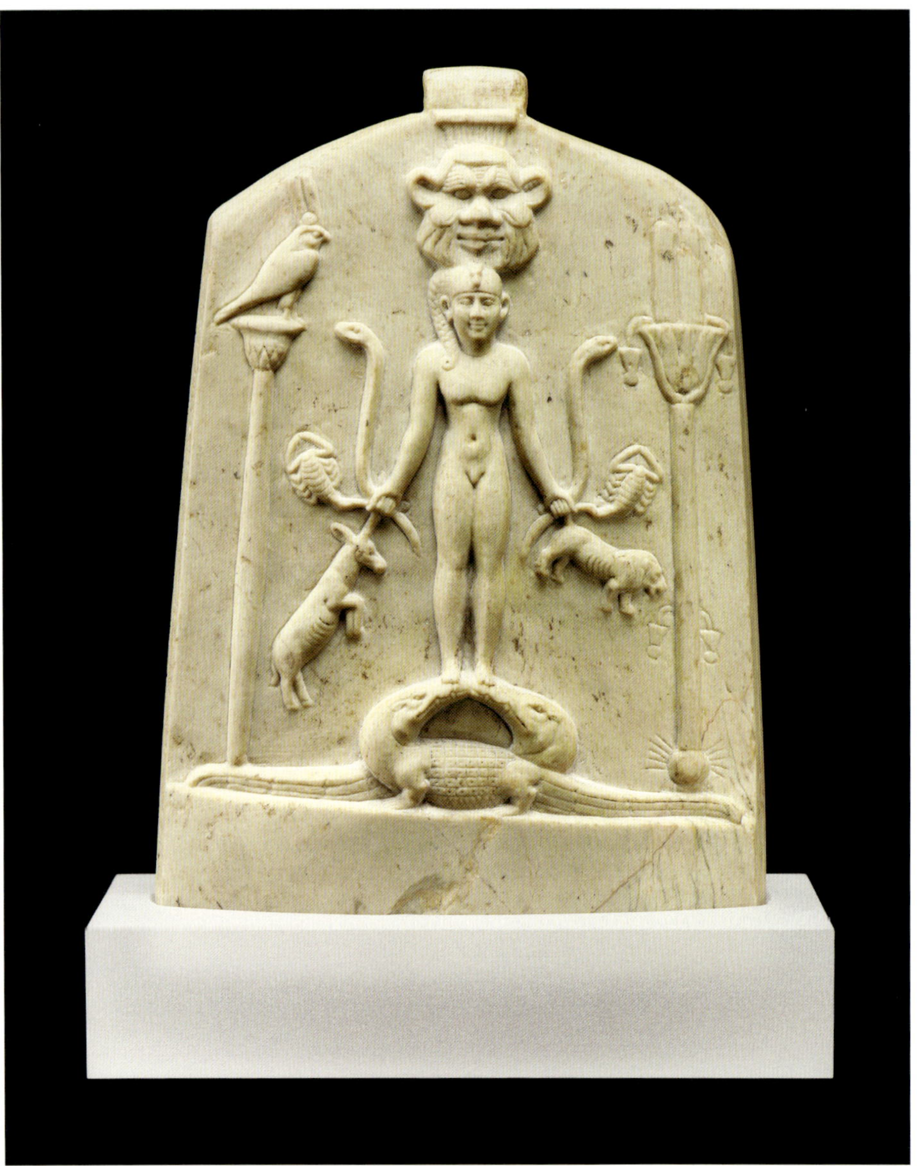

The front of this cippus is sculpted in raised relief and designed with a focus on the principal figure, a nude youth, whose hair is closely cropped (compare cat. 88) and provided with a sidelock (compare cat. 68) and fronted by a uraeus. Above is a head of a Bes-image. The legs of the youth are erect, with the soles of each foot placed on the upper jaw of one of two juxtaposed crocodiles, whose heads are turned around over their bodies to form a circle. The nude youth holds, at left, a serpent, a scorpion, and a horned cervid, perhaps to be identified as an oryx and, at right, a serpent, a scorpion, and a lion. The column to the right features the open flower of a lotus supporting two plumes from which are suspended a pair of counterpoises, with another pair suspended lower on its shaft. These motifs are often associated with the god Nefertum (compare cat. 71). The column to the left features a papyrus umbel on which a falcon, wearing double plumes fronted by a sun disk, perches.

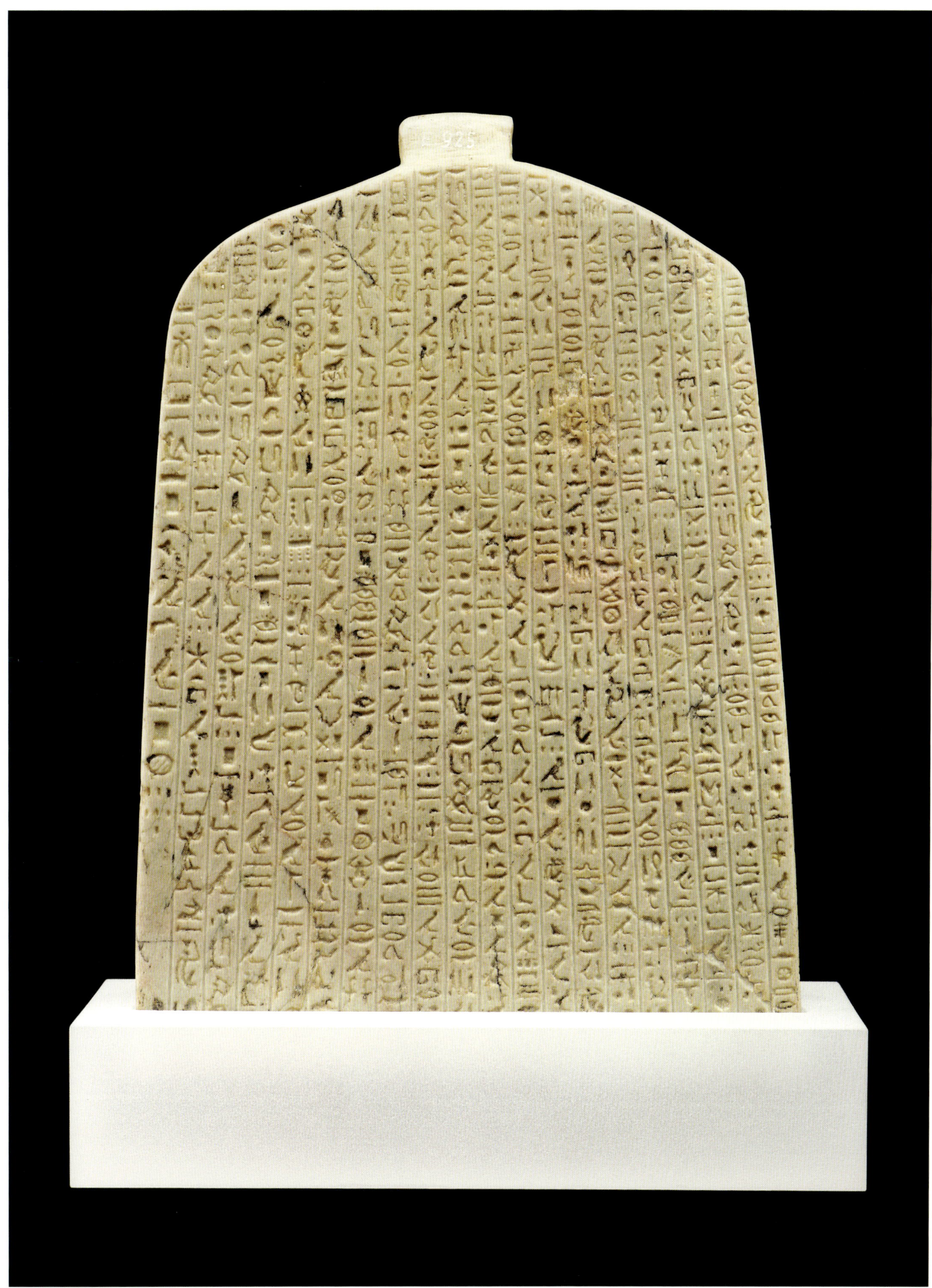

Cat. 17, Seen from the back

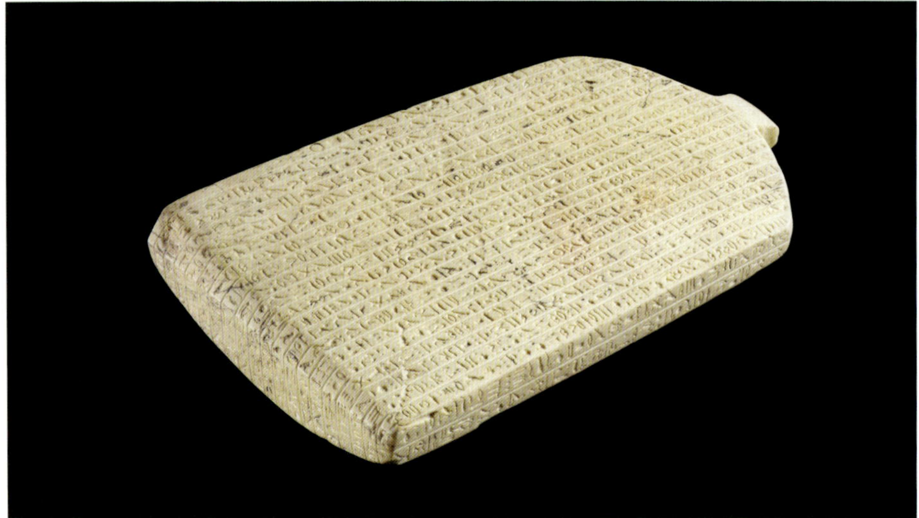

The back and sides of this cippus are covered with hieroglyphic inscriptions containing variations of a known corpus of apotropaic spells against venomous bites of snakes, scorpions, and other noxious beasts. The principal defender is Horus, whose image on the front connotes his powers because, nude and unarmed, he is menaced neither by the crocodiles on which he stands nor by the beasts that he holds. It is suggested that these venomous and noxious beasts are to be understood both literally and figuratively, with the result that their depictions represent malevolent, dangerous forces in general, against which such cippi serve as prophylactics.

The role of Horus in this context developed during the Old Kingdom but gained popularity during the Third Intermediate Period, when the earliest cippi with this type appear. Scholars suggest that the efficacy of these cippi might be activated in one of several ways. One might do the following: recite the prayers; pour a liquid, generally water, over the cippus, which would then be collected and drunk, with the belief that the water had become infused with the power inherent in the image and inscriptions; apply the cippus directly to the wound in order to effect the physical transference of curative powers of the cippus to the body; or simply kiss it. Such cippi have also been found in tombs, where they were thought to protect the dead as well as the living from similar dangers.

The spells appearing on cippi have been modernly divided into groupings, of which two are inscribed on this example. Here Spell B exhibits some peculiar variants; Spell C is the longest and, hence, most complete version of that Spell known to date. Some of these on this cippus may be translated as

> *Do not approach! Nahaher renders you offense-less!*
>
> *Turn your feet away from me, o you foes!*
>
> *He orders your massacre!*
>
> *The four great gods who protect Osiris, these are the ones*
> *who are also protecting the one who is on his water.*

This cippus is inscribed for Nehaher, and, on the basis of parallels, it is suggested to date to the early Ptolemaic Period.

Published: Chappaz and Chamay, *Reflets du divin*, 2001, pp. 122–23, no. 115; Gasse, "Une stèle d'Horus," 2005, pp. 23–37 with pl. VII–IX; Schwentzel, *Images d'Alexandre*, 1999, pp. 172–75.

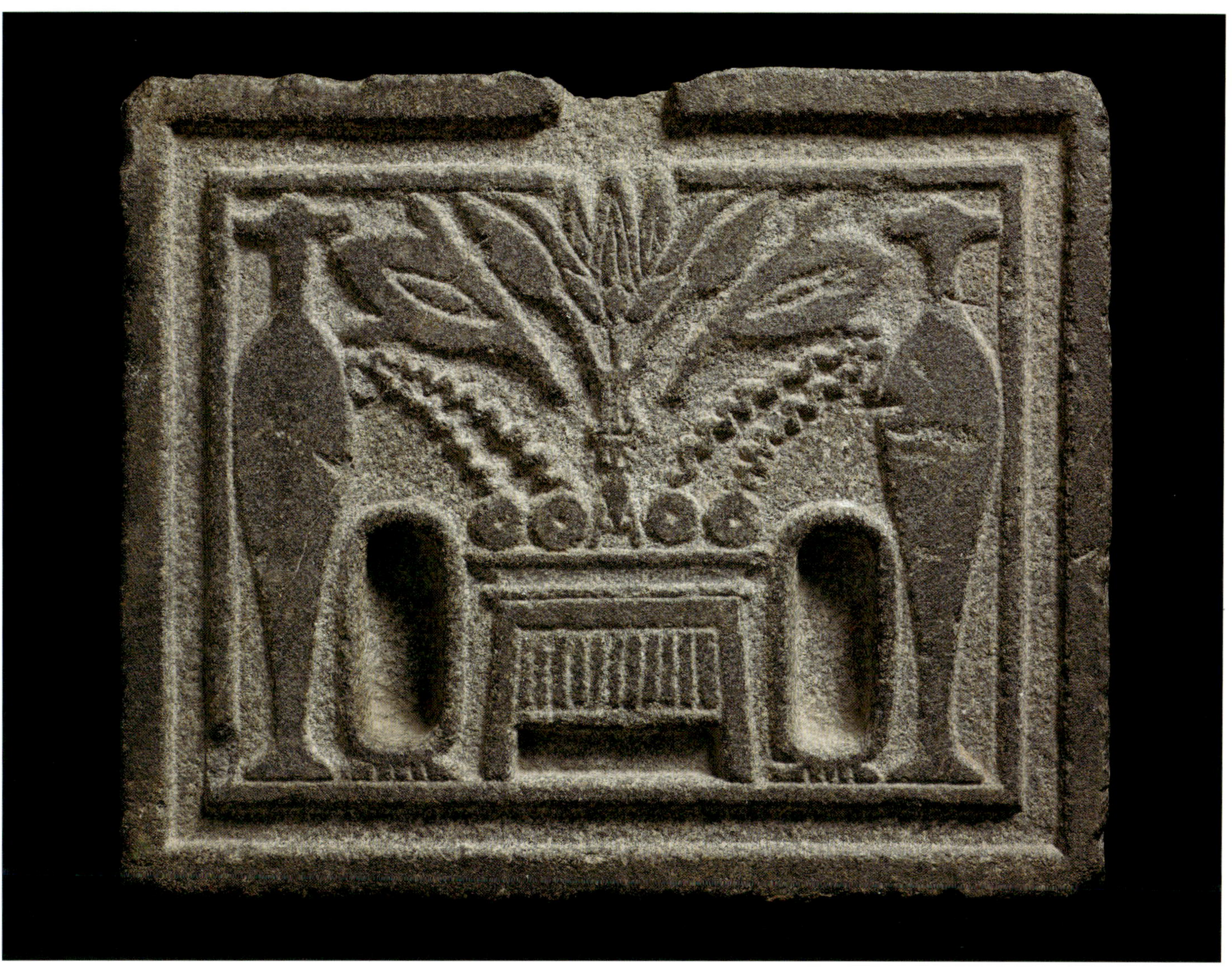

18.

An Offering Table

Ptolemaic Period, 305–30 BC
Granodiorite
Length 16 ⅛ in.
Inv. no. EG-17

This rectangular offering table is very contemporary in its look and in the symmetrical arrangement of its motifs. The center is occupied by the depiction of a table, designed as a shrine with battered corners and a cavetto cornice. Its interior vertical bands are intended to represent wooden slats. A fan-shaped bouquet consisting of a central lotus flower flanked by buds appears to have been placed into a miniature vase supported by a stand in the center of the tabletop. To the left and right are four circular objects, with dotted centers, which are to be identified as loaves of bread. The largest objects are two tall ewers, right and left, to each of which are attached two somewhat diagonal zigzag lines, each touching the top of one of the loaves of bread. Two depressions, in the form of cartouches, occupy the space between one side of the table and a ewer. This symmetrical composition is doubly framed with a tall, wide raised border around its outer edge and a second shorter, thinner raised border within.

The zigzag lines are themselves elongated versions of the hieroglyph for "water" and represent that liquid pouring forth from the ewers for the purposes of ritual purification. That water may also be associated with the environment in which the lotus grows. The spent water was then metaphorically collected in each of the two cartouche-shaped reservoirs.

In practice, such an offering table was designed for use within a tomb or temple to receive actual water libations for the benefit of a deity or the deceased (compare cat. 1). The libation poured onto the table would collect until its flow was evacuated through the space above the lotus flower of the inner frame, which conducted the water through the gap in the outer frame. Because ancient Egyptian art is hieroglyphic and because the hieroglyphs could magically become animated, the images on this offering table created in stone would represent the perpetual performance of this purification rite without recourse to human agency.

One must stress that the combination of only five motifs—offering table, loaves of bread, a lotus bouquet, ewers, and two cartouche-shaped reservoirs—belies the complexity of meaning inherent in those motifs. The loaves of bread represent the single most important source of food for the benefit of the deceased by virtue of the fact that bread invariably stands at the head of all commodities listed in the funerary offering prayer. The lotus was observed to open as it was struck by the rays of the dawning sun and to close up again upon its setting. It thus became a potent symbol for resurrection and could, in some contexts, serve as the equivalent of the ankh, or sign of life, via the principle of the rebus, or visual pun (compare cat. 1). Through this same rebus principle, the cartouche became the noun for "name," which the deceased wished would be pronounced in order to ensure eternal life. One can only admire the creative genius of the ancient Egyptian elite, who were able to imbue such a seemingly simple and very limited number of ordinary objects with such a profound system of interlocking connotations.

The object is dated to the Ptolemaic Period on the basis of parallels.

Published: Chappaz and Chamay, *Reflets du divin*, 2001, p. 66, no. 51.

19.

A Statuette of a Woman

Predynastic Period, about 4000–3200 BC
Ivory
Height 7 ⅞ in.
Inv. no. EG-174

At the very dawn of ancient Egyptian civilization, in a period that witnessed the gradual emergence of the elite but well before its members introduced the hieroglyphs and established the canonical principles for representation, anonymous artisans appear to have laid the foundations upon which those subsequent design tenets would be based, as the stylistic characteristics of this delicately crafted statuette reveal.

The figure is sculpted from a single piece of (elephant?) ivory in broad planes, which swell out to articulate her wide hips and mound to form her small breasts set relatively high up on her chest. Here the modeling is both restrained and minimal, so that the elbows and knees of the arms and legs are not indicated. Two tiny projections on either side of the proportionately small head suggest ears, and a second projection, vertical and thin, represents the nose. Incision becomes the means by which detail is rendered, particularly in the faint horizontal line suggesting the mouth and the bolder outline forming the pubic triangle within which a random, dotted pattern suggests her pubes. A deep circular depression articulates the navel and two more, somewhat

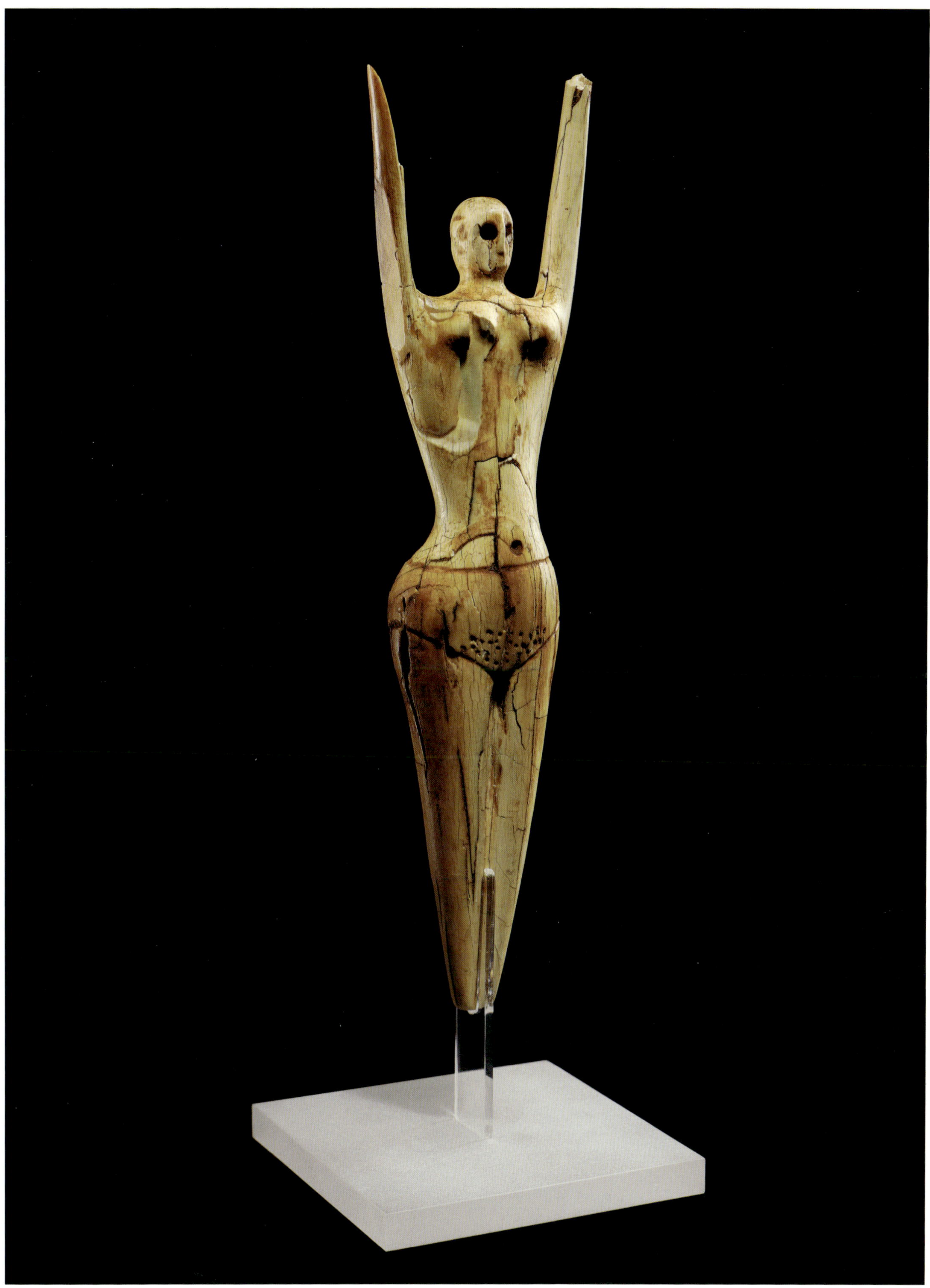

deeper, suggesting that they were originally inlaid, form the eyes. There is no doubt, therefore, that the time-honored design principles of relying upon modeling in broad planes with detail rendered by incision in a composition further enhanced by inlays were already formulated in this remote period.

Evocative of a movement in dance performed by an accomplished prima ballerina, the elegant design of the figure is imbued with a subtle polyvalence. The conical legs connote protective powers, as comparison with the corpus of similarly designed objects from the Predynastic Period suggests, but this shape, together with the uplifted arms, is virtually the same as that used for the depictions of certain plants in the art of the Predynastic Period. This congruence suggests that the female figure may be regarded as a tree goddess. Taken together, one should interpret this figure as symbolic of the religious forces intended to support a positive afterlife.

Published: Chappaz and Chamay, *Reflets du divin*, 2001, p. 18, no. 1;
Lessing and Vernus, *Dieux*, 1996, pp. 40 and 199.

References: Anonymous, "Les ivoires de Beersheba," 1995, pp. 60–61; The Brooklyn Museum: 07.447.502: Needler, *Predynastic*, 1984 , pp. 338–39; Hendrickx, "Iconography," 1997, pp. 75–80 and 217–19, respectively. Perrot, "Statuettes en ivoire," 1959, pp. 8–13, with pl. II–III; Petrie, *Naqada and Ballas*, 1896, pl. LIX, 6; Ucko, "Ivory Figures," 1865, pp. 214–39; Vandier, *Manuel*, 1952.

20.

A Statuette of a Male Figure

Predynastic Period, 4000–3200 BC
Ivory
Height 9 5/16 in.
Inv. no. EG-175

The observations made for the female figure (cat. 19) apply equally to this male figure, sculpted from a single piece of (hippopotamus?) ivory. The deep holes representing his eyes and those randomly placed on his head suggest the presence of now-lost inlays. The figure is depicted nude, with the exception of a phallus sheath (compare cat. 86 and cat. 87), which is more frequently represented in the Predynastic Period than in any other epoch of Egypt's history. It is a garment worn by exceptional individuals, most of whom can be identified as gods. It appears to be associated with rebirth and virility, suggesting a connection to the ankh-sign.

The dating of this statuette to the Predynastic Period is assured on the basis of a stylistically similar figure excavated at Mahasna, now in the collections of the Egyptian Museum, Cairo.

Published: Chappaz and Chamay, *Reflets du divin*, 2001, pp. 18–19, no. 2; Lessing and Vernus, *Dieux*, 1996, pp. 41 and 199.

References: Baumgartel, *Cultures*, 1955–60, pp. 60–561, with pl. IV; For phallus sheaths, see both Ucko, "The Predynastic Cemetery," 1967, pp. 345–453, and Baines, "Ankh-sign," 1975, pp. 1–24.

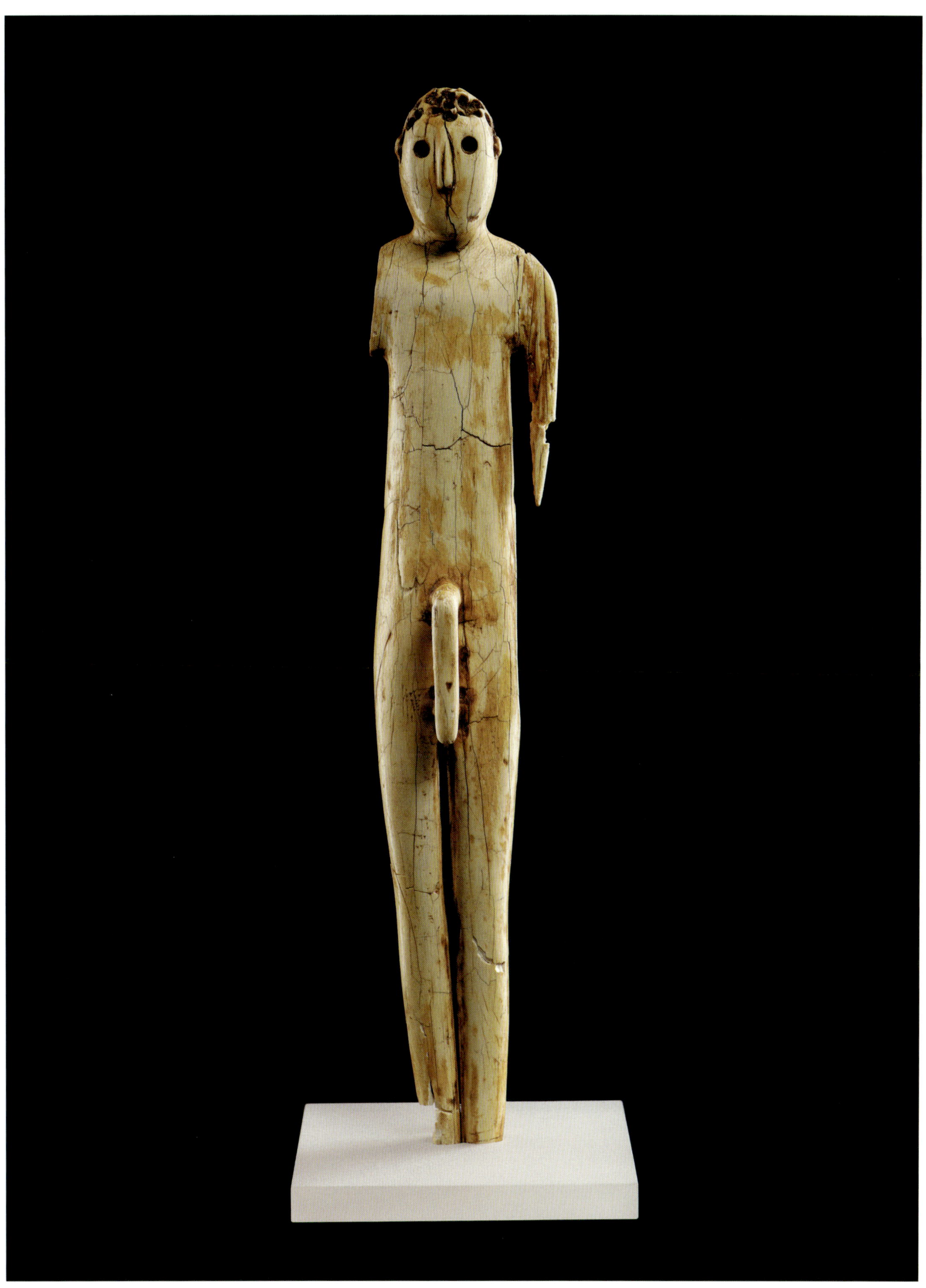

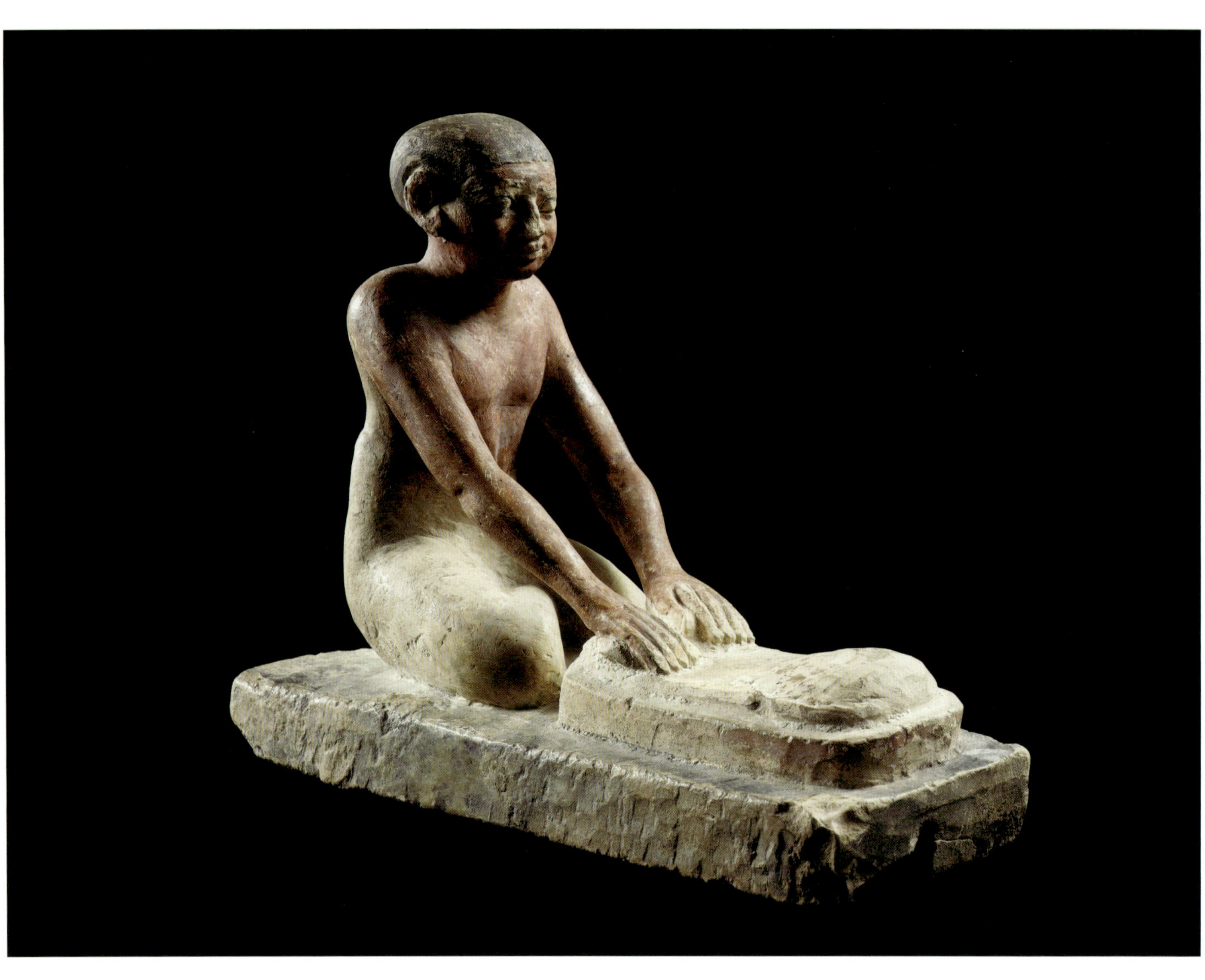

21.

A Statuette of a Baker

Dynasty VI, 2290–2155 BC
Painted limestone
Height 11 5/8 in.
Inv. no. EG-343

The baker and his kneading stone are sculpted from a single block of limestone, with an integral plinth on which both rest. The baker is wearing a plain kilt that reaches to his knees and does not appear to be belted. His pose is exceptional. He does not kneel, as would be expected. On the contrary, he is asymmetrically sitting on the ground, with his right leg bent at the knee and placed under and behind the left leg, which bears the weight of his body. So posed, he extends his arms to the front, with his hands kneading dough on a raised stone. His hair is closely cropped and his visage characterized by naso-labial furrows, which convey the impression of an older man, in keeping with one artistic tenet governing the appearance of laborers. The gender-specific use of color in the Old Kingdom mandates that his skin tones are painted red.

Painted limestone statuettes of bakers, both male and female, are not uncommon in tombs of the Old Kingdom and are found in numerous collections. These statuettes, like the hieroglyphs and objects depicted on tombs of the Old Kingdom (compare cat. 1) were symbolically possessed with the ability to become animate in order to perpetuate the eternal supply of food and commodities for the benefit of the deceased in the hereafter.

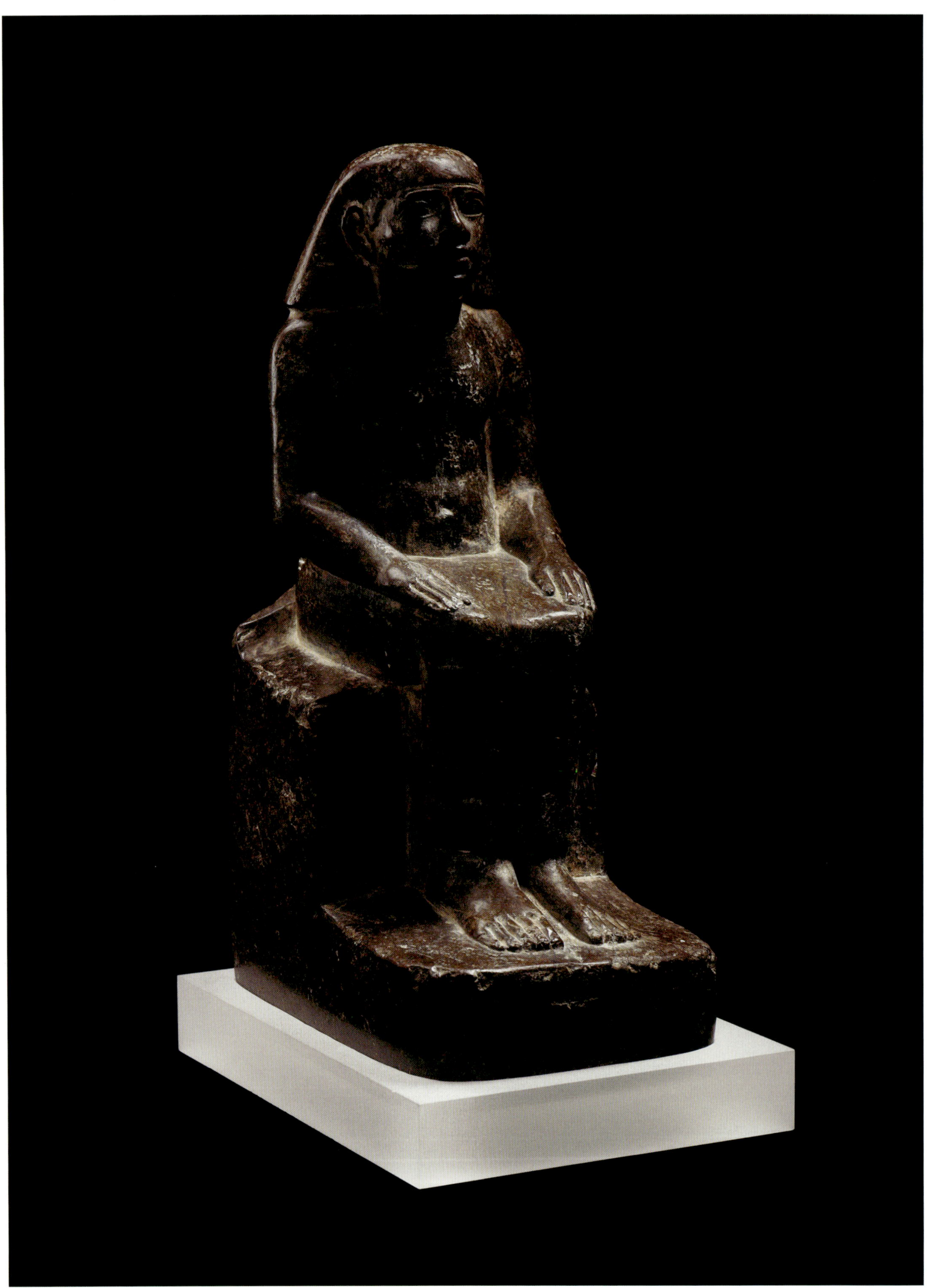

22.

A Statuette of an Enthroned Member of the Elite

Dynasty XII, 1991–1785 BC
Serpentine with traces of red polychromy
Height 10 in.
Inv. no. EG-252

The figure is seated on a chair, to which is affixed a back pillar, not inscribed, which reaches to the level of his shoulder blades. His bare feet rest parallel to one another on the projecting front of the chair. He is wearing a long, ankle-length skirt, unbelted and unadorned, with his arms held along his torso and bent at the elbow so that the open palms of his hand rest on his thighs. A wide, plain wig, falling to the shoulders, frames his face but exposes his disproportionately large ears, which may symbolically enhance his aural facilities. The features of the face of his raised head are dominated by large eyes, over which are plastic, or sculpted, brows. His narrow-bridged nose ends in wide wings with prominent nostrils, set above a small mouth with fleshy lips, their corners drilled.

The modeling of the torso is noteworthy inasmuch as it exhibits tripartition, in which the pectoral region, rib cage, and lower abdomen are articulated. Such modeling is a departure from the expected bipartite design of the nude male torso, in which the pectoral region and rib cage coalesce into one unit. Such tripartite modeling is rare, but attested, and is revived in the Late Period via the principle of archaizing. Its reappearance at that time has little to do with the burgeoning Greek presence in Egypt. The statuette was originally painted, traces of which are still visible along the arms and at the feet.

On the basis of parallels, one can assign this figure to Dynasty XII of the Middle Kingdom.

Published: Malek et al., *Topographical Bibliography*, 1999, nos. 801-431-550.

23.

A Bust of an Elite Official

Dynasty XII, 1991–1785 BC
Granodiorite
Height 10 ½ in.
Inv. no. EG-185

The position of the arms, bent at the elbow and projecting forward along the line of the thigh, suggested by the shape of the break under the right arm, indicates that this figure was originally sitting. His image is modeled in broad planes, clearly evident in the bipartite treatment of the chest, which avoids an articulated rib cage, although the nipples of the pectorals are indicated. A wide wig with its strands of hair indicated by incision, frames his face, and does not cover his disproportionately large ears, which may have been designed to emphasize a symbolically enhanced ability to hear. The pupils of his almond-shaped, hieroglyphic eyes are plastically rendered as thin, raised disks, and his eyebrows are formed as raised ridges.

The processes by which ancient Egyptian stone sculpture was created are clearly indicated by certain details exhibited by this statue. The smoothly polished surfaces of the face and wig, for example, contrast with the rougher, less polished surfaces of the negative space, particularly evident between the arms and torso.

The figure's physiognomy is characterized by signs of age that imbue the face, when regarded by Western standards, with a certain introspective melancholy. This has led some commentators to suggest that the concept of portraiture may have been pioneered in these institutionally affiliated craft ateliers of the Middle Kingdom. Such images are not, however, to be regarded as portraits, defined as identifiable likenesses of individuals by the application of Western art historical principles. The Middle Kingdom was a period of constant struggle, with members of the elite attempting to become pharaohs in their own right. These struggles resulted in sumptuary laws aimed at curbing the overt display of wealth by the elite so as not to overshadow similar, but apparently less opulent, royal displays. They also led to assassination attempts against several pharaohs of the period.

Within such social strife, the principal vehicle for self-presentation was visual. As Dynasty XII began, royals elected to represent themselves in the idealizing style that so dominates the sculptural repertoire of ancient Egypt. The members of the competing elite, wishing to distance themselves from these royal depictions, elected to pioneer a visual style that was immediately recognizable as the antipode of that idealizing. They consequently introduced images characterized by signs of age, for which this bust may be taken as an example. The existence of two diametrically opposed idioms for self-representation—one ideal, the other nonideal, characterized as it was by signs of age—visually segregated the two groups. Ateliers creating works for the pharaoh soon aped the principles of the elite and employed them for the production of nonidealizing royal images. Viewed from this vantage, images in ancient Egyptian art are expressions of ideology, and cannot be taken at face value as portraits in the Western sense.

Certain aspects of the culture of the Middle Kingdom were to inform future generations of the elite. So, for example, the very design of hieroglyphs and their arrangement became models for later generations to emulate; the literature of the period became the classics, forming an equivalent of a Western canon of great books; and sculptural styles and types became sources of inspiration, based on the principle of archaizing, which later generations reinterpreted for their present purposes (compare cat. 24).

Published: Chappaz and Chamay, *Reflets du divin*, 2001, p. 62–63, no. 47.

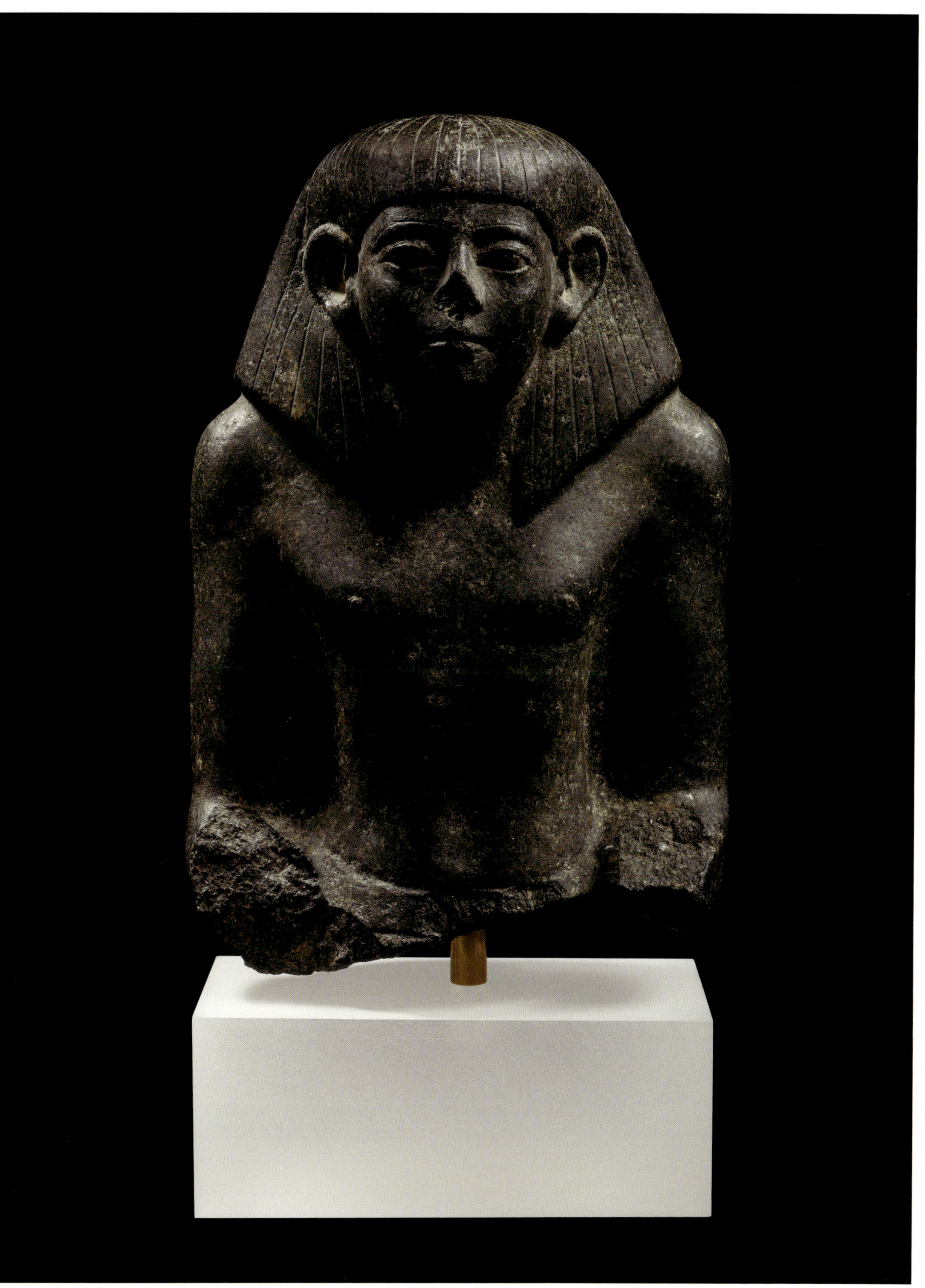

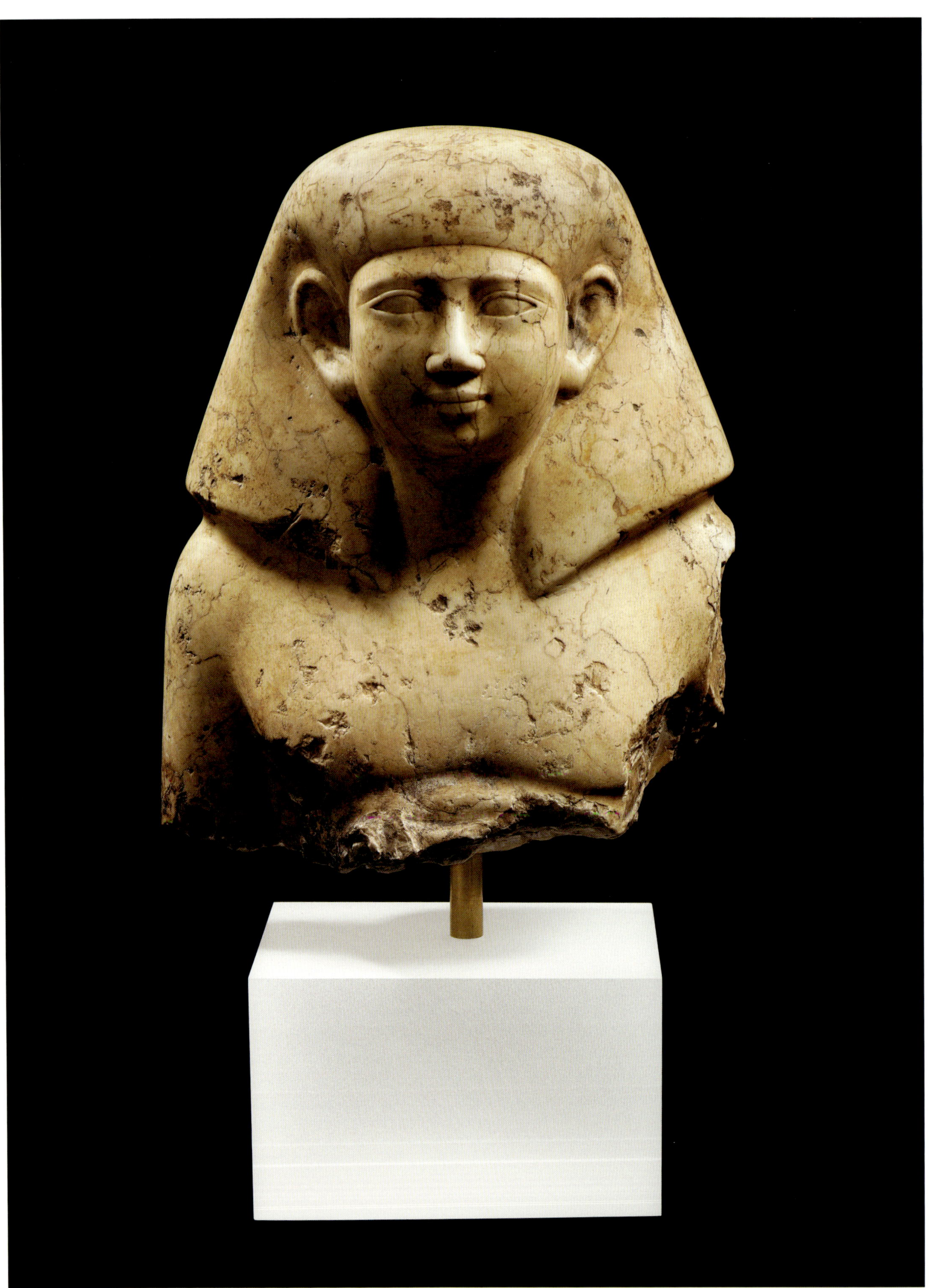

24.

A Bust of an Elite Male Member of Society

Dynasty XXVI, 664–525 BC
Crystalline limestone (possibly marble)
Height 9 ½ in.
Inv. no. EG-30

Sculpted in polished broad planes with linear adjuncts, this bust represents an elite member of society. He wears a wide, undecorated wig, which leaves both ears, disproportionately large, free. The lappets of the wig end in sharp diagonals resting on the top of his chest. The shape of the break at the bottom of the chest would seem to indicate that the figure was depicted wearing a wraparound skirt, recalling the appearance of that worn by others (compare cat. 25).

The features of the face are idealized, with almond-shaped rimmed eyes set beneath a horizontally accentuated brow, a thin-bridged nose with slightly flaring wings, and a small mouth. The modeling of the pectoral region of the chest suggests a degree of corpulence, which served as an index of rank and social standing rather than of the actual appearance of the individual.

At first glance, the bust appears to be a creation of the Middle Kingdom, an epoch during which the skirt was often wrapped around a body exhibiting a corpulent torso, which was found in association with similarly designed wigs behind disproportionately large ears. Certain details of the face and the manner in which the corpulence of the torso is designed and executed suggest that this bust was created at a later date, perhaps during Dynasty XXV–XXVI, when models from the past, particularly those created during the Middle Kingdom, were revived (compare cat. 23).

Such a date seems confirmed by the choice of stone, but its geological identification is difficult to establish visually. It appears to relate to that used for at least one royal image dated to Dynasty XVIII and perhaps for a statue of a queen dated to the Ptolemaic Period. Whether this stone is a type of marble remains moot, inasmuch as received wisdom maintains that Egypt is marble poor. The pitting of the surfaces and the veins would seem to suggest that the material is alabaster, a stone prized because its white color connotes qualities of purity. Such a quality would be desirable for statues of this type, which were habitually erected in temples in order to become a perpetual, integrated recipient of all of the cultic practices performed therein.

Published: Chappaz and Chamay, *Reflets du divin*, 2001, p. 65, no. 49.

References: Bianchi, "Images of Cleopatra," 2001, p. 22 n. 58; Eggebrecht, *Ägyptens Aufstieg*, 1987, pp. 186–87, no. 103.

25.

A Statue of an Elite Member of Egyptian Society

Dynasty XII, 1991–1785 BC
Basalt
Height 9½ in.
Inv. no. EG-29

This figure of an elite male is designed with an integral base. He is depicted in the canonical pose of a stride with the left foot advanced, his arms pressed to the sides of his body. The wig on his head is round and volumetrically circular (compare cat. 60). He is both barefoot and bare-chested, without any accessories, and wears only a long, wraparound skirt tucked in above the navel in the way one might modernly wrap and secure either a beach or bath towel around one's body. The folded tuck is represented in accordance with visual tenets demanding visual clarity rather than an illusion of reality. The sculpting method relies on modeling in broad planes, polishing, and adding linear adjuncts for details.

Naturalism was not an objective in this sculptural system, which relied instead upon the principles of visual clarity. In keeping with this avoidance of strict realism, the arms should not be judged by Western standards and characterized as disproportionately elongated. The fingers of the flat hands are sausagelike, without any indication of either knuckles or nails, as found on the toes as well. In keeping within the imperatives of these artistic principles, the face is somewhat idealized. Its features might, at first glance, seem inconsistent with the nascent corpulence of the pectoral region of the chest. There is no contradiction. In its avoidance of naturalism, corpulence becomes an index of status, connoting importance and elevated social standing; it is applied to a torso selectively and independently of other anatomical treatments in order to convey this specific meaning.

On the basis of parallels, this statue can be dated to the early Middle Kingdom. It was placed within a tomb where it might serve as an equivalent of the deceased, eternally perpetuating both his memory and participation in all requisite cultic activity.

Published: Chappaz and Chamay, *Reflets du divin*, 2001, p. 62, no. 46.

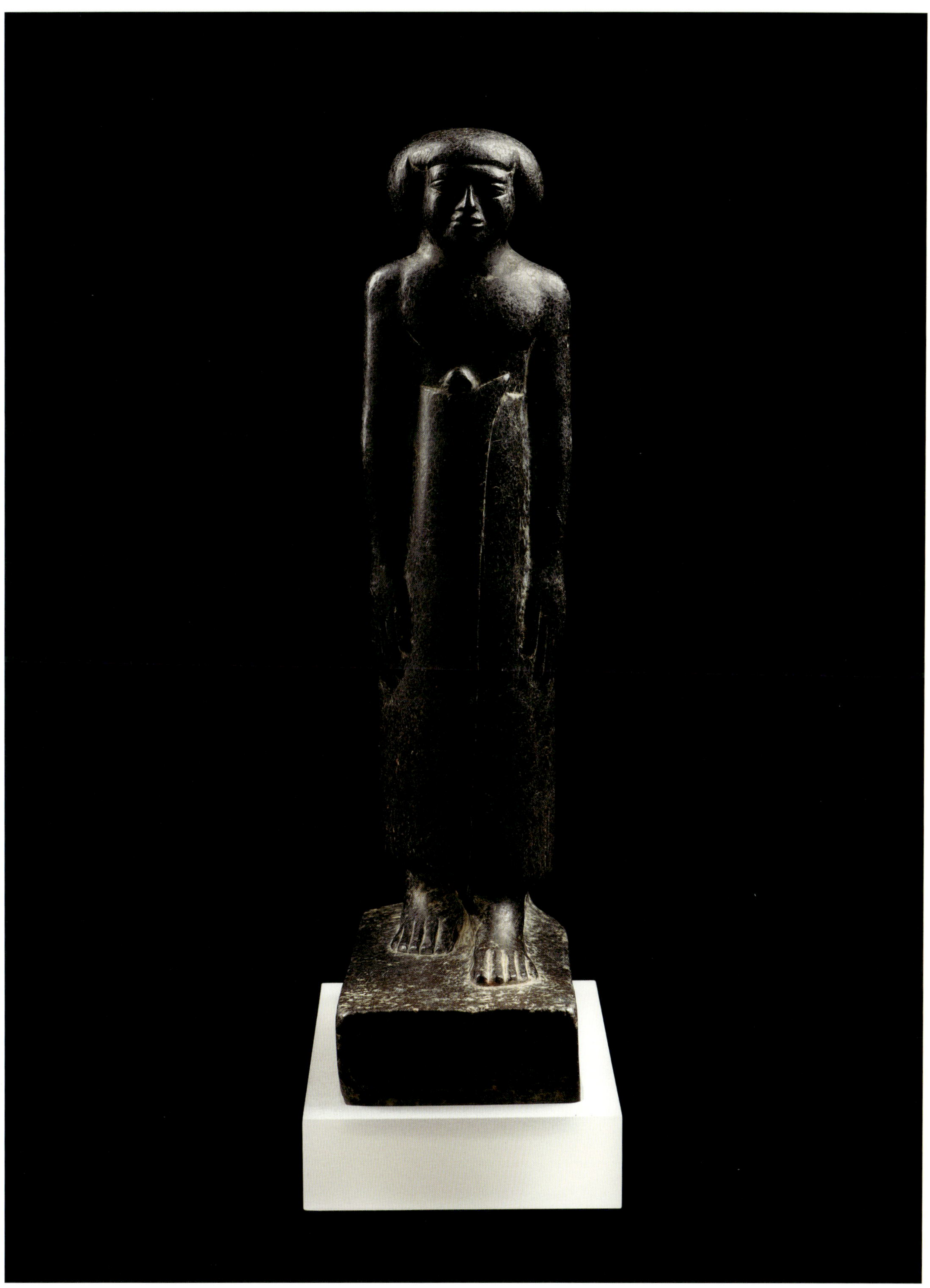

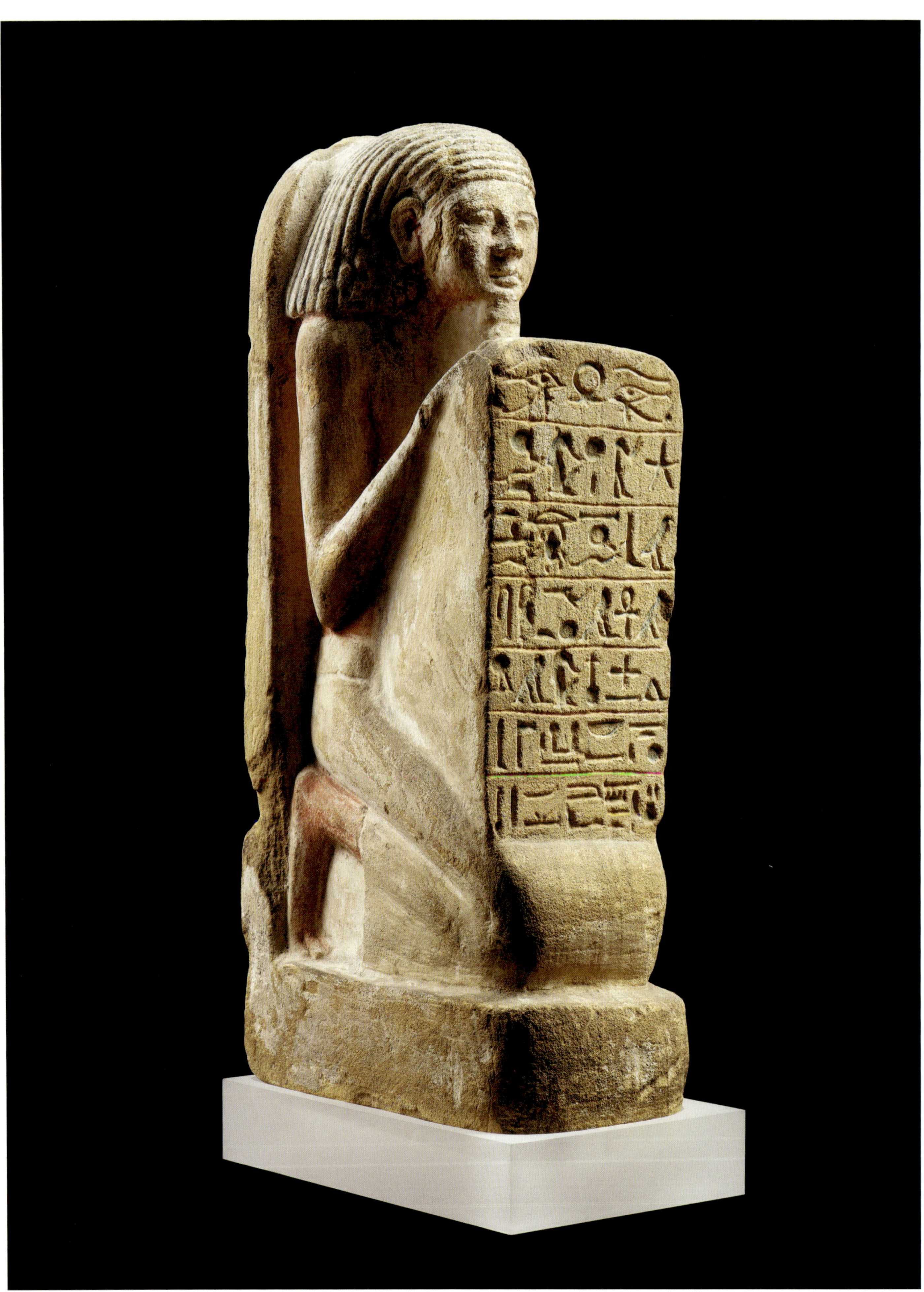

26.

Mahu Presenting a Sun Stela

Dynasty XVIII, reign of Pharaoh Amenhotep II, 1439–1413 BC
Painted sandstone
Height 16 ½ in.
Inv. no. EG-44

The contours of this statue conform to the block of stone from which it was sculpted. That conformity reaffirms the observation that the ancient Egyptians employed both cost-effective and efficient methods in the procurement of stone, which was never much larger than the planned finished product. These imperatives can also be observed in the fact that the rectangular base with its rounded front is integral to the statue and was not made separately.

Mahu wears a long, flaring skirt, belted at the waist, as he kneels on the ground in order to steady a stela, resting on his thighs, with his two raised hands. He wears a striated wig and sports a goatee, only articulated in the frontal view, where he appears to be raising his head above the rounded top of his stela. The ancient Egyptians were reluctant to cut heads, arms, and legs free from the block of stone, with the result that the negative space most evident in the area between Mahu's chin and the back of the stela has not been removed. Mahu's back is flush with a round-topped, uninscribed back pillar.

The lunette of the stela features a centrally placed shen-sign flanked by wadjet eyes, beneath which are inscribed six rows of hieroglyphs:

> *Worshipping the sun god Re when he dawns in order to come into being and when he sets in life in the entourage of Wenenefer in accordance with the diurnal imperatives which are repeated daily...for the ka of the second prophet of the god Amun.*

The statue represents Mahu, a common Egyptian name, frozen eternally in time as he offers his inscribed stela honoring Re, the sun god, who becomes alive at dawn when he rises and is transformed into Wenenefer, a form of the god Osiris, when he sets. The ancient Egyptian theologians suggested a link between Re and Osiris by which the dead Osiris was magically morphed into Re. Mahu wishes to enjoy the same transformation when he is identified with Osiris in death and with Re in resurrection.

This desire is reaffirmed by the design of the statue which, like virtually every ancient Egyptian statue, promoted the front view as the primary one. When so viewed, Mahu's head is raised with his view cast heavenward. On one level, this attitude may suggest that Mahu's eyes are focused in the direction of the rising sun who, as Re, is the principal recipient of his prayer. On another level, the front view equates Mahu's head with the sun disk rising from the horizon, making manifest his aspired identification with Re.

The sandstone connotes permanence and stability. Red is used extensively. Although it is the traditional color for the representation of the flesh of men, it also has solar associations, and its use imbues the figure of Mahu with characteristics of Re, with whom he wishes to be identified.

This statue of Mahu can be narrowly dated in time on the basis of parallels for both the design of the statue and the details of its accompanying inscription.

Published: Chappaz and Chamay, *Reflets du divin*, 2001, p. 60, no. 44; Künzi et al., *Les trésors*, n.d., fig. 167, pp. 116–17.

References: Copenhagen, Ny Carlsberg Glyptotek AEIN 663: Jorgensen, *Catalogue III*, 1998, pp. 70–71.

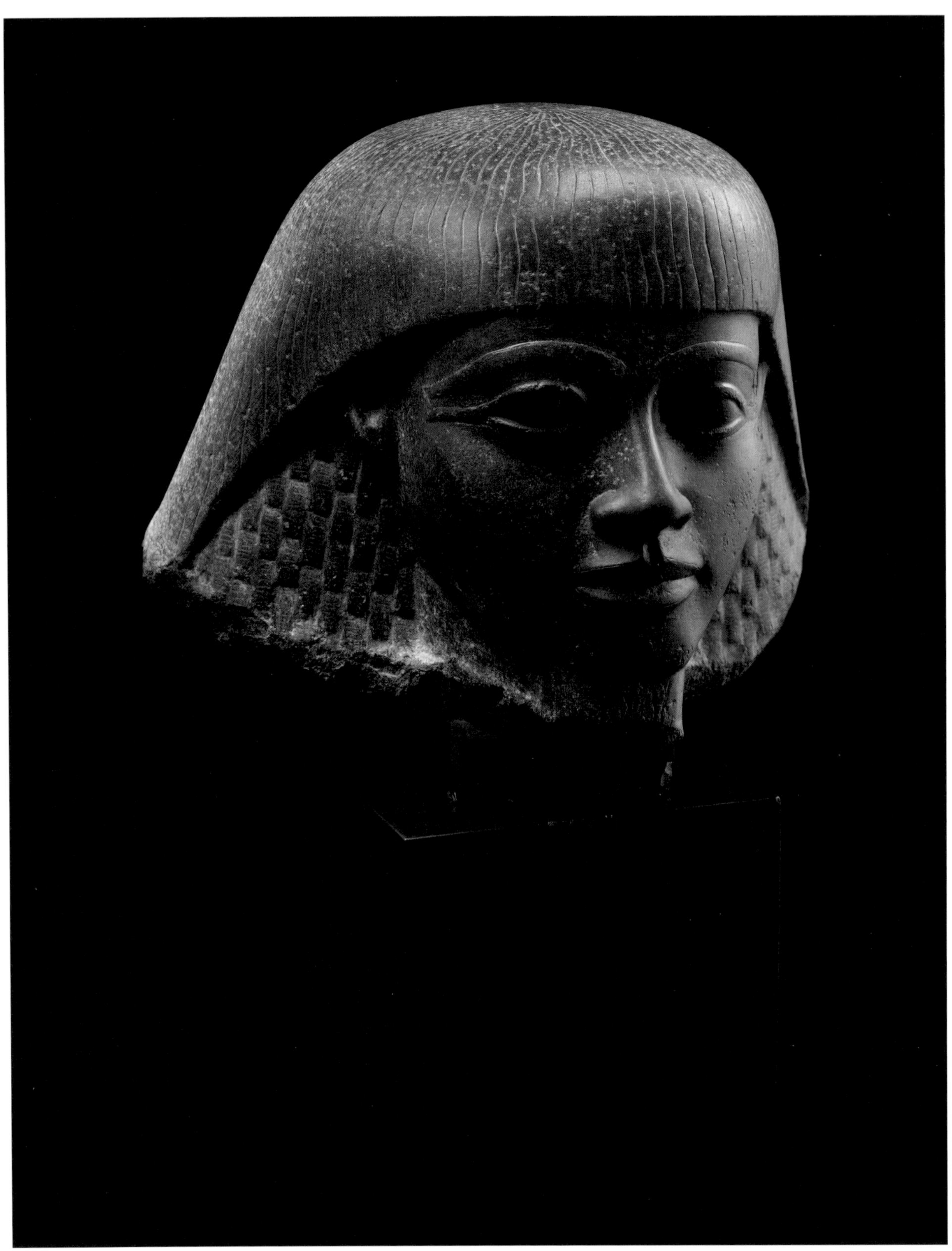

27.

A Portrait of an Official

Dynasty XVIII, 1554–1305 BC
Granodiorite
Height 10 ⅝ in.
Inv. no. EG-5

This life-sized image of an Egyptian official depicts him wearing a double-echeloned wig, the upper part of which consists of fine strands of hair coiffed in wavy curls that overlay a regular pattern of alternating columns of larger, rectangular curls, arranged behind the ears, the bottom halves of which are not covered (compare cat. 9). The face is dominated by large eyes, termed hieroglyphic because their appearance clones the hieroglyph for "eye." Their thick, plastically rendered (sculpted in bold relief) upper and lower lids extend toward the ears to indicate paint stripes, emphasizing the tear duct in their inner corners. These eyes are set into sockets over which are eyebrows, each in bold relief and formed as a gently curving arch that coalesces into the thin bridge of the nose, ending in slightly flaring wings. The fleshy lips are horizontally aligned, the upper dominated by the philtrum.

The face exhibits the idealizing features often associated with ancient Egyptian art, but is designed in such a way that clear naso-labial furrows are introduced to suggest age, one on each side of the nose framing its wings and extending toward the outer corners of the lips. The resulting image portrays the individual as a mature bureaucrat (compare cat. 23).

The appearance of the double-echeloned wig, the manner in which the hieroglyphic eyes are designed in relation to their paint stripes and plastic brows, the philtrum on the upper lip, and the naso-labial furrows imbuing the image with mature characteristics are features found in images created during the reign of pharaoh Amenhotep III. These features are particularly evident in statues of Amenhotep, the son of Hapu, one of that pharaoh's important administrators. These similarities incline one to date this image into that period.

The ancient Egyptian processes for sculpting stone relied upon the technique of abrasion, by which materials of a higher value on the Mohs scale of hardness were used to remove unwanted material from the block of stone being worked which was of a lower value on the same scale. The process is illustrated in a vignette in the Tomb of Rekhmire, an official in the employ of Pharaoh Tuthmosis III, that represents sculptors at work (fig. 26).

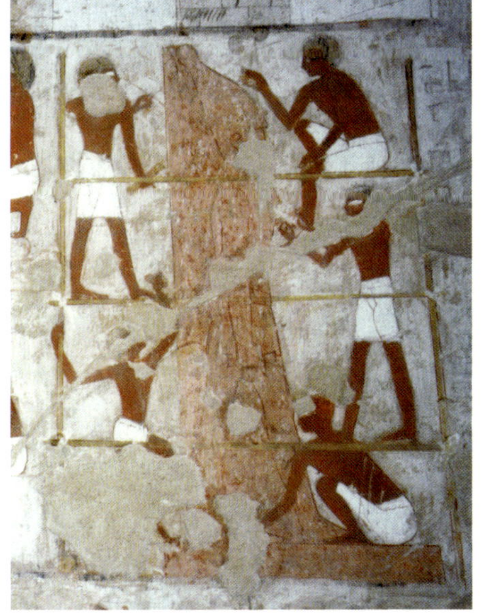

Figure 26
Detail of a scene from the Tomb of Rekhmire depicting stone sculptors at work on a statue, Dynasty XVIII

Published: Chappaz and Chamay, *Reflets du divin*, 2001, p. 64, no. 48; Künzi et al., *Les trésors*, nd, fig. 169, pp. 120–21.

References: Hill and Wilkinson, *Egyptian Wall Paintings*, 1983 p. 96, no. 30.4.90; Schulz, Die Entwicklung, 1992.

This painstakingly laborious process resulted in an object characterized by broad planes, clearly visible in this image in the modeling of the wig and of the face. When the process of modeling the objects in broad planes was complete, details were incised, or cut into, the stone, as a series of linear adjuncts. These linear details are most evident in the striations in the wig over the crown of the head. The surfaces were then polished with materials, again in various hardnesses on the Mohs scale, giving most of the surfaces of this image their shining, shimmering quality. The craftsmen were, however, unable to finely polish the rectangular locks of this double-echeloned wig because of its irregular raised pattern. As a result, this area of the wig appears lighter in color and exhibits rougher surfaces.

An examination of the break on the bottom suggests that the head was broken from a much wider surface, indicating that the head originally belonged to a block statue, so called because its final shape preserves the outline of the original block of stone from which it was sculpted. Such statues were traditionally dedicated in temples, so that the owner might be in perpetual communication with the deities worshipped therein and both might partake of the rituals performed there. In order to achieve that union, a ceremony of opening the mouth was performed upon the statue in order to animate it. The aspiration that the statue might remain in such a perpetual communication is reinforced by the use of granodiorite. Such a stone was extremely durable and imbued the image with the quality of permanence.

28.

The Pharaoh Rameses II, called Rameses the Great

Dynasty XIX, reign of Pharaoh Rameses II, 1290–1224 BC
Red granite
Height 28 ¼ in.
Inv. no. EG-133

This impressive red granite bust is sculpted in broad planes that clearly reveal the bipartition of the male torso, divided vertically by the sternal notch into symmetrical mirror images with emphasis on the pectoral region, coalescing into the lower abdomen. Characteristic of ancient Egyptian conventions, it avoids the depiction of the rib cage. There is a suggested emphasis on the clavicles, or collar bones, as well as on the sinuses of the neck. The round head is dominated by almond-shaped hieroglyphic eyes, the upper and lower lids clearly indicated as raised planes, above which lie plastically rendered eyebrows, the ends of which trail off toward the ears. The bridge of the nose is wide, with flaring wings in which the nostrils are visible from front view. The mouth, horizontally aligned, features full but small lips, from each corner of which a sign of age, imbuing the face with characteristics of maturity, descends toward the rounded chin which protrudes slightly from the lower jaw (compare cat. 27). The ears are disproportionately large when judged by Western criteria, but their size may very well be symbolic, convening an enhanced aural ability on the part of the statue when animated, as assuredly it was, to hear prayers addressed to it. The head is covered with a nemes-headcloth, its characteristic striping indicated by incision, with emphasis placed on its plain, undecorated head band. Over this is found the protective uraeus, or sacred cobra, part of its body in a double coil behind its hood, the remainder curling backward over the crown of the head. The use of red granite not only conveys the characteristics of durability and permanence to the image but also imbues it with solar associations because of its color.

Although not inscribed, the identity of the statue as a depiction of Rameses II, called the Great, of Dynasty XIX of the New Kingdom, is assumed by the circumstances of its discovery. Edouard Naville, the renowned Swiss Egyptologist, excavated this impressive bust in 1891 in the Temple of Heryshef, one of several creator gods who emerged from the primeval water of the mythical sacred lake. The suggested maturity of the image, conveyed by the signs of age, conforms to other images of Rameses II and would seem to confirm the identity of the statue.

Rameses II was one of the longest lived of all the ancient Egyptian pharaohs and commissioned temples throughout the land. Of these, Abu Simbel is perhaps the best known.

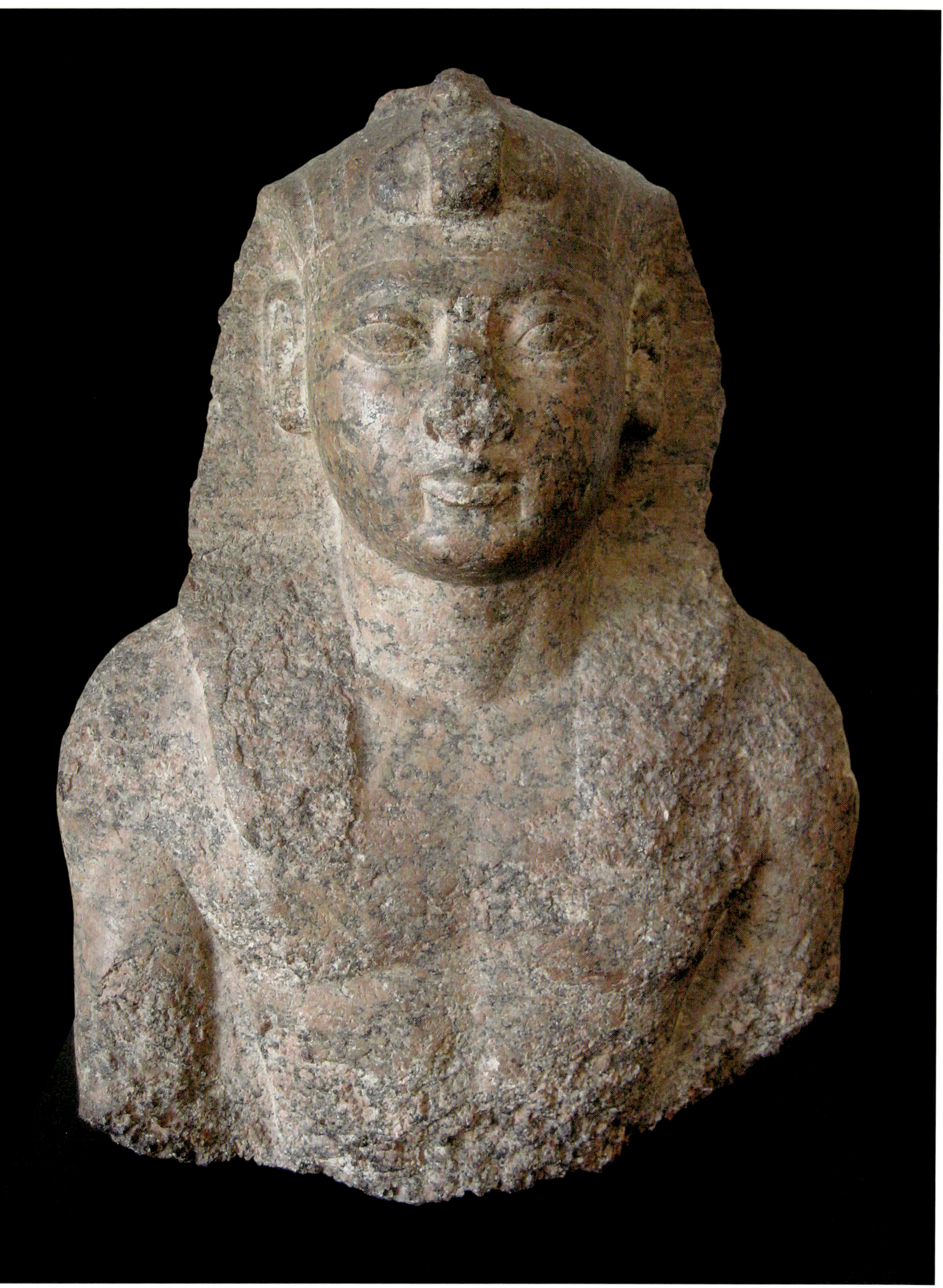

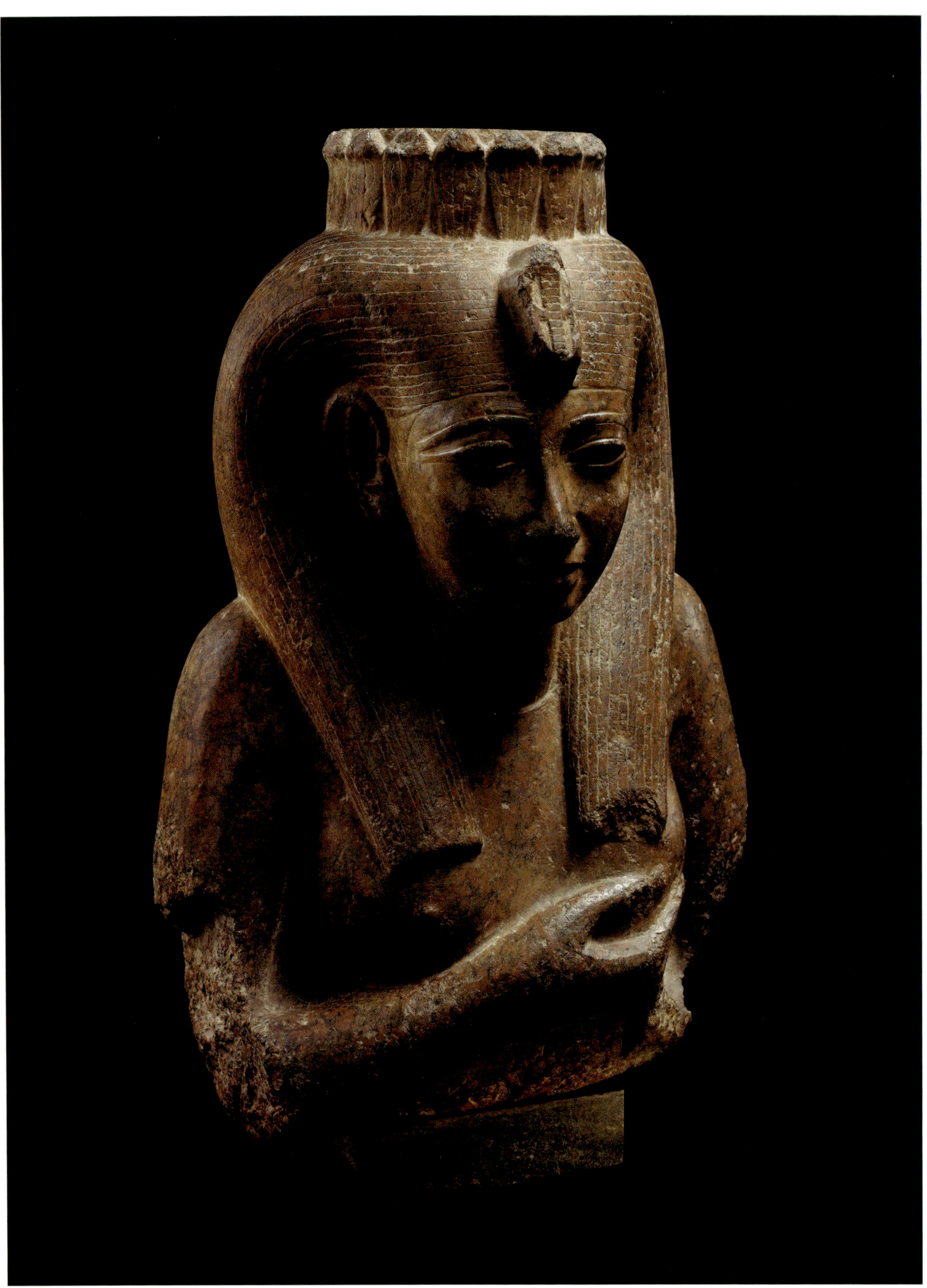

29.

A Life-Sized Bust of a Nursing Woman

Dynasty XXV–XXVI, 745–525 BC
Red granite
Height 22 ⅜ in.
Inv. no. EG-9

The statue, despite the lack of a body from the level of the navel down, may be restored in the mind's eye as a seated woman with a child on her lap whom she nurses with her offered left breast, the nipple of the right breast clearly articulated as a raised dot (compare cat. 75). The artistic tenets governing its design stress visual clarity rather than illusions of reality, which is the reason behind depicting this goddess wearing a tightly fitting sheath, as the presence of the curved neckline between the lappets of her headdress reveal.

She is modeled in highly polished broad planes, with linear adjuncts employed for the depiction of the locks of her tripartite wig, which falls behind the ears; the uraeus fronting her brow; and those forming the modius, or circlet, on her head. This anchored a now-missing attribute, as the presence of the mortise within it suggests (compare cat. 77).

The representation of a mother nursing her child was established as an iconic image in ancient Egyptian art from the time of its first appearance during the Old Kingdom. Over time, the image was reserved for the goddess Isis and her divine son, Horus, and was often appropriated for depictions of queens who wished to to be identified with her. This particular statue may very well depict one of those queens assimilated to Isis. The lack of an accompanying inscription renders her precise identification moot, but such ambiguity is consistent with the polyvalent nature of ancient Egyptian art, in which any given motif has multilayered, interlocking meanings. The inclination to identify the bust as a royal rather than as a goddess may be supported by the use of granite, because its red color, which is imbued with solar associations, would tend to reinforce a queen's aspired identification with a goddess.

On the basis of the design of the face, one can suggest a dating for this statue into Dynasty XXV–XXVI, when the style of the late Kushite Period was perpetuated into the early Saite Period. The Kushite pharaohs of Dynasty XXV, originating from lands now located in the modern nation state of the Republic of the Sudan, promoted the worship of child gods, with whom those monarchs were particularly identified (compare cat. 68).

Published: Chappaz and Chamay, *Reflets du divin*, 2001, pp. 58–59, no. 43; Künzi et al., *Les trésors*, n.d., fig. 170, pp. 122–23.

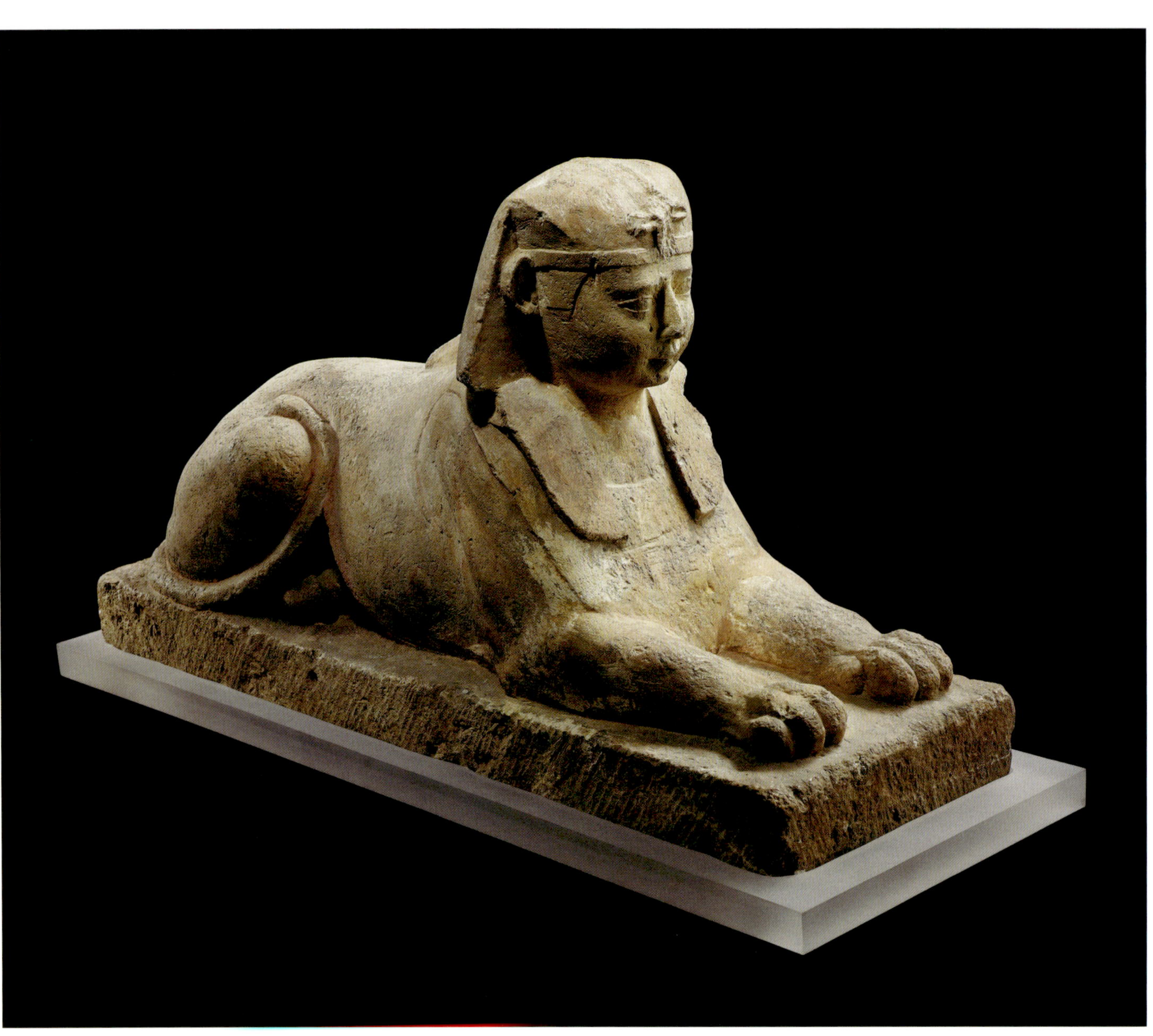

30.

A Sphinx

Ptolemaic Period, 305–30 BC
Limestone with traces of red pigment
Length 26 ¾ in.
Inv. no. EG-126

Ancient Egyptian art is populated with a virtual menagerie of composite beasts in which a leonine body is combined with a variety of heads—ram, falcon, and human. Some are even provided with the tail of a crocodile. Each of these may be designated as a sphinx, a word universally applied to such creatures, which derives from an ancient Greek term meaning "strangler," but whom the ancient Egyptians called *shepsep ankh*, "the living image." Of all the species of sphinxes, none, perhaps, is as well-known or captures the popular imagination as the one that features a human head on the body of the king of beasts. In keeping with the polyvalent nature of ancient Egyptian cultural norms, the sphinx represented both the pharaoh and the sun god, coexisting without any apparent Aristotelian contradiction.

From the time of the New Kingdom through the Ptolemaic and Roman periods, dromoi, or causeways, both fronting temples and linking those in close proximity with one another, were lined on either side with such images. Their function was both to protect these sacred avenues from danger and to proclaim the might and power of the reigning pharaoh. This example, despite its scale, appears to have served a similar function, to judge from its shared similarities with a group in Paris, excavated in the nineteenth century at Saqqara by Auguste Mariette.

This sphinx is modeled in broad planes and poised, recumbent, on an integral rectangular plinth, with attention to such details as the toes with their claws and the creases of its skin. The statue was once lavishly painted, tantalizing traces of which can still be detected, noticeably in the polychromy articulating the striped pattern of the nemes-headdress. Over this is placed a hair band, overlapped in part by the hood of a uraeus, whose coils trail off over the crown of the head.

The sphinx itself was first polished, after which it was painted, as the traces of red pigment, a color with solar associations, suggest. The unfinished state of its integral plinth need not be taken as evidence that the sculpture was not completed, because the proper left-hand long side of the plinth appears to have contained an inscription (in Greek?) painted in red letters, with an alpha and tau(?) still visible. It is entirely possible that this inscription was anciently added some time after it was made, because the surface on which it is painted would have originally been concealed if, as is suggested, the entire object was set into a larger pedestal intended to elevate the sculpture.

Its facial features are designed in an idealizing manner, although Western sensibilities may discern an unintended melancholy in its expression. Some commentators have attempted to use that perceived expression as the means by which to adduce the identity of the pharaoh represented. Such attempts, however, are flawed because portraiture, as defined by Western art historical principles, was not a concern of the Egyptian elite. Revisionist approaches to the question of portraiture suggest that such images, in keeping with the generic nature of the hieroglyphs, should be regarded as expressions of kingship and authority, erected along avenues of temples to proclaim the might and power of reigning pharaohs.

Published: Chappaz and Chamay, *Reflets du divin*, 2001, p. 53, no. 40; Künzi et al., *Les trésors*, n.d., fig. 171, pp. 124–25.

References: Bianchi, "Elite Image," 1992, pp. 34–48; Lembke, "Die Sphinxallee," 1998, pp. 267–73.

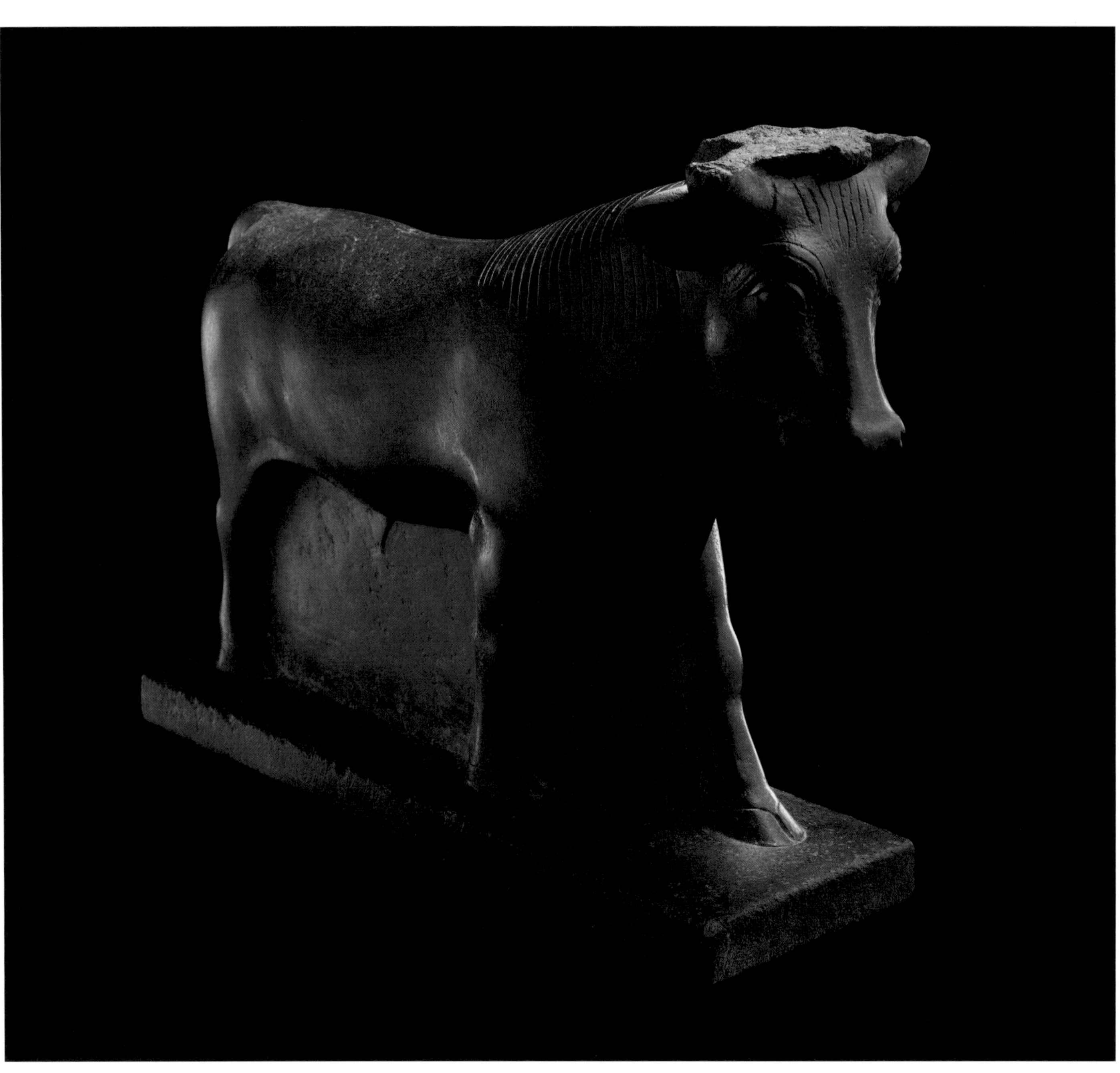

31.

Statue of an Apis Bull

Ptolemaic Period, 305–30 BC
Granodiorite
Length 22 ⅞ in.
Inv. no. EG-32

One of the more endearing characteristics of ancient Egyptian art is its ability, shared with hieroglyphs, of capturing the essence of the animal depicted. Both representation and sign distill and capture the nature of the beast as a generic image. Here, that image is brought to life by modeling the bovine in broad planes which are polished to a gleaming shine. The planes clearly reveal the undulating nature of the bull's musculature. Details are applied in the form of linear adjuncts to articulate coat, head, tail, genitalia, and hooves. The negative space both between the belly of the bull and the integral base as well as between the legs and tail has been purposefully left in a rougher, less well-polished state so as not to be confused as part of the animal depicted.

The damaged attribute, visible in front view and cradled by the horns, is a sun disk fronted by a uraeus. This attribute is the visual indicator that this representation is that of a sacred rather than ordinary animal. In accordance with the polyvalent nature of ancient Egyptian art, the bull serves as the hypostasis of several deities, among whom are the Apis, Buchis, and Mnevis bulls.

The identification and dating of this statue as an Apis bull created during the Ptolemaic Period, is suggested by its close stylistic affinities with examples excavated at Saqqara, where the Apis bull was both mummified and buried. As the hypostasis, or alternate form, of Ptah, the creator god, the Apis symbolizes the mighty cosmic, generative forces of that god (compare cat. 85).

Published: Chappaz and Charnay, *Reflets du divin*, 2001, p. 24, no. 4.

References: Cleveland, The Cleveland Museum 69.118;
Bianchi, *Cleopatra's Egypt*, 1988, cat. 105, pp. 211–12.

32.

A Colossal Royal Head

Ptolemaic Period, 305–30 BC
Limestone with traces of red and blue polychromy and gilding
Height 15 ¾ in.
Inv. no. EG-355

This colossal head, more than likely from a sphinx, is characterized by a round face with hieroglyphic eyes and plastic eyebrows with a thin-bridged nose and fleshier wings. The mouth is small, with fleshy lips, the upper designed as a Cupid's bow, the corners of which are drilled. The pharaoh is shown wearing a nemes-headdress fronted by a uraeus, its body in a figure-8 configuration beneath its hood and its tail trailing off over the crown of the head.

The stippled surfaces of the nemes-headdress and the rough surfaces of the face belie its original condition, which must have been impressive since it was lavishly painted in blue and red and gilded, traces of which remain here and there.

The idealizing features of the face preclude an exact identification, but a dating within the Ptolemaic Period seems assured, as comparisons with sphinxes recently inventoried reveal (see cat. 30). The provocative assertion that such idealizing physiognomies, characterizing the faces on representations of pharaohs as sphinxes such as these, are not to be understood as images of individual pharaohs, but are to be understood as generic expressions of kingship.

References: Lembke, "Die Sphinxallee," 1998, pp. 267–73.

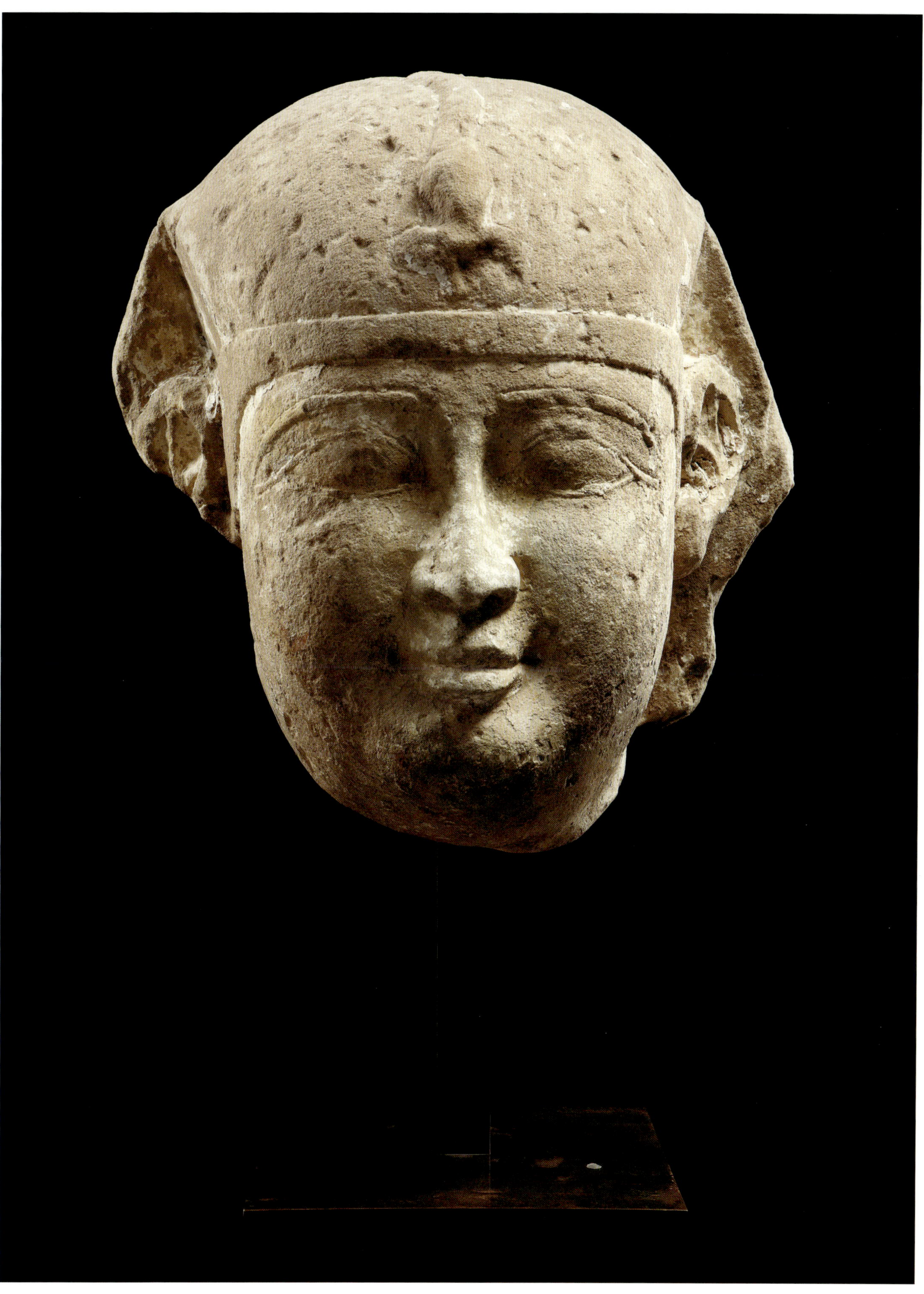

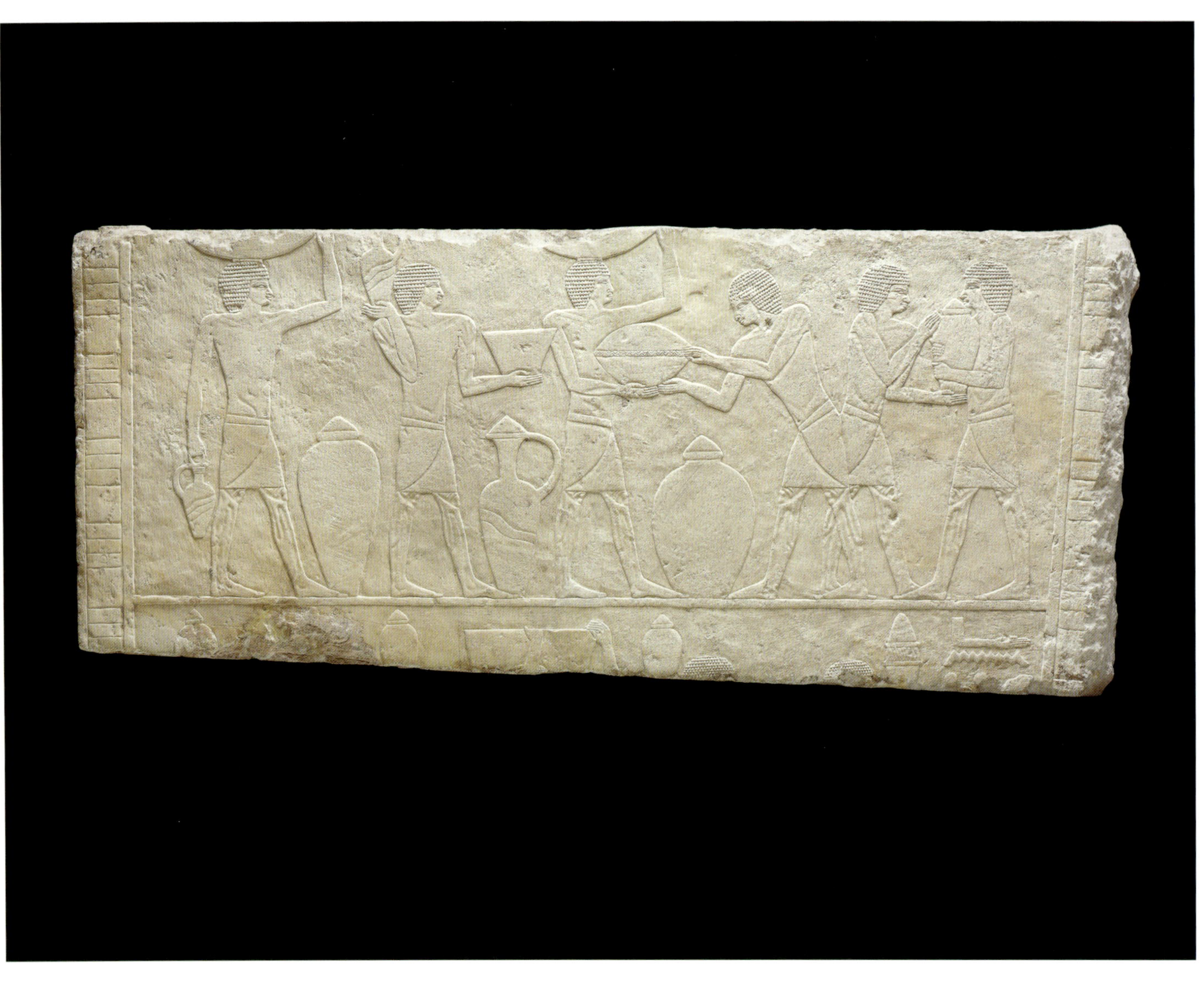

33.

A Neo-Memphite Relief with Offering Bearers and their Vases

Dynasty XXV–XXVI, 745–525 BC
Limestone
Length 43 ½ in.
Inv. no. EG-291

Sculpted in wafer-thin relief that rises ever so slightly from the background, the better preserved of the two scenes represents a group of six men, their wigs coiffed in short, tight curls and their bodies clothed simply in identically fashioned short, belted kilts. The musculature of their legs is emphasized by an incised linear pattern, which is so stylized and mannered as to suggest its model was created during the Old Kingdom. This detail, together with the design of the torsos of the two figures to the far right, which appear almost in profile, and that of the raised arm, bent at the elbow, of the second figure from the left, are indices of archaizing, which classify the relief as Neo-Memphite. That classification applies to a series of reliefs decorating tombs created during the Late Period that consciously evoke the style of the wall decoration of tombs created at Saqqara, the necropolis of the capital city of Memphis, during the Old Kingdom.

The fragmentary scene below appears to have depicted a similar group of offering bearers to judge from the preserved tops of their identical wigs. The single group of hieroglyphs appearing here at the far right spells the noun "myrrh." Consequently, these figures are bringing vases containing balms, ointments, and aromatics for use of the tomb owner. The offering bearers in the better-preserved upper register are to be understood as carrying and arranging vases filled with foodstuffs and liquids for the benefit of the deceased. Those vases were created in alabaster, as the preserved wavy lines ornamenting some reveal.

The subject matter of this relief places the several vessels in this exhibition into their funerary context and emphasizes the primacy of alabaster as the stone of choice for such containers.

Published: Anonymous, "La porte du rêve," 2007, p. 44.

References: Kuhlmann and Schenel, *Das Grab des Ibi*, 1983, pls. 26, 27, and 30.

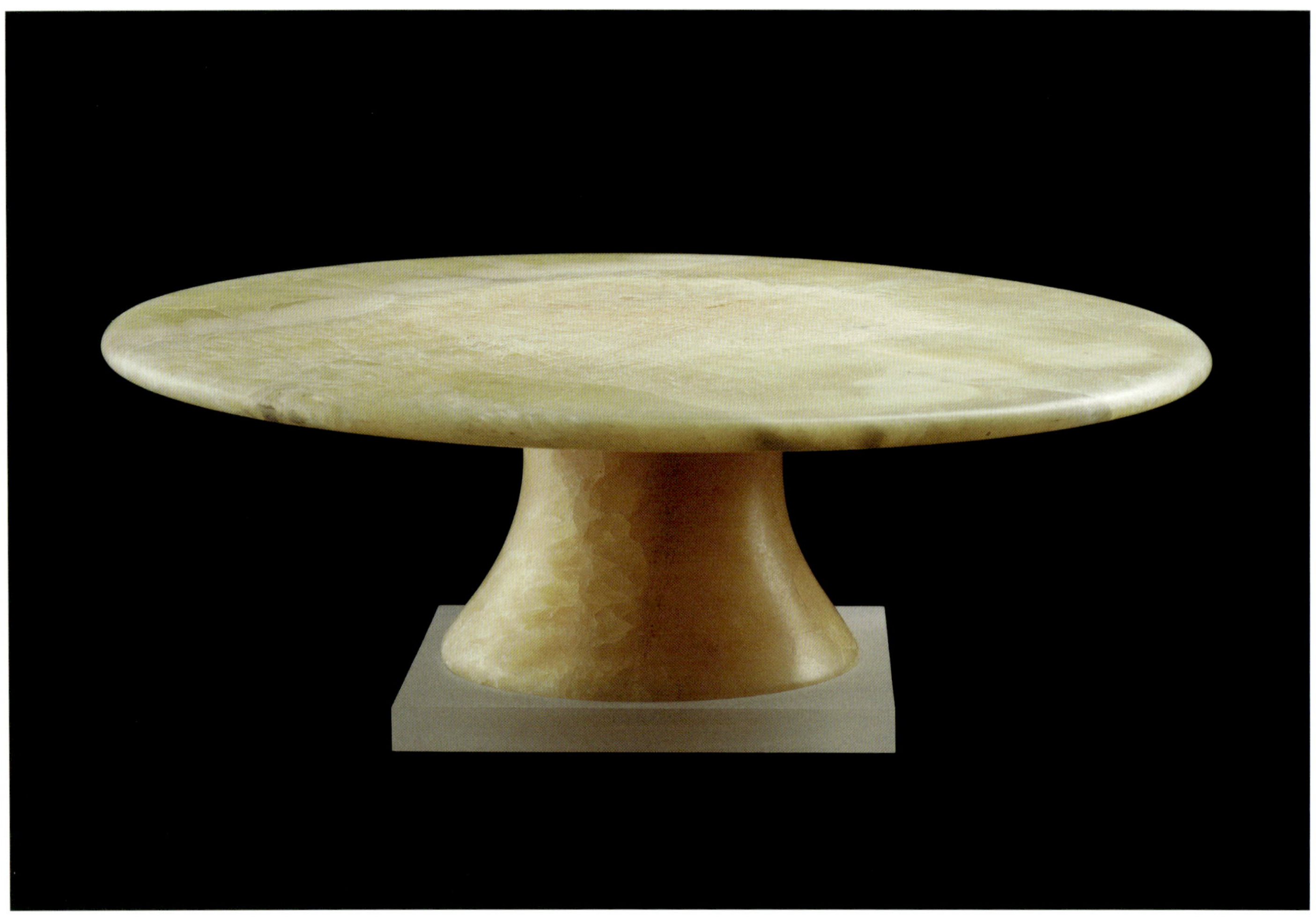

34.

A Model Table

Dynasty V–VI, 2450–2155 BC
Banded alabaster
Diameter 11 ⅞ in.
Inv. no. EG-222

This object, crafted from a single block of translucent alabaster, features a central support designed in the shape of an hourglass topped by a thin, wide disk. Excavated examples demonstrate that such objects functioned as miniature tables that formed parts of services, complete with vessels of various shapes and designs, some of which were actually placed on the tops of the tables. These sets often included miniature ewers for holding water so that the deceased might symbolically be able to wash before and after partaking of the foodstuffs so arranged in his tomb. These objects were substitutes for the costlier and bulkier full-sized services that they replaced in the tomb. Despite their smaller scale, they were just as efficacious. The use of alabaster imbued those services with characteristics of purity and permanence.

References: New York, The Metropolitan Museum of Art, 11.150.2; Hayes, *Scepter* I, 1953, pp. 118–19, with fig. 72; MMA, *Age of the Pyramids*, 1999, pp. 492–93, cat. 214.

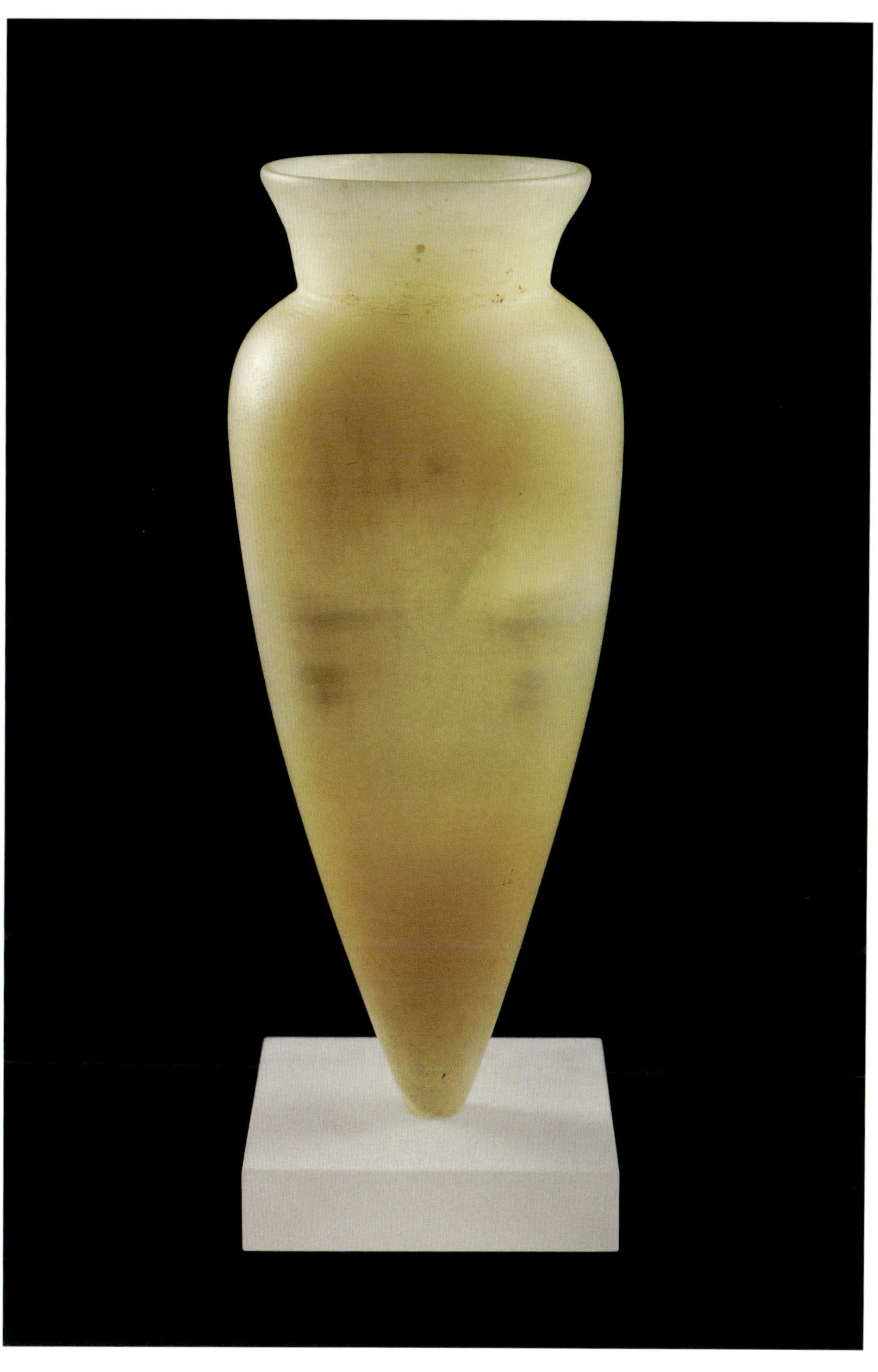

35.

A Piriform Vessel

Dynasty VI, 2290–2155 BC
Alabaster
Height 5 ¼ in.
Inv. no. EG-250

This vessel, sculpted from a single block of stone, is characterized by a narrow, sharply tapering body with a short shoulder and conical neck, exhibiting a faintly everted lip. Its size and shape suggest it originally held a balm or unguent associated with funerary rites.

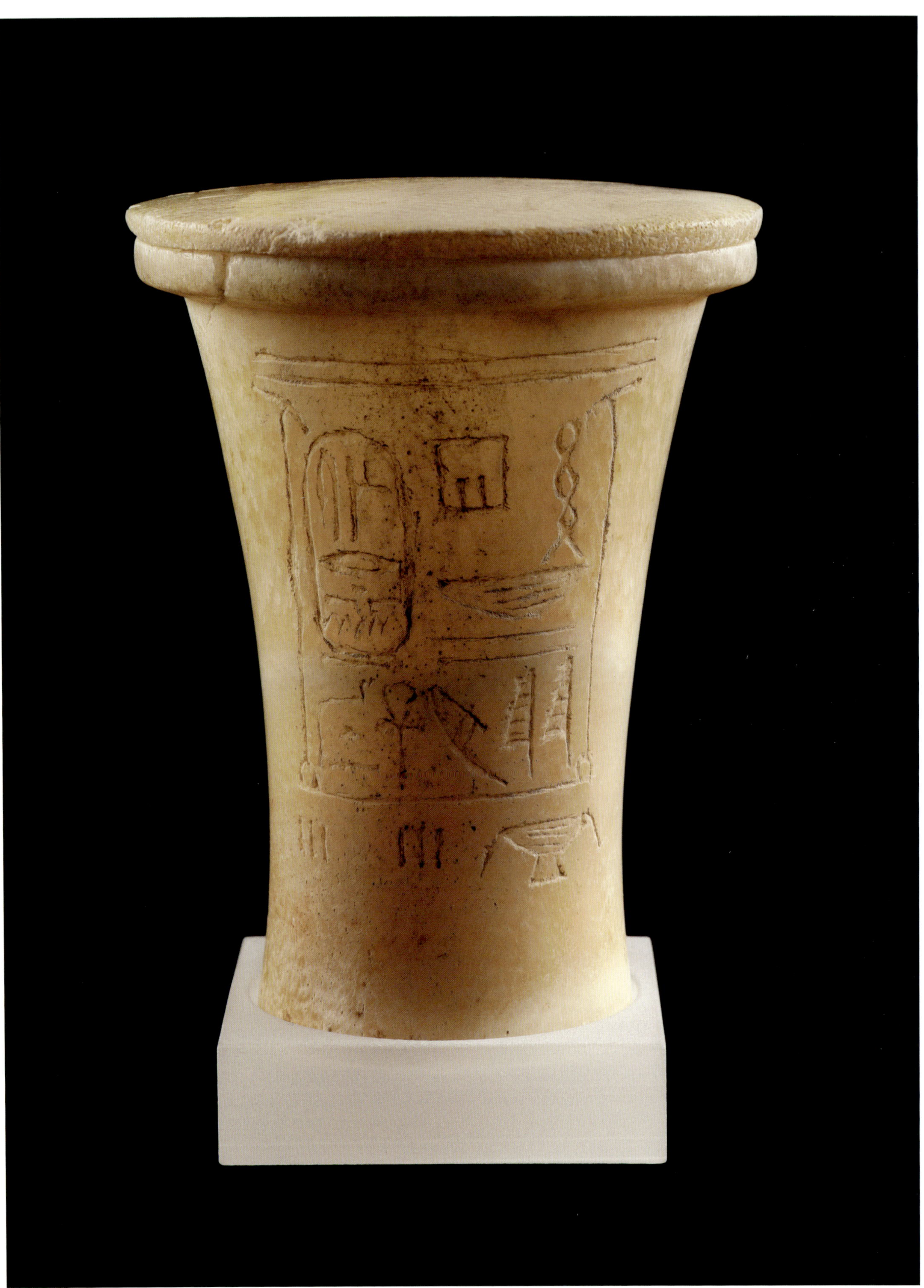

36.

Vase Inscribed for a Pharaoh Sesostris, with its Lid

Dynasty XII, 1991–1785 BC
Limestone
Height 3 3/16 in.
Inv. no. EG-168

The diameter of this conically-shaped vase increases with its height, so that it is wider at the top than at the bottom. Designed without any indication of a foot, its top terminates in a disk-shaped rim that just overhangs its vertical wall. The circular lid was created with a boss, or circular projection, centered on its underside, which fits into the mouth of the vase to ensure that it was tightly closed when lidded. Such vases were anciently called *baket* (compare cat. 42).

One face of the vase is decorated with a carefully planned and executed incised scene. Its left- and right-hand sides are framed by upright was-scepters and hieroglyphs representing the nouns "dominion" and "lordship." These in turn support a *pet*-sign, representing the noun for "the sky," and rest on a ground line. Together these elements form a four-sided frame within which is found a hieroglyphic inscription which includes the cartouche of a pharaoh

> *Sesostris, the one beloved of the god Ptah, the lord of the Two Lands [Egypt], may he live eternally!*

There is an enigmatic inscription beneath the ground line that consists of the hieroglyph for the noun "gold" followed by six short, vertical strokes, in two groups of three, widely separated from one another. The form of this inscription suggests that the hieroglyph for gold indicates the precious nature of the substance originally contained within this vessel, which is otherwise not indicated. The six strokes taken together would then seem to indicate the quantity, again not specified, of that substance.

The ancient Egyptians thought that the sky was supported by four columns, one placed at each of its corners, which rested on the earth. That concept is conveyed by the design of the frame, which creates a symbolic universe within which a pharaoh Sesostris metaphorically exists by virtue of the principle by which the name of an individual and that individual's person are one and the same. One might, therefore, tentatively conclude that the costly or precious substance contained within this vessel, presumably intended for funerary purposes, was thought to contribute to the aspired eternal existence of the pharaoh named. Such an aspiration would be consistent with the use of alabaster, a white stone that was imbued with connotations of permanence and purity.

The dating of this vessel is assured by the presence of the cartouche of a Sesostris. Because there were several pharaohs of Dynasty XII named "Sesostris," one is hard-pressed to identify any of them with the one named on the inscription because of the lack of additional information in the form of other names, titles, and the like.

Published: Chappaz and Chamay, *Reflets du divin*, 2001, p. 67, no. 52.

37.

A Canaanite-Shaped Amphora inscribed for Pharaoh Amenhotep II

Dynasty XVIII, reign of Pharaoh Amenhotep II, 1439–1413 BC
Alabaster with blue-paste pigment
Height 10 ¾ in.
Inv. no. EG-353

The shape of this alabaster vessel imitates that of contemporary Canaanite ceramic amphorae, a name applied to such vessels with two handles, deriving from the ancient Greek etymology, "to carry on both sides."

These earthenware vessels exhibit a somewhat conical shape in their modified piriform bodies that both enabled their contents to settle and eased their loading for transport on oceangoing cargo ships, in which they were nested, like eggs in their cartons, in straw-cushioned racks. Its Canaanite shape is appropriate for the period because Egyptian involvement in the Near East at this time is well-documented. The region lay within the expanding spheres of Egyptian influence in general and its location fostered a brisk trade that promoted cultural exchanges. Its dating is assured by the presence of a single column of hieroglyphs on the front of its belly, which can be translated as

> *the good god, Aa-kheperu-re [the prenomen of Amenhotep II], given life.*

In keeping with the Canaanite model, this vessel, although sculpted from a single block of stone, has a wide neck, the interior of which is V-shaped. This is separated from the shoulder by an incised line. The rolled rim, disk-shaped, overhangs the wall of the neck. The vertically aligned handles were created by drilling, but traces of that process are still visible because the handles were not completed polished.

The vessel exhibits the unusual use of projections, termed "collars," at the top and bottom of its handles, which are not found on its Canaanite model (compare cat. 51). In addition, the vase is somewhat asymmetrical, not only in the execution of its neck but also in the orientation of the handles, which are not strictly aligned with one another on a level, horizontal plane. These anomalies, which may seem awkward by the application of Western design principles, appear to have been of little concern to the ancient Egyptians, because this same awkwardness is discernible in any number of other alabaster vessels inscribed with names of pharaohs of the same dynasty. Western characterizations such as "awkward" are very subjective and do not seem to reflect the concerns of the ancient Egyptian elite. One must, therefore, devote additional time to the study of these stone vessels in order to determine why pharaonic ateliers, capable of producing aesthetically accomplished objects in stones of all types in all classifications, should content themselves with such productions. For the present, such is the nature of one aspect of royal Egyptian art during Dynasty XVIII (compare cat. 9).

The ornamentation of the individual hieroglyphs with pigmented paste on such royal vessels of Dynasty XVIII was common practice, as was, apparently, their design, which appears to have been formulaic, prefixing the prenomen and suffixing it with the phrase *the good god and given life*, respectively. The use of alabaster imbued the vessel's contents with qualities of permanence and purity, the colored paste with those of resurrection and regeneration. The adopted foreign shape may also have connoted the exotic, a meaning perhaps intended to encompass desirable foreign imports.

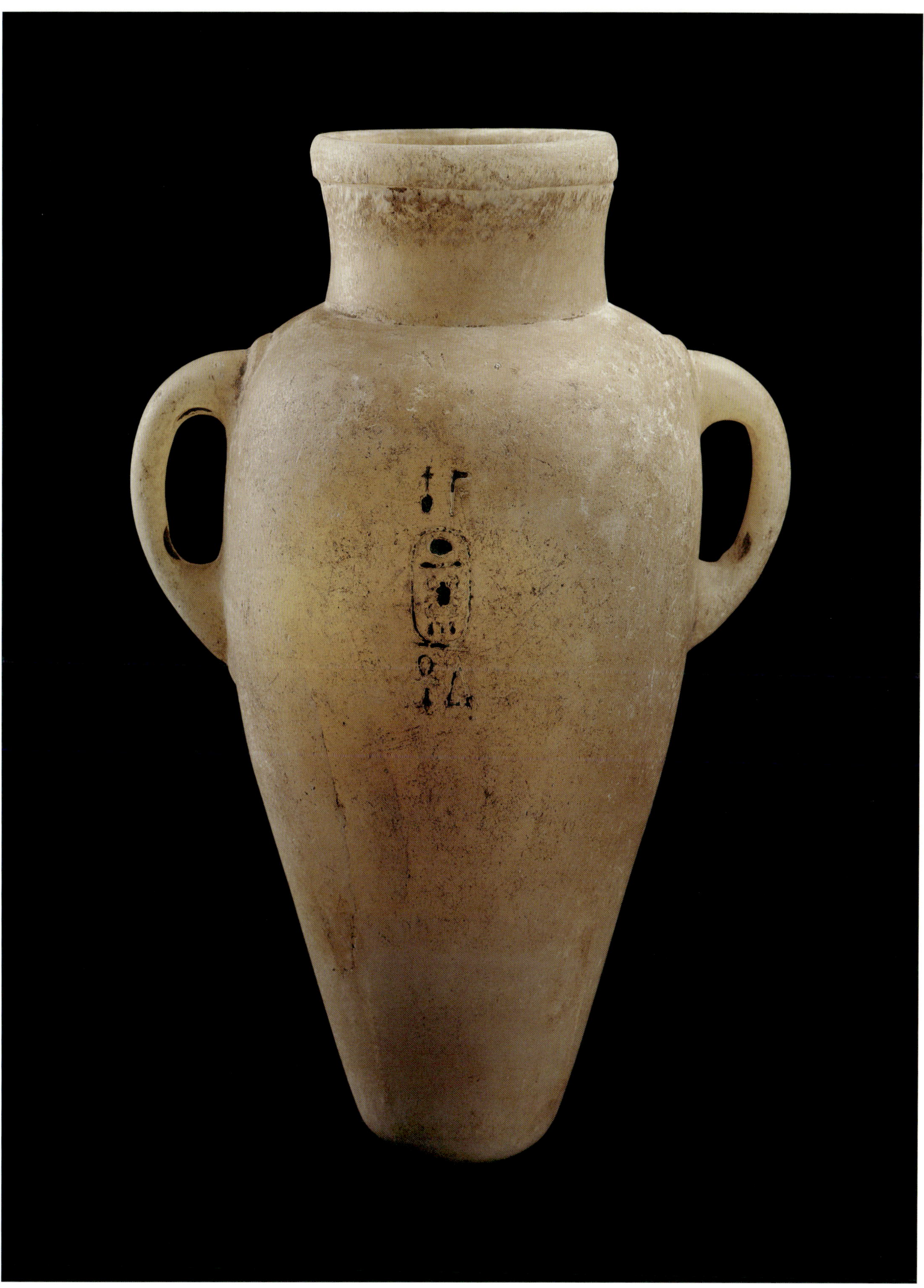

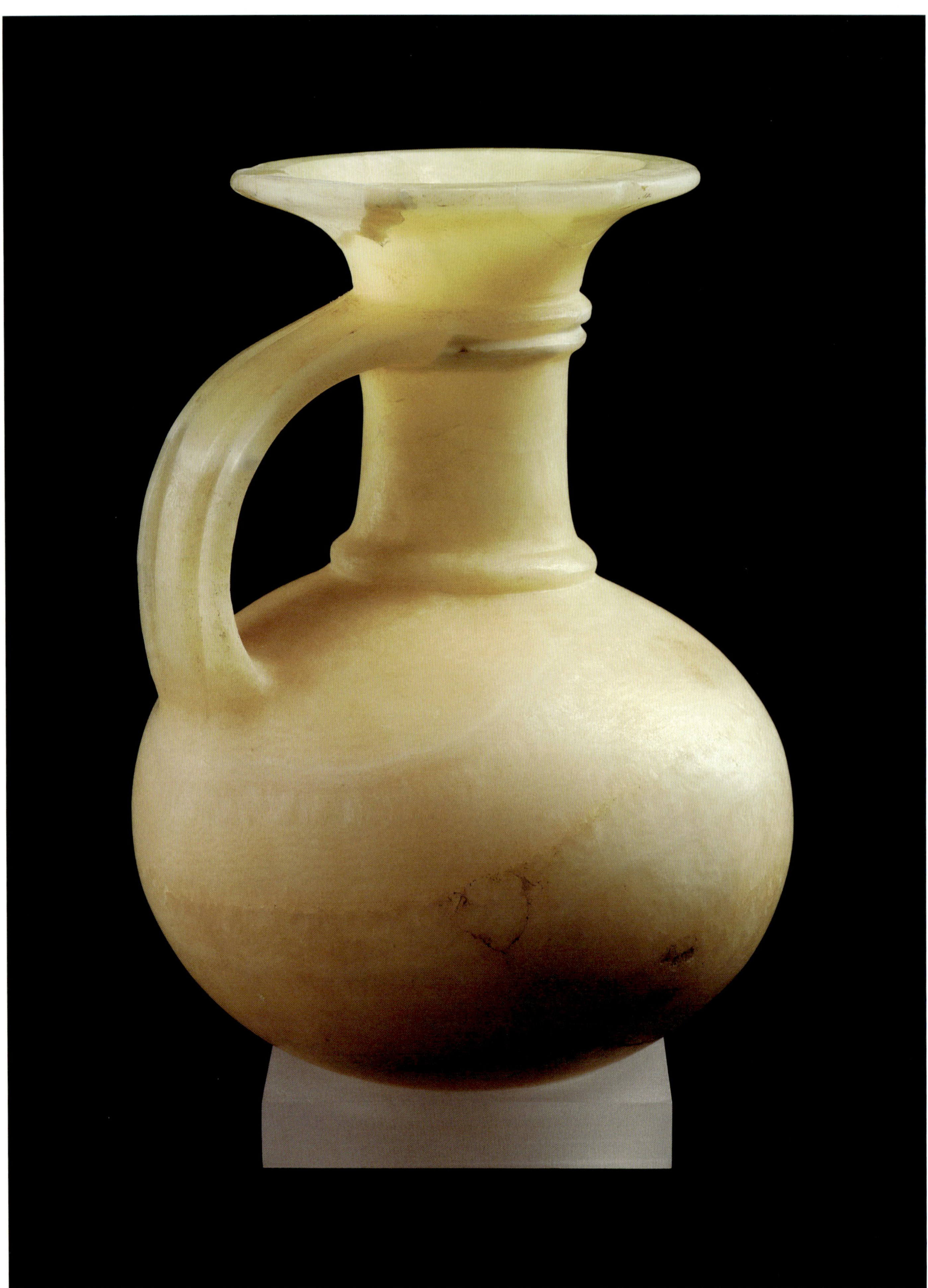

38.

A Jug

Dynasty XVIII, 1554–1305 BC
Alabaster
Height 5 ¾ in.
Inv. no. EG-290

This vessel, sculpted from a single block of stone, exhibits a globular body with a cylindrical neck that swells to a trumpetlike flaring mouth. It is provided with a strap handle, ornamented with two parallel incised lines, which springs from the shoulder to the neck, at the juncture of which are two convex bands. A single convex band is found at the juncture of the neck with the shoulder.

The jug appears to be a variant of a shape inspired by vases created on the island of Cyprus (compare cat. 39). One suggests that it originally contained scented oils or fats used as a balm.

39.

A Pitcher

Dynasty XVIII, 1554–1305 BC
Alabaster
Height 8 ½ in.
Inv. no. EG-311

This vessel is an Egyptian translation into stone of a pottery type, associated with the island of Cyprus, that belongs to a classification termed base-ring ware because of the distinctive circular shape of its articulated foot, here splayed and concave underneath. The body of the pitcher is ovoid, with a slender, long, and slightly flaring neck, terminating in a flat, overhanging rim. Its tapering handle, designed with notches suggested to represent cords, is attached to the neck. Its base and top are ornamented with horizontal ribbing. The entire vessel was sculptured from a single block of stone.

The Cypriote examples, first attested as imports during the Second Intermediate Period, continued to enter Egypt until the end of Dynasty XVIII. The Egyptians also translated this shape into faience and glass, suggesting its popularity. That popularity, however, seems to have been based not on an Egyptian fondness for this foreign shape, but rather on the Egyptian preference for its contents, suggested to have been a honey laced with opium that was highly regarded for its medicinal, rather than its recreational, properties. The design of this particular vessel type appears to have been inspired by the seed pod of the opium poppy. The efficacy of the drug was believed to be enhanced by the shape of its container, symbolically adding even more opium to its contents.

The substances contained within these pitchers of Egyptian manufacture appear to have been scented animal fats or almond oils used as cosmetics, rather than the Cypriote pharmaceutical drug. The present example is dated to Dynasty XVIII on the basis of parallels.

References: Bourriau, "Pitcher," 1982, p. 129, no. 118.

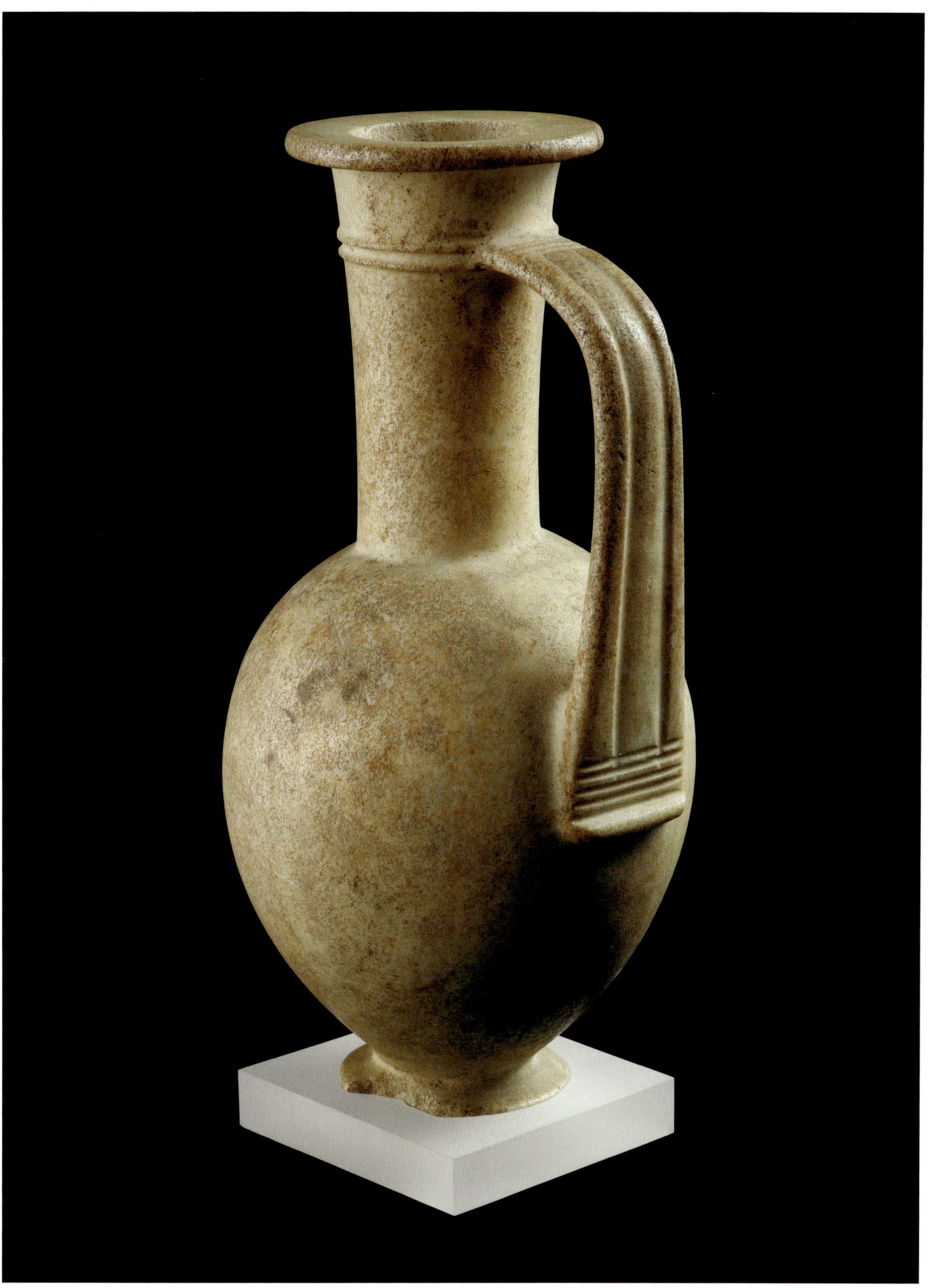

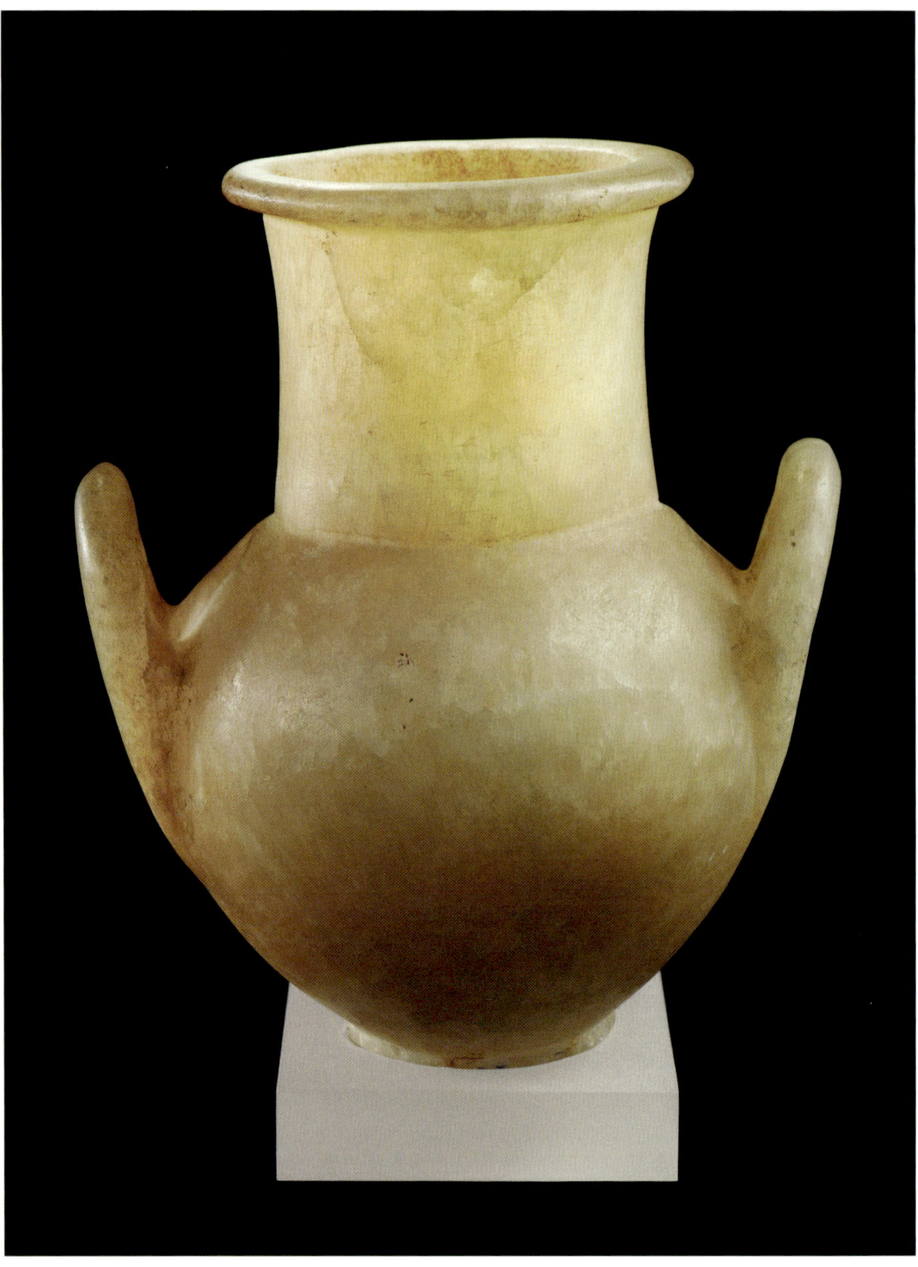

40.

An Amphora

Dynasty XVIII, 1554–1305 BC
Alabaster
Height 5 ¾ in.
Inv. no. EG-314

Sculpted from a single block of stone, the ovoid body of this amphora rests on a disk foot. The tall, slightly concave neck is set off from the shoulder by an incised line, and a second separates it from its everted, rounded rim. The vessel has two looped handles, vertically projecting from its belly. Such containers were originally provided with lids. The shape was extremely popular, with examples created in pottery, glass, and faience as well.

This particular example is instructive because it exhibits the method of its manufacture. The stonemason employed a drill in order to hollow out both looped handles, but in the process created an unwanted dimple on each shoulder where the drill apparently hit the wall of the vessel.

The dating of this example to Dynasty XVIII is based on inscribed parallels, some of which indicate that their contents were liquid, in one case identified simply as "a brown ointment."

References: Bourriau, "Amphora," 1982, p. 127, no. 114.

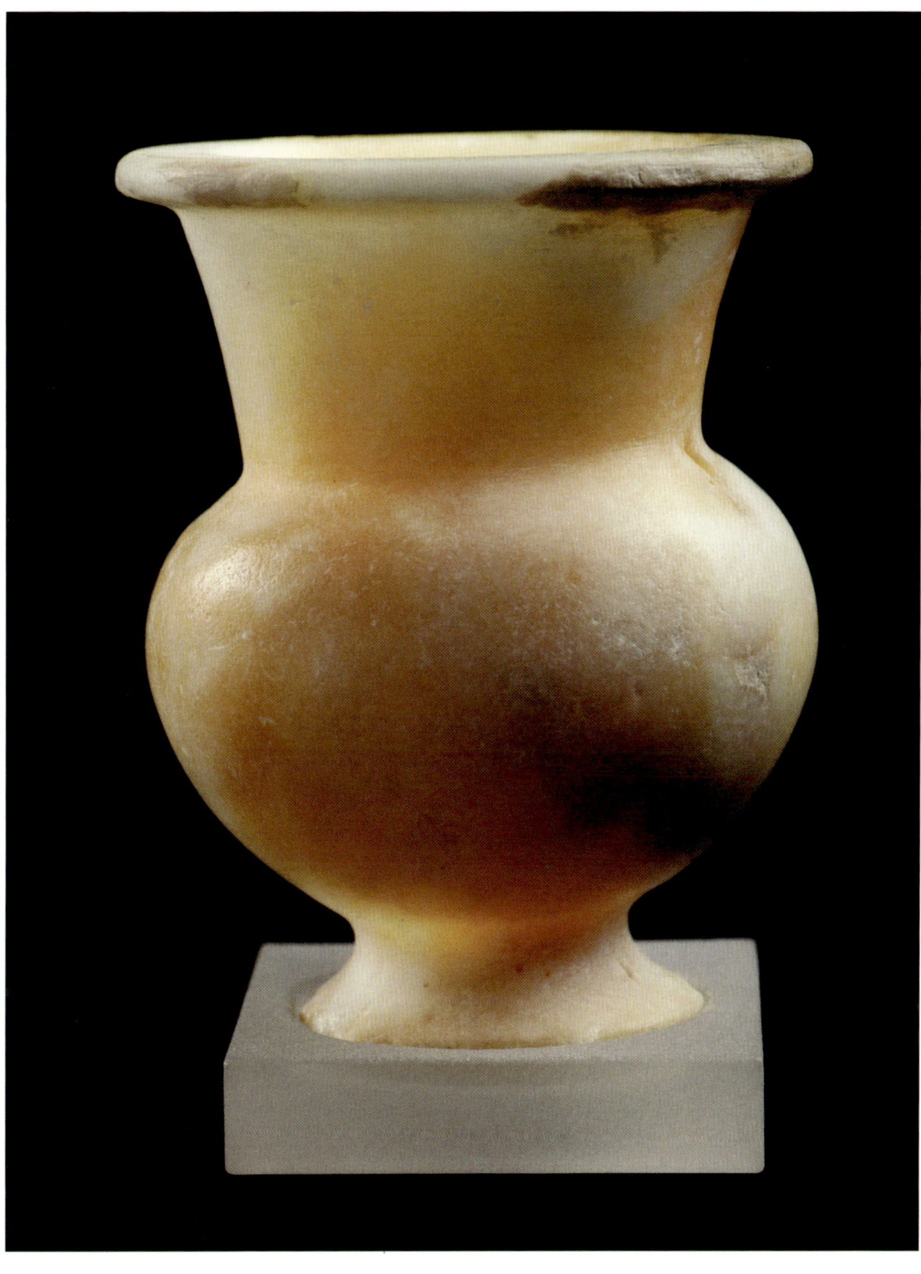

41.

A Miniature Thistle Vase

Dynasty XVIII, 1554–1305 BC
Alabaster
Height 1 ¾ in.
Inv. no. EG-373

These vases are called "thistle vessels" because their profiles resemble that flower. They were so popular that they were created in a variety of materials and in a variety of sizes. The exacting adherence of all of these thistle vases, regardless of material and scale, to a common model strongly argues in favor of the existence of pattern books or templates available to elite overseers for use in institutionally affiliated ateliers (compare cat. 47 and cat. 48).

Thistle vases are suggested to have held expensive unguents, employed in funerary rites, temple rituals, and celebrations featuring the pharaoh. Their archaeological context suggests that they date to Dynasty XVIII, and the present example may in fact be the smallest known representative of the type.

42.

A Palette for the Seven Sacred Oils

Dynasty V, 2450–2290 BC
Alabaster
Length 6 ¾ in.
Inv. no. EG-334

This rectangular palette is designed with a single line of unframed hieroglyphs along the top and seven somewhat equally spaced columns below, separated by divider lines, aligned with seven corresponding circular wells along its bottom edge. The single line is inscribed with the name and titles of its owner:

> *The sole companion, the lector-priest, the overseer of the secrets of the house of mourning [whose name is] Sa-inut.*

The phrase, the house of mourning, is traditionally written with the hieroglyph for a human hand, its palm empty, as its first sign. The hieroglyph employed as the first sign of that phrase on this palette is written with a liquid pouring forth from the palm of the human hand (see detail at right). This seemingly insignificant detail is instructive. The overseer of the house of mourning is charged with the ritual act of dressing the pharaoh and attending to his toilette. In the performance of these duties, Sa-inut probably touched the pharaoh's person, so that the hieroglyph of liquid pouring from the open palm symbolically represents one of his actual duties.

The seven vertical columns of inscription contain the Egyptian nouns for each of these seven sacred oils, from right to left: 1) *Setj-heb*, 2) *Heknu*, 3) *Sefeti*, 4) *Ni-chenem*, 5) *Tewat*, 6) the best *Ash*, and (7) the best *Tiehenu*. The hieroglyphs for these words are followed by one in the form of a specific type of lidded ointment jar (compare cat. 36), in which the oil named was symbolically thought to be contained. The ancient Egyptian name for such a vase appears to have been *baket*. The meaning of those vases is further emphasized by the presence of the circular wells, which serve as additional receptacles.

The modern equivalent or composition of many of these seven sacred oils remains unknown. Nevertheless, those unguents and balms, first attested on jar labels discovered within the royal tombs of Dynasty I at Abydos, were important for both Egyptian burial and offering rituals. Beginning in Dynasty V, the seven sacred oils were often inscribed on false doors, but they might also be the subject of individual tablets, such as the example under discussion. The spelling and sequence of these oils appear to have been invariable. Excavated examples have always been found in the burial chambers proper, and one suggests that the circular wells were intended to contain a small amount of each oil named, where they would be readily available to the deceased.

References: Cour-Marty, "Les Textes," 1994, pp. 123–39; Koura, *7-Heiligen*, 1999; Manniche, *Sacred Luxuries*, 1999, pp. 37ff; Strudwick, "12. Oil Tablet," 1988, pp. 81–82.

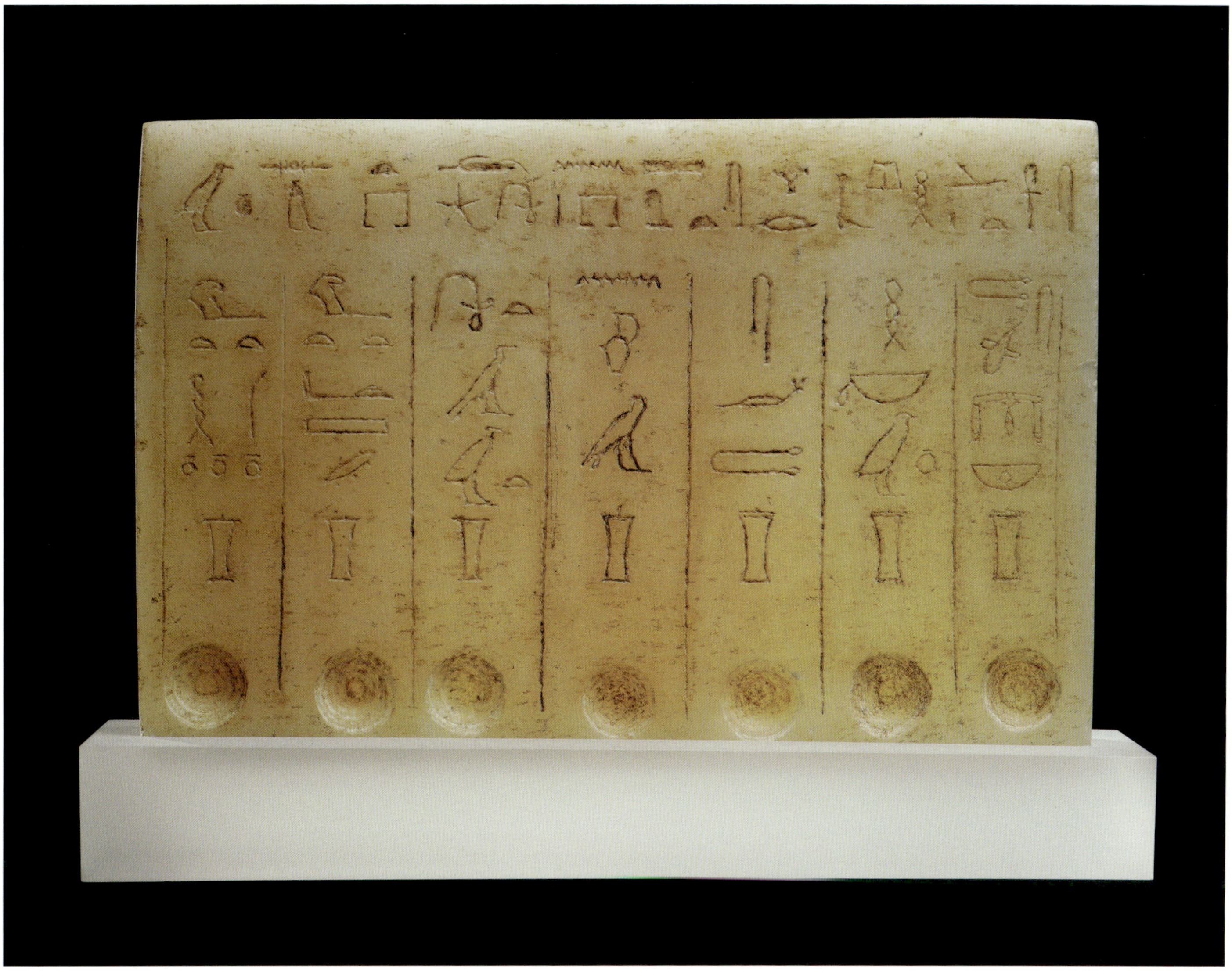

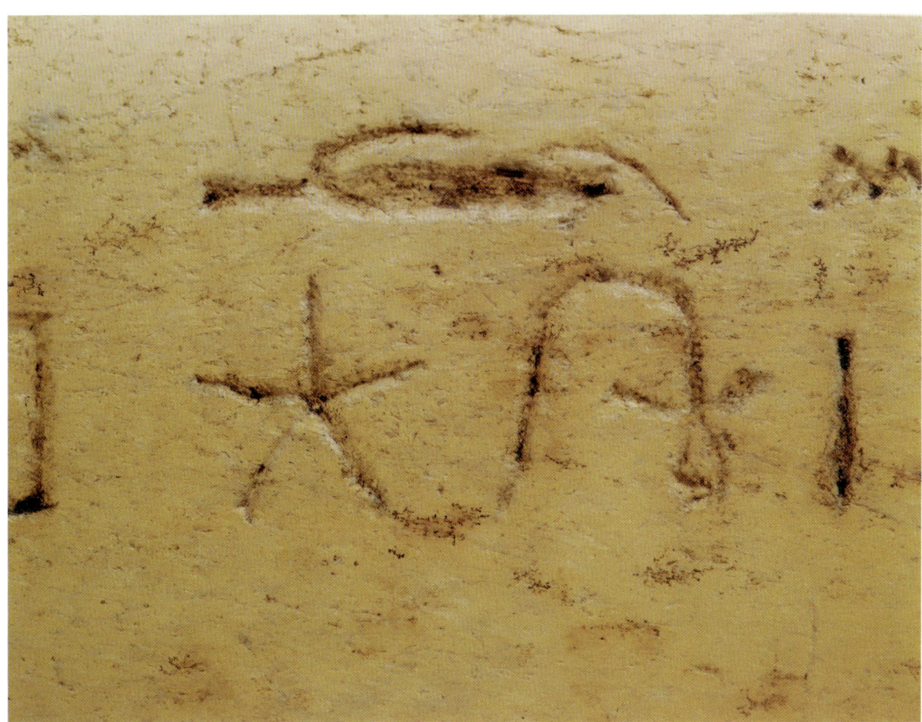

Cat. 42 Detail of hieroglyph

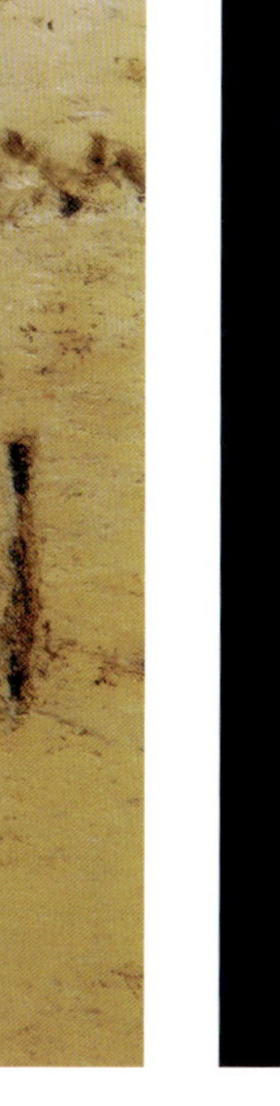

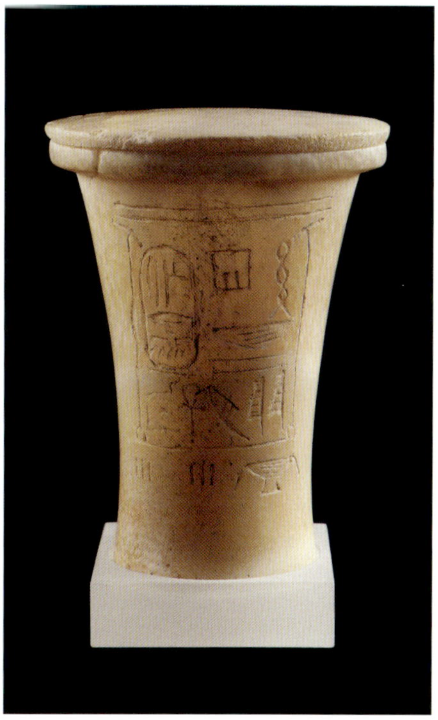

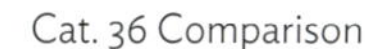

Cat. 36 Comparison

43.

A Cosmetic Spoon

Dynasty XVIII, 1554-1305 BC
Alabaster
Length 9 5/8 in.
Inv. no. EG-69

Ancient Egyptian hieroglyphs can be designed in such a way that component parts of two or more objects seen in the real world can be combined into one sign in a manner both pleasing and harmonious to Western aesthetic sensibilities. The design of this object conforms to those ancient Egyptian design tenets. The lanceolate design of its bowl is attached to its handle by a transition zone in the form of two curvilinear projections adapted from a stylized papyrus plant. The handle itself tapers and terminates in a finial in the form of the head of a duck, its head dominated by an hour-glass-shaped bill curved back so that it faces the bowl.

In keeping with ancient Egyptian sculptural processes, the spoon was created by the abrasion technique which has resulted in its delicately modeled broad planes. One calls particular attention to the bottom of the bowl with its bilateral design subtly suggested by a slightly raised medial rib. These planes have been ornamented with linear adjuncts particularly evident in the articulation of the papyrus element and the head of the duck. The skill of the craftsmen is evident, not only in the paper-thin thickness of the walls of the bowl which imbues them with a delightful translucence, but also in the way the head of the duck has been created in the round, freeing it entirely from the fabric of the handle's shaft.

The lanceolate shape of the bowl suggests that it was modeled on a motif found in the floral kingdom. Yet, the artistic principles governing the design of objects in ancient Egyptian art that insist on capturing their generic nature in terms of visual clarity, rather than as allusions of reality, preclude a precise identification. Nevertheless, its lanceolate form suggests that the model may have been a zucchini-like elongated squash or perhaps the contours of a bunch of grapes, both of which figure prominently in piled offerings depicted in tombs of the Eighteenth Dynasty.

The presence of the duck may allude to the god Amun, a solar deity par excellence who is often associated with a duck. The papyrus suggests the primeval marsh from which creation arose when the rays of the first dawning sun struck the surface of its waters. The fruit, perhaps representing the floral kingdom in general, connotes concepts of rebirth and regeneration on analogy with the floral kingdom's ability to sprout anew after a period of dormancy. Taken together, these images singly and collectively connote concepts of renewal in general and rebirth in particular. These connotations are appropriate for the function of this object, its bowl suggested to have been used as a receptacle for special unguents or perfumes, although admittedly no residues of any such cosmetics have ever been found in any object of this type.

In the popular imagination, cosmetics represent a salient feature of the material culture of ancient Egypt. One is, therefore, initially inclined to associate such objects with the toilette of elite women. Accordingly, the possibility exists that such objects may have been used in life. The archaeological record, on the other hand, suggests either a funerary or sacred, rather than a domestic, context for such objects. Whereas it may be argued that such objects of daily life were then interred in tombs for the benefit of the deceased in the hereafter, an alternative view regards the creation of such objects specifically for their funerary function. The craft of embalming elite members of society relied upon the extensive use of costly and exotic balms and unguents with

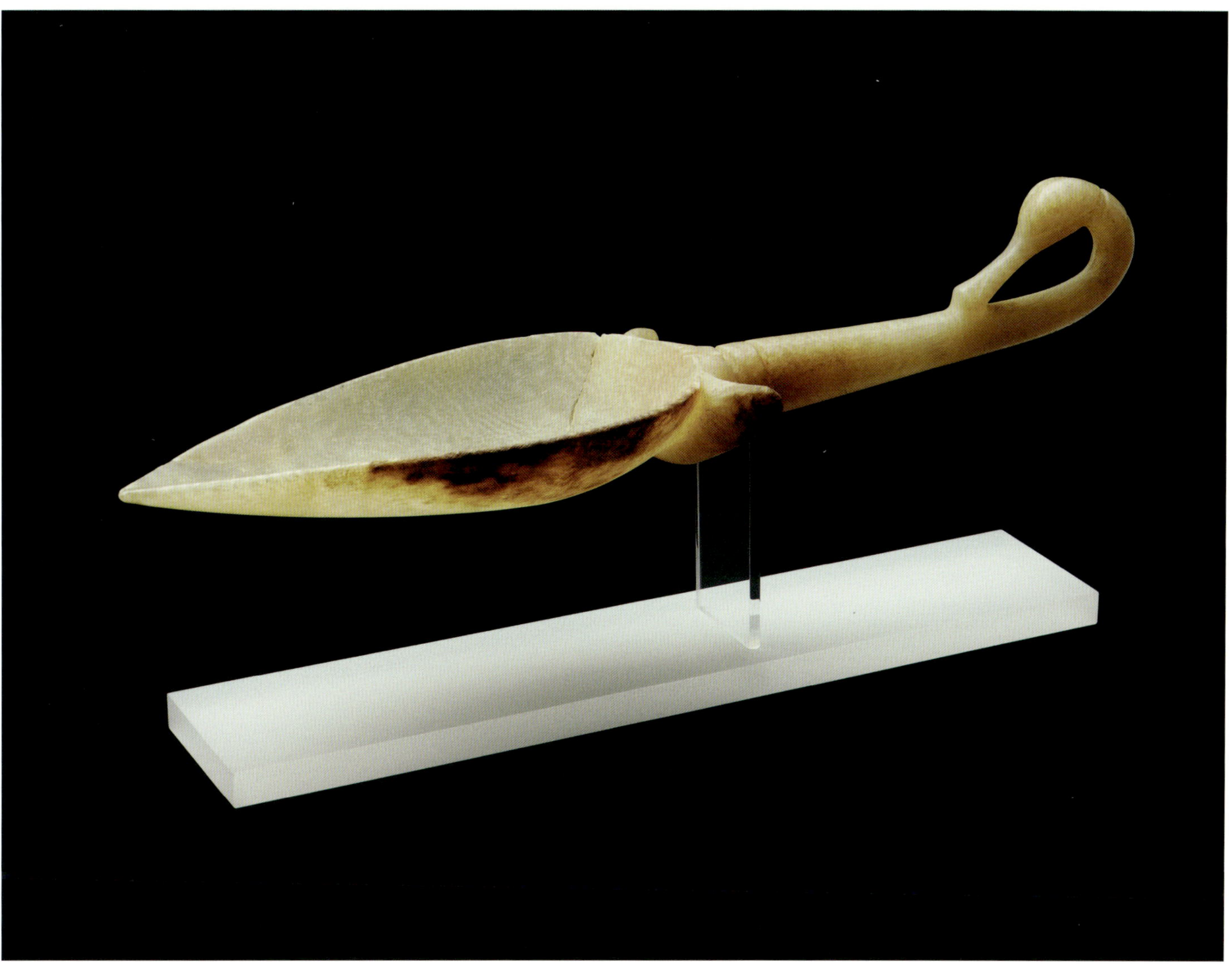

which the corpse was bathed and anointed so that the deceased might realize aspired resurrection. This spoon is suggested to have contained such cosmetics and is designed with motifs which singly and collectively connote concepts of rebirth and regeneration.

In like manner, ancient Egyptian sources, such as *The Daily Cult Ritual*, inform us that deities in temples were awakened, and hence animated, by the dawn's early light, after which priests performed a series of rites on the cult statue including anointing it with balms and unguents similar to those used in the embalming process. Such cosmetics might have likewise been contained in the bowl of this cosmetic spoon, the motifs of which, due to the polyvalence inherent in Egyptian philosophical discourse, resonate with connotations of cosmic regeneration and renewal.

Of these alternative interpretations, one is inclined to endorse the funerary function of this cosmetic spoon based on its perfect condition. It is a given in archaeology that objects placed into tombs, when excavated, are generally in better physical condition than those found in either domestic or religious contexts because funerary objects, sealed within the tomb, were less likely to be disturbed and damaged (compare cat. 44).

Published: Chappaz and Chamay, *Reflets du divin*, 2001, p. 72, no. 61; Germond, "Bestiaire," 2002–3, pp. 75–94, particularly pp. 87–88 with fig. 14; Künzi et al., *Les trésors*, n.d., fig. 178, pp. 136–37.

References: Moret, *Rituel*, 1902.

44.

A So-called Cosmetic Spoon in the Form of a Trussed Goose

Dynasty XXV, 745–655 BC
Unglazed steatite (possibly indurate limestone)
Length 5 ⅝ in.
Inv. no. EG-345

This object is created from an unusual material, the nature of which is difficult to identify, because visually it resembles either glazed steatite or a form of indurated limestone. It is designed as a dressed goose with its legs tucked up over its body, its web feet spread and its head turned to one side. The modeling is in broad planes with details incised. The body is hollow in order to contain a presumed cosmetic, but no example has been found that contains traces of its original contents (compare cat. 43). There does not appear to be any provision for the attachment of a lid.

In the popular imagination, cosmetics represent a salient feature of the material culture of ancient Egypt and evoke images of Cleopatra. The archaeological record suggests, on the contrary, that such objects were primarily funerary in nature, exemplified by the extensive use of balms and unguents in the processes of mummification. Objects such as these cosmetic spoons are suggested to have contained samples of such substances placed eternally at the disposal of the deceased. Similar cosmetics were also used in daily life in the rituals preformed on behalf of deities and their cult statues in temples and were likewise employed in ceremonies performed on behalf of the living pharaoh. (compare cat. 45 and cat. 46).

The duck is a frequent symbol of regeneration (compare cat. 56) and is often found as a motif associated with cosmetic spoons (compare cat. 43) in funerary contexts, in which it exhibits a remarkable polyvalence, both because of its associations with the primeval marsh from which creation arose and because it is specified as an essential offering for the deceased in the traditional prayer,

> *1,000 of bread and 1,000 of beer, and 1,000 of oxen and 1,000 of fowl.*

This ointment spoon finds a very close parallel, somewhat smaller, in Paris (Musée du Louvre), which is suggested to date to Dynasty XXV, the Kushite Period, the period to which this example is also assigned.

References: Bulté, "Cuillères d'offrandes," 2008, pp. 75–94.

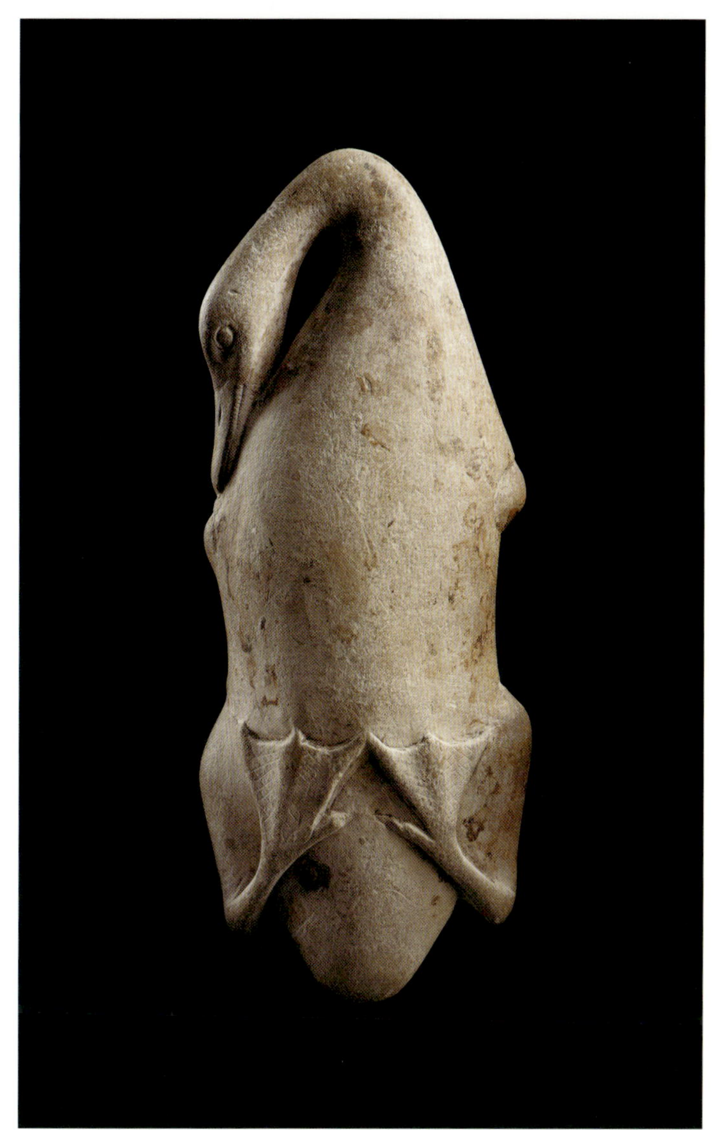

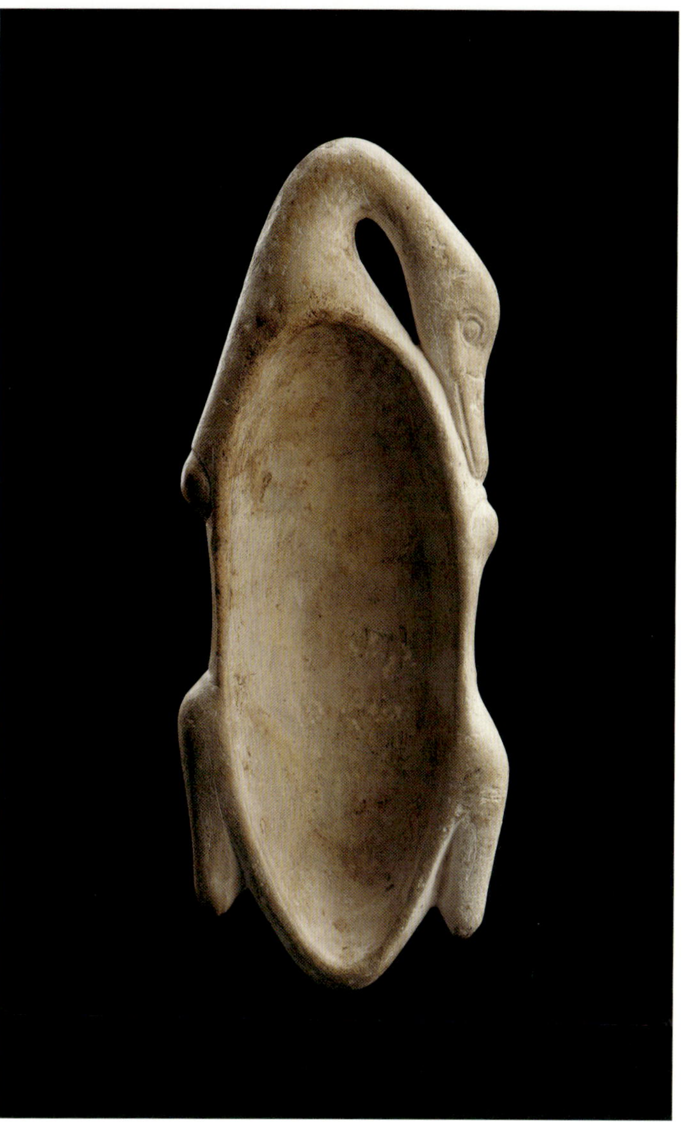

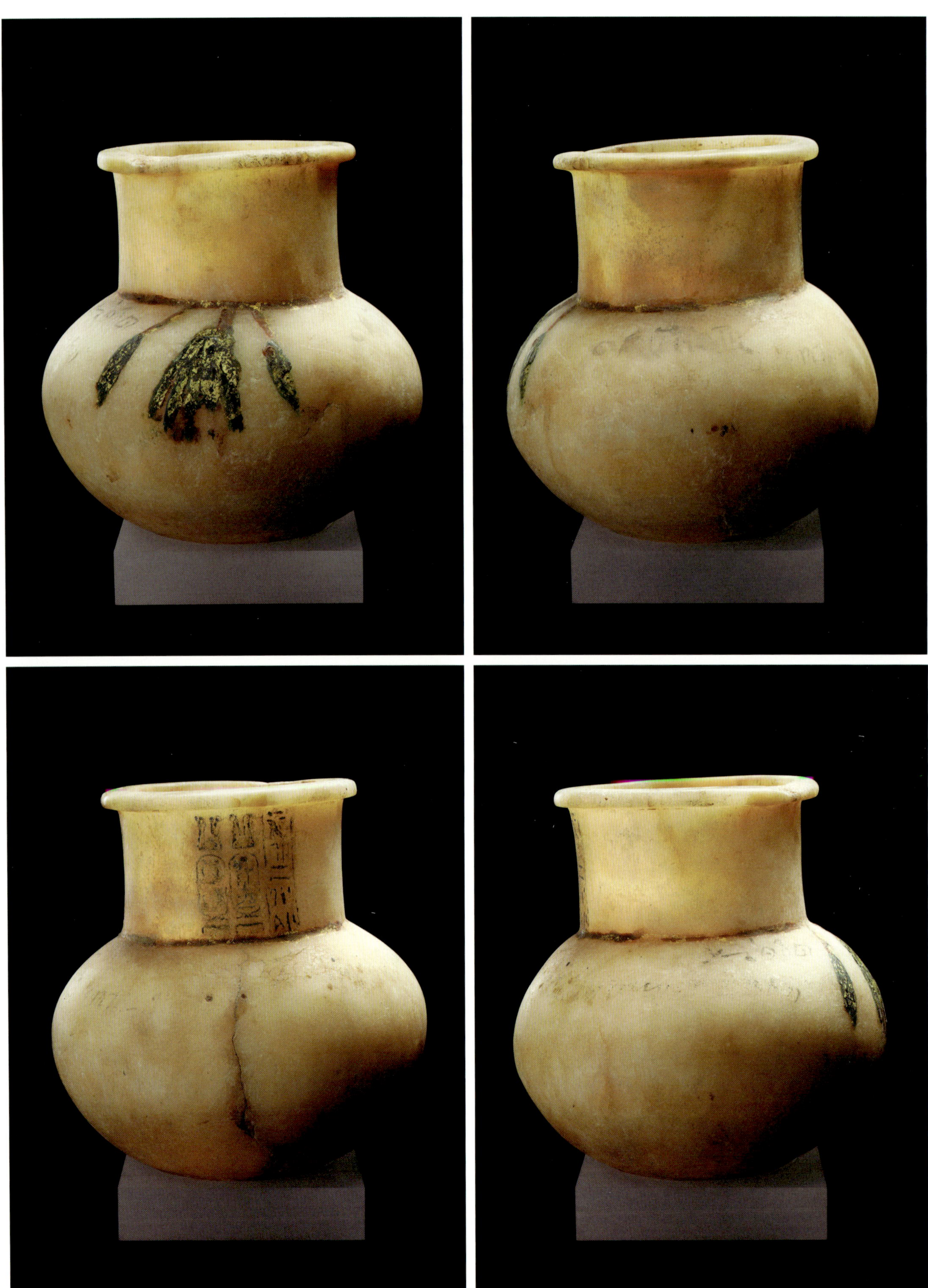

45.

A Vase Inscribed with the Name of Rameses II

Dynasty XIX, reign of Pharaoh Rameses II, 1290–1224 BC
Alabaster, encaustic, and gilded
Height 8 ⅞ in.
Inv. no. EG-7

The body of this globular vessel possesses a very narrow shoulder that abruptly transitions into a cylindrical neck, almost as tall as the body, which is provided with a disk-shaped rim overhanging the wall of the neck.

The vase is decorated on two sides. The first contains three columns of hieroglyphs incised onto the neck, which still retain traces of their gilded pigments. These contain the name of Rameses II in two cartouches, surmounted by double plumes fronted by a sun disk at the top and a neb-sign below. The presence of these names established the dating for this vase:

Wesermaatre Sepepenre Rameses, beloved of the god Rehorakhty, the great god, the lord of heaven, the prince of Heliopolis.

The transition zone at the juncture of the neck and the shoulder is designed as a stem-like ribbon to which are attached a single lotus flower and two of its blossoms, which hang upside down on their bellies opposite the inscribed neck.

The undecorated side of the belly of the vase has been inscribed in black ink in hieratic, a cursive form of the hieroglyphs, but these signs are so faded and indistinct that even the use of infrared technology did not contribute to their legibility. One suggests that this inscription specified both the contents of the vessel and its capacity, perhaps still represented by the traces of an unanalyzed residue with the vase's body. The laboratory of the Museum of Art and History in Geneva determined that the capacity of this vessel, when filled to within a centimeter of its lip, was 3.47 liters, or about 3 5/8 quarts. Presumably its contents were intended for use in ceremonies performed on behalf of Rameses II.

Published: Chappaz and Chamay, *Reflets du divin*, 2001, p. 68, no. 54.

46.

An Amphora

Dynasty XIX, 1305–1196 BC
Alabaster, encaustic, and wood
Height 16 ¼ in.
Inv. no. EG-323

Resting on a slightly projecting disk base, the tall, ovoid body of this amphora exhibits a very narrow shoulder, from which springs a tall, cylindrical neck with rounded rim. The two handles of the vessel are in the form of an integral head and upper neck of an ibex, the base of which is set at the shoulder level and the horns of which spring upward to form the handles. The entire vase was sculpted from a single block of stone, designed to accommodate the ears of these ibexes, which were separately made of wood, one of which is still preserved in its original position.

As early as the Predynastic period, Egyptian pottery might include animal protomes. Over time, both human and animal bodies might be designed as vessels in their own right. This unlimited creativity manifested itself in the remarkable variety of alabaster vessels found in the tomb of Tutankhamun. The ancient Egyptian artisans, with this tradition extending back in time for millennia, could design vessels in alabaster in almost any conceivable form. The ibex heads as handles on this amphora belongs to this tradition of innovation and may have, in fact, been inspired by the motif of the ibex employed by the Asiatics of the Syrian-Palestine region. Such horned animals appear as elements ornamenting vases depicted on a wall of the mortuary temple of the pharaoh Rameses III presented to that king by Western Semitic peoples.

This alabaster vessel has been decorated in encaustic, a technique in which pigments are suspended in molten wax, which is then painted on to the surface of an object. That decoration takes the form of two strands of necklacelike ornamentation on the neck. The body exhibits a U-shaped collar-like floral form, its center occupied by an inverted lotus blossom.

At least one vessel of this type is inscribed for the pharaoh Rameses II, the contents of which included linen, sand, natron, resin, and organic debris connected with the processes of mummification. Similar vases have been excavated in the Valley of the Kings and were associated with the funerary equipment of the pharaoh Merenptah, the son and successor of Rameses II. These parallels suggest the dating of this vessel.

This vase is inscribed with a partially preserved inscription in hieratic, a cursive form of hieroglyphs, on the neck, which may be translated as

> *a wreath [garland] and bread of the gods...*

The text suggests that the function of this vessel was likewise funerary.

References: Burlington Fine Arts Club, *Catalogue*, 1992, p. 1,A and plate XXXII; P. Lacovara in Burlington Fine Arts Club, *Catalogue*, 1992, and Lacovara, P., and B. T. Trope, *Collector's Eye*, 2001, pp. 124–25; D'Avennes, *Atlas*, 1868–78/1991, p. ii, 83rd plate; Reeves and Wilkinson, *Valley of the Kings*, 1996, p. 148.

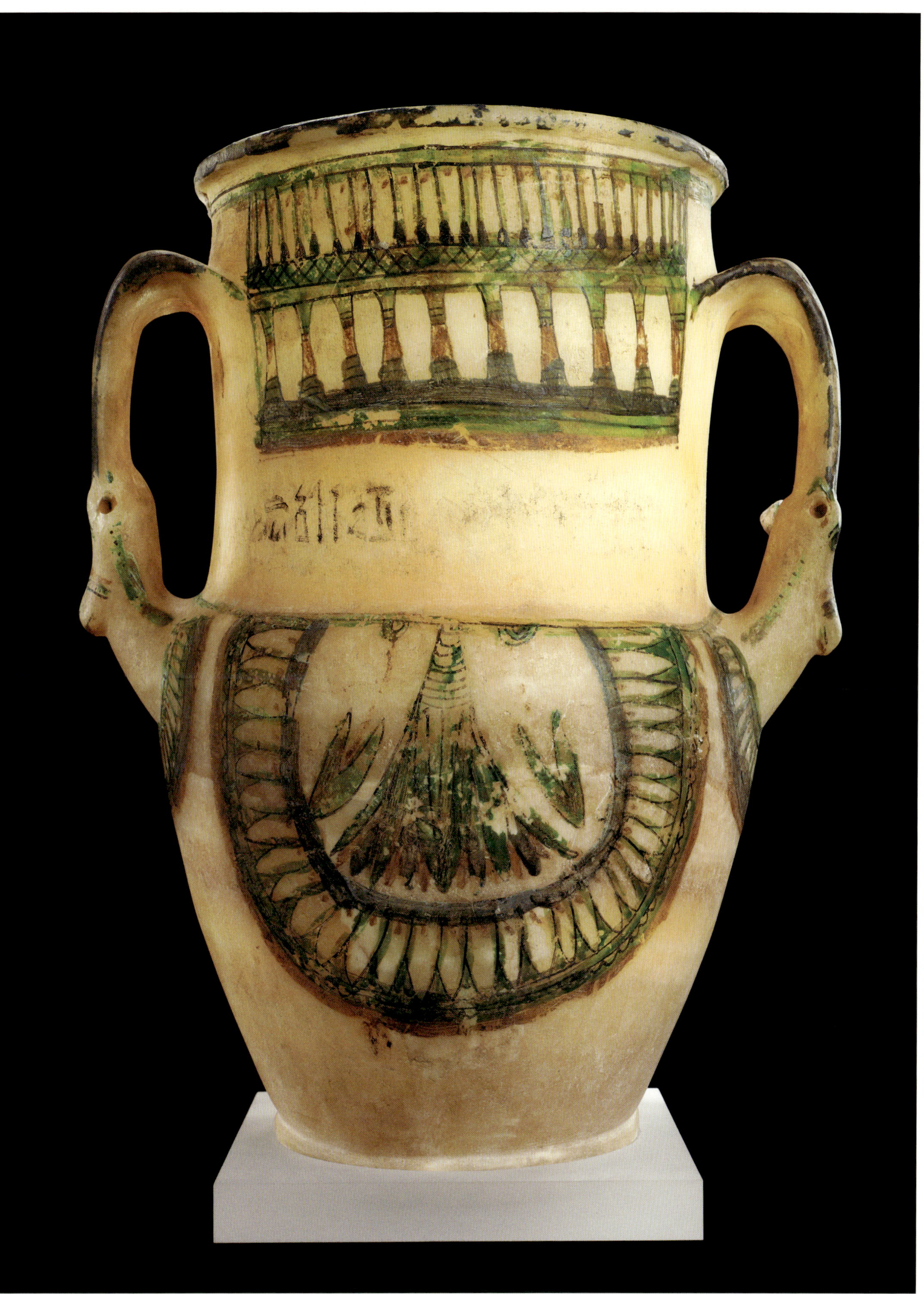

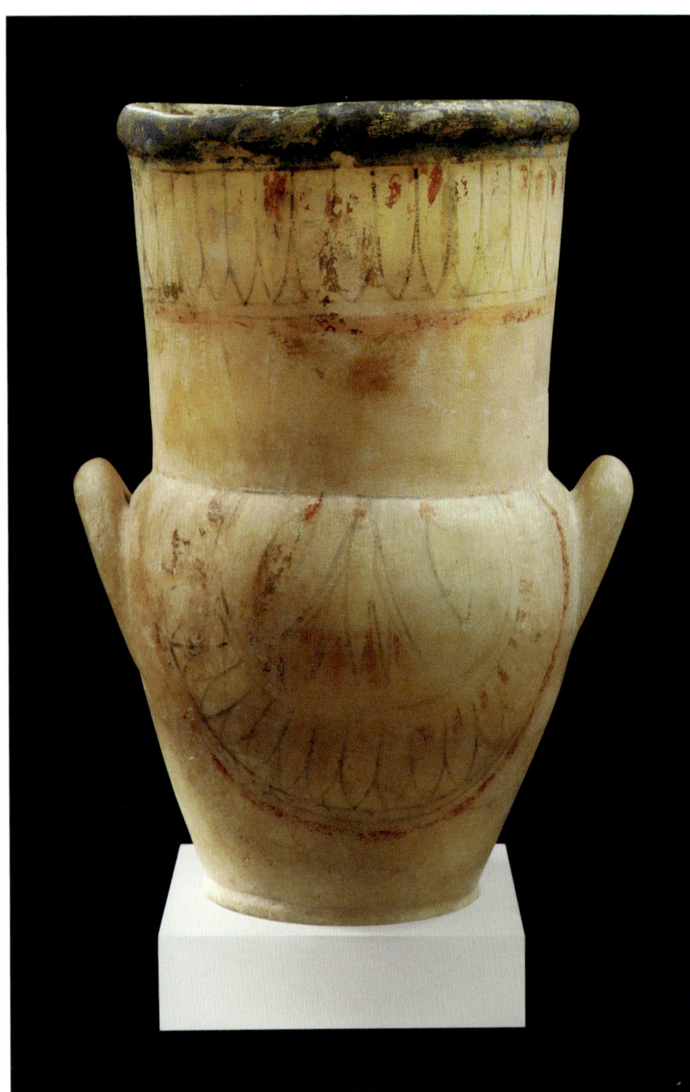

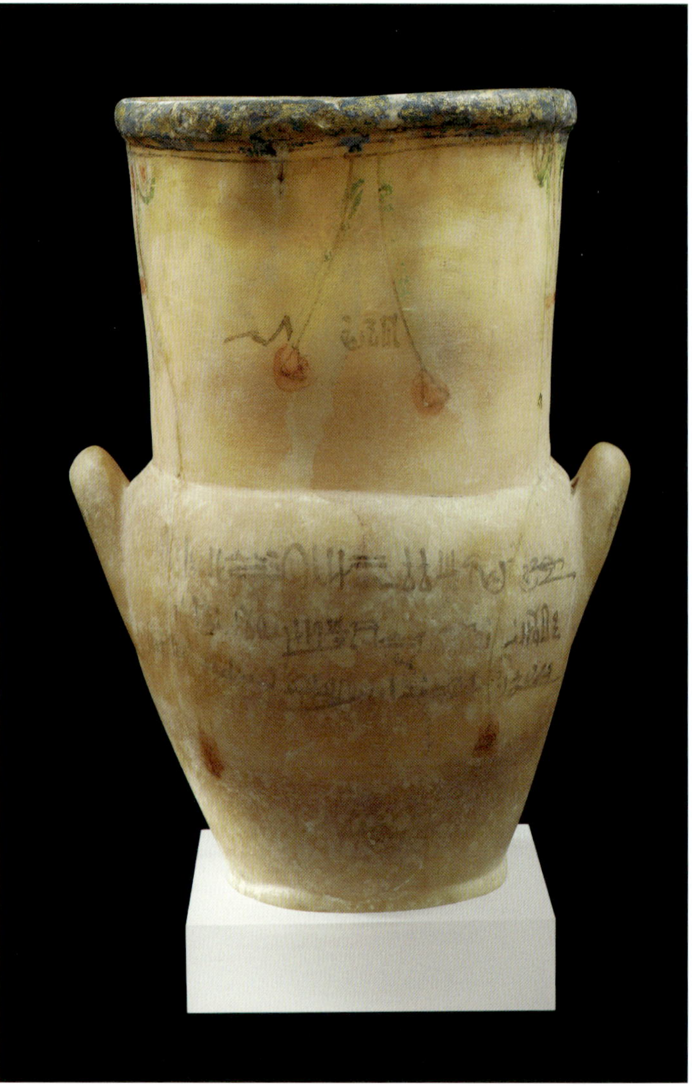

47.

An Inscribed Vase

Dynasty XIX–XX, 1305–1080 BC
Painted alabaster
Height 14 3/16 in.
Inv. no. EG-127

Sculpted from a single block of alabaster, the characteristics of which imbue its contents with both purity and permanence, this vessel exhibits a conical belly resting on an offset disk foot. The belly is equipped with two thick straplike handles of an inverted U-shape, attached obliquely. An exceptionally tall neck rises from its proportionately short shoulder, exhibiting a rounded lip that overhangs its wall (compare cat. 48).

The encaustic technique is employed for the green decoration of its lip, where red and green polychromy are used for the remainder of the decoration, which depicts floral motifs. These take the form of a horizontal bunting secured to the neck by a floral cord, the two ends of which appear as budded stems knotted to form an inverted V-shape on what may be regarded as the back of the vase. The bunting is framed below by a red stripe. The belly is ornamented with a lotus framed on either side by a bud, designed as if tied and hanging upside down from the juncture of the shoulder and neck. The principles of design preclude determining whether the floral images below forming a simple broad collar are to be understood as part of the lotus ensemble or if they form a separate element.

The suggested back of the vessel is inscribed in black ink with three lines of hieratic, a cursive form of hieroglyphs. These specify that a high official named Ptahmes was charged with the preparation of its contents,

> *oil of the first quality, excellent styrax, prepared in the ateliers of pharaoh.*

Styrax (or storax) has been defined as a balsam resin, derived from trees native to Asia Minor, the Aegean littoral between modern Greece and Turkey. It is a turbid, viscid liquid, gray in color, with an odor like benzoin resembling a light camphor-like smell.

The inscription further specifies that this vessel contained seventeen *hins* of styrax. A *hin* is an Egyptian unit of measure, equal to approximately half a liter or about .53 quarts. Seventeen *hins* would amount to about 2.02 gallons, or 8.09 quarts. That is surprisingly close to the 7.650 liters that this vessel could hold, measured to within one centimeter of its rim, in experiments conducted by the laboratory of the Museum of Art and History in Geneva.

It is assumed that this quantity of styrax, produced in royal ateliers overseen by Ptahmes, was used in religious ceremonies involving the pharaoh. Such ceremonies might include jubilees and the like, but because styrax was also employed as a balm in mummification, its use for that purpose cannot be automatically excluded.

A dating of this vase to the Ramesside Period is suggested by the style of its hieratic inscription, which would have been more precise if that inscription had contained a regnal year, as one finds in similar texts.

Published: Chappaz and Chamay, *Reflets du divin*, 2001, p. 69, no. 55.

References: Lucas, *Materials*, 1989, p. 116.

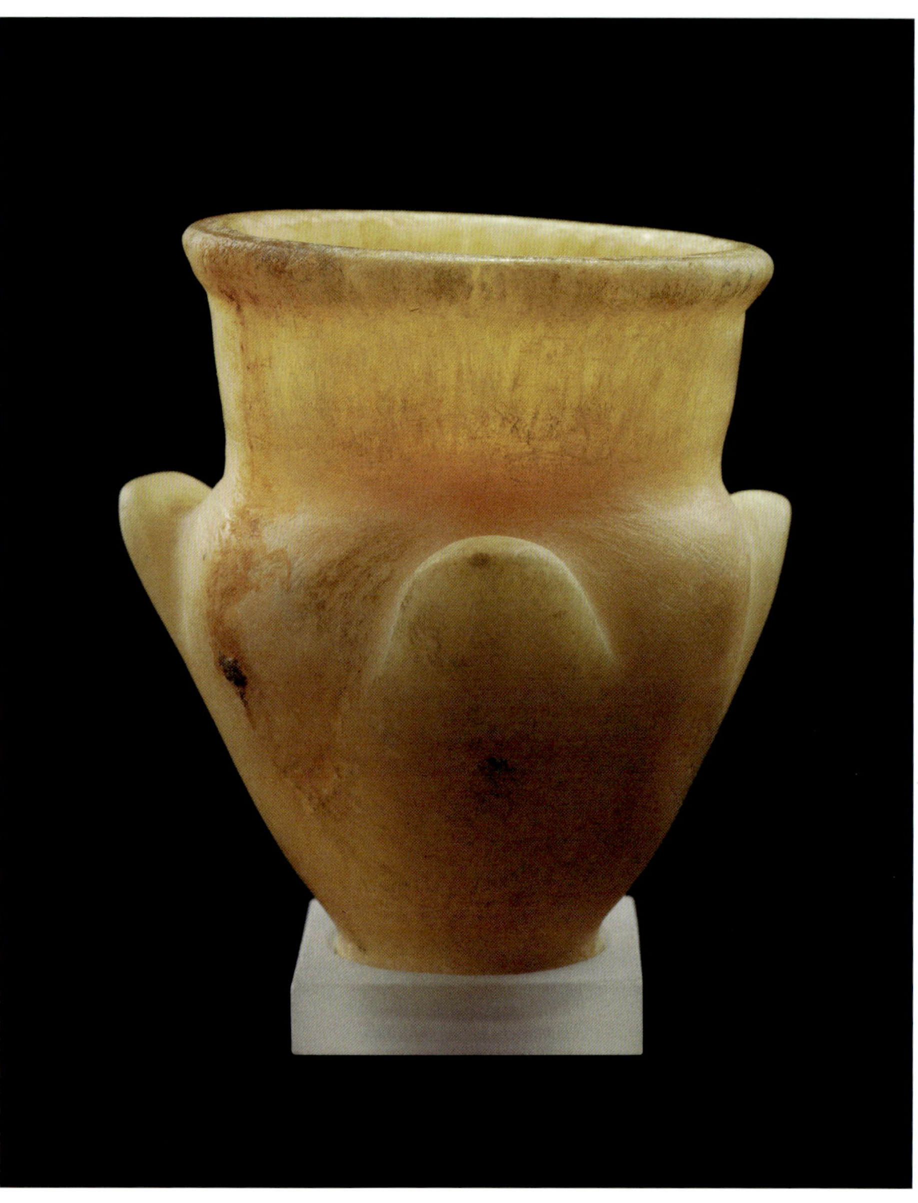

48.

A Stone Vessel

Dynasty XIX–XX, 1305–1080 BC
Alabaster
Height 2 in.
Inv. no. EG-277

This vessel is sculpted from a single block of white alabaster, the color and material of which lends its contents both purity and permanence. Its conical belly is equipped with three thick, straplike handles of an inverted U-shape, attached obliquely, but not cut free, so that their interiors still retain the negative stone of the original alabaster block. The belly rests on an offset disk foot. An exceptionally tall neck rises from a proportionately short shoulder, exhibiting a rounded lip which overhangs its wall. Larger versions of the same general shape, with two rather than three handles, are sometimes inscribed with their capacity in *hin*, an ancient Egyptian measure used principally for liquids (compare cat. 47). One can suggest, therefore, that such a vessel held a precious unguent.

This vessel is a miniature version of another alabaster one in this exhibition (cat. 47), almost an exact clone, in fact. This similarity strongly suggests that the institutionally affiliated ateliers in which such vessels were being manufactured had recourse to pattern books or other instructional material, which served as a model: numerous, exactingly similar examples could be created at will.

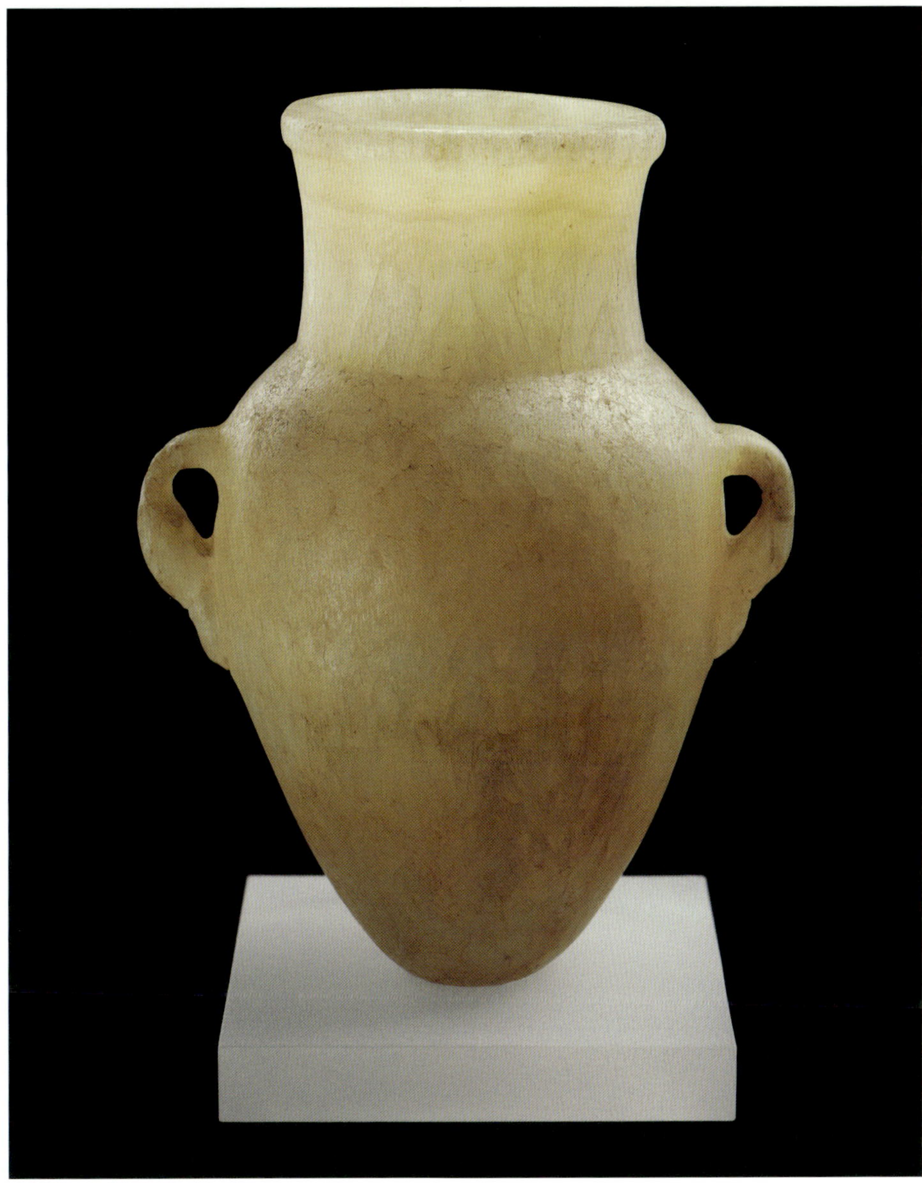

49.

A Vase with Duck-Headed Handles

Dynasty XVIII–XX, 1554–1080 BC
Alabaster
Height 3 ¾ in.
Inv. no. EG-307

The profile of this alabaster vessel is a variation of the design popular in the New Kingdom (compare cat. 47 and cat. 48). Sculpted from a single block of stone, it features a piriform belly which replaces the footed, conical belly of its variants. The use of white alabaster would have lent the contents its associated qualities of permanence and purity.

The design of this vessel is deceptive because of its small size. At first glance, it causes one to overlook the careful execution of its two handles, which end in the heads of ducks. Such elaborately designed, zoomorphic handles appear on stone vessels for the first time during Dynasty XVIII and continue to be created into the Ramesside Period (compare cat. 46). The duck-shaped handles suggest that the contents of this vessel may have been a precious balm or unguent (compare cat. 43).

50.

An Inscribed Vase

Dynasty XXI–XXV, 1080–655 BC
Alabaster
Height 19 in.
Inv. no. EG-308

This massive vessel, sculpted from a single block of stone, exhibits a cylindrical body with a tapering base below and a flat, shelflike shoulder above, with a short, concave neck, and everted, very thin lip. Two angular handles, circular in cross section, begin at the juncture of the body with the neck and end just below the single band of hieroglyphs, framed top and bottom with a single incised line. The single line of inscription may be translated as:

> *For Nesamunenipet, prophet of the god Amun at Karnak, prophet of the goddess Isis, mistress of Hebyt, who also served as scribe[?] of the army.*

It is suggested that the contents of the vessel were intended for the funerary use of its owner. Parallels indicate a dating within the Third Intermediate Period.

References: Gamer-Wallert, *Ägyptische und ägyptisierende Funde*, 1978, pl. 22–24; Aston, *Stone Vessels*, 1994, p. 164.

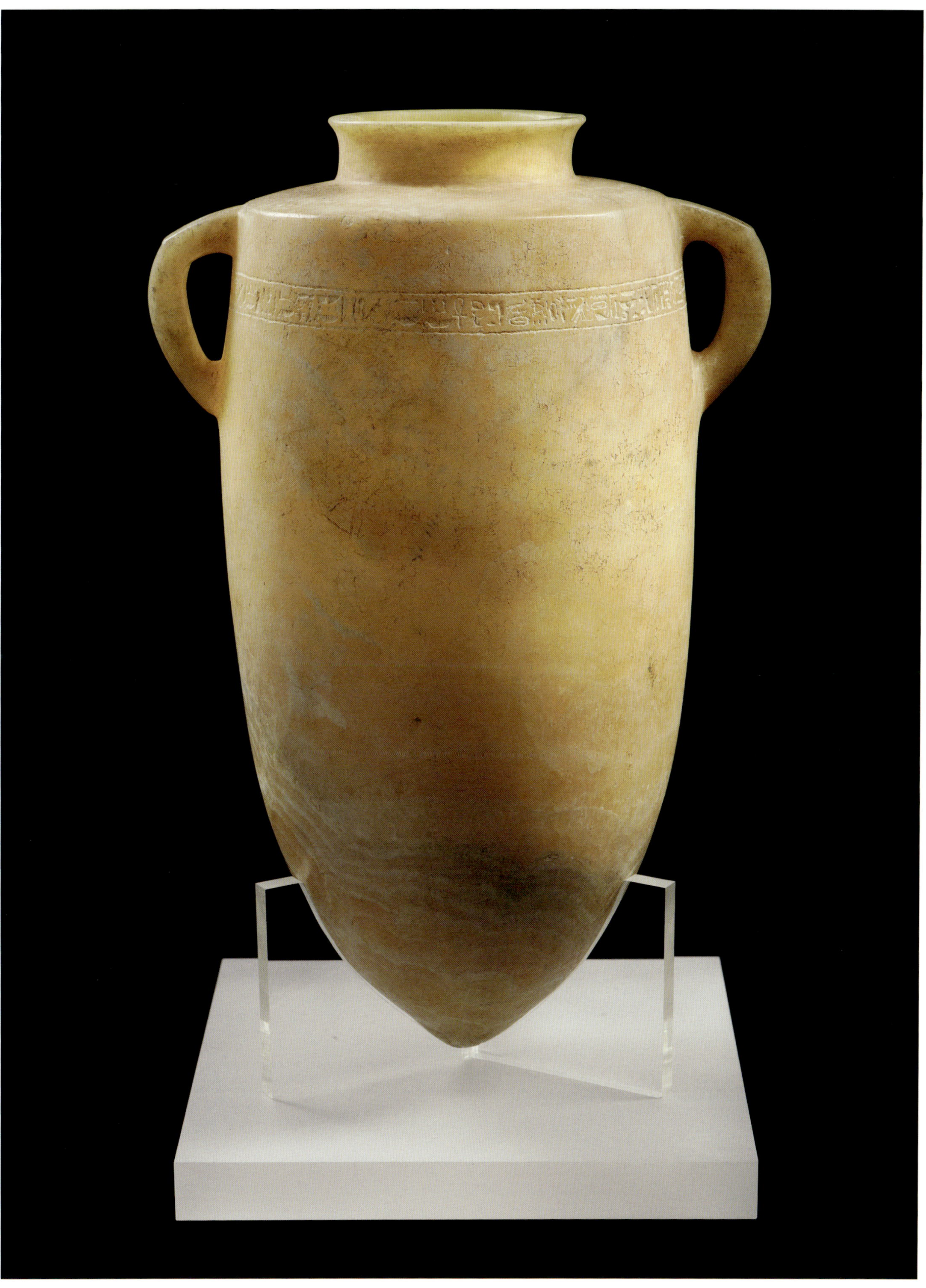

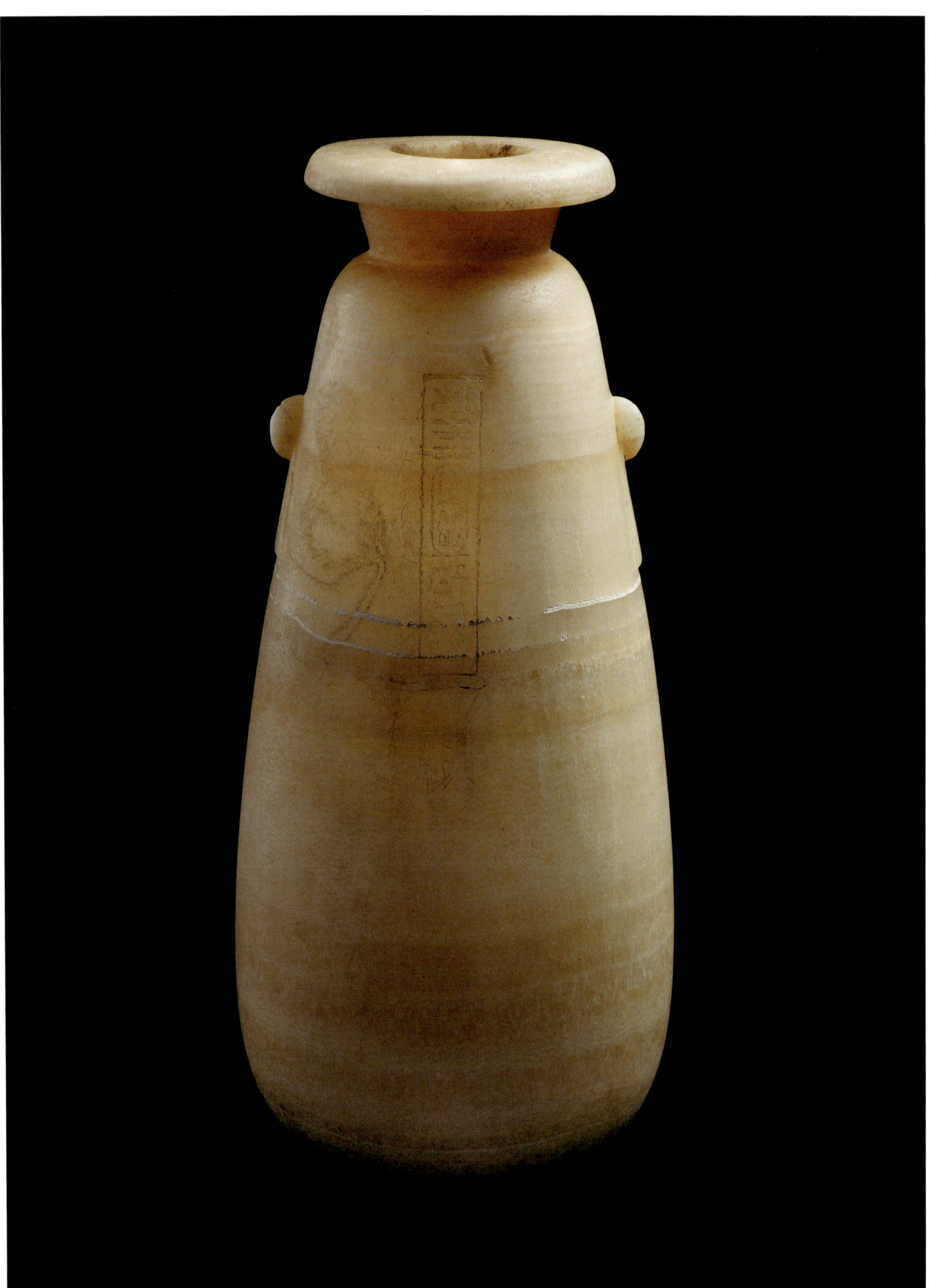

51.

A Vase Inscribed for Darius I

Dynasty XXVII, the First Persian Period, Regnal Year 33 of King Darius I, 489 BC
Banded alabaster
Height 12 ⅛ in.
Inv. no. EG-356

This vase is an outsized version of an alabastron (compare cat. 52) with an upward-tapered globular body, an offset, short, slightly flared neck beneath a disc-shaped lip. Its lug handles are provided with trapezoidal flanges below, representing a somewhat stylized version of a Near Eastern design aesthetic (compare cat. 37).

The vase is ornamented with a vertical panel that begins just above the top of the lug handles. This is inscribed in hieroglyphs with the titles and cartouche of Darius I, King of Persia, followed by a year date,

> *The King of Upper and Lower Egypt, the Lord of the Two Lands [named] Intirucha [the Egyptian hieroglyphic version of the name Darius], living forever, Regnal Year 33*

An inventory of stone vessels created in Egypt and inscribed in hieroglyphs for Persian kings, compiled by George Posener, found over sixty examples, preserved either in their entirety or as fragments. Of that number, only six are inscribed for Darius I. Of these six, five are fragments, all of which are in the collections of the Musée du Louvre. The present example is an addition to the catalogued examples and joins the second, found in 1931 in Syria, as one of only two complete vases created in Egypt and inscribed in hieroglyphs for that ruler.

Furthermore, this vase is the only one of these seven inscribed vases and/or fragments created in alabaster, an ancient Egyptian material. The other six, the complete one found in Syria and the remaining five fragments (found in Susa), are of aragonite, a non-Egyptian stone. One can suggest, therefore, that this particular vase was created in Egypt and was subsequently exported to Persia.

It shares other characteristics with the other six examples in this group. All seven of these vessels are inscribed only in Egyptian hieroglyphs; none bears a cuneiform inscription. The column of hieroglyphs in all cases is framed by a vertical panel, the top of which is designed as the sky, or *pt*-sign. The hieroglyphs of all seven vases share in the same orientation; they begin at the top and face right. The writing of the name of Darius in all seven cases is identical, and the signs used to write this name represent the hieroglyphic form of the name of Darius as it was current toward the end of his reign. This late form of his name is consistent with the observation that only three of the seven in this group bear a complete year date. This example is inscribed for Regnal Year 33, the equivalent of 489 BC. This is the same year inscribed on the second complete vase found in Syria. Only one of the five fragments in the Louvre is inscribed, for Regnal Year 34, the equivalent of 488 BC.

These correspondences suggest that all the vases were created by a royal decree specifying the manner in which they were to be inscribed. They were subsequently crafted in institutionally affiliated ateliers under the supervision of native Egyptian overseers. Their collaboration with the Persian overlords of Egypt is well documented. One such elite member of Egyptian society credits himself with creating the name and title of Darius in hieroglyphs. Such close cooperation between elite and ruler is characteristic of Egyptian culture. It is suggested that these vases were commissioned on an annual basis, because they are dated to specific regnal years, for use in Persia, the purposes of which have yet to be identified.

References: Posener, *Première Domination*, 1936, pp. 137–40.

52.

An Alabastron

Ptolemaic Period, 305–30 BC
Alabaster
Height 9 ⅞ in.
Inv. no. EG-199

The consummate skill of the ancient Egyptian stoneworkers is perhaps nowhere more graphically demonstrated than in their creation of this exceptional vessel, which features a thin, elliptically shaped body. The vessel's profile ends in a sharply pointed taper. Its wider belly then transitions into a slightly less wide, and proportionately long neck, hourglass in shape, which is horizontally equipped with an integral disk before terminating in a shorter, flaring cone.

This vessel type is termed an alabastron, a name that originally referred to a bag-like, or cylindrically shaped, container in which cosmetics were stored (compare cat. 51). The term is Greek, but ultimately derives from the Egyptian phrase, *inr-Bastet, the stone of the goddess Bastet* (compare cat. 73). That stone was generally alabaster. The Greeks appropriated the phrase during the course of the seventh century BC. The designation has thence been traditionally applied in general to vessels such as this, which may have originally contained ointment.

Similar examples of such alabastron, several without a disk on the neck sculpted from the same block of stone, have been excavated. Among these, the best parallel is the example from the necropolis at Gabbari, a district of Alexandria, which was designed as three separate pieces—body, disk, and neck—and is about a third as tall as the example under discussion. The archaeological context of this Alexandrian parallel suggests a dating into the second half of the third century BC for both vessels.

References: Günther and Wellauer, *Ägyptische Steingefässe*, 1988, p. 66 and pl. 20 and 43; the example from Gabbari GA98.50400.19.1+50400.21.1+50400.18.5:Nenna et al., "Mobilier," 2003, p. 513, no. 4.

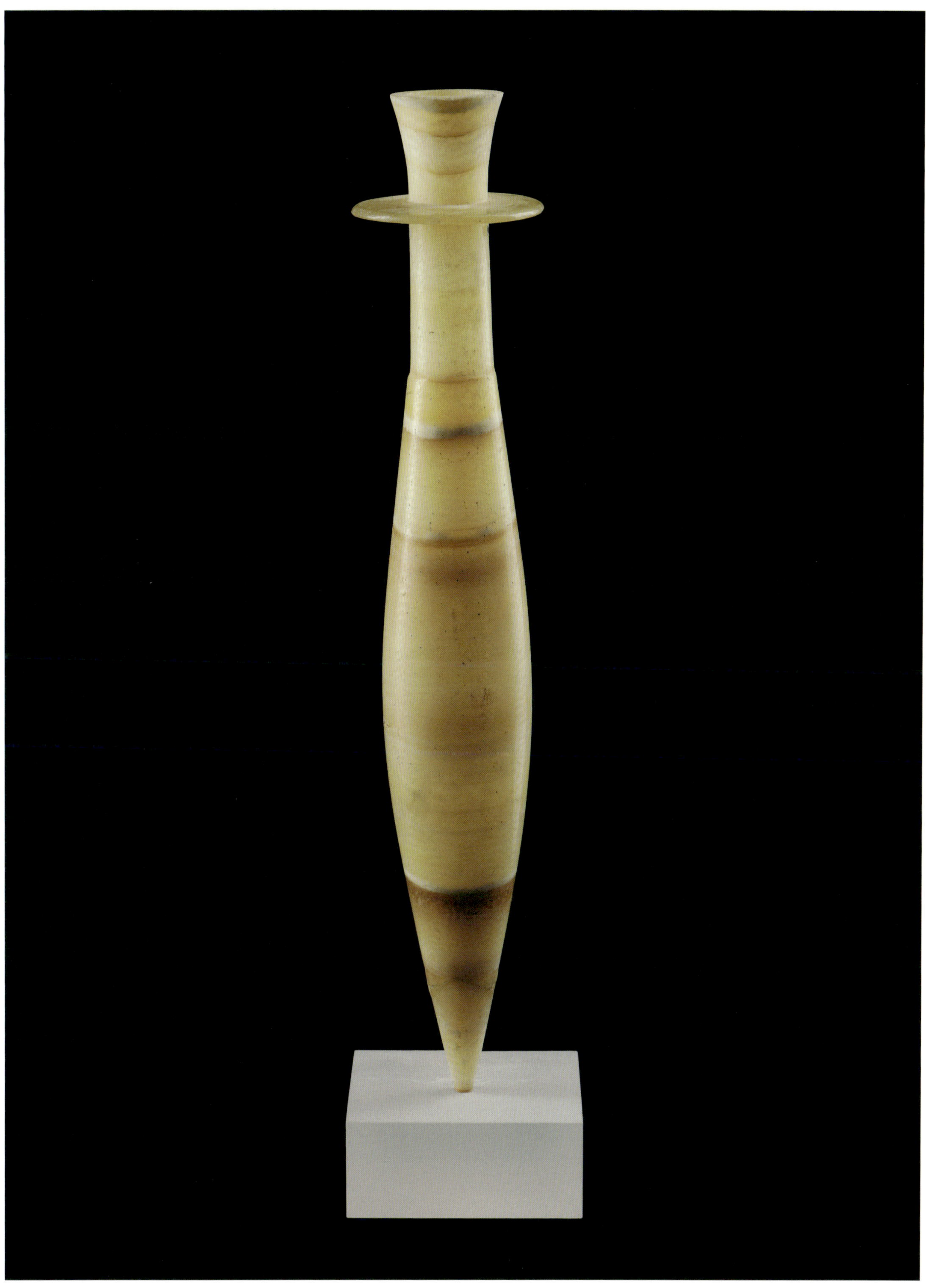

53.

A Scene of Weighing the Heart from the So-called Book of the Dead

Ptolemaic Period, 305–30 BC
Papyrus and black ink
Length 44 in.
Inv. no. EG-157

The most famous vignette found within *The Book of the Dead*, the ancient title of which was *The Book of Going Forth by Day*, is the "Weighing of the Heart," illustrating Spell 125. The design of the present illustration for that Spell avoids Western conventions of narrative and combines into one scene a series of episodes. One is to imagine that these sequential episodes unfolded within the Hall of Judgment, although the assessors, or judges, are not depicted.

At the far left is a personification of Maat, a female figure whose head is replaced by an ostrich feather, *maat* in the ancient Egyptian language. *Maat* is usually translated as "truth," but the word encompasses concepts of cosmic equilibrium, order, stability, and harmony. Her raised hand rests on the back of the deceased, the owner of the papyrus, depicted as a male figure wearing a long kilt and bandolier. He is barefoot, with closely-cropped hair, and he raises his arms in a gesture indicating that he is "true of voice." He is preceded by three goddesses, all wearing similar wigs and tightly fitting sheathlike dresses, their arms in various gestures of adoration. Before them is the scale on whose horizontal bar sits a baboon, a hypostasis of Thoth, god of scribes, whose task it was to ensure the accuracy of the weight. Anubis, the jackal-headed god of mummification, steadies one of the pans, in which is placed the heart of the deceased. To the left, the falcon-headed Horus steadies the pan in which a seated figure of Maat, substituting for the feather, is placed. Thoth, the ibis-headed god of wisdom, stands before the scale with arm raised, holding a scribal palette with which he will record the outcome of the weighing.

Ammit, the devourer, a mythical creature whose body combines features of a crocodile, a hippopotamus, a lion, and a sow, sits on a pedestal with its mouth open and tongue extended. Should the heart of the deceased indicate perjury, it would be fed to Ammit and the deceased would cease to live, perish forever, because Egyptian religion did not include a concept comparable to the Christian Purgatory.

A table piled high with offerings and a floral bouquet is placed between Ammit and an open lotus flower on top of which stand mummiform representations of the Four Sons of Horus, before an enthroned Osiris behind whom is his sister-wife, Isis.

The three columns of hieroglyphs in the field in front of Osiris may be translated as

> *Osiris, the lord of the West, the great god, the lord of Abydos, [and the god] Ptah-Sokar-Osiris, the great god, the one who resides in his sanctuary, [and the god] Anubis, lord of the necropolis, Anubis who presides over the divine booth.*

The fact that Anubis is twice mentioned should cause no surprise, because different aspects of the same deity are often indicated by the repetition of the name of the god followed by a different epithet. It is for the same reason that Thoth appears here on the balance beam as a baboon and again as an ibis-headed male figure (compare cat. 16).

The large amount of empty space may indicate that the papyrus is unfinished, which seems to gain confirmation by the fact that the assessors are not represented. To this

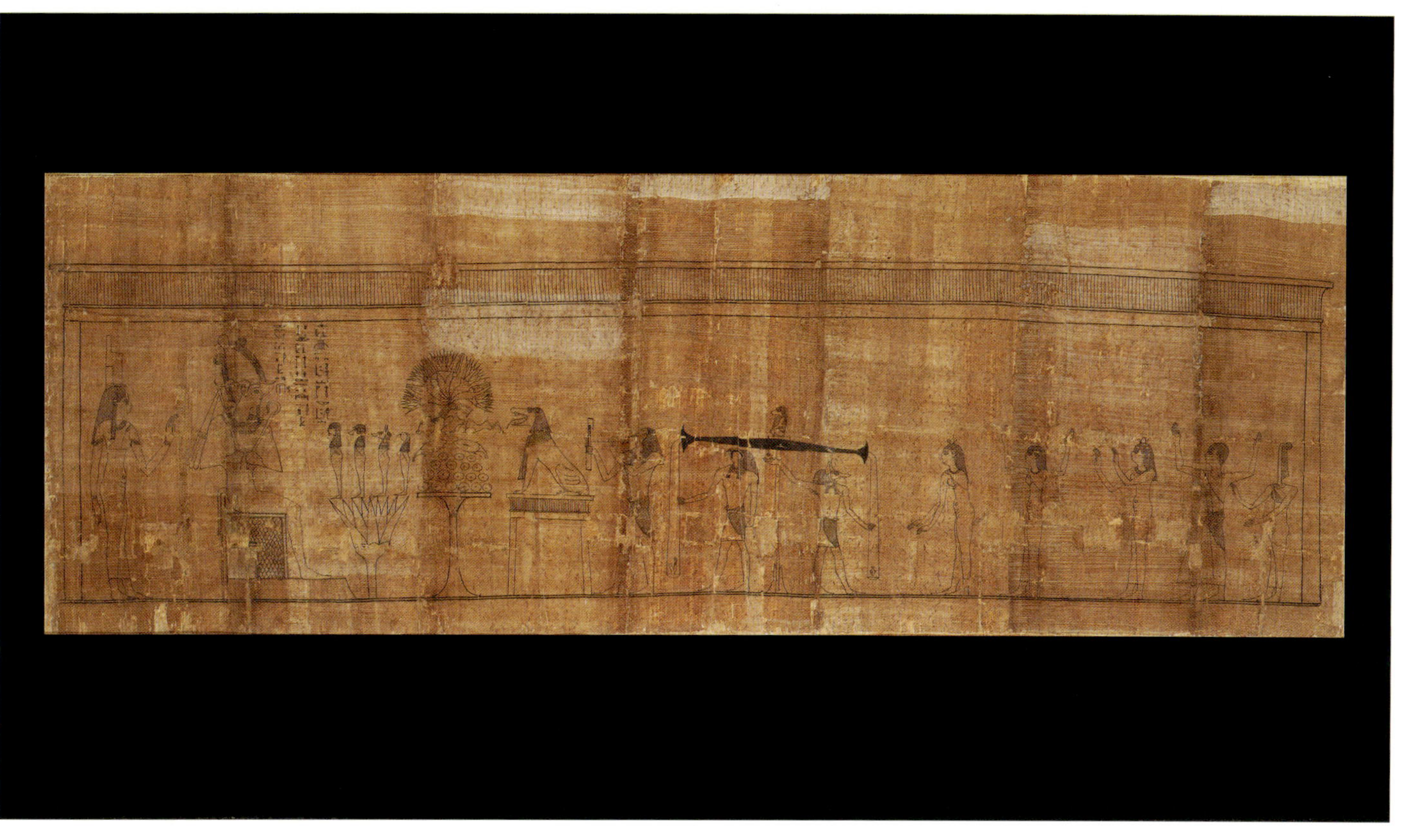

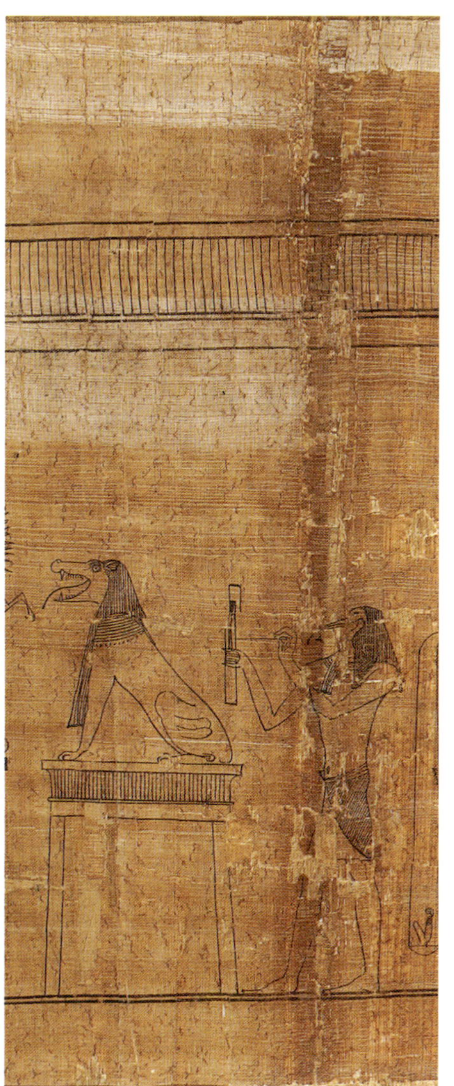

should be added the observation that the suggested owner of this papyrus was Lady Ta-net-wesir, the daughter of Nes-min and Tes-en-amun. Her coffin and additional fragments of what are thought to be part of the scroll from which this vignette came were known in the nineteenth century. Her depiction as a male may indicate that this papyrus was acquired "off the rack," that is, created in advance to be customized for its eventual owner. On the other hand, the representation of Ta-net-wesir as a male is of little consequence, because the epithet, "The Osiris," was not gender-specific and was habitually applied to both male and female members of the elite. Variations in detail are so common to all vignettes in this corpus that the choice of what to include or exclude appears to been a decision made by the elite foreman in charge of the atelier. In fact, there is neither a canonical order nor an imperative to include each and every spell in *The Book of the Dead* in any given scroll. Such variability distances this particular work from the modern religions of The Book: Judaism, Christianity, and Islam.

The conceit of weighing the deceased's heart against a feather of truth requires comment. During the proceedings that are here illustrated, the deceased was required to recite "The Negative Confession." Then, the heart was weighed to determine whether the deceased had committed perjury. Because ancient Egyptians believed that the heart was the seat of one's conscience, one's heart could not lie. Weighing it against the feather became the final witness in determining the fate of the deceased. The presence and primacy of the scale in this vignette for Spell 125 has seduced Western commentators into suggesting that the heart should not be heavier than the feather against which it is weighed. This suggestion is at variance with the connotative meanings of the word *maat* and runs counter to the ancient Egyptian worldview. That worldview demands equilibrium, in terms of the connotative meanings of *maat* as cosmic order and harmony. By repeating "The Negative Confession," the deceased, as a member of elite society, is not reaffirming strict adherence to any religiously dominated practice. On the contrary, he or she affirms adherence to a set of moral and ethical values:

> *I have done no wrong; I have not robbed; I have not slain people; I have not told lies; I have not caused anyone to weep; I have not been*

hot tempered; I have not confounded truth; I have not done harm to animals; I have done no harm to mankind; I have not carried off the milk for the mouth of the babe; I have not acted wickedly.

By acting and conducting one's life in a socially responsible manner, the deceased maintained order and harmony, promoting the ancient Egyptian way of life, which may very well explain the ardent desire to be resurrected, because ancient Egyptian life, for the elite, was good. The vignette of Spell 125 was a means of ensuring this desired equilibrium.

Published: Chappaz and Chamay, *Reflets du divin*, 2001, p. 81, no. 67.

References: Faulkner, *Book of the Dead*, 1994; Taylor, *Journey*, 2010.

54.

A Necklace with Fifteen Amulets

Dynasty XXVI–XXX, 664–342 BC
Lapis lazuli and gold
Length as modernly strung: 13 ¾ in.
Inv. no. EG-285

Each of the amulets comprising this necklace is made of sheet gold, with incised details, designed in conformity with their hieroglyphic counterparts. The amulets include an elaborate apron, a ba-bird, a broad collar, a crook, a *djed*-pillar, a *djet*-serpent, a flail, an amulet in the form of the head of a snake, three similarly designed uraei, two similarly designed vultures, and a wadjet-eye.

Many of these amulets correlate with illustrated spells found in *The Book of the Dead* and other religious treatises inscribed on either papyrus or linen, which can be dated to the Late Period. From such evidence, one can estimate that mummies of elite members of Egyptian society were provided with at least sixty such gold foil amulets, the cumulative force of which was to assist in the owner's aspired resurrection. The gold symbolically imparted to the deceased the characteristics of divine flesh, and the color of lapis lazuli lent associations of regeneration, the waxing of the moon, the primordial waters from which creation arose, and associations with the floral kingdom.

The dating of this necklace is based on parallels.

References: Andrews, *Amulets*, 1994, pp. 6–9; Andrews, *Mummies*, 1984, p. 31, fig. 31; Williams, New-York Historical Society, 1924, pp. 154–55.

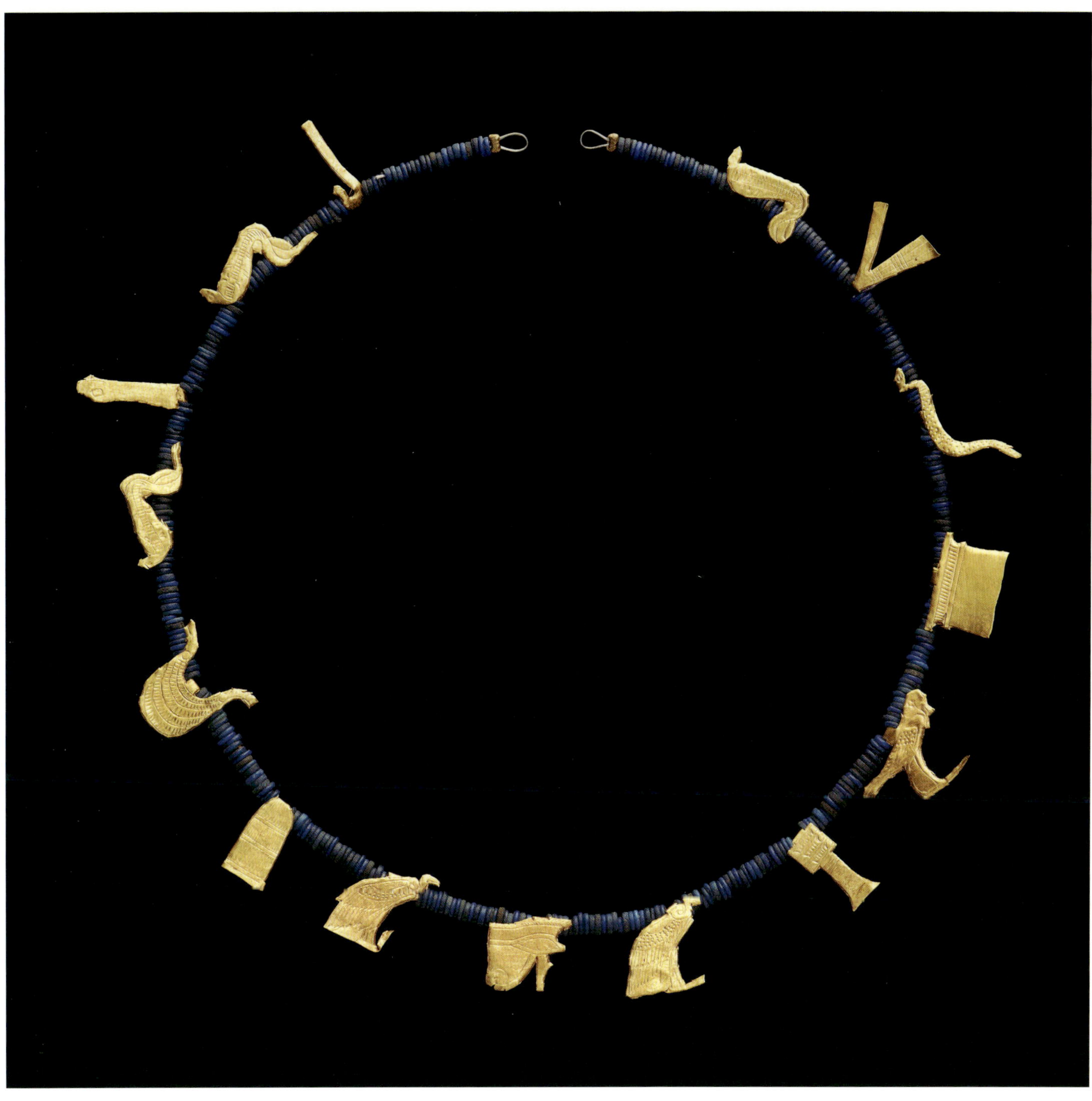

55.

Part of a Funerary Broad Collar with Falcon-Headed Terminals

Ptolemaic Period, 305–30 BC
Gold, with inlays of semiprecious stones and glass paste
Length 17 ⅜ in.
Inv. no. EG-184

One should envision the original appearance of this necklace as a series of paired strands, one above the other, of which only one pair is presently preserved. Such multistrand necklaces are referred to as broad collars because of their size when measured side to side. The paired strands of this broad collar end in mirror images of the head of a falcon, facing in opposite directions, which serve not only to secure the strands but also to attach them to the braided chain that was placed around the neck when worn. The chain is fastened by passing its J-shaped hook through the loop at its opposite end. The principal paired strands serve as a frame from which is suspended a third strand that forms V-shaped patterns as it is strung between and fastened to the top and bottom of the pair. Seven ankhs, or signs of life, are suspended within as pendants.

Broad collars featuring falcons (compare cat. 82) are part of the funerary panoply specified in the very short Spell 158 of *The Book of the Dead*. This laconic spell defines the function of such broad collars as the means by which the deceased might be freed from the mummy bandages enveloping the body:

> *Spell for a collar of gold to be placed on the neck of the deceased. Recitation by Osiris N. "O my father! O my brother! O my mother Isis! Unswathe me! Behold me! I am one of the unswathed ones who see Gēb!"*

Several complex conceits, drawn from the real world of natural phenomena, are seamlessly united in this ostensibly simple spell and were employed as analogies with which to explain resurrection in the hereafter. The stands of this broad collar, when worn as illustrated, would dip to form a U-shaped arrangement on the chest, a shape that intentionally recalled the horizon from which the sun rises and sets. That horizon was anciently compared to a valley bounded on each side by a high mountain. Each of these mountains was thought to be guarded, as here, by a falcon, with its backs to the valley in order to protect it. This image of a valley bordered on each side by a high mountain might also be equated with the loins of a woman in labor as the child emerged. Within the polyvalent nature of ancient Egyptian theological discourse, the legs of the birthing woman were equivalents of these two mountains, and her loins from which the neonate emerged were associated with the valley. The concept of physical birth with the head of the child emerging first, and that of the sun disk breaking the horizon at dawn, becomes synonymous visual puns. When the broad collar was placed on the mummy, the head would appear to be rising from it in much the same way as the sun would rise from the valley flanked by mountains guarded by falcons. The act of a child emerging from the loins of its mother was then associated with that rising sun, so that these natural phenomena were regarded as equivalents of one another, employed as analogies to explain how the deceased was thought to be released from the mummy bandages.

The materials used for the creation of this broad collar further its function. The color of the sun is reflected in the use of gold, itself the material from which the flesh of Egyptian deities was made. The predominately blue color of the inlays was associated with the floral kingdom, members of which sprouted after a period of dormancy. By means of these materials and their colors, the broad collar symbolically possesses

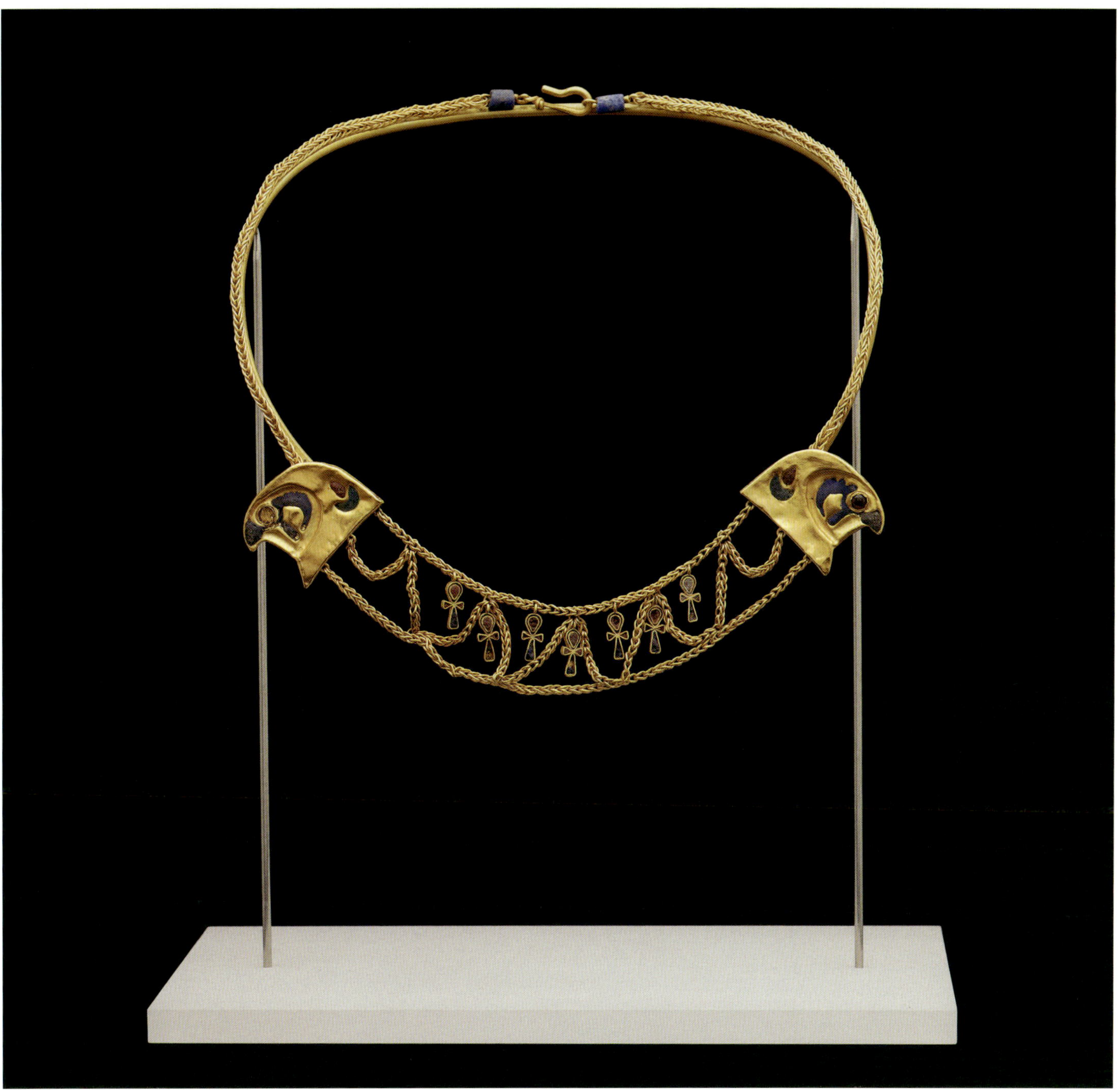

characteristics of the sun, the deities, and the floral kingdom. Their properties were thought to be transmitted to the deceased, so that resurrection, identification with solar deities, and deification might be magically and symbolically assured.

This broad collar is dated to the Ptolemaic Period on the basis of two techniques used for its manufacture. Ancient goldsmiths had not developed the technology of drawing gold through a plate for the manufacture of wire. They relied instead on cutting hammered gold sheets into thin strips, which were then rolled to create the wire from which the braid was created. The inlays set into the gold find their closest parallel in a single falcon-headed terminal, created in gold and inlaid in the same way, which has been universally dated to the Ptolemaic Period.

Published: Chappaz and Chamay, *Reflets du divin*, 2001, p. 96, no. 82.

References: Brooklyn, Brooklyn Museum 65.3.2: Fazzini, *Images*, 1975, p. 126, no. 112.

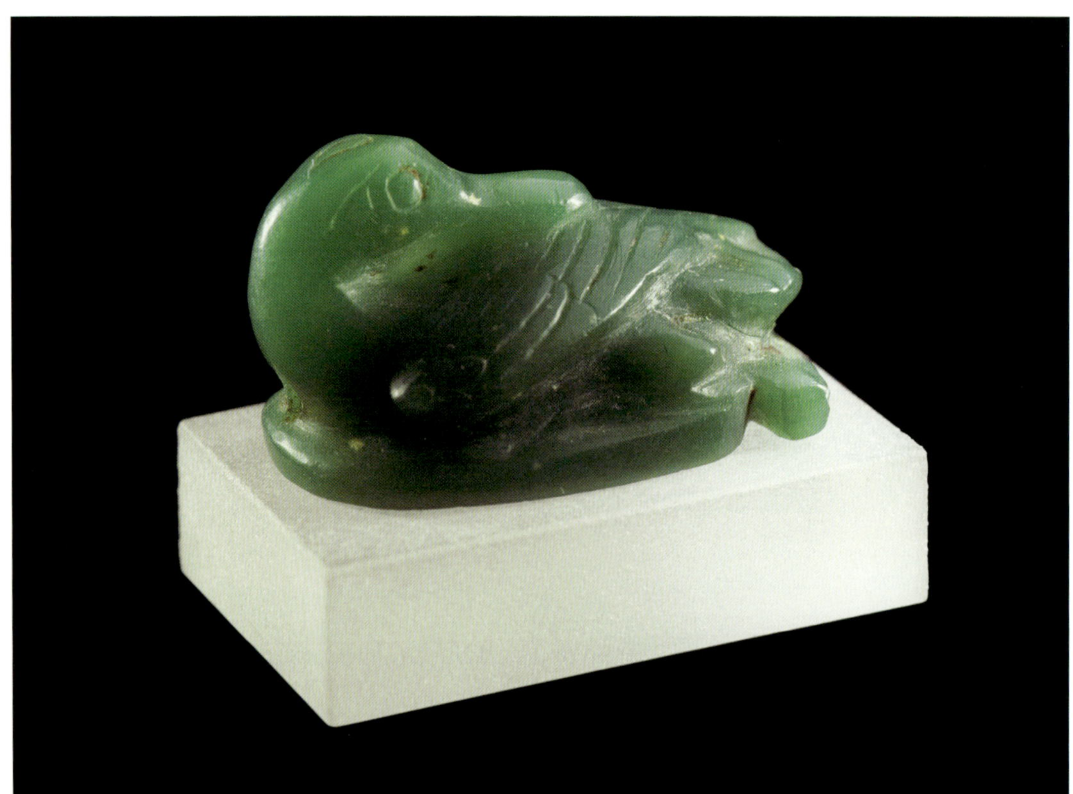

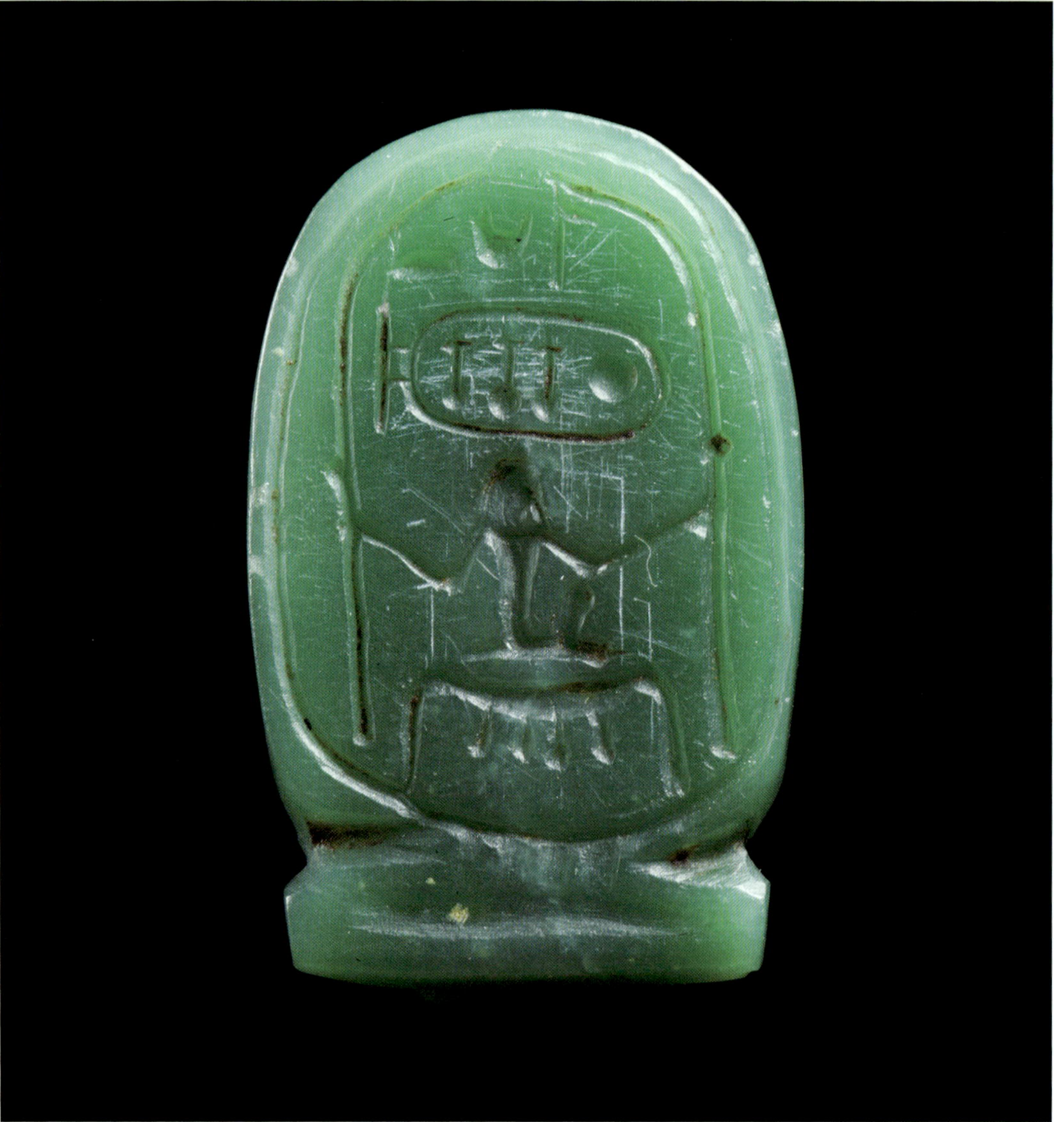

56.

An Amulet in the form of a Duck Inscribed for Princess Neferu-re

Dynasty XVIII, time of Pharaoh Hatshepsut, 1490–1470 BC
Green chrysoprase (a form of chalcedony)
Length 13/16 in.
Inv. no. EG-166

Ancient Egyptian art is characterized by its monumentality, as exhibited by the Great Pyramids of Giza and the Sphinx. But the ancient Egyptians were also capable of creating exquisite objects in miniature, such as this amulet. The jewel-like, precise execution of its design belies its small scale. It depicts a duck with its wings folded under its beak, its head turned back so that it aligns with the axis of its spine. The object's integral base is in the form of a cartouche, or royal ring, representing a lasso that literally surrounds those hieroglyphs that spell a royal name. The hieroglyphs within this cartouche and its introductory title may be translated as

> *the wife of the god [whose name is] Neferu-re.*

Neferu-re is known from historical sources. She was the only daughter born to Tuthmosis II and Hatshepsut. The death of Tuthmosis II elevated his young son Tuthmosis III to the throne, with Hatshepsut initially serving as his regent. Seven years later, after proclaiming herself pharaoh, Hatshepsut relinquished her claim to the title, god's wife, which she then bestowed upon Neferu-re, who discharged the functions of that office for a decade.

These hieroglyphs are framed by a male figure wearing a striated wig and false beard who kneels on the hieroglyph for gold and holds a palm frond in each hand. This figure is Heh, a deity who supports the sky, suggested by the presence of the palm fronds which also represent the noun "year." Via a complex series of its interlocking associations conveyed by these images, the amulet symbolically affords Neferu-re continuance in office and numerous years of life. The green color of the chrysoprase reinforces those themes.

Published: Berlandini, "Amenhotep III," 1993, pp. 11–28, particularly pp. 20-21 with fig. 7; Germond, "Bestiaire," 2002–3, pp. 75–94, particularly pp. 90–91, with fig. 17; Künzi et al., *Les trésors*, n.d., fig. 189, pp. 156–57.

References: Pittsburgh, The Carnegie Museum of Natural History 1917-201: Patch, *Reflections of Greatness*, 1990, p. 106; Roehrig, *Hatshepsut*, 2005.

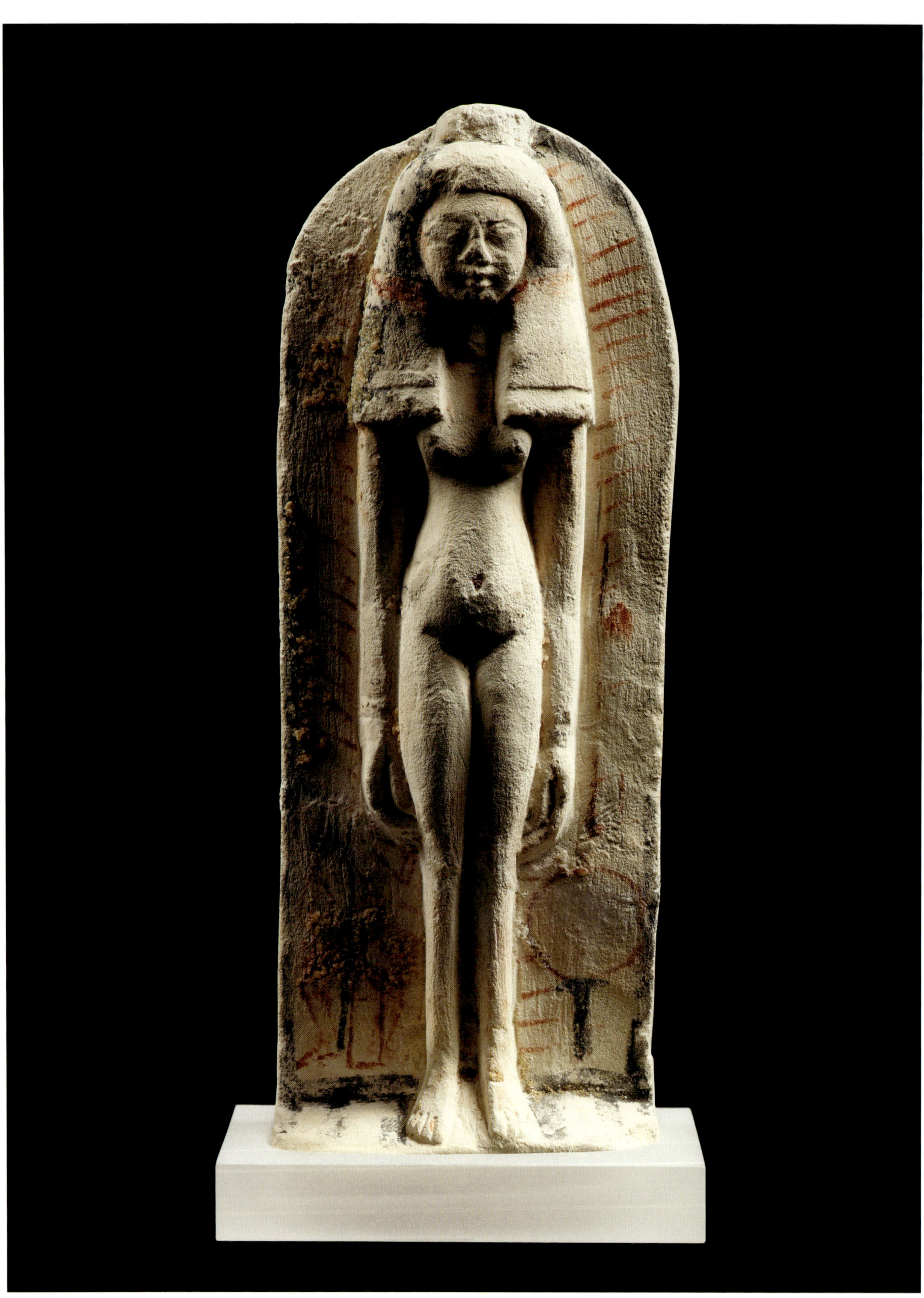

57.

A Female Figure Lying on a Bed

Dynasty XVIII–XX, 1554–1080 BC
Painted limestone
Length 6 ¼ in.
Inv. no. EG-303

Sculpted from a single block of limestone, this object depicts a woman in raised, bold relief set off from a round-topped background. The female figure appears to be completely nude, but wears a full wig, painted black, that falls over her shoulders, its lappets secured on either side by a red ribbon and reaching the tops of her breasts. The wig is surmounted by a modius, which is to be interpreted as a stylization of the so-called ointment cone, symbolic of the aura of the deceased in their altered, resurrected state. As such, these attributes are precursors of Christian haloes. The figure is shown wearing bracelets as well, painted in black.

The round-topped background against which the figure emerges recalls stelae of similar design, but its red and black ornamentation suggests that it is to be regarded as a bed. Indeed, the foot end is designed at a ninety-degree angle to the tall back and its black, reticulated design is in imitation of a wooden footboard characteristic of ancient Egyptian beds in general. The red diagonal lines on either side of the figure may then represent the lattice work of the "springs/mattress" of the bed proper.

The erotic overtones of the elaborate wig worn by this female figure are well known. Those are reinforced by the presence of a disk-shaped mirror to the (proper) left of the figure and of a baboon to the (proper) right of the figure. The identification of the latter as a baboon is assured by the articulation in black paint of his head with its characteristic muzzle. The attitude of the arms of the baboon may suggest that he was playing a musical stringed instrument, such as a lute. The interpretation of the complex imagery on this object presupposes an in-depth understanding of ancient Egyptian erotic symbolism used in a fecundity context that might apply in life or in death.

The mirror, although regarded as an *objet de toilette* of daily life, was regarded as a celestial symbol, standing for either the sun or the moon (compare cat. 58). Each of these celestial bodies referenced the recurring cosmic cycles because of the daily rising and setting of the sun and the transformations of the moon during its monthly cycle. In this case, the mirror must be regarded as solar due to the presence of the baboon. Ancient Egyptian religion maintained that the sun rose accompanied by the "secret language" of the baboons, who were observed in nature to "speak" by making a great deal of noise at dawn. Their secret language was accompanied by music. Within this context, then, the nude female figure may be regarded as Hathor-like, although her voluminous wig does not exhibit Hathor's characteristic curls.

Taken together, then, the images on this object are possessed of solar associations, for which there are contemporary parallels, many in terracotta, several of which come from Thebes.

The use of such objects is clearly cultic. They were either dedicated in sanctuaries by parents in expectation of, or in thanks for, a successful pregnancy, or in funerary contexts for the aspired resurrection of the deceased.

References: Traunecker, "Amenophis IV et Nefertiti," 1986, p. 34.

58.

A Mirror

Dynasty XVIII, 1554–1305 BC
Bronze
Height 8 1/16 in.
Inv. no. EG-401

This mirror was constructed by assembling its solid cast handle and disk by means of a rivet, which is still in place but has loosened with the passage of time. Its handle is in the form of a nude woman with her pubic triangle articulated. She stands with her legs and feet together on a small, integral base, with her arms pressed close to the sides of her body, the palms of her hands open and resting on her thighs. She wears a long wig and a necklace. A papyrus umbel, with incised ornamentation, is secured to her head and serves as the anchor for the disk of the mirror, to which it is affixed by means of a rivet. The disk itself is not a perfect circle.

There are several words and phrases in the ancient Egyptian lexicon that can be translated as "mirror." These include *maah her*, "the object that views the face," *wen-her*, "the object that reveals the face," and *aton*, "the disk." In the Ptolemaic and Roman Periods, ancient Egyptian mirrors were often called ankh, "that which lives."

Although often associated with cosmetics and daily life, mirrors, as their designation *aton*, "the disk," reveals, were associated with both the sun and the moon. In the Ptolemaic and Roman periods, the ritual of offering mirrors regarded these objects as the equivalents for those two heavenly bodies. As a result, they were regarded as resurrection symbols, appropriate objects to be placed in tombs.

The fact that the disks on many ancient Egyptian mirrors are not in the form of a perfect circle but appear to be slightly wider than tall, as on this example, seems to be based on natural observations of the rising sun. Scholars have often commented that the rising sun appears to be flattened on top due to optical illusions caused by the sun's rays interacting with the atmosphere. As a result, the shape of these disks is an attempt to depict the sun at the moment that it instantaneously rises from the horizon at dawn.

This re-creation of the rising sun is reinforced by the fact that the disk, as the metaphorical equivalent of the sun, is attached to an open papyrus umbel. According to one of the creation legends of the ancient Egyptians, the sun rose from a papyrus swamp. The combination of the disk and the papyrus umbel alludes to this original myth and reinforces the symbolism of resurrection. That symbolism is further reinforced by the design of the handle in the form of a nude, nubile young lady, seductively attired in an elaborate wig and broad collar. This image is inherently erotic and suggests that cosmic regeneration in the form of the daily rising of the sun is linked to physical procreation. Human procreation resonates with the myth of Osiris, whose posthumous union with his sister-wife Isis created their son and heir Horus.

In a very sophisticated manner, the ancient Egyptians were able to create a composition uniting disparate elements—sun disk, open papyrus umbel, and nude female figure—all contributing to the significance of the mirror as a symbol of resurrection and cosmic regeneration (compare cat. 57).

This mirror finds close parallels in others dated to Dynasty XVIII, supporting its assignment to that period.

References: Bénédite, *Miroirs*, 1907, pp. ii–iii; Bianchi, "Reflections," 1985, pp. 10ff; Husson, *Miroir*, 1977.

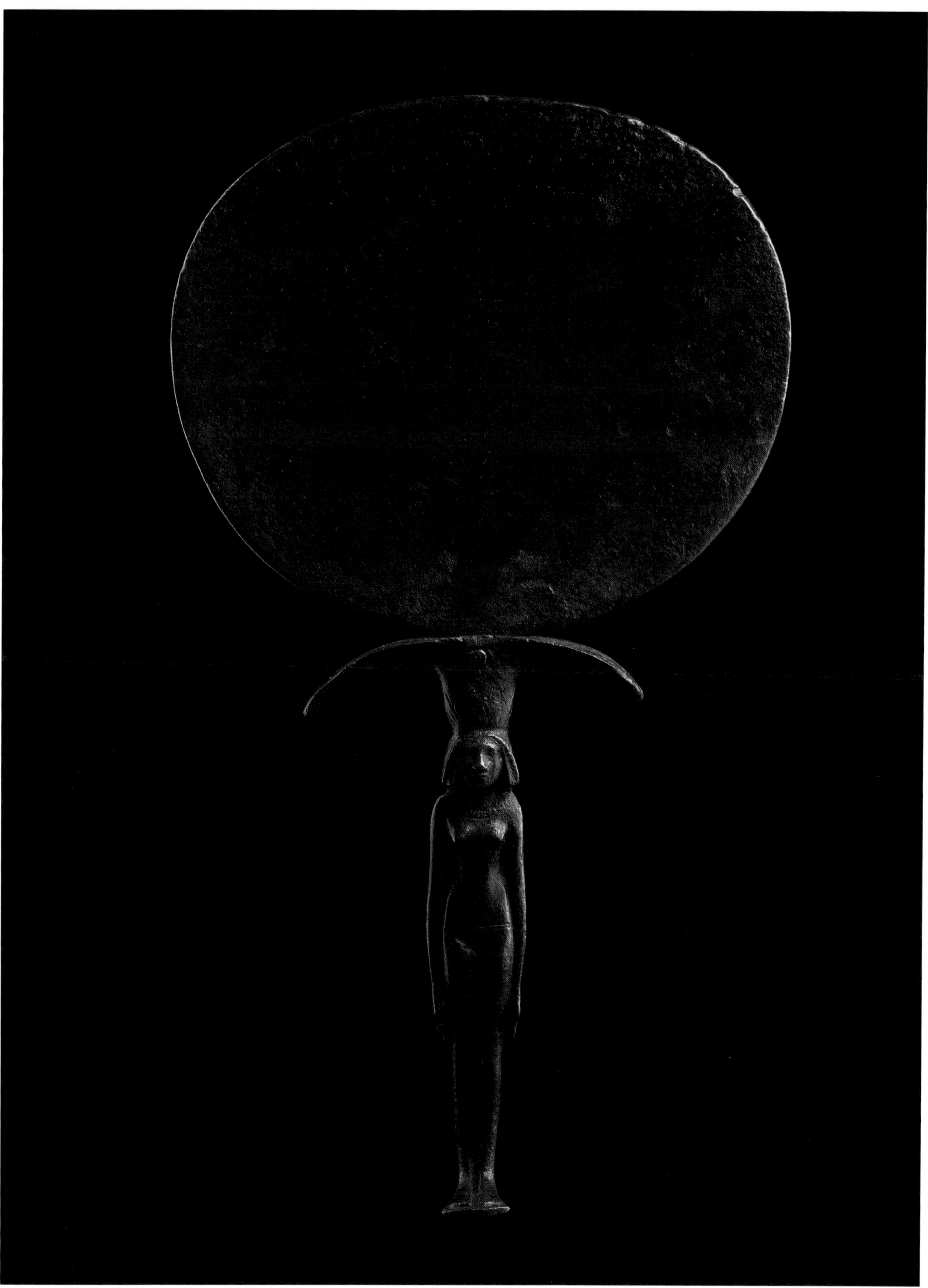

59.

A "Pillow" from a Headrest

Dynasty XVIII, 1550–1305 BC
Possibly cedar
Length 6 ¼ in.
Inv. no. EG-206

The design of ancient Egyptian beds, known from actual examples as well as from depictions, places the foot end at a lower elevation than the head end. These beds were equipped with headrests, designed as T-shaped objects in which the pillow, usually of concave form, was affixed to an upright, often provided with a foot for added stability.

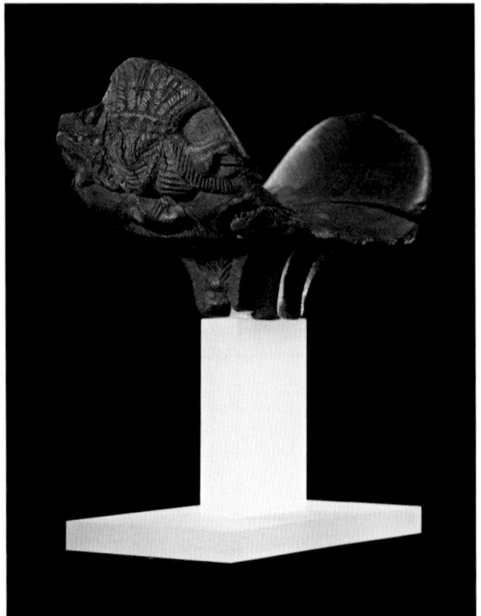

This object represents the pillow from such a headrest, seen from the bottom because the top surface is plain and undecorated. The now-missing vertical support was inserted into the rectangular slot in the object's center. The bilaterally symmetrical decoration is traditionally formed by relying, as it does, upon modeling in broad planes, with detail added as linear adjuncts. Its composition takes the form of mirrored heads of a Bes-image rising from a floral element, perhaps to be identified as a lotus. The vertical support would have been incorporated into this design, specifically resembling a stem of that flower or suggesting, by its vertical alignment, its presence.

These Bes-images represent one of several genii of like appearance who populated the ancient Egyptian pantheon (compare cat. 80). Over the course of time these Bes-images gradually acquired potent, protective characteristics, enhanced by their tongues sticking out of their mouths, a pose which anthropologists would interpret as apotropaic. They were intended to ward off evil by frightening away malevolent forces. The protective characteristics of these Bes-images were transferred to pieces of furniture such as these headrests, as well as to beds, which came into direct contact with the bodies of elite members of society, as a means of protecting them from surmised nocturnal dangers.

A recent inventory has catalogued approximately 125 examples of such headrests, all dated to Dynasty XVIII, of which ninety are decorated, one-third of that number exhibiting Bes-images. These parallels provide the suggested date for this example.

It is possible, however, that such headrests were entirely funerary in nature. Spell 166 of the so-called *Book of the Dead* is a spell for a headrest.

> *May the pigeons awaken you when you are asleep, O Ani, may they awaken your head at the horizon. Raise yourself...you are Horus son of Hathor, the male and female fiery serpents, to whom was given a head after it had been cut off. Your head shall not be taken from you afterwards, your head shall not be taken from you forever!*

The act of lifting one's head up from a pillow in the morning is here compared to the awakening of the deceased from death. The spell continues to assure the deceased that he will not be decapitated, an idea perhaps derived from the fact that the desiccation of the body during the mummification process so weakened the connection of the head to the spinal column that such separations may have been all too common. The spell is intended, therefore, to prevent one from losing one's head.

Published: Chappaz, *Akhénaton et Nefértiti*, 2008, p. 181, no. 23.

References: Eggebrecht, *Ägyptens Aufstieg*, 1987, p. 278, catalogue no. 222; Faulkner, *Book of the Dead*, 1994, plate 32, 166. Hannover, Kestner-Museum 2890: Dettmer, *...den Sinn für das Schöne erwecken*, 1998, p. 58; Hill, L., "Their Heads to Keep," 2009 in ARCE, *60th Annual Meeting*, 2009, p. 53; Schoske, *Schönheit*, 1990, pp. 124–25; Taylor, *Journey*, 2010, pp. 109–110, and 175, no. 83.

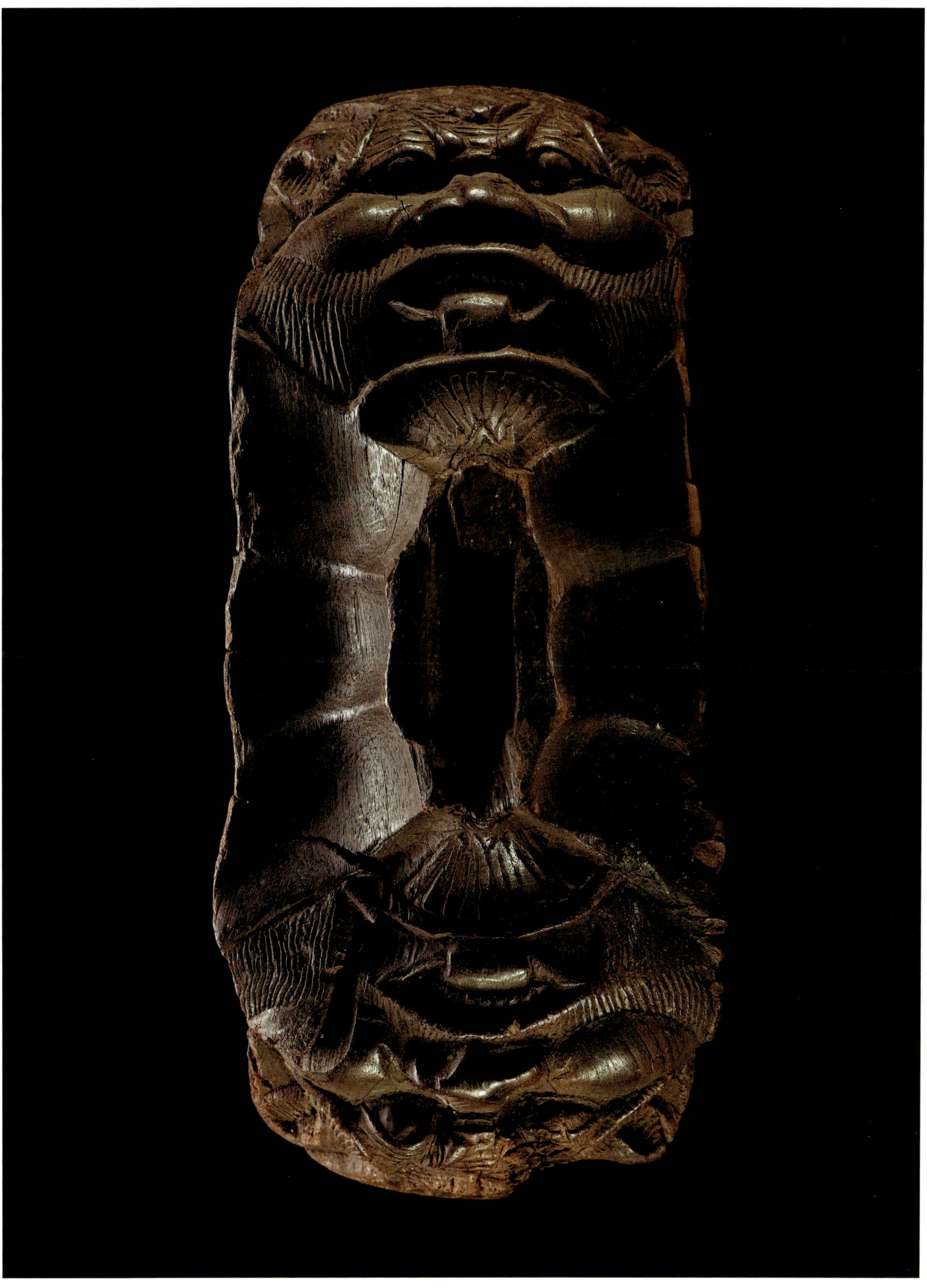

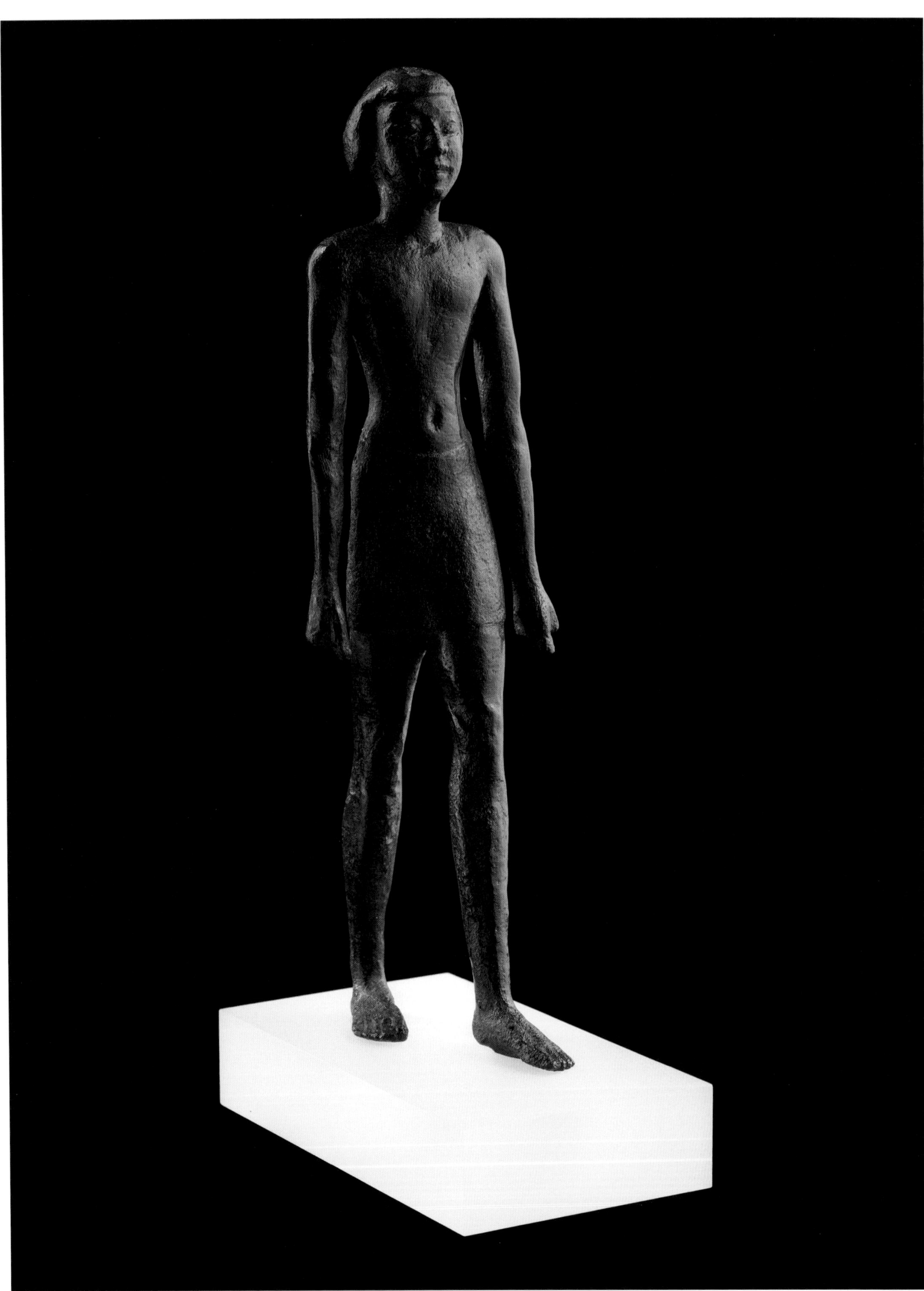

60.

A Statuette of a Striding Elite Male

Dynasty VII–XI, 2155–1991 BC
Copper-based alloy
Height 7 3/8 in.
Inv. no. EG-246

The principles governing the design of sculpture in the round are applied to all statues without regard to their medium, as an examination of this figure reveals. He strides forward with his left leg advanced, his arms hanging down along the sides of his body, their hands fisted and empty. He wears but a simple, undecorated kilt without any indication of a belt. His hair or wig is coiffed as an unarticulated globe that frames the face and covers the ears (compare cat. 25). The features of the face include hieroglyphically shaped eyes set into fairly deep sockets, a short, thin-bridged nose with flaring wings, and a horizontally aligned mouth with stylized lips, the upper relatively longer than the lower. The torso is wasp-waisted with a teardrop-shaped navel and an interest in the pectoral regions. A V-shaped depression divides the torso into two symmetrical halves which avoids defining the rib cage. The arms, with the thumbs of their hands, as well as the legs, are elongated.

The statue represents a nascent attempt on the part of metalworking ateliers to create a solid-cast image in the round. Heretofore, ancient Egyptian metal statuary, if preserved earlier examples are representative, relied exclusively upon forming images from sheet metal. The craftsmen responsible for this statuette clearly recognized the tensile strength of their chosen medium and, with the exception of a triangular area in the region of the armpits, avoided the incorporation of negative metal, so that the arms and legs are free and rendered in the round.

An inventory, compiled within the last decade, of known statuettes in cupreous alloys has catalogued approximately fifty known examples, fewer than ten of which are stylistically related to this statuette. Although traditionally dated to the Middle Kingdom, the archaeological contexts of some of the inventoried examples suggest that their appearance may have begun as early as Dynasty VI of the Old Kingdom. Virtually all of these have come from burials, suggesting exclusive funerary function as surrogates for the deceased. If the transformation of copper from its mined to its worked state obtains for the period in which these statuettes were created, the metal would imbue the statuette with connotations of order triumphing over chaos, reinforcing the aspired resurrection of the deceased, who was obliged to triumph over malevolent forces en route to rebirth.

References: Baltimore, The Walters Art Museum 54.407: Hill, *Gift for the Gods*, 2007, pp. 14–15, figs. 8, 16, and 201; Hill, *Royal Bronze Statuary*, 2004, pp. 9–11.

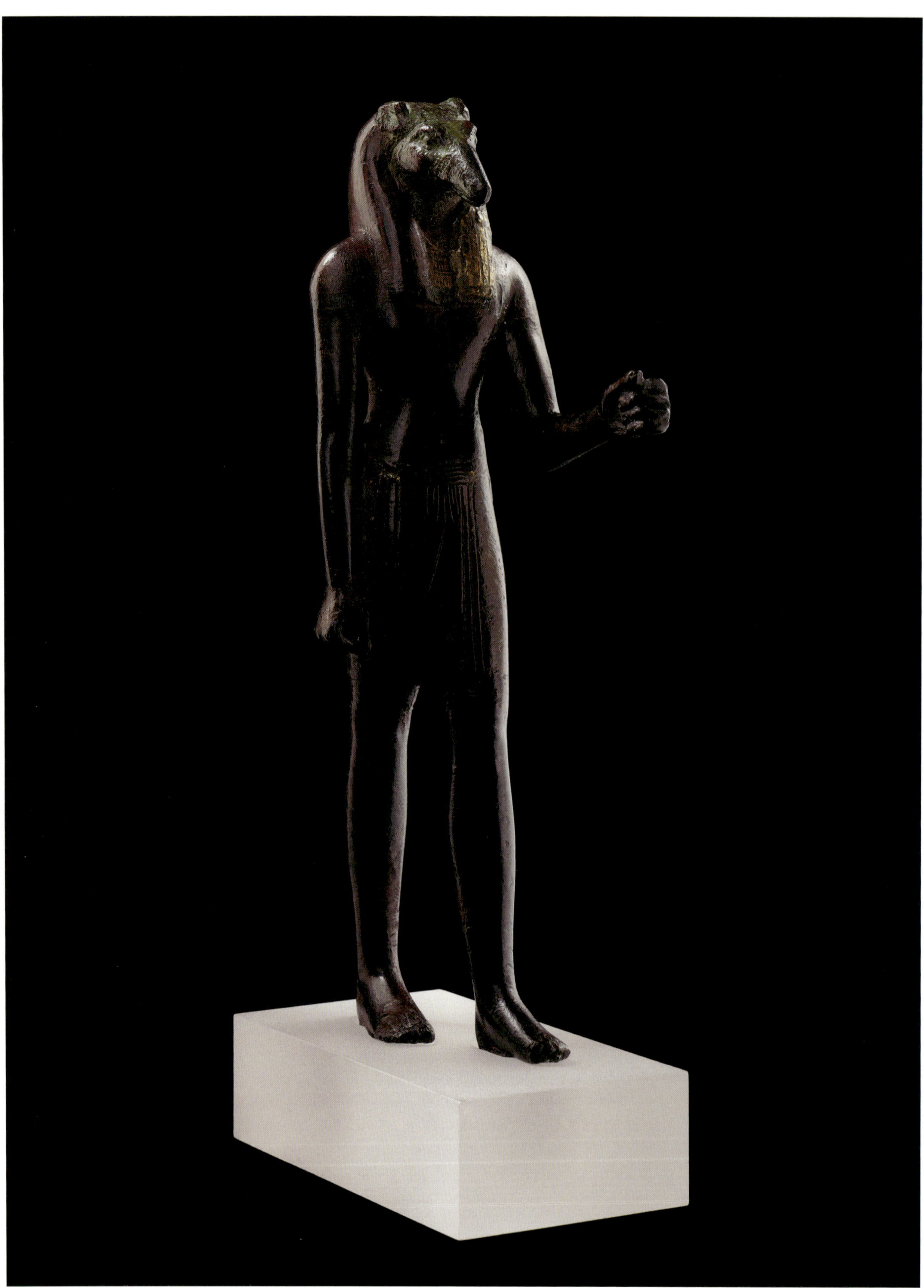

61.

A Statuette of the God Seth

Dynasty XIX, 1305–1196 BC
Gilded bronze
Height 6 ¾ in.
Inv. no. EG-251

This composite deity can be confidently identified as a representation of the god Seth because of its characteristic head, the species of which cannot be determined. Although Seth is associated with both the pig and the hippopotamus, various scholars have identified his animal hypostasis, characterized by a long snout and ears, as an ass, a jackal, an orycterope, an okapi, and so forth. The most recent academic discussions on this issue, however, conclude that this hypostasis is not a depiction of an actual animal, but is rather a fanciful, composite beast created by the imaginative minds of the Egyptian elite, perhaps combining features from several creatures (compare cat. 53).

The deity is depicted in the canonical ancient Egyptian pose of the striding male figure, with his left leg advanced. In keeping with that traditional pose, the god is both barefoot and bare-chested. He is wearing a striated kilt with a front flap secured in place by a horizontally striated belt, from which is suspended "the knot of Isis," termed *tjt* in ancient Egyptian (compare cat. 9). There is a broad collar visible between the lappets of his striated, tripartite wig. His ears protrude from the top of the wig. His right arm hangs down alongside his body, and his left arm, bent at the elbow, is extended to the front and slightly raised. Both of the hands are fisted and hollow to accommodate now-missing attributes, perhaps to be restored as a scepter and staff. The entire statuette was originally gilded, extensive traces of which are still preserved.

The cult of the god Seth was already established during the course of the Old Kingdom. He was popular at Avaris (Tell ed-Daba) during the course of the Second Intermediate Period because of his associations with Canaanite deities worshipped by the Hyksos, who were ruling from that Eastern Delta city, which served as their capital. The cult of this god became very popular during the course of Dynasty XIX, particularly since several pharaohs of that dynasty were named in honor of Seth.

The ancient Egyptians were ambivalent about the character of the god Seth. He might be portrayed as the god of confusion, whose evil powers threatened the order and harmony of the Egyptian cosmos, but he was also regarded as a protector, who destroyed the forces of evil, often personified as the serpent Apophis. It is for this reason that Seth often appears in the company of the sun gods on solar barques of the New Kingdom.

During the course of the Third Intermediate Period, however, the cult of Seth began to decline in popularity, and his malevolent connotations as the murderer of Osiris began to eclipse his beneficent role as the defender of the sun god. From that time on, Seth was considered to be an incarnation of evil itself, and those associations continued to be perpetuated by later Jewish and Christian traditions.

The ambivalent character of Seth, simultaneously benevolent and malevolent, may account for the present condition of his imperfectly preserved ears in this statuette. A careful examination of those ears reveals that they were intentionally damaged in antiquity, as were the ears of another bronze statuette of Seth. Such deliberate physical damage was regarded as a symbolic mutilation intended, one suggests, to render harmless the god's malevolent characteristics without diminishing his benevolent powers. One is not certain about the date of the mutilation of his ears, but parallels suggest that such bronze statuettes were long-lived. These alterations may have been visible and functioning for several centuries.

The appearance of the *tjt* amulet suspended from the belt of Seth deserves comment. The amulet represents bands of linen associated with the menstrual blood of the goddess Isis, which, by means of a series of complex religious conceits, played a central role in the creation of human life. The *tjt* may, therefore, be regarded as powerfully charged. It offers protection against the forces of evil. This function is clearly stated in Spell 156 of *The Book of the Dead*; the title of this Spell is *A Spell for a tjt-Amulet of Red Jasper*

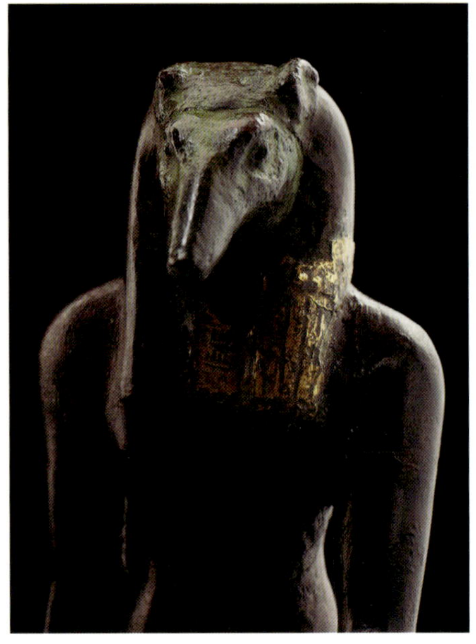

> *You have your blood, O Isis; you have your power, O Isis; you have your magic, O Isis. The tjt-amulet is a protection for this Great One which will drive away whoever would commit a crime against him.*

Furthermore, Spell 75 of The Book of the Dead describes how wearing the tjt amulet places its owner

> *in the Eastern sky in which the sun god Re appears and in which the sun god Re is daily exalted...*

The *tjt* amulet is, therefore, an appropriate emblem for the god Seth in his function as one who protects the sun god from the forces of evil during his nocturnal journey across the night sky. This amulet also enabled Seth to act as a guide, as is clearly stated in the Spell of the *tjt* amulet in the *Book of the Dead*

> *...no path will be hidden from him, and one side of him will be towards the sky and the other towards the earth...*

In keeping with the complexities of ancient Egyptian religious beliefs, which are often filled with inconsistencies that are difficult for a Western mind to comprehend, the positive characteristics of Seth as the protector of the sun god entitled him to receive any attribute or amulet in the ancient Egyptian repertoire that would positively contribute to his function. The *tjt* amulet of Isis, which symbolized creation, therefore becomes a suitable attribute of Seth because, in his role as the protector, he ensured that the sun god would rise each morning at dawn in a cyclic act that symbolized creation for the ancient Egyptians.

Published: Schorsch, "Seth," 2009, in ARCE, *60th Annual Meeting*, 2009, pp. 102–03.

References: Andrews, *Amulets*, 1994, pp. 44–45; Aubert and Aubert, *Bronzes et or*, 2001, pp. 104–07; Begelsbacher-Fischer, *Untersuchungen zur Götterwelt*, 1981, pp. 178ff; Bietak, "Zur Herjunft des Seth," 1990, pp. 9–16; Daressy, "L'animal séthien," 1920, pp. 165ff; DuQuesne, "Seth," 1998, pp. 613–28; Frechkop, "L'orycterope," 1946, pp. 91ff; Keimer, "Die falschlich," 1950, pp. 110–12; McDonald, "Tall Tails," 2000, pp. 75–81; Newberry, "Pig," 1928, pp. 211ff; Schorsch, "Metal Statuary," 2007, in Hill, *Gift for the Gods*, 2007, pp. 188–99; te Velde, *Seth*, 1967.

62.

A Statuette of a Priestess

Dynasty XXI–XXV, 1080–655 BC
Bronze, inlaid with glass paste colored blue, red, and black
Height 11 5/8 in.
Inv. no. EG-179

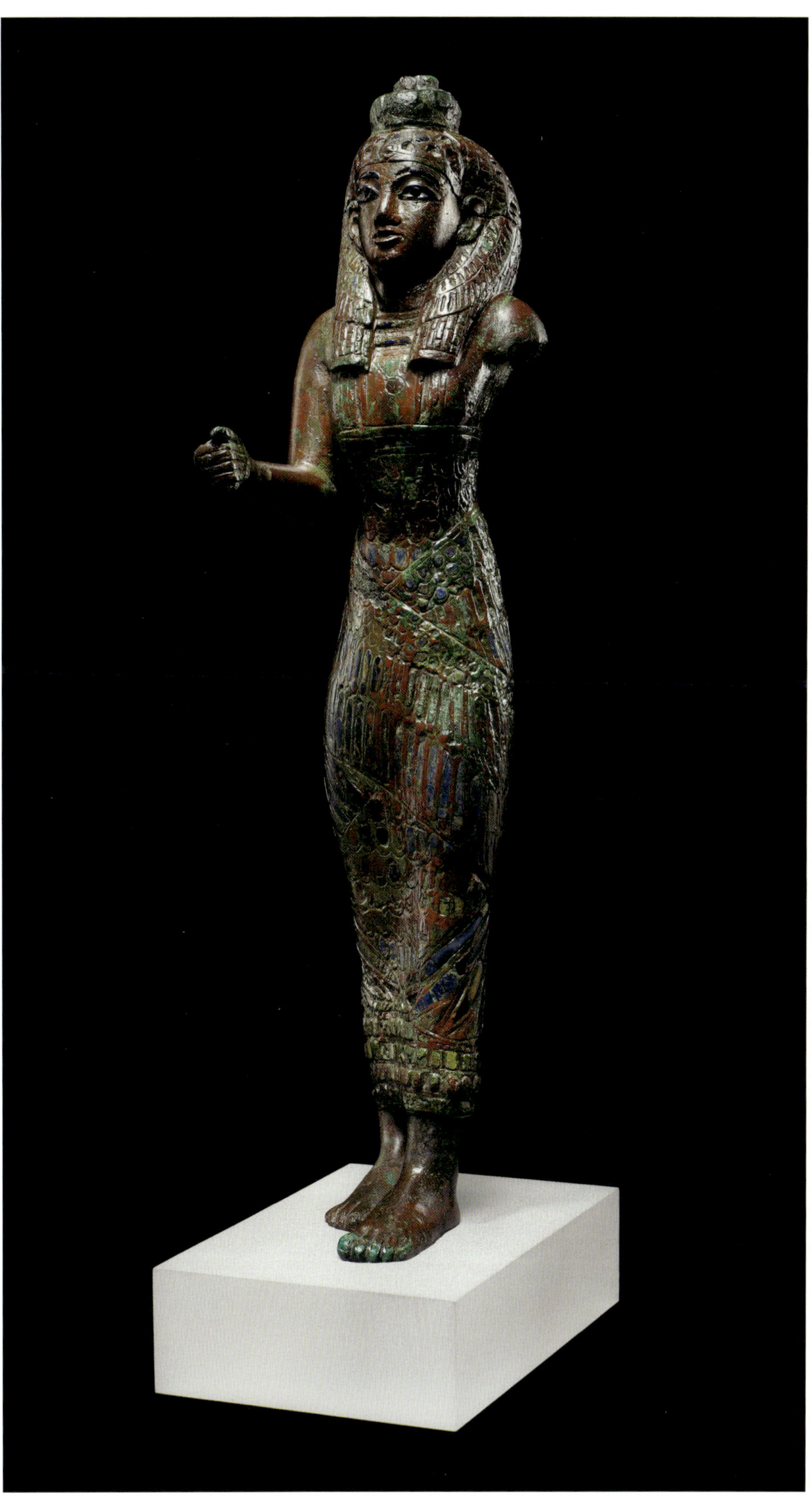

This cast, inlaid bronze statuette of a priestess depicts her striding, with her left leg advanced and her right arm, bent at the elbow, held out in front of her body with its fisted, hollow hand originally holding a now-missing attribute. The form of the body is well modeled, as seen in the physiognomic features of her face, with their emphasis on the inlaid eyes, and in her bare feet, the toes and nails of which are clearly articulated.

The figure wears a tripartite wig that leaves the ears free, the individual locks of which are designed as alternating, vertically aligned rectangles, with a horizontal fascia at the end of each lappet suggested to represent a ribbon or tie (compare cat. 75). The headdress supports a circular modius, the top of which reveals the base of its attribute, which is no longer extant. This wig is covered in part by a vulture headdress, designed to accentuate the bird's head, talons, and wings (compare cat. 77). She wears a dress, the bodice of which resembles a modern tank top, to which has been sewn two wide straps that are worn over each shoulder, joining its top as they cover the breasts. This elaborate costume, richly inlaid with secondary materials, is ornamented at the back with the figure of a falcon with a sun disk atop its head, whose wings wrap around the figure's waist.

Although not inscribed, contemporary inlaid bronze statuettes such as this example represent elite women in high ecclesiastical positions. The process of mining and transporting ore and its ultimate fashioning into works of art was considered a symbolic transformation by which the forces of chaos morphed into those of harmony. The inclusion of inlays furthered that conceit and was thought to imbue the image with all of the powerful, symbolic properties inherent in the mineral wealth of Mother Earth. Those powers are then shared with the solar falcon, whose wings wrap around the figure's body in a symbolic embrace of protection. The female represented may, therefore, be correctly identified as an elite priestess, powerfully charged and divinely protected.

The figure may be dated to the Third Intermediate Period, when such stylistically similar, opulently inlaid bronze statuettes of elite women were particularly popular.

Published: Chappaz and Chamay, *Reflets du divin*, 2001, pp. 58–59, no. 43.

References: Bianchi, "Egyptian Metal Statuary," 1990, pp. 61ff;
Hill, *Royal Bronze Statuary*, 2004; Ziegler, "Les arts du métal," 1987, pp. 85–101.

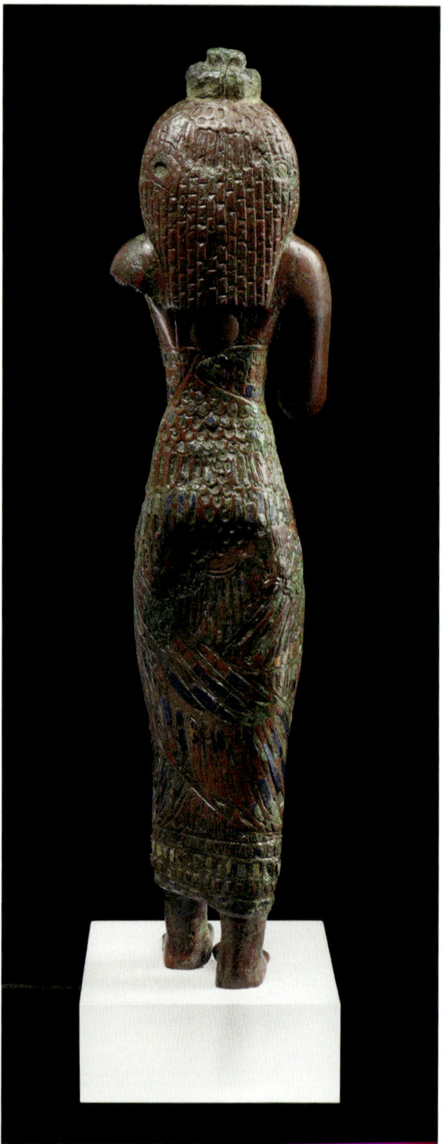

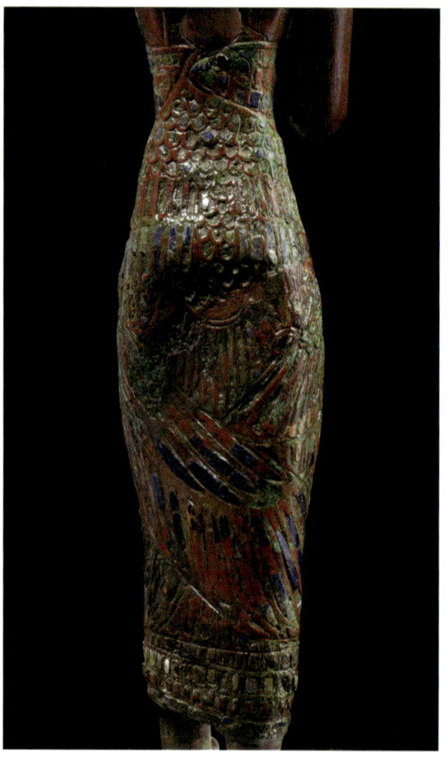

63.

A Bes-Image Serving as a Finial for a Staff

Dynasty XXI–XXV, 1080–BC
Bronze
Height 8 ¾ in.
Inv. no. EG-23

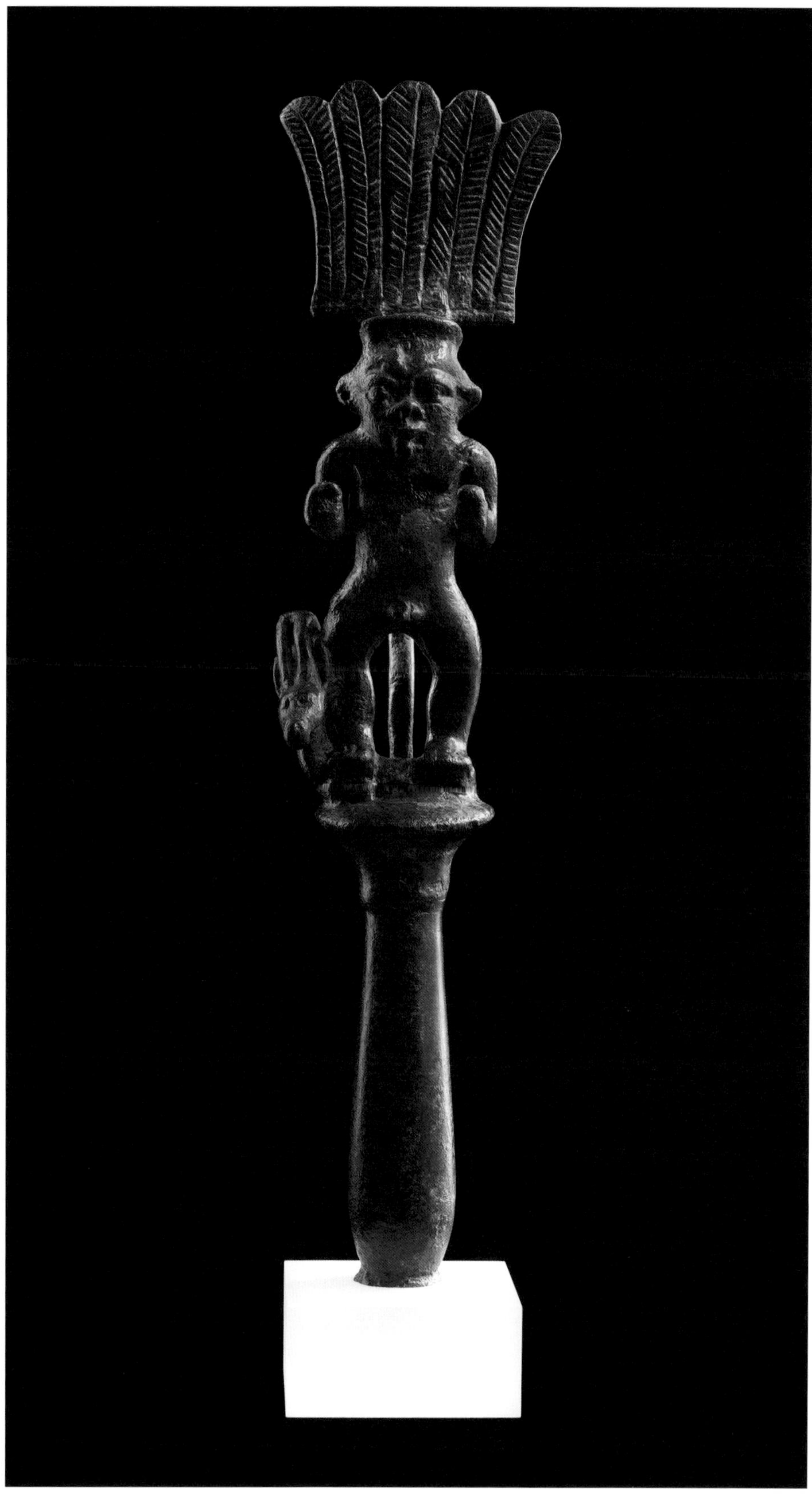

The bandy-legged, leonine-faced Bes-image (compare cat. 80) is attached to a stylized, open papyrus umbel by the soles of the feet of his spread legs and by his elongated phallus, a characteristically emphasized part of his anatomy. His arms are bent at the elbow and held out in front of his body, slightly raised so that their fisted hands might have originally held a now-missing attribute. He wears his canonical headdress, composed of a series of vertically arranged feathers attached to a horizontal support. The body of a horned animal—perhaps a gazelle, an antelope, or an oryx—lies horizontally beneath his right foot, with its head turned ninety degrees and represented in frontal view against his right knee.

The Bes-image was used for the depiction of several similarly designed protective genii of the ancient Egyptian pantheon. Within this context, the horned African animal here represents forces of evil in general, which are being controlled by lying underfoot, metaphorically trampled.

This composition is suggested to have served as a finial of a staff that may have been carried in religious processions, the use of which was apotropaic, to ward off evil (compare cat. 65 and 66). The function of the series of vertically aligned suspension loops remains to be satisfactorily explained (compare cat. 71).

Such objects are frequently dated to the Third Intermediate Period, to which one assigns this object.

Published: Chappaz and Chamay, *Reflets du divin*, 2001, p. 121, no. 114.

64.

An Amulet in the form of a Scorpion

Dynasty XXVI–Ptolemaic Period, 664–30 BC
Gold
Length 15/16 in.
Inv. no. EG-112

The principles governing hieroglyphs are operative in the design of this composite figure, which seamlessly combines the head of a human being with the body of a scorpion. Modeled in broad planes, linear incision is effectively used to articulate the features of the human head and wig that are unequivocally those of a woman, representing a goddess. The scales of the body and the segmented appearance of the tail with its stinger, although stylized, are convincingly represented. Two small, vertically aligned suspension loops under the lappets of the wig were used to suspend this pendant from a necklace or other object. A now-missing attribute may have originally been affixed to the modius, rising from the crown of her head, as its traces, still visible in the center, suggest.

The principle of *alexikakos*, from the ancient Greek phrase meaning, "to exchange evil," enabled ancient theologians to convert the malevolent characteristics of potentially dangerous animals into benevolent characteristics for the advantage of the elite, an analogy, perhaps, with the modern principle of "fighting fire with fire." As a result,

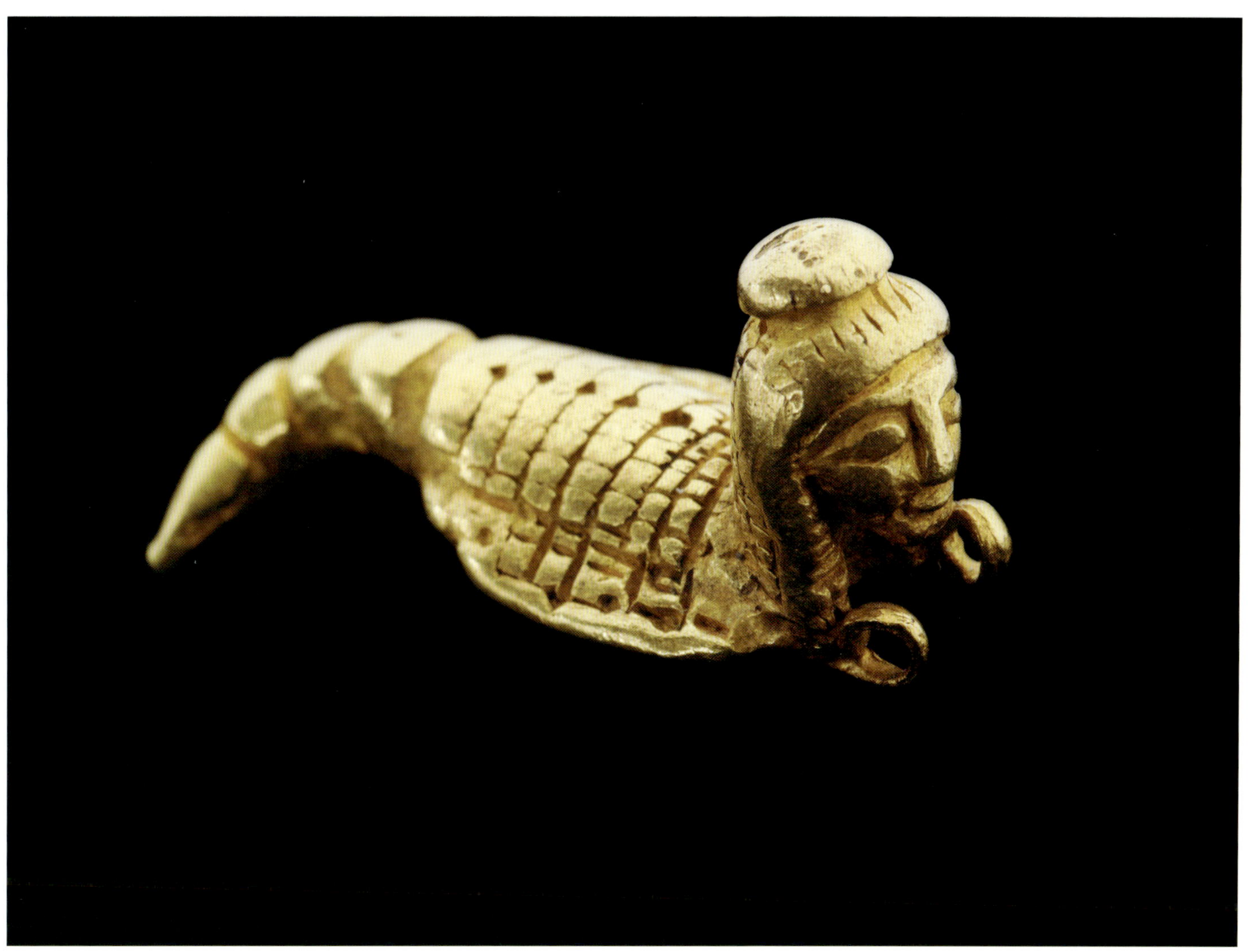

the harmful, and on occasion, lethal sting of the scorpion was harnessed for use against other malevolent beings and forces.

A definitive identification of the goddess depicted is precluded, inasmuch as the amulet lacks both a distinctive attribute and an accompanying inscription. Within the Egyptian pantheon, the scorpion is frequently found as a hypostasis of the goddess Selket on the basis of her name, which means "the one who causes the throat to breathe," presumably for her powers to neutralize the asphyxiating effects of the scorpion's venom. A similar amulet, in Bologna, has been identified as this goddess and is dated to the Late Period, Dynasty XXVI or later. Although one is inclined to accept a similar date for this amulet, its identification as Selket can be challenged, because the composite deity might plausibly represent Isis (compare cat. 65). It would be prudent, therefore, to conclude that this amulet exhibits characteristics of any goddess whose powers avert evil. Demanding an exact identification is an exercise in futility, given the polyvalent nature of Egyptian images in general, particularly when they are not inscribed.

References: Bologna, Museo Civico Archeologico KS 321: Tiradritti, *Harwa*, 1999, pp. 70 and 166, cat. 161.

65.

Statuette of Isis as a Scorpion Serving as a Staff's Finial

Dynasty XXI–XXV, 1080–655 BC
Bronze
Height 4 ⅜ in.
Inv. no. EG-205

This statuette is designed in accordance with principles established for the creation of composite beings, which here seamlessly combine a human head with the body of a scorpion. The result compares favorably with the amulet in gold of a scorpion suggested to represent Selket (compare cat. 64). There are, however, subtle differences between the two. This statuette, unlike the gold amulet, exhibits a vulture headdress worn on top of the striated wig.

This composite figure sits sphinxlike on an integral, rectangular plinth, its tail poised in the air, with the stinger turned to the right. A series of struts serves to attach the integral base to the top of a closed papyrus bud. The composition is suggested to have served as a finial, with the long stem of the papyrus accommodated to the shaft of a staff, which may have been carried in religious processions. Its function was apotropaic, to ward off evil (compare cat. 63 and cat. 66).

The hieroglyphic inscription on the integral plinth, which perhaps contained the name of its owner in the lacuna, can be translated as

> *may the goddess Isis grant life to...*

This inscription is instructive because it demonstrates quite clearly that the scorpion, traditionally identified as Selket, is here identified as Isis. The polyvalence inherent in all Egyptian imagery, whereby one image may represent several competing and perhaps contradictory concepts, cautions one against insisting that any image is possessed of a single meaning.

The scorpion goddess depicted here can be unequivocally identified with Isis. Whether the presence of a vulture headdress is her iconographic signifier distinguishing her from Selket as a human-headed scorpion requires further investigation. Nevertheless, the hypostasis of Isis as a scorpion is apotropaic, turning evil on its head, and appears to connote powers similar to those of Selket.

Such objects are frequently dated to the Third Intermediate Period, to which one assigns this object.

References: Copenhagen, Ny Carlsberg Glyptothek 6363: ING Belgique et Fonds, *Sphinx*, 2006, cat. 237, pp. 136–37 and 263.

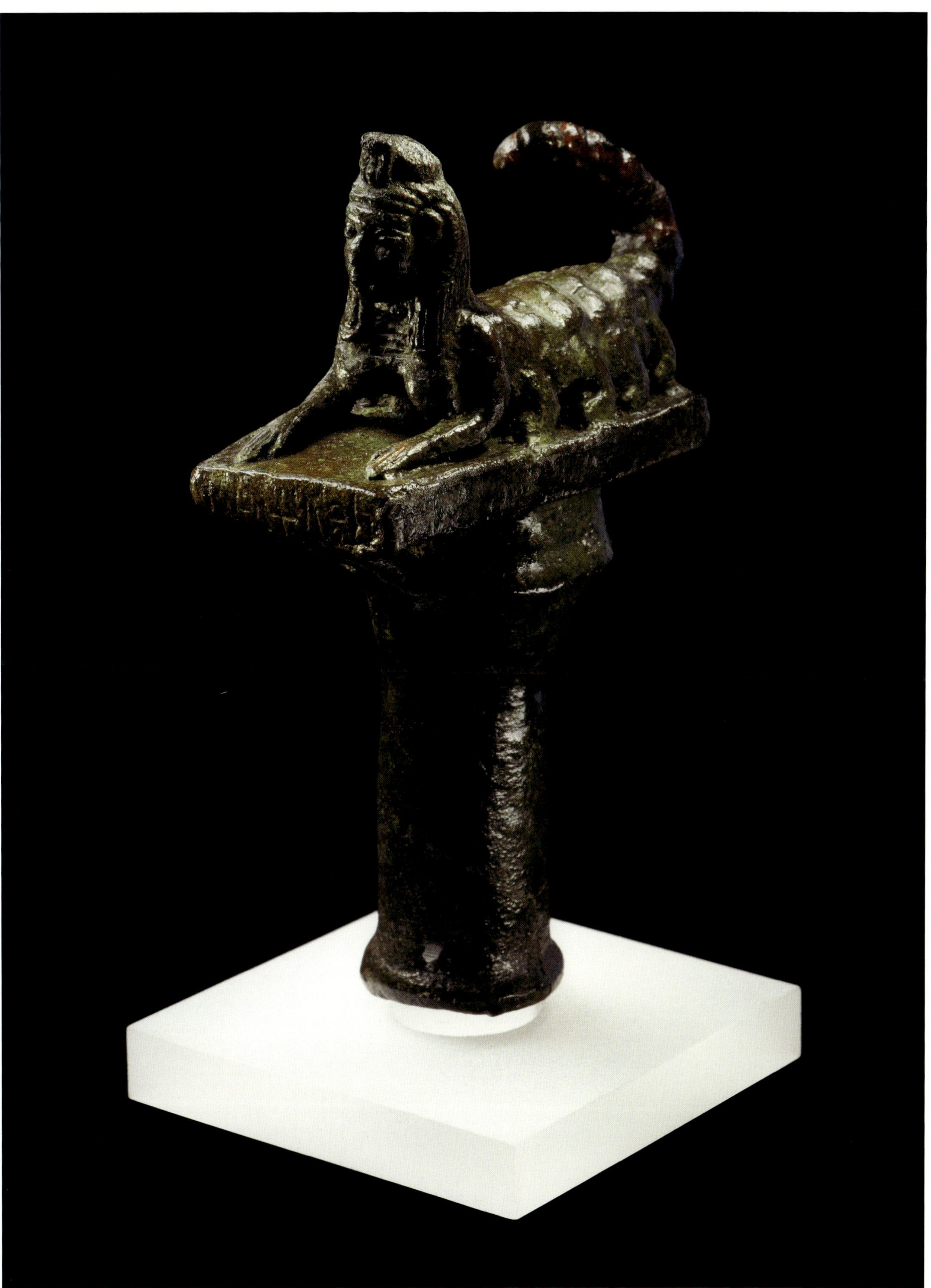

66.

A Palm-Leaf Capital with a Finial in the Form of a Baboon

Dynasty XXI–XXV, 1080–655 BC
Bronze
Height 6 5/8 in.
Inv. no. EG-404

This object appears to have been solid cast as one piece (compare cat. 63 and cat. 65). The bottom is in the form of a cylindrical column, with five horizontal rings at the juncture of its palm-formed capital, to which is attached its finial in the form of a crouching baboon. The baboon has been cast with an integral, thin base, and is designed in the traditional crouching position, its forepaws resting upon its thighs and knees. A celestial disk framed from a horizontally aligned crescent serves as the attribute identifying this baboon as one of the hypostases of Thoth, god of writing and patron of scribes. The details of this object have been finely rendered as a series of thin linear adjuncts.

This type of object—a bronze column surmounted by a bronze image of a deity or animal—is not uncommon within the repertoire of ancient Egyptian bronzes. It has been cogently suggested that such objects were attached to staves, possibly of wood, and were carried in ritual processions either by priests or worshippers in general. An alternative suggestion, that such objects decorated pieces of furniture, cannot be dismissed out of hand.

The disk and crescent, serving as attributes, represent the full and waning moon, respectively. These are appropriate emblems for Thoth, because the moon was regarded as the second eye of Re, the sun god. Furthermore, the monthly changes of the lunar cycle were regarded as marking the passage of time, which Thoth habitually recorded.

The presence of this disk may also be polyvalent and might be interpreted as the sun disk (compare cat. 58). In the wild, baboons were observed to awaken as the sun rose, at which time they chattered incessantly and jumped about, raising their forepaws in the air. The ancient Egyptians interpreted this behavior as a form of sun worship and thought that the chattering of the baboons at dawn was a hymn to the rising sun, recited in their own secret language. Within this context, the floral form of the shaft may allude to the primeval swamp from which the sun rose (implied by the behavior of baboons at dawn), suggesting that this composition might serve as an analogue.

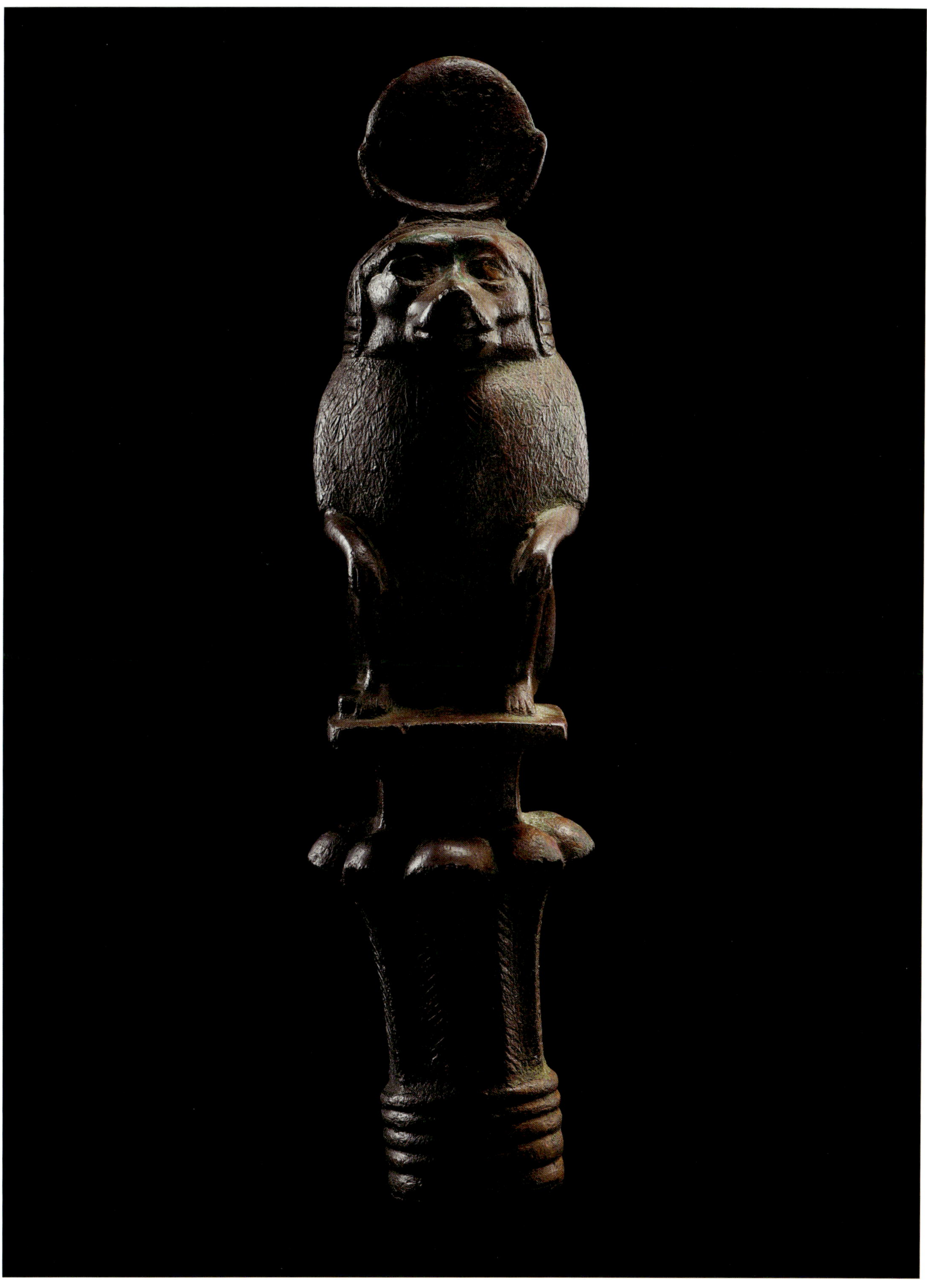

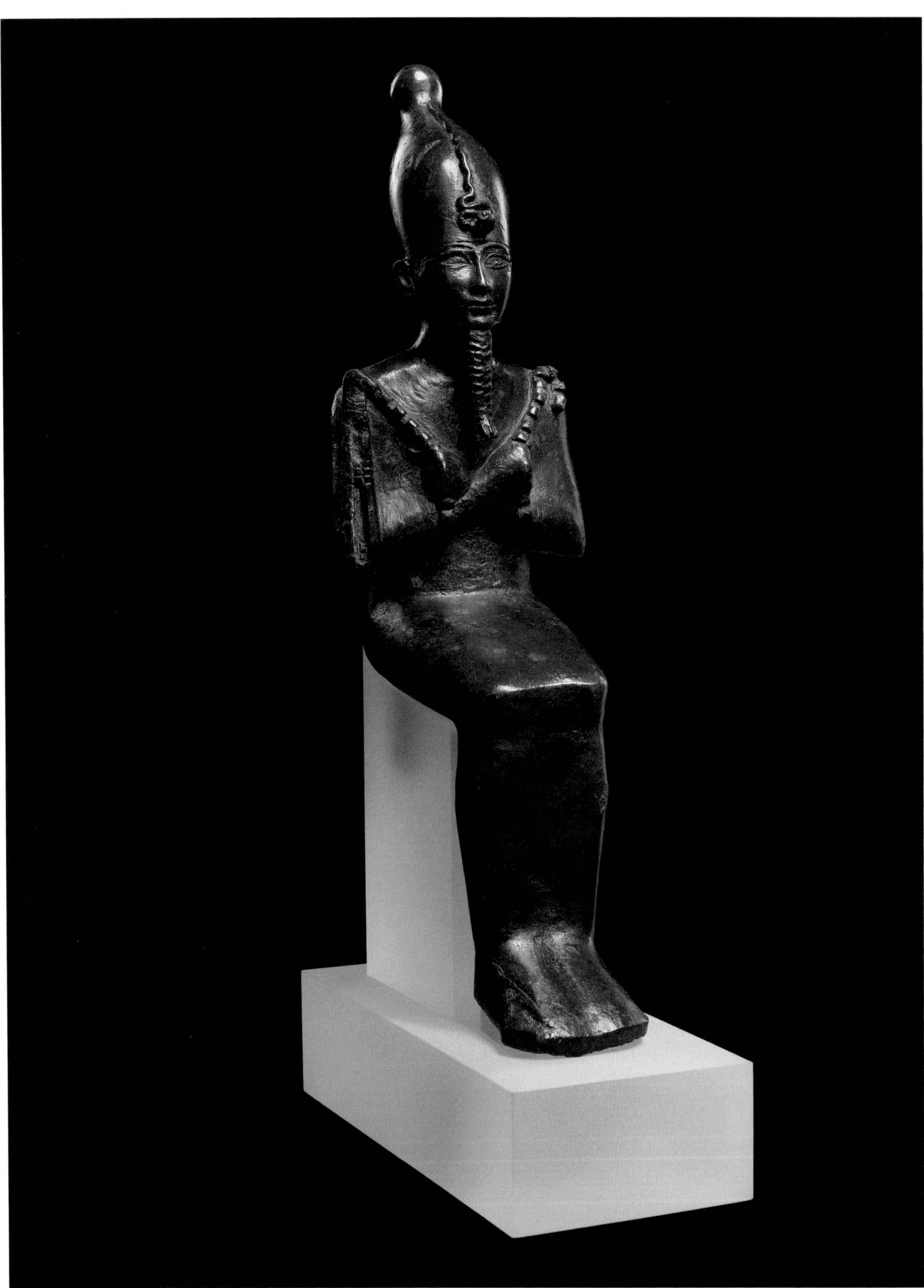

67.

A Statuette of Osiris Enthroned

Dynasty XXI–XXV, 1080–656 BC
Bronze, originally lavishly inlaid
Height 10 ½ in.
Inv. no. EG-301

Although not inscribed, this statuette may with a degree of confidence be identified as a depiction of the god Osiris, one of the few deities of the Egyptian pantheon whose iconography appears fixed. The legend of Osiris, his defeat at the hands of his malicious brother Seth, his subsequent dismemberment, rememberment, posthumous knowledge of his sister-wife Isis, and final investiture as the lord of the hereafter, are well known, principally through the account of Plutarch writing in Greek in the second century AD. Surprisingly, there is not a single ancient Egyptian source that contains all of the episodes of the Osiris narrative.

The god is represented completely enveloped in a garment, which is equated with his mummy bandages, from beneath which the forms of his body appear (compare cat. 77). His accessories include a broad collar; a thin, plaited false beard; a White Crown fronted by a uraeus; and a crook and flail. The idealizing features of his face are dominated by once-inlaid eyes.

The original profusion of inlays on this statuette, which can be dated to the Third Intermediate Period on the basis of its style and related features, was not merely decorative. Each of the inlays could represent one of the minerals of the earth, imbued with its own powers because of the close correspondence between color and mineral. Inlaying the statue metaphorically transferred those powers to the image, which was then considered to be "mineralized," that is, symbolically charged with all of the powers inherent in the earth's mineral wealth.

References: Aufrère, "Evolution des idées," 1998, pp. 31–42; Bianchi, "Stones," pp. 109–17.

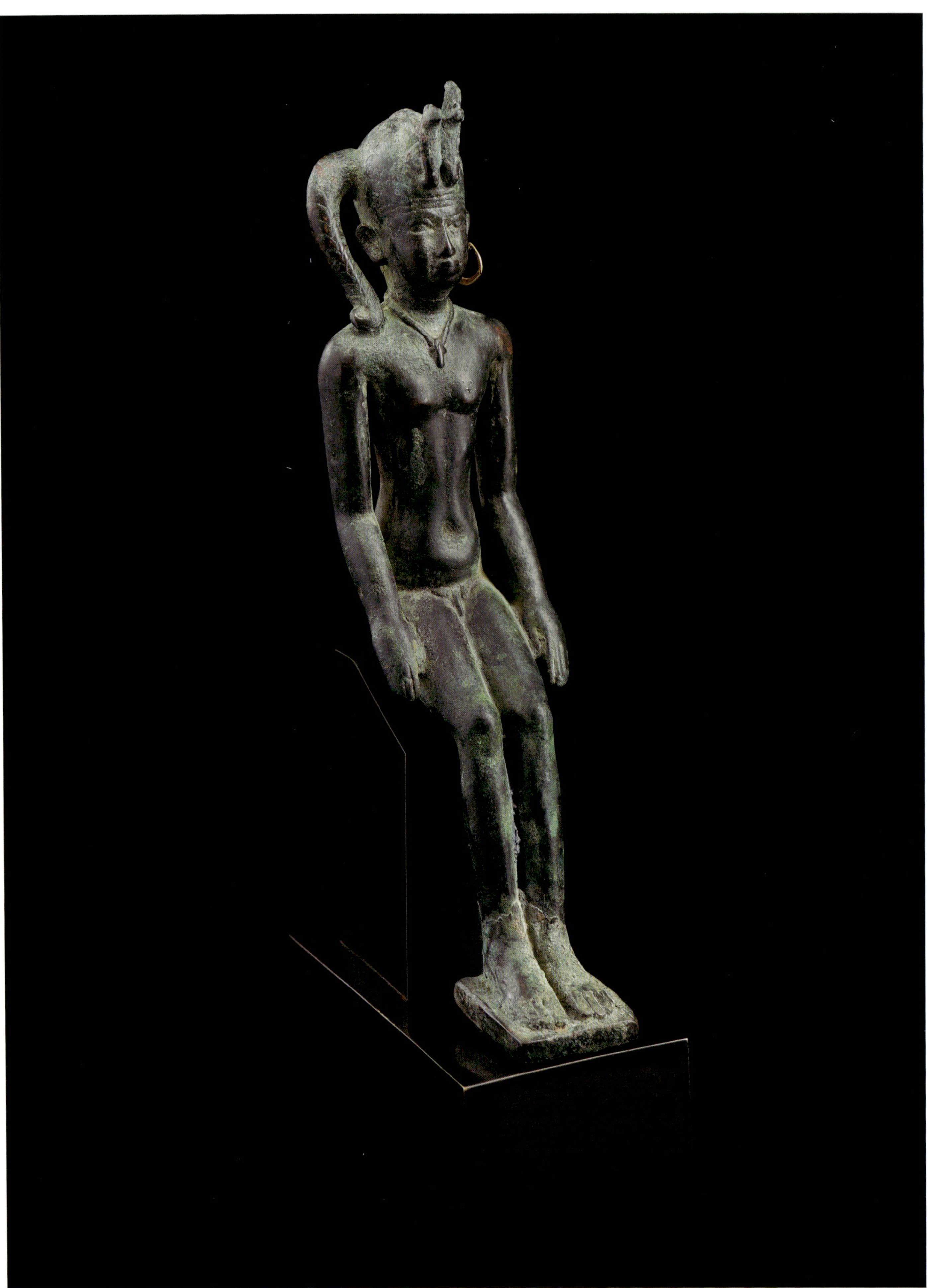

68.

A Statuette of a Child God

Dynasty XXV, 745–655 BC
Bronze and gold
Height 7 in.
Inv. no. EG-361

This statuette was formerly in the collection of Omar Pascha Sultan, which was formed in the late nineteenth and early twentieth century, perhaps in Middle Egypt in the vicinity of Minya. The collection was catalogued by a group of anonymous authors and published in Paris in 1929, but it was not until after April 1975 that objects in the collection were first offered—and to this day, apparently, continue to be offered—for sale.

This statuette depicts a nude youth in a seated position with his feet attached to an integral, square plinth. Both of his arms are parallel to his torso. The palms of his hands are open and facing down, with the thumbs touching the thighs.

The dating of this statuette to Dynasty XXV is suggested by certain features that are now recognized as characteristic for statuary created at that time. These include the shape of the round head, with its somewhat nonidealizing features that, via the principle of archaizing, were utilized to represent the physiognomies of the Kushites, or Nubians, who had entered Egypt from further south and established themselves as the Black Pharaohs of that dynasty. Their characteristic headdress, reserved for depictions of Kushite pharaohs, is termed a cap-crown. It fit snugly on the head in the manner of a modern swimmer's bathing cap, although there is scholarly debate about whether this element is a cap at all or is actually a stylized convention for the depiction of curly hair. The side-lock is traditionally the emblem indicating the figure so represented is a child. His forehead is adorned with the double uraeus, or paired cobras, which serve as the insignia par excellence for identifying Kushite pharaohs, although the exact significance of paired cobras in this particular Nubian context remains elusive (compare cat. 98).

His other accessories include a necklace, from which a single heart-shaped pendant hangs, and a single gold earring. It is quite possible that the earlobe was originally pierced, because there are other documented representations of child gods wearing similarly designed hoop-shaped earrings. Whether the present one is original or not is moot, because numerous examples of ancient Egyptian bronze statuettes of cats also exhibit pierced ears preserved without this accessory. The earring on this figure may very well have been modernly added in accordance with the well-attested practice of certain antiquarians who, on occasion, added a gold singleton to one ear of bronze cats.

The cap-crown fronted by the double uraeus is an element of royal regalia reserved for the Kushite pharaoh. The cult of the child god is well attested in the Third Intermediate/Kushite Period, and, although not inscribed, this statuette may very well be intended to represent one of the Kushite kings of Dynasty XXV as the divine child god, with whose cult he aspired to be identified.

References: Fazzini, *Iconography*, 1988, pp. 8ff.

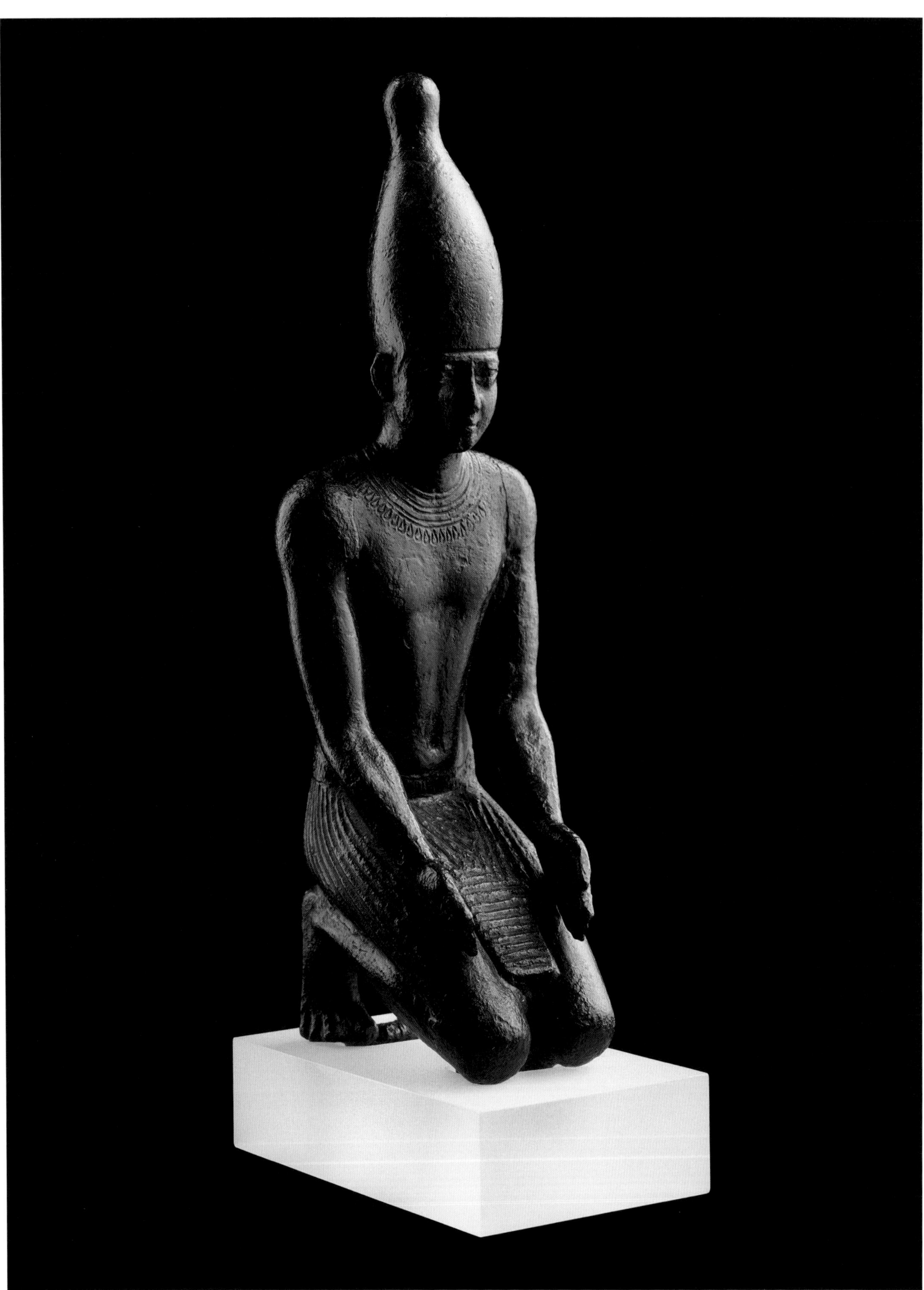

69.

A Statuette of a Kneeling Pharaoh in a White Crown

Dynasty XXVI, 664–525 BC
Bronze
Height 6 ½ in.
Inv. no. EG-12

This cast bronze statuette depicts a pharaoh kneeling on the ground with his arms bent at the elbow and lowered so that his hands rest on his thighs. He is shown wearing a striated kilt, secured at the waist with an ornamented belt, a six-strand broad collar, and the White Crown of Upper Egypt, once fronted by a now-missing uraeus. The features of his face are carefully modeled, as are his fingers and toes, which are detailed to the point of representing the nails themselves. His wasp-waisted torso is designed in bipartition, both sides of the sternal notch mirror images of one another, with the rib cage suppressed so that the pectoral regions and lower abdomen are one. The belt of his kilt rides low on his hips, beneath a deeply recessed, almost teardrop-shaped, navel.

The gesture of his hands, held vertically with palms open and facing each other, with their fingers close together, suggest that the statuette once supported a now-missing attribute, which may have been either a divine image or a piece of religious furniture in the form of a shrine, perhaps with a divine image within. The elliptical depression in the center of the chest at the level of the biceps appears to be the trace of a point of contact or attachment between this attribute and the statuette. The tang at the bottom of the feet indicates that this statuette was originally affixed to a larger base forming part of a group composition, perhaps kneeling before a deity or inserted into the deck of a ceremonial boat carried in procession (compare cat. 79).

Bronze statuettes of pharaohs with idealizing physiognomic features and lacking accompanying inscriptions are notoriously difficult to date. The somewhat round head of this example, and the observation that the crown rests very low on the forehead where it almost touches the eyebrows, invites comparison with monumental stone sculpture inscribed for pharaohs of Dynasty XXVI, the suggested date for this example.

Published: Chappaz and Chamay, *Reflets du divin,* 2001, pp. 54 and 56, no. 41; Hill, *Royal Bronze Statuary,* 2004, pp. 86, 195–95, no. 127 [LPPt-6].

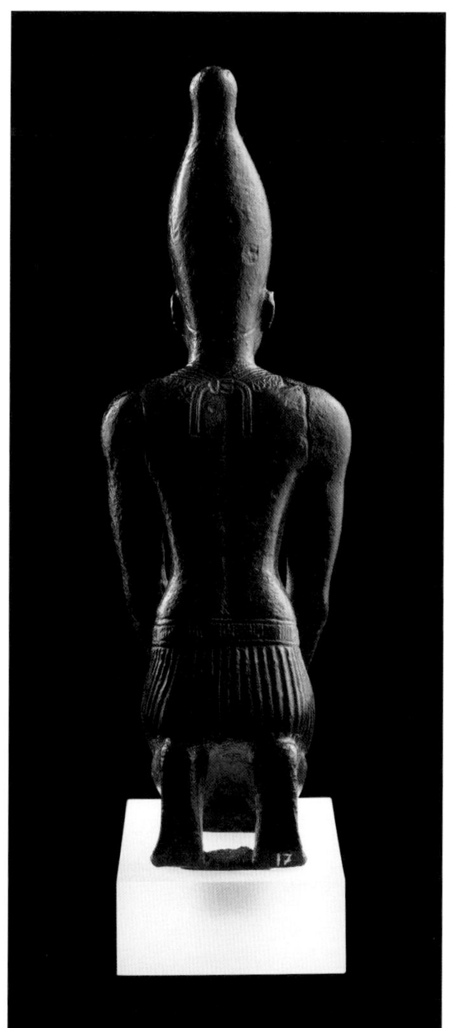

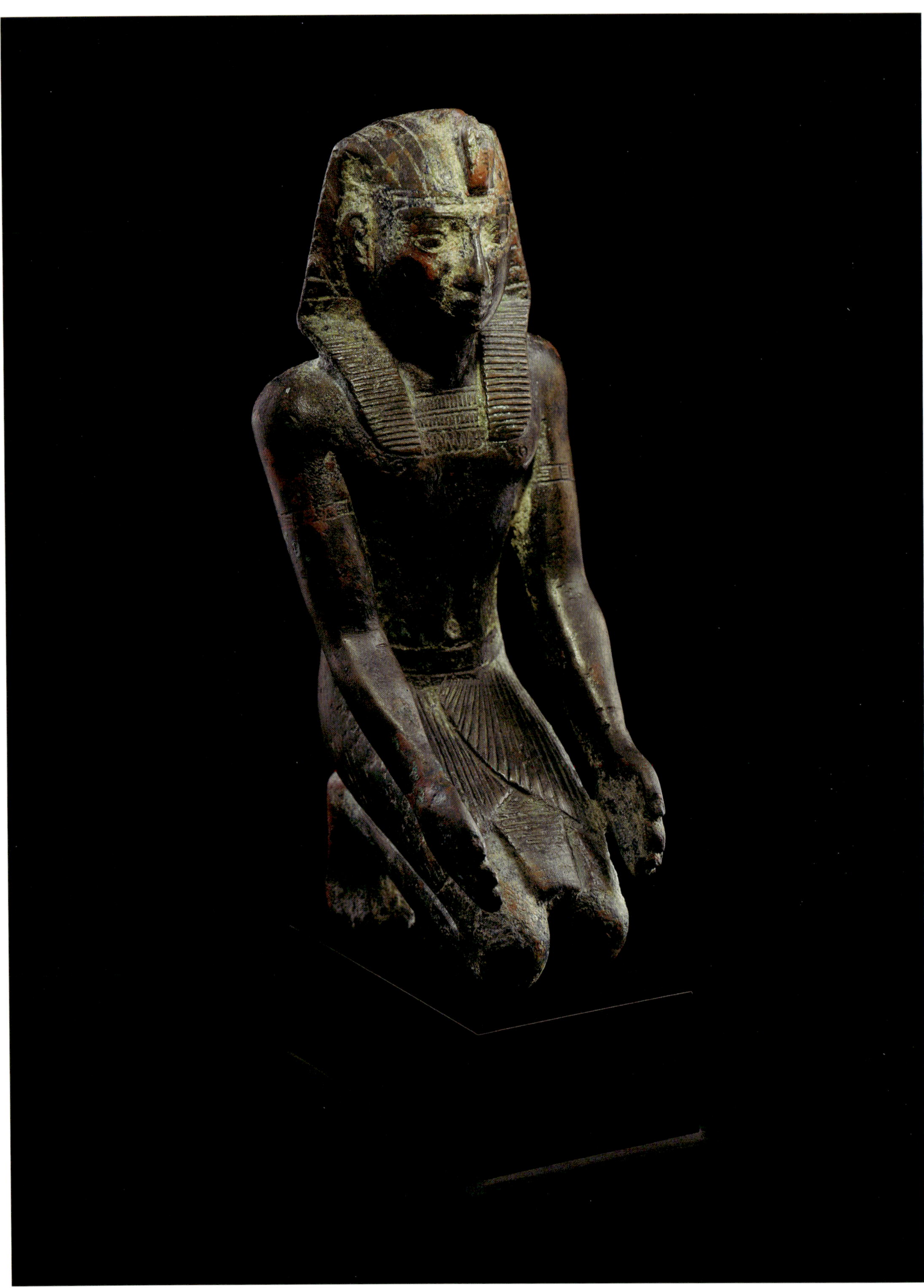

70.

A Statuette Inscribed for a Pharaoh Named Psametik

Dynasty XXVI, 664–525 BC
Bronze
Height 6 ¾ in.
Inv. no. EG-358

This statuette depicts a pharaoh in a kneeling position, wearing a striated, belted kilt and striped nemes-headdress fronted by a cobra. His accessories include a broad collar, bracelets, and armlets. His arms are placed alongside his body following the outline of both the torso and thighs, with his hands open, palms facing inward, suggesting that he was holding an object, either a shrine, termed a naos, or statuette.

There is a cartouche on the biceps of his left arm inscribed with the nomen Psametik, common to three like-named individuals who ruled during Dynasty XXVI. Although there are few representations securely identified as depictions of Psametik I in the round, certain elements of this statuette, such as the edge of the nemes-headdress, which is pulled down over the forehead so that it almost touches his eyebrows and leaves very little of the height of the forehead exposed, is a feature found on two kneeling figures inscribed for Necho II, the successor of Psametik I. On the basis of these parallels, one would suggest that this statuette may be a depiction of Psametik I.

The statuette was attached to a separately made base, as the tang under the legs reveals. Its presence suggests that this statuette may have been part of a larger group composition, perhaps designed with this image of the kneeling pharaoh offering to a large figure of a deity. Alternatively, the statuette may have been attached to a sacred processional barque, on analogy with examples of similar depictions of two-dimensional kneeling pharaohs on such boats (compare cat. 69 and cat. 79).

References: Philadelphia, University of Pennsylvania Museum of Archaeology and Anthropology E13004 and Brooklyn, Brooklyn Museum 71.11: Hill, *Royal Bronze Statuary*, 2004, nos. 24 and 25, respectively.

71.

A Statuette of the God Nefertum

Dynasty XXVI, 664–525 BC
Bronze
Height 8 ½ in.
Inv. no. EG-21

The deity is depicted in the canonical Egyptian pose of striding forward with the left foot advanced. He is clothed in a striated kilt secured at the waist with a plain belt. A tripartite, striated wig fronted by a uraeus rests on his head and supports an attribute designed as an open lotus with two plumes attached, joined side to side. A single menat, or counterpoise used to steady a necklace when worn, is attached to each side of the open lotus, serving both as an additional attribute and functioning to secure the lotus and feathers to the headdress of the statue (compare cat. 17). A khepesh, or dagger-like weapon with curved blade that is perhaps the precursor to an Islamic scimitar, is designed as a stylization of a bull's powerful rear leg, the shape imbuing the dagger with symbolic might. The figure is attached to an integral, rectangular plinth, which is not inscribed. The center of its bottom is equipped with a tang for insertion into a larger base, suggesting that this figure may have been part of a larger group composition.

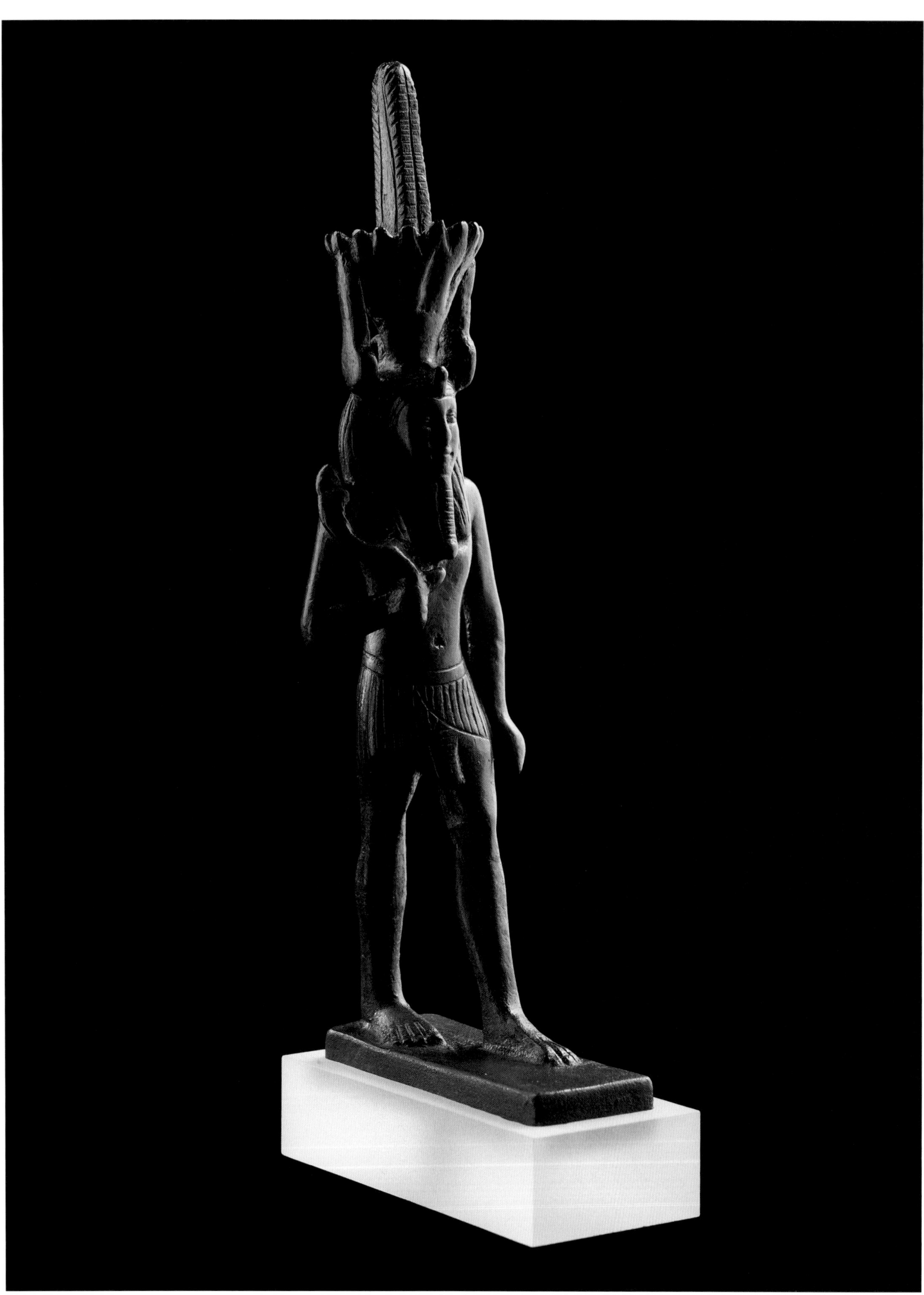

The characteristic headdress focusing on the lotus clearly identifies this figure as Nefertum, the god of the primeval lotus. The lotus was observed to open when hit by the rays of the dawning sun and to close when the sun set. The natural behavior of this flower was then used as an alternative but equivalent image of the valley between the two high mountains from which the sun rises and into which it sets. In keeping with the polyvalent nature of the hieroglyphs, concrete objects are pressed into service to explain abstract concepts. This equivalence then associated Nefertum with the sun god, one of the generators of creation. The two plumes and menats, which serve as this deity's additional attributes, are associated with goddesses of fecundity, particularly Hathor, and reinforce the creative, life-giving powers of this deity, whose weapon might be used to ward off malevolent forces.

Spell 266 of The Pyramid Texts, composed during the Old Kingdom as an aid for the resurrection of the pharaoh, specifically mention this flower:

> *the lotus blossom which is before the nose of Re.*

This passage provides the context in which one can understand the function of the lotus as a life-giving instrument, because it is placed to the nose of a deity to impart the breath of life. It is for this reason that the lotus may replace the ankh-sign in representations of the elite who are depicted in the act of sniffing it. These depictions, often described as an individual enjoying the flower's pleasant scent, are imbued with symbolic associations, because the lotus becomes the equivalent of the ankh-sign, which deities offer exclusively to the pharoah's nose. By replacing the ankh with the lotus, members of the elite can receive "the breath of life" in a coded system that avoids issues of *lèse majesté* (compare cat. 1 and cat. 5).

The statuette exhibits a vertically oriented suspension loop attached to the back of the head at the juncture of the bottom of the stem of the lotus with the top of the headdress. The sheer size of the statuette and the observation that it was set into another base, as the presence of the tang indicates, suggests that the resulting object would have been even larger in size and somewhat cumbersome, if not uncomfortable, if this bronze composition were intended to be worn as a pendant suspended from a necklace. But this Western, so-called logical approach fails to take into account representations that depict elite members of society actually wearing such large bronze statuettes as pendants, secured by a necklacelike chain, covering their chests from the region of the Adam's apple to that of the navel. These images, often dedicated in temples, assure the participation of the elite so represented in the cult of the deity, whose image is worn as just such an outsized pendant.

On the basis of parallels, this bronze statuette of the god Nefertum is suggested to date to Dynasty XXVI.

Published: Chappaz and Chamay, *Reflets du divin*, 2001, p. 40, no. 25.

72.

A Monumental Image of the Goddess Wadjet Enthroned

Dynasty XXVI–XXX, 664–BC
Bronze with limestone inlay and polychromy
Height 20 ½ in.
Inv. no. EG-413

This gynomorphic, composite goddess is clearly identified as Wadjet in her accompanying hieroglyphic inscription. One inventory suggests that there are about fifty known monumental bronze images depicting enthroned deities preserved worldwide, to which this example belongs. The presence of a tang suggests that this statuette formed part of an even larger group composition in bronze. The goddess is wearing a tightly fitting sheathlike garment suggested to have been woven of fine linen that reveals the feminine forms of her body, particularly her small, indented navel. She is depicted with a leonine head and human female body and is seated on a low-backed chair, conforming in its design to the hieroglyph for "throne." This throne is decorated in incision on both of its sides and its back.

The features of her leonine head are modeled in broad planes, as is evident in the treatment of her muzzle and sockets of her eyes, which are inlaid with limestone highlighted with black-painted circles for eyeballs. She is wearing a tripartite wig, ornamented with parallel vertical incisions, which falls to a level just above her breast, the lappets of which are covered by her mane, encircling her head and ornamented with incised flamelike elements. An unadorned sun disk rests on her head, nestled between her ears, themselves articulated by incision, as is the hood of the uraeus, or sacred cobra, rising from her forehead and fronting the sun disk. Its tail is continued along the crown of her head toward its back and extends on to the tripartite wig. The uraeus is also functional because it acts as a strut, clearly understandable in the profile views, to lend strength to what would otherwise be an unsupported, vertically aligned sun disk.

Her arms are bent at the elbow and rest on her thighs, both fisted hands hollow to receive now-missing attributes that appear to have been separately cast and added. These are suggested to have been a papyrus scepter, the traditional emblem of goddesses, and an ankh-sign. Her feet rest on an integral plinth attached to the lower part of the throne by a strut.

The throne is decorated with incisions on three of its sides. The back is divided into two horizontal registers. The smaller, top register features a vulture with outstretched wings, understood as protectively embracing the deity. Beneath is a stylized feather pattern, generally found decorating the thrones of goddesses. The left side features Wadjet, enthroned as she appears in this statuette. She holds a papyrus scepter and is seated before a brazier on which a duck is roasting. The hieroglyphic caption may be translated as "A recitation by Wadjet..." but continues in a manner which is at present difficult to understand. The corresponding right side of the throne is decorated with an image of an enthroned, falcon-headed deity, clearly identified in the accompanying inscription as Horus, seated before an offering table laden with loaves of bread. He wears a double crown and holds a was-scepter in one hand and an ankh in the other. The accompanying caption in hieroglyphs may be translated as "A recitation by Horus of Pe." The front of the base is also inscribed in hieroglyphs; it reads "A recitation by Horus of Pe [and] by Wadjet that they may grant all life and all health to..."

The goddess Wadjet was associated with both Horus and the shrew (compare cat. 100). The nocturnal shrew, connected with the night, darkness, and blindness, was

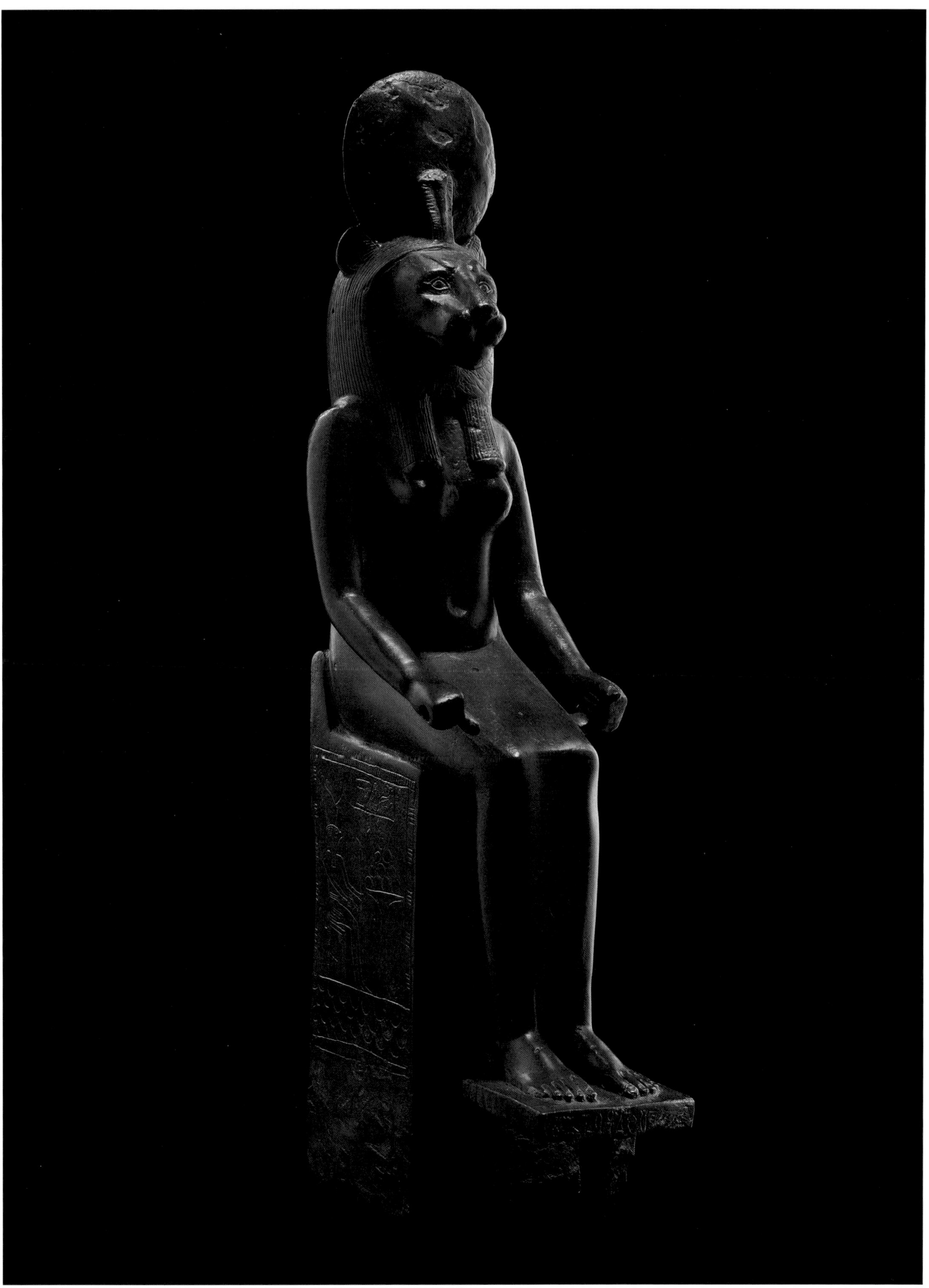

therefore an appropriate guide for the deceased as they made their nocturnal journey toward resurrection. The Blind Horus was believed to have appeared as a shrew when the evil god Seth blinded him in the struggle to avenge Osiris. In this connection, the shrew was also sacred to Wadjet, who was personified as the cobra/uraeus. Taking this form, the goddess helped Horus escape from Seth at another point during their struggle.

The dating of this statuette is based on parallels that are inscribed with names of pharaohs known to have ruled in both Dynasty XXVI and XXX.

References: Aubert and Aubert, *Bronzes et or*, 2001, pp. 199–203; Coche, "Une nouvelle statue," 1970, pp. 51–62; Vanider, "Ouadjet," 1967, pp. 7–75; Vernus in Vernus and Yoyotte, *Bestiaire*, 2005 p. 614, s.v., "Musaraigne."

73.

A Statue of the Cat-Headed Goddess Bastet

Dynasty XXX, 380–342 BC
Bronze and gold
Height 4 in.
Inv. no. EG-95

In keeping with ancient Egyptian principles of design, this composite goddess seamlessly combines the head of a cat with the body of a woman. The figure, designed on an integral rectangular plinth, strides forward with her left leg advanced. The goddess is depicted wearing an ensemble that consists of a long dress, reaching to just above her ankles, and a shawl draped over both shoulders, the bottom of which covers her back and extends to the region of her buttocks. The linear patterns of the costume suggest that it was tailored from decorated textiles, either woven into the fabric or added as embroidery. This detail is noteworthy inasmuch as the depiction of ancient Egyptian costumes in general avoids all such ornamentation. Because they were woven from linen, created from flax, which has no natural mordants, any introduced color would be fugitive and would wash away when the garments were laundered. The ears of the goddess are pierced, one of which sports a gold earring (compare cat. 68).

Her right arm is bent at the elbow with its forearm slightly raised and held out in front of the body. Its fisted hand once held a now-missing attribute, suggested to have been a sistrum, or sacred rattle. Her left arm is likewise bent at the elbow and is held in front of her breasts, with its hand holding an *aegis*, an ancient Greek word for "shield," which is traditionally used in Egyptological literature to designate a U-shaped broad collar to which the head of a deity is attached, in this case that of a ram (compare cat. 79).

Although the object is not inscribed, composite images of cat-headed female figures who wear costumes with decoration suggesting patterned textiles and who hold both an *aegis* and sistrum prove invariably to be images of the goddess Bastet, whose name is related to the noun, *bast*, which designates a particular type of ointment jar (compare cat. 52). Her principal cult center was Bubastis, in the Eastern Delta. The polyvalence of Egyptian theological thought regarded Bastet both as the daughter of the sun god, one of whose hypostases was the ram, featured on the *aegis* she holds, as well as one of several mother goddesses whose primary function was protective.

The dating of this statuette to the Late Period, perhaps more specifically to Dynasty XXX, is based on the design of the shawl, which appears to have been starched because of its stiff contours and rigid shape. Such a stiff, rigidly shaped shawl is characteristic of a handful of other bronze statuettes, also suggested to date to that period.

Published: Chappaz and Chamay, *Reflets du divin*, 2001, p. 39, no. 23.

References: Málek, Cat, 1993, pp. 27, 57, 73–74, *passim*.

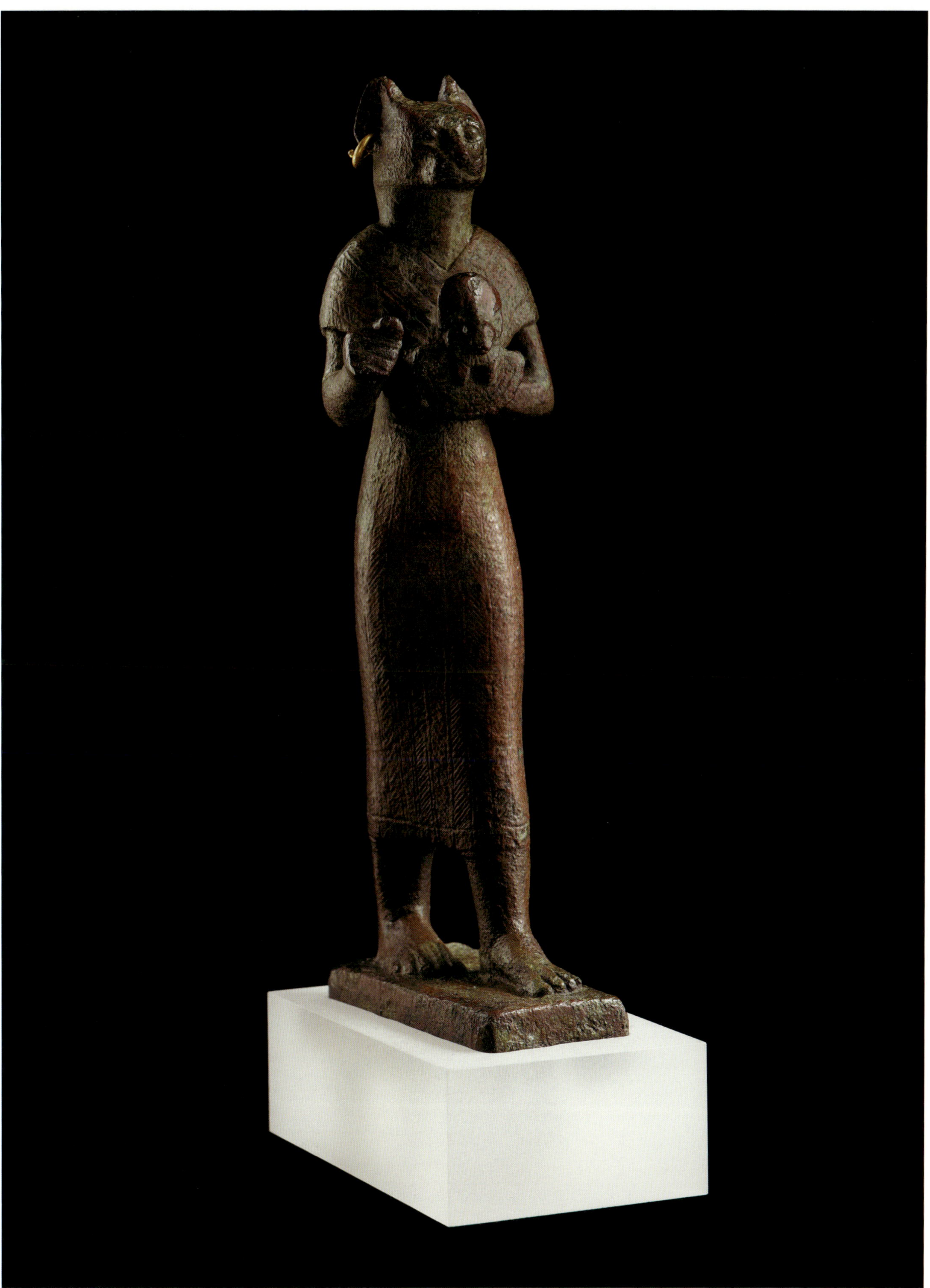

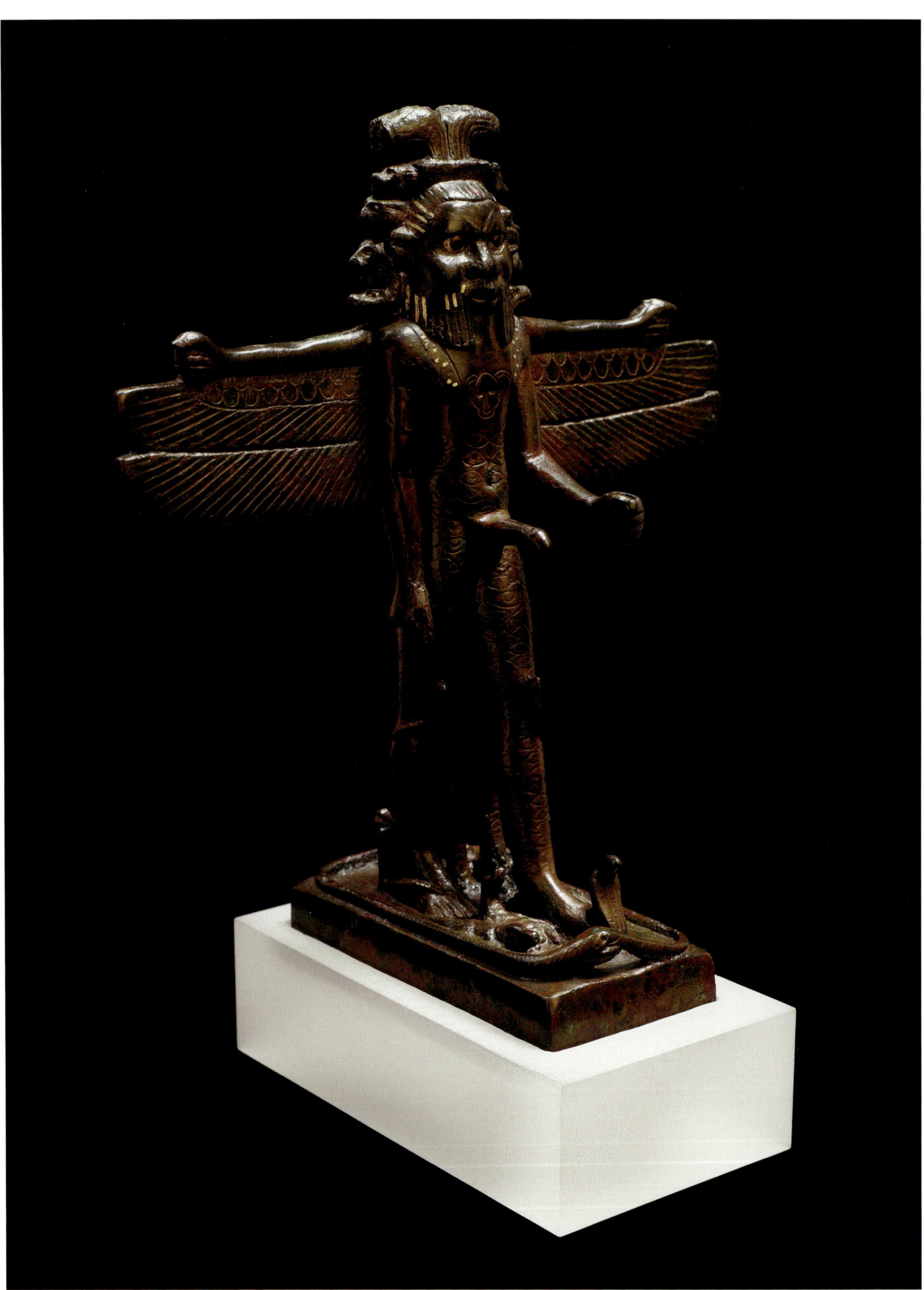

74.

The State God Amun and his Bas, or Multiple Manifestations of his Elemental Powers

Dynasty XXVI–Ptolemaic Period, 664–30 BC
Bronze inlaid with gold
Height 8 3/8 in.
Inv. no. EG-170

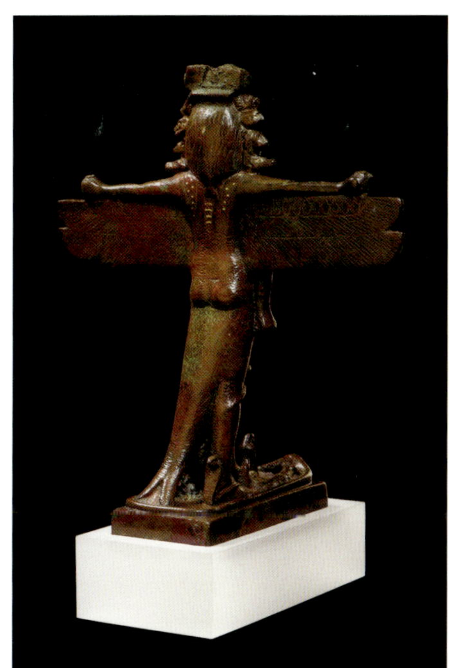

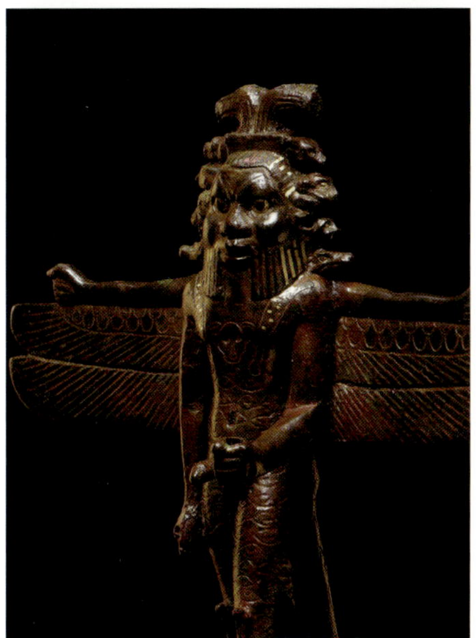

This statuette is perhaps over the top, even within the design principles that admit the creation of composite creatures, because of its reliance upon combining into one image a seemingly large number of disparate elements. The principal figure is that of a nude, ithyphallic male, striding forward on an integral, rectangular base with his left foot advanced. His right arm is held down alongside his body, with its fisted hand resting on his thigh. His left arm is bent at the elbow and extended perpendicularly in front of his body, its fisted hand hollow, into which was set a now-missing attribute. The torso and legs of his nude body are ornamented with any number of incised, small eyes. His only accessory appears to be a necklacelike affair, designed as a strap over each shoulder, to which is attached the head of a panther, incised in the middle of his pectoral region. These straps, all inlaid with gold, are also visible at the back.

He is provided with an additional set of arms, their fisted hands once holding attributes. These are arranged perpendicularly to his body and rest on top of the first of two parallel pairs of wings, their feather patterning incised.

The outer edge of the top of the integral plinth is framed by an ouroboros, a serpent with its tail placed into its mouth. A pair of scorpions and another of crocodiles rest on this base. A cobra wraps its body around his right leg, with its head appearing in front of his left, while two others are attached to his lower legs with their heads resting at the level of his knees. The wings of a bird are attached to his lower buttocks as if to serve as a tail.

The design of the head and face of this composite beast, parts of which are inlaid with gold, resembles that which is frequently associated with Bes-images (compare cat. 63 and cat. 80). Smaller heads of four pairs of animals appear to protrude from each side of his larger head: a baboon, a falcon, a lion, and a canine on the right, and a bovine, ram, cat, and crocodile on the left. There was an additional attribute attached to the top of his head, of which only fragmentary traces now remain.

Earlier scholars, seduced by the seemingly identical appearance of all heads of Bes-images, identified this composite being as a hypostasis of one of the forms of those genii. Such an interpretation, however, fails to take into account the polyvalent nature of ancient Egyptian philosophical discourse, based on hieroglyphs, in which any one physical image may connote a number of different and, on occasion, contradictory meanings. The identification of this figure as a depiction of the state god Amun is confirmed by the appearance of identical figures, with all of their complex imagery intact, found on papyri where the identification and role of this hypostasis of Amun are specifically mentioned. All of these disparate images are pressed into service to suggest in visible terms his universal omnipotence. The expression of those myriad powers is to be found in each of the disparate elements, which are combined in this statuette of Amun, who is described in some ancient Egyptian texts as *the lord of the sky, the earth, the netherworld, the water, and the mountains. He is the one who keeps his name mysterious before the gods and who is a giant of a million cubits in height, who fastens the sky on his head...the one from whose nose air emerges to give life to all noses, the one who rises as the sun to brighten the earth, from the effluxes of whose body the inundation flows to give life to every mouth.*

The dating of this statuette of Amun is suggested by the date of the aforementioned papyri on which identical figures of this aspect of Amun are found and described.

Published: Chappaz and Chamay, *Reflets du divin*, 2001, pp. 118–19, no. 110.

References: Koenig, *Magie*, 1994, pp. 127–28; Brooklyn, Brooklyn Museum 47.218.156: Sauneron, *Le papyrus magique*, 1970; Paris, Musée du Louvre E11554: Ziegler, *Naissance de l'écriture*, 1996, p. 304; and Ziegler, "Jalons," 1996, pp. 26–38, especially p. 32.

75.

A Statuette of a Mother Goddess Nursing her Divine Son

Dynasty XXVI–Ptolemaic Period, 664–30 BC
Bronze
Height 15 5/16 in.
Inv. no. EG-128

This cast bronze statuette represents a goddess wearing a wig. The head of the vulture belonging to that headdress replaces the uraeus on her forehead. A modius in the shape of a circlet composed of uraei rests on her head and anchors the attribute of cow's horns framing a sun disk (compare cat. 29 and cat. 77).

The nude child-god, a young boy so designated by the side-lock of youth on the right side of his head, whose forehead is adorned with a uraeus, sits on his mother's lap with his legs together and arms parallel to the sides of his body. In keeping with the design tenets for such group compositions, the principal view of each figure remains the frontal one. Consequently, the child is seated in such a way that the vertical axis of his body is perpendicular to that of his mother. The design tenets for each figure are respected, with the result that the one is not integrated into the other. It is for this reason that the mother independently cups her left breast with her right hand and that breast makes no contact with her son's lips.

Without an accompanying inscription or other independent evidence, it is unwise to insist on the identification of these two figures, although received wisdom habitually regards them as the goddess Isis nursing her divine son Horus (compare cat. 29).

The feet of the goddess rest on an integral rectangular plinth, the bottom of which is provided with a thin, rectangular tenon for insertion into a now-missing larger base. This suggests that this group may have been part of an even larger composition. Dating is suggested by any number of stylistically similar examples.

Published: Chappaz and Chamay, *Reflets du divin*, 2001, p. 101, no. 187.

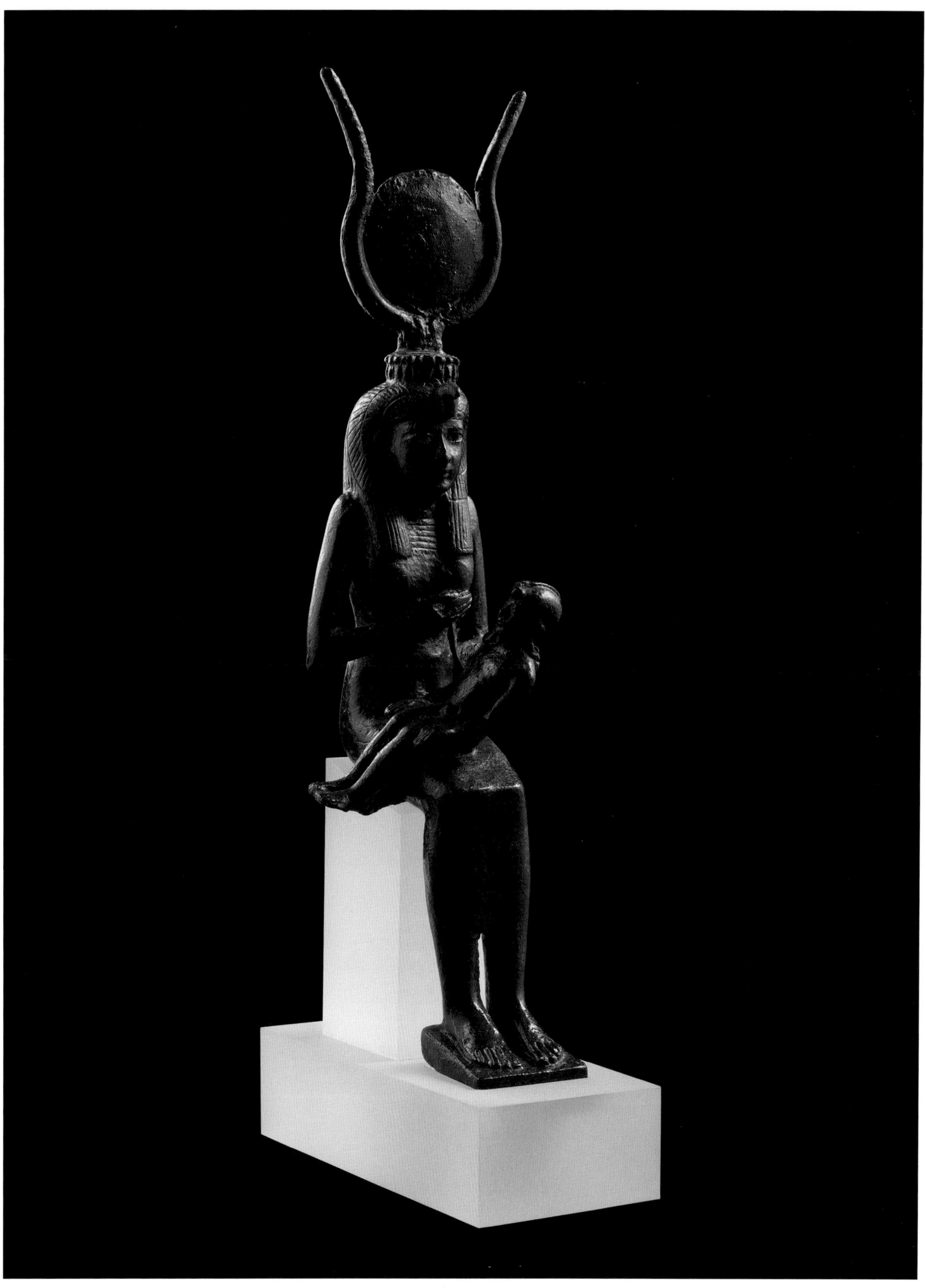

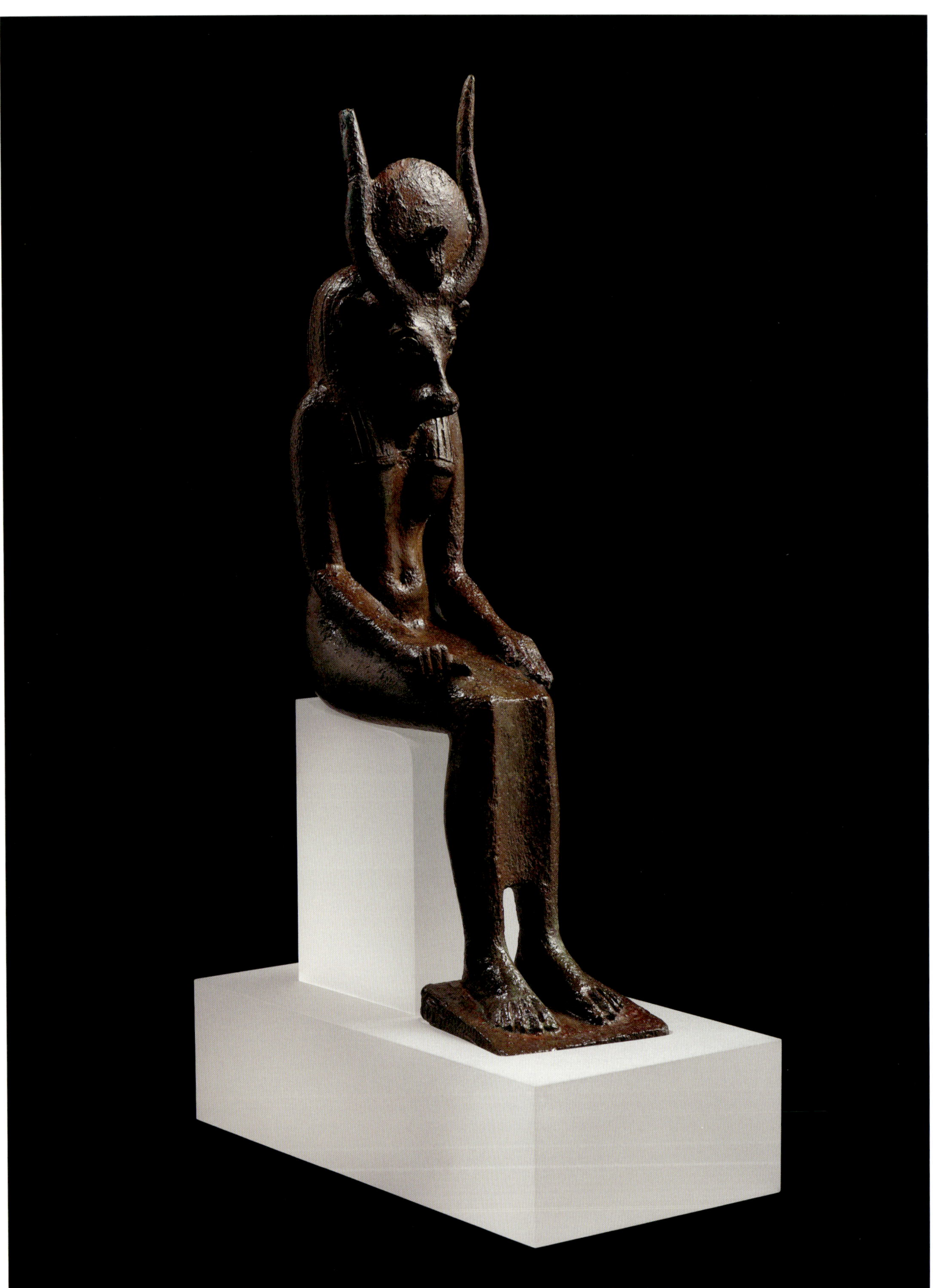

76.

Statuette of a Cow-Headed Goddess, Identified as Hesat

Dynasty XXVI–Ptolemaic Period, 664–30 BC
Bronze with gold inlays
Height 11 7/16 in.
Inv. no. EG-31

In accordance with the design tenets of hieroglyphs that admit composite signs, so, too, this statuette is designed as a composite beast, in which the head of a bovine is combined with a human female body. So harmonious is the integration of these disparate parts that the resulting figure, a deity, is imbued with a feeling of calm and tranquility.

The statuette was carefully designed and cast, as demonstrated by the detailing of the generalized features of her bovine head, including its ears and the modeling of the fingers and toes of her hands and feet. The goddess is shown seated on a now-missing throne. Her figure has been cast together with a thin, square-shaped plinth on which her feet, placed parallel to one another, rest. She is depicted wearing the time-honored, form-fitting sheath and a tripartite, striated wig, the lappets of which appear to end in a horizontal band, perhaps suggesting a ribbon. Her attribute consists of a large sun disk, fronted by a uraeus, framed by the tall, tapering horns of a cow. The rectangular tang affixed near the back of the integral plinth suggests that this figure was inserted into a larger base, which may have included additional figures.

The polyvalent nature of hieroglyphs extends to images of the real world, so that the cow was the hypostasis of several goddesses, foremost among whom were Hathor and Isis, the latter considered to be the mother of the Apis Bull (compare cat. 31 and cat. 85). Without an accompanying inscription, it is risky and unscientific to insist upon the strict identification of any such cow-headed goddess. The goddess represented on this statuette, however, is incontrovertibly assured to be Hesat by the inscription in hieroglyphs on the base, which, although possessed of difficulties, nevertheless can be translated in part as

> *the pure priest, the overseer of the secrets of the goddess Hesat,*
> *whose name is Hotepimen, the son of Khary[?].*

Hotepimen dedicated this statuette to Hesat, in whose cult he served. This goddess was identified as the mother of the Mnevis Bull, regarded as a hypostasis of the sun god of Heliopolis.

A dating of this statuette is suggested both by its style and by the name of its owner/dedicator.

Published: Chappaz and Chamay, *Reflets du divin,* 2001, p. 106, no. 93.

77.

A Goddess with Her Aniconic Child

Dynasty XXVI–Ptolemaic Period, 664–30 BC
Bronze
Height 9 5/16 in.
Inv. no. EG-90

The artistic tenets that govern the processes by which ancient Egyptian three-dimensional images were created are magnificently brought to bear on the subject and meaning of this most enigmatic of images. Those techniques rely on modeling the figure in broad planes, to which are added linear adjuncts for the articulation of detail. In the case of this particular statuette, linear detail has, for the most part, been suppressed, and the broadly modeled planes have been designed in such a way as to suggest the presence of concealed forms which, when understood, elucidate the meaning of the image (compare cat. 67).

The image represents a figure so completely covered in an enveloping shroudlike sheet, which even conceals the integral rectangular plinth on which the figure is placed, so that only its head is revealed. The round face exhibits somewhat idealizing features, although one might argue that the nose is wide and the lips thick. The head is framed by a tripartite, but otherwise unadorned, wig, with its lappets extending to the tops of circular protrusions on the chest that can only be understood as breasts and identify the figure as female. This is confirmed by the presence of the head of a vulture, replacing the expected uraeus, on her forehead. The vulture, so positioned, is generally an exclusive feminine insignia (compare cat. 101) as is the circlet, sculpted for the most part in the round, in the form of a modius resting on the crown of the head (compare cat. 29), to which a sun disk framed by cow's horns is affixed (compare cat. 75).

Vertical forms to either side of the figure are detectable beneath the shroudlike sheet, which suggests a throne and back pillar, and indicates that the female figure is seated. The massive form occupying the space between the left side of the figure's torso and the frontal plane must be understood as a child, which in ancient Egyptian art habitually sits at a right angle to its mother's lap and torso. That identification enables one to visualize her right hand offering her breast in a nursing gesture (compare cat. 29 and cat. 75).

The image appears to be unique and has no ready parallels within the repertoire of Egyptian statuary, but it does relate to a small group of iconographic examples in two-dimensional representations, confined for the most part to Thebes. These are now recognized as depicting the god Amun in his aniconic, or nonrepresentational, manifestation, likewise concealed from view, designed as forms subtly discernible beneath an enveloping shroudlike covering. These aniconic images of the state god Amun at Thebes convey his powers of regeneration and allude to the universal birth of the cosmos. One can argue that the representation under discussion is its analogue. This aniconic image of a nursing mother can profitably be regarded as an equivalent image, in which universal birth and concepts of regeneration are couched in terms of the female. The recognition by the ancient Egyptian theologians that human procreation is only possible if the male and female components are equally contributory to inception, confirms this equivalence. It is for this reason that a woman could legitimately take her place as pharaoh.

The dating of this figure is problematic, but one suggests it should be assigned to the Late Period on the basis of its general style.

Published: Aubert and Aubert, *Bronzes et or*, 2001, p. 223; Chappaz and Chamay, *Reflets du divin*, 2001, p. 108, no. 96.

References: Daressy, "Nouvelle forme," 1908, pp. 64ff; Kuhlmann, *Das Ammoneion*, 1988, pp. 111–25; Traunecker, *Coptos. Hommes et dieux*, 1992, pp. 202–5.

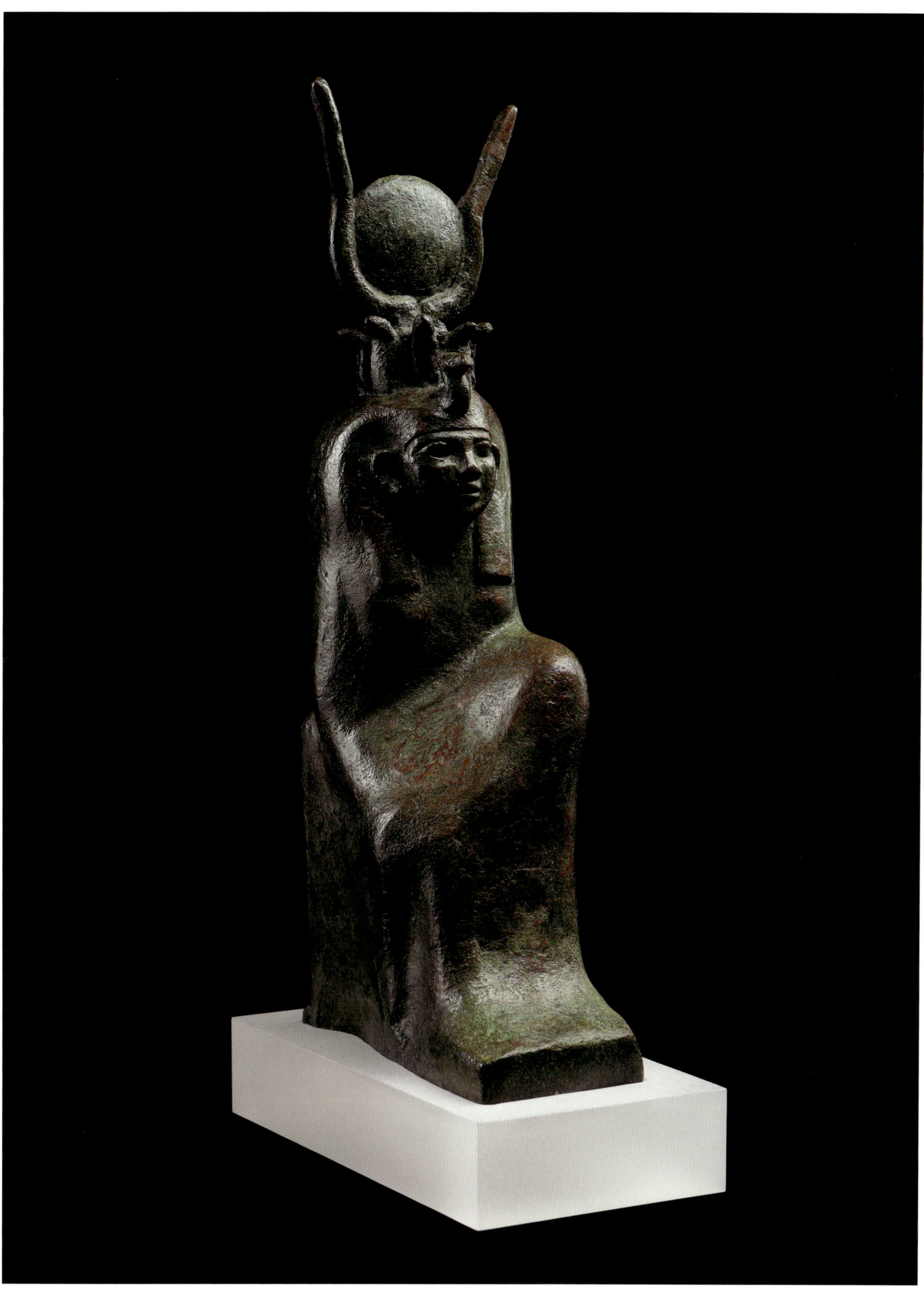

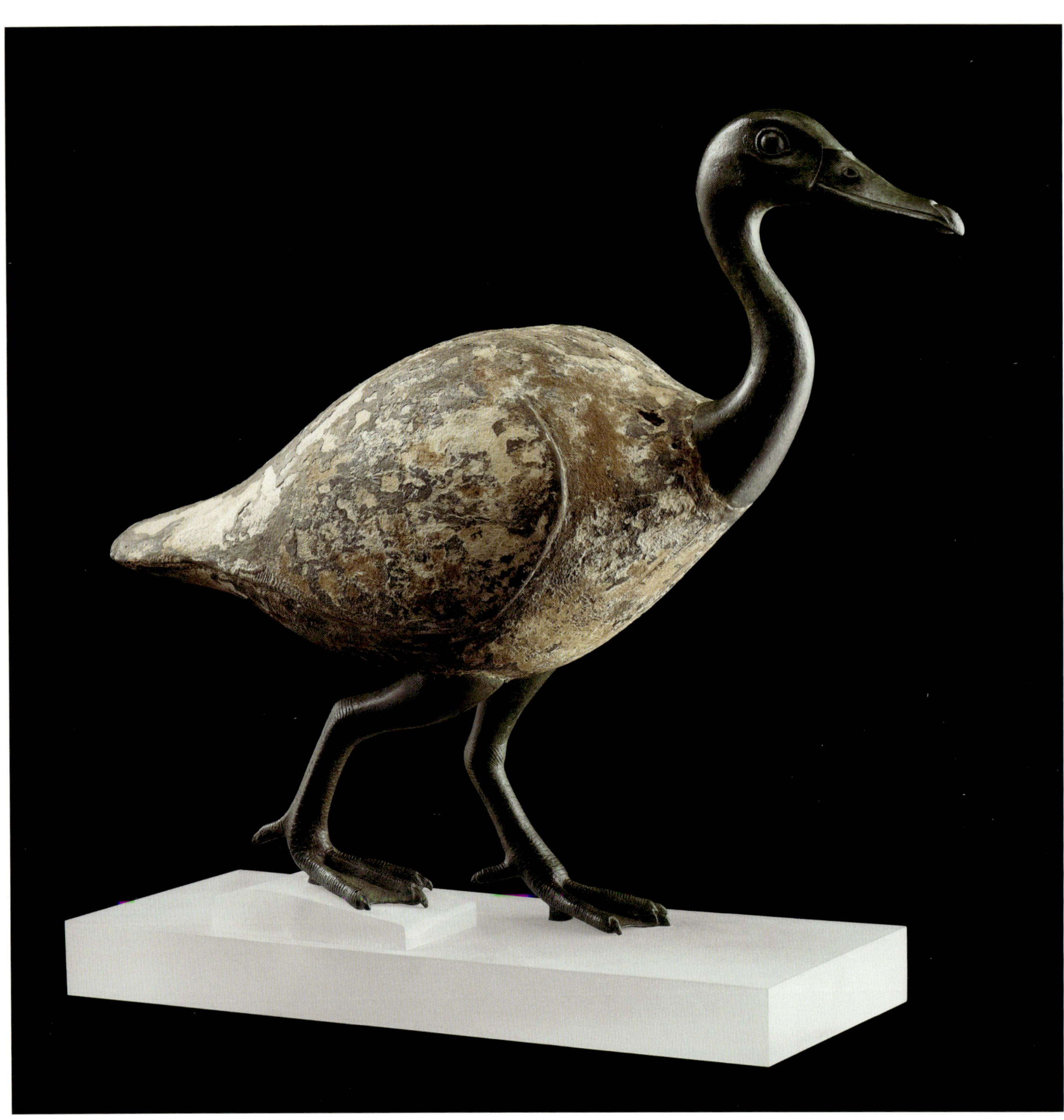

78.

A Statuette of a Goose

Dynasty XVIII, 1554–1305 BC
Gessoed and painted wood with bronze
Length 13 in.
Inv. no. EG-67

This convincing representation of a goose, captured in mid-stride with its head erect and eyes alert, is an excellent example of just how accomplished the ancient Egyptians were in capturing the essence of the animal depicted. The wooden body, modeled in broad planes, has been coated with a layer of gesso, a type of plaster, which was then painted, if the traces of black pigment can be so interpreted. The legs and their webbed feet, and the head, from the bottom of its neck to the end of its beak, have been separately cast in bronze, but have been modeled in broad planes with details incised, before being attached to the body. The use of bronze connotes harmony over chaos, reinforcing the regenerative character of the wood. These characteristics suggest that this goose is a hypostasis of a deity, rather than a farm animal (compare cat. 79).

Two very similar statuettes of geese have been discovered in the Valley of the Kings. The first was found standing in the southeastern corner of Burial Chamber (D) in the Tomb of Tutankhamun, while the second was found in the Sarcophagus Hall (H) in the Tomb of the pharaoh Tuthmosis III. Both of these geese are regarded as hypostases of the god Amun. These images were doubtless placed into those royal tombs because Amun's status as the supreme deity of the Theban pantheon during Dynasty XVIII and his associations as the prime creator were compatible with the aspired resurrection of those pharaohs. One can, therefore, cautiously suggest that this wooden and bronze statuette of a goose dates to the same period, and might even have come from a royal tomb in the Valley of the Kings.

Published: Aubert and Aubert, *Bronzes et or*, 2001, p. 260; Chappaz and Chamay, *Reflets du divin*, 2001, p. 29, no. 11; Künzi et al., *Les trésors*, n.d., fig. 164, pp. 110–11.

References: Wiese and Brodbeck, *Golden Beyond*, 2000, pp. 88–89, with fig. 14, and p. 98, with fig. 36, respectively.

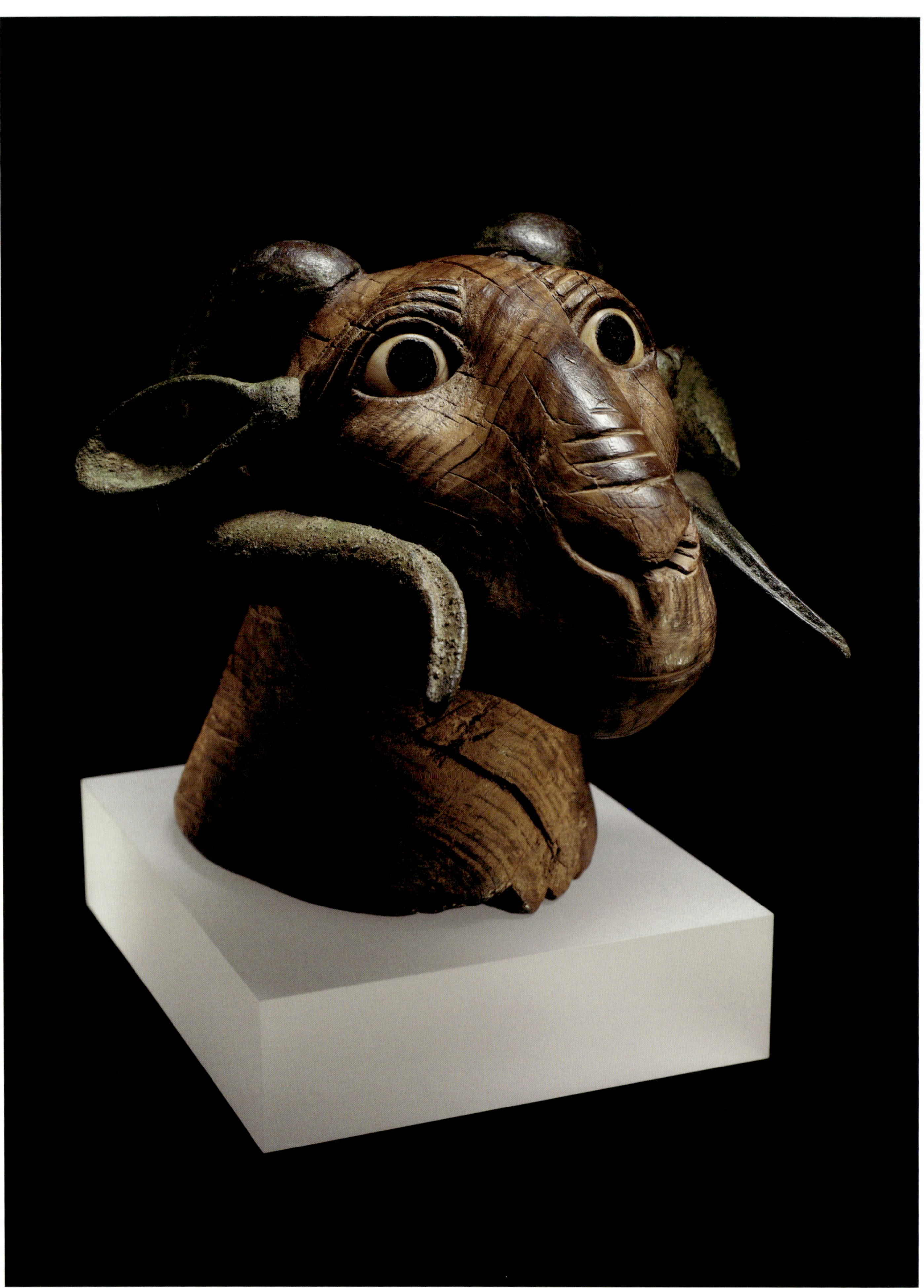

79.

A Head of a Ram

Dynasty XXV–XXVII, 745–404 BC
Wood with black-and-white stone inlays and bronze additions
Length 7 5/8 in.
Inv. no. EG-28

Although sculpted in wood, the processes utilized for the creation of this head of a ram are consistent with those used for stone statues and bronze statuettes. The figure is modeled in broad planes, here more readily evident in the formation of the forehead and muzzle, and then polished. That polishing removed all traces of the tool(s) used, so that the surfaces, thus smoothed, might be articulated with linear adjuncts detailing the regions around both eyes and the muzzle. The eyes themselves were inlaid with an opaque white (alabaster?) and black stone. Both the horns and the ears around which they curve were separately cast in bronze and then attached to the head. The use of secondary materials in the form of stone inlays and bronze additions is one of the hallmarks of ancient Egyptian art, which imbued objects with the symbolic properties inherent in those materials. The stones suggest permanence and the bronze harmony over chaos, reinforcing the regenerative character of wood from which the head was principally made (compare cat. 78).

Such connotations are suitable for the image of a deity, rather than for one of a farm animal. Although the ram served as the hypostasis for several gods of the Egyptian pantheon, the horns curling around the ears clearly identify this object as the hypostasis of the god Amun (compare cat. 83).

The head represents a complete, finished work of art and is not to be considered a fragment, as the smoothed, level surface of the bottom of the neck reveals. That surface exhibits a mortise in its center, indicating that the head was attached to another object. The angle of that break and the presence of the mortise suggest that it was not fastened to the body of a ram, but rather served another function, attached to either the prow or stern of a sacred boat which priests carried in procession (fig. 27). The transition zone between the neck of this ram and the prow or stern of the vessel was doubtless effected by the presence of an *aegis* (compare cat. 73), as indicated in two-dimensional depictions of such sacred boats (compare cat. 70).

Such figureheads were the visual means by which the largely illiterate agricultural community of the land could identify the deity whose closed and covered shrine was placed on the deck of those processional boats. Numerous two-dimensional vignettes sculpted on the walls of temples dating from the New Kingdom to the Ptolemaic Period feature such figure-headed sacred barques, and provide us with the suggested appearance of the one to which this head was attached.

Although one should always exercise an enhanced degree of caution and skepticism when scientific testing is offered for either authenticating or dating an ancient work of art, Carbon 14 testing of the wood by Professor G. Bonani of the Ecole polytechnique fédérale de Zurich suggests a date for this object between 765–414 BC. This dating gains confirmation from that suggested for the head of lion with bronze secondary elements in the collections of the Brooklyn Museum.

Published: Anonymous, "La porte du rêve," 2007, p. 40; Chappaz and Chamay, *Reflets du divin*, 2001, pp. 30–31, no. 12; Künzi et al., *Les trésors*, n.d., fig. 165, pp. 112–13.

References: Cooney, "Persian Influence," 1965, pp. 39–63, for Brooklyn 37.261E.; Dunand et al., *Des animaux*, 2005, p. 39, fig. 20.

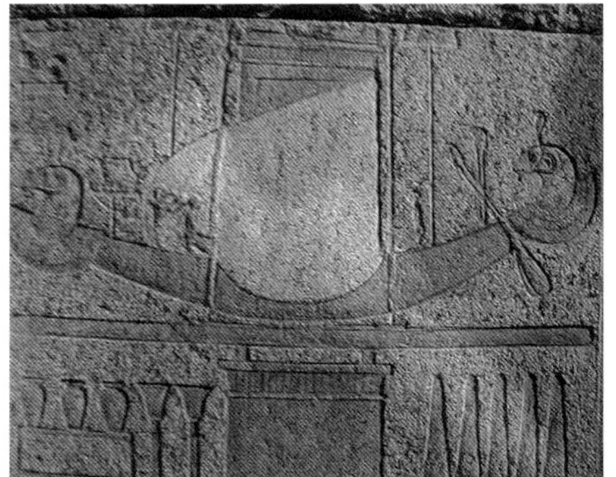

Figure 27
Detail of the Sacred Barque of the God Amun, Prow and Stern Adorned with Heads of Rams, from the Granite Sanctuary at Karnak, Macedonian Period

80.

A Bes-Image

Dynasty XXVI–Ptolemaic Period, 664–30 BC
Wood inlaid with ivory
Height 4 5/8 in.
Inv. no. EG-37

Depicted standing with his hands, palm open with fingers spread, resting on his knees, and his long phallus trailing on the ground between his legs, this bandy-legged, somewhat grotesquely comical image represents one of several genii within the ancient Egyptian pantheon. All are characterized by a leonine face, framed by ears placed perpendicularly to the head, and an open mouth from which the tongue usually protrudes (compare cat. 59 and cat. 63). The polyvalent nature of ancient Egyptian visual images precludes an exact identification, because this image was pressed into service for the representation of several, virtually identical-looking minor gods. The most popular among those was Bes, whose name has become synonymous in the popular imagination with such images. Unless there is an accompanying inscription specifically identifying such an image or other compelling evidence to support the identification, such figures should more properly be termed Bes-images.

In the past, scholars have proposed any number of origins for this figure, which is now suggested to have developed from a lion-masked priest attested in the Old Kingdom. Such an origin adequately explains the leonine, fishhook-like curls of his mane and the feline markings found on his face and ears. The image is often clothed, as here, in the skin of a big cat, believed to be a leopard because of its ornamentation in the form of circles, thought to represent stylized versions of that animal's spots. The head of that skin was originally sculpted on the ivory inlay placed in the center of the figure's chest, but its features have been effaced. Ivory heightened the protective powers of such figures, as its use as a material for a series of magical knives suggests.

These Bes-images gradually acquired potent, protective characteristics, enhanced by their phalli and tongues sticking out of the mouths, body parts that anthropologists would interpret as apotropaic, intended to ward off evil by frightening away malevolent forces. The protective characteristics of Bes-images, employed on pieces of furniture such as beds and headrests (compare cat. 59) that came into direct contact with the bodies of elite members of society, were transferred to the user, shielding them from nocturnal dangers.

Mirror disks were anciently regarded as images of the sun and the moon, celestial bodies whose daily and monthly cycles symbolized both rebirth and the recurrence of cosmic cycles. Some handles of these bronze mirrors designed in the form of female figures exhibit a Bes-image on one of their thighs, which some interpret as a tattoo. Exactly this same type of body decoration is seen on figures of women painted on walls over benches found in elite homes of the Ramesside Period. These benches are suggested to have been used for birthing. Such contexts clearly reveal the role of these Bes-images as protectors of pregnant women and their neonates.

Although extremely popular and frequently represented in art, these genii were never the recipients of major temples in the pharaonic periods, although Bes does appear to have been the principal deity in a temple dated to the Ptolemaic and Roman Periods, erected at El-Bawiti in the Bahariya Oasis.

Stylistic comparison with other Bes-images, some of which are inscribed, suggest the dating for this particular work.

Published: Chappaz and Chamay, *Reflets du divin*, 2001, p. 121, no. 113.

References: Altenmüller, *Die Apotropaia*, 1965; Hawass, *Valley*, 2000, pp. 168–73; Meeks, "Le nom du dieu Bes," 1992, 14ff; Romano, "Bes-Image," 1980, pp. 39–56.

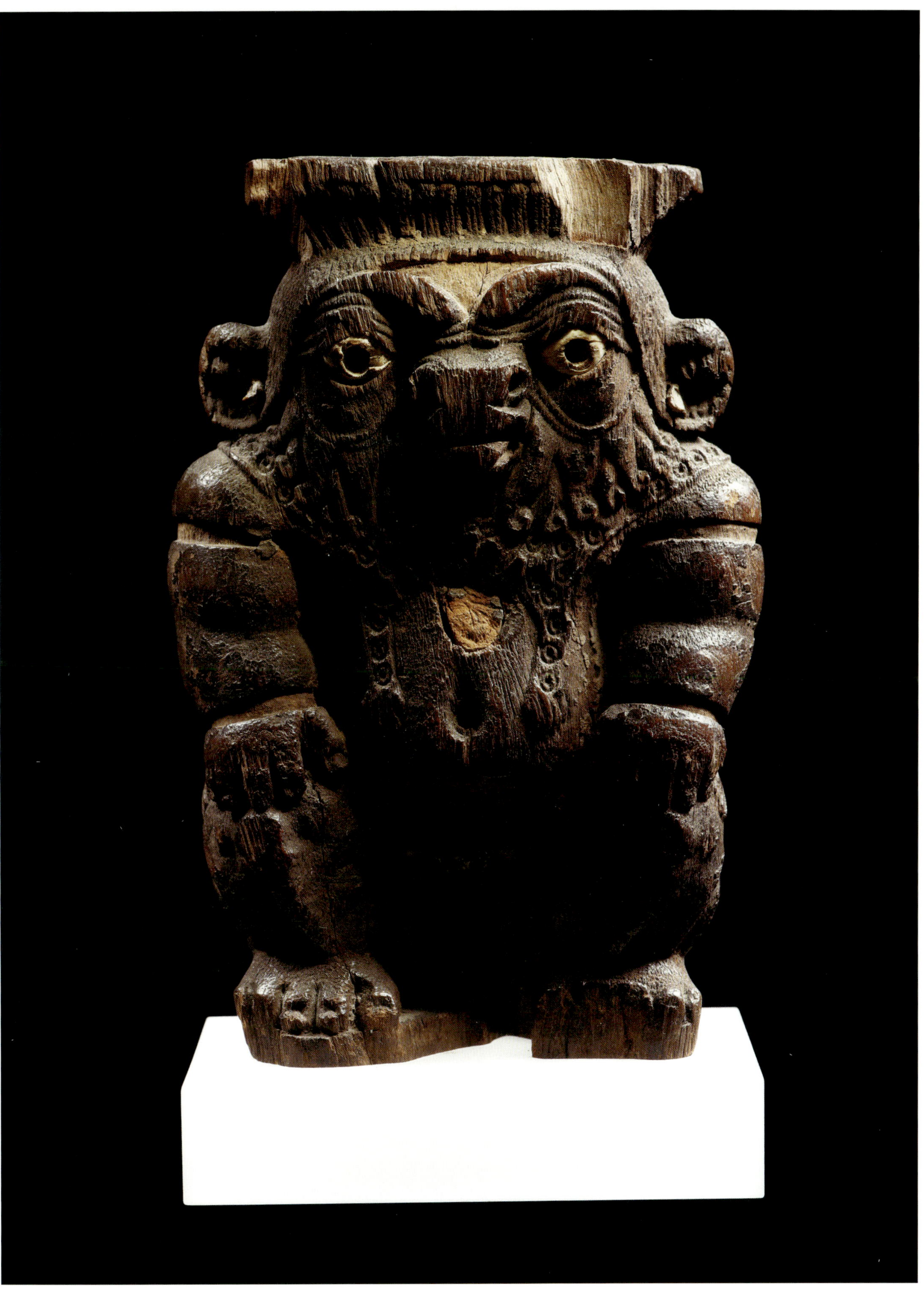

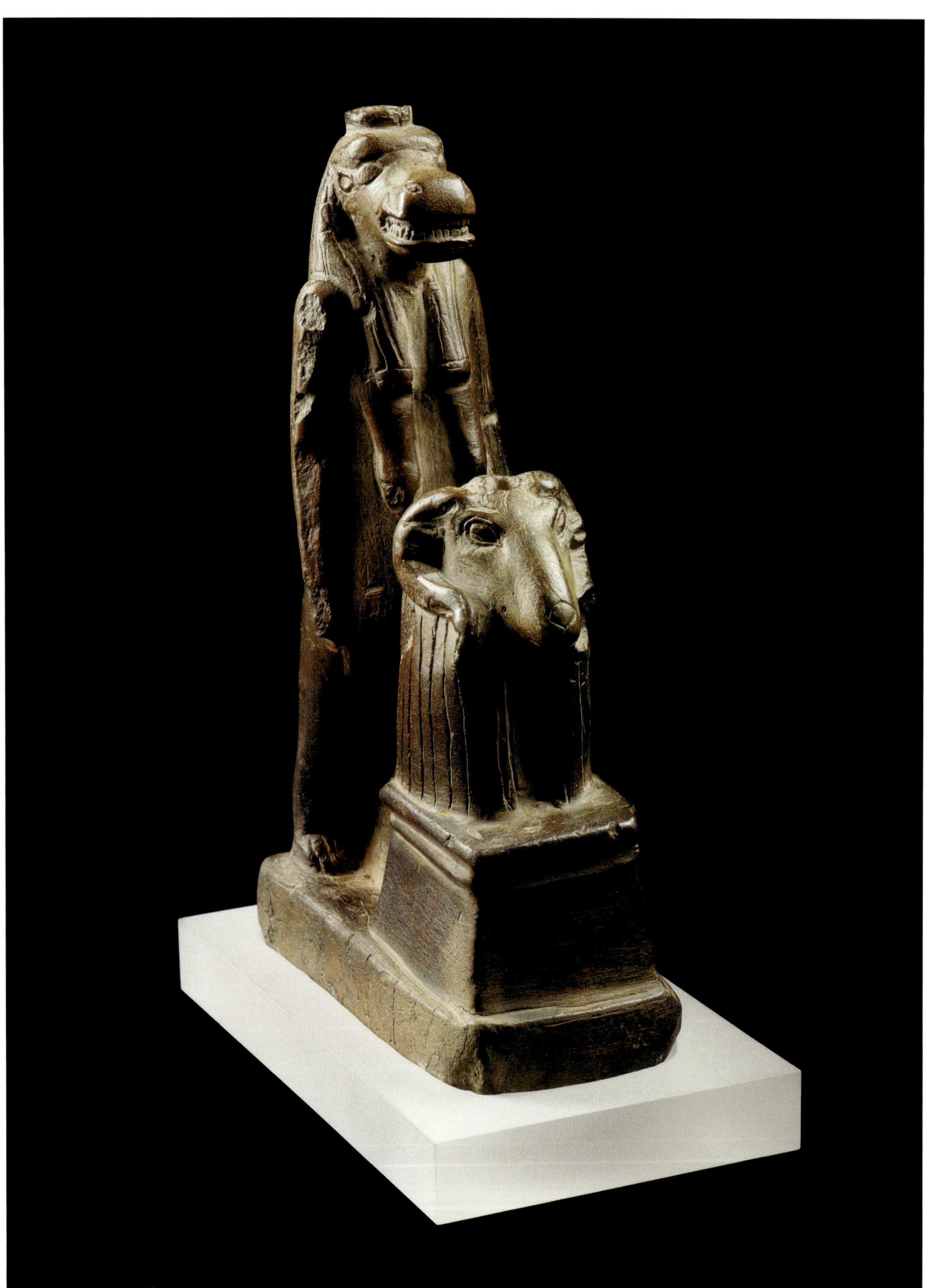

81.

The Goddess Taweret Offering Amun

Dynasty XVIII–XX, 1554–1080 BC
Graywacke (schist)
Height 6 ⅝ in.
Inv. no. EG-293

The principal figure is a representation in the round of one of several composite deities, designed with the body of a hippopotamus, to whose chest is added a pair of pendulous human, female breasts that combined with her swollen lower abdomen to suggest pregnancy. Her arms and legs are modifications of the legs of a lioness. The vertical line of her spine is designed as the tail of a crocodile, here ornamented with a chevron pattern. Such figures are traditionally depicted open-mouthed, generally revealing teeth, which seem to be omitted here. The combination of these various zoomorphic elements was intended to imbue the figure with specific powers.

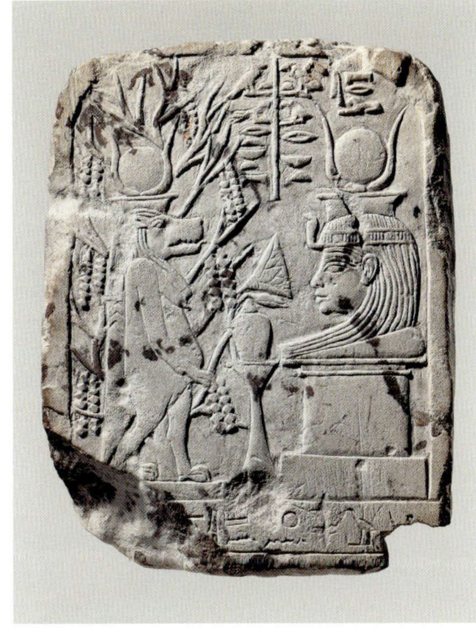

Figure 28
Votive stela with figures of Goddesses Taweret and Mut of Isheru.
Egyptian, possibly from Thebes, Dier el-Medina, New Kingdom, reign of Amenhotep III, ca. 1390–1352 BC, limestone with paint
Metropolitan Museum of Art, New York
Dodge Fund, 1947; 47.105.4

The figure stands upon an integral, rectangular plinth, in front of which is a naos, or shrine, to which she is joined by a bridge of negative stone. A ram's head has been placed on its top. The horns of that ram identify it as a hypostasis of Amun (compare cat. 79 and cat. 83).

This group composition may be explained by reference to a stela in The Metropolitan Museum of Art, New York, reportedly from Deir el-Medineh in Western Thebes (fig. 28), which is dated to the New Kingdom, with which this group is roughly contemporary. Its figural scene represents a standing hippopotamus to the left facing a naos, or shrine, on the top of which is the head of a goddess. This scene may be regarded as a two-dimensional variant of the group under discussion. The caption identifies the hippopotamus goddess and head of the goddess as, respectively,

> *Taweret, the Mistress of Heaven*
>
> *Mut, the Great One, the Mistress of Isheru [a sacred lake in her precinct]*

The depiction of the goddess Mut on this stela in the form of a female head divorced from her body is not exceptional (compare cat. 86 and cat. 87). The hieroglyphic basis of ancient Egyptian art permits the use of parts separated from the whole to serve as both independent hieroglyphs as well as independent motifs, each possessed of specific meaning. It is within this long tradition that use of the heads of animals and humans as independent works of art arises. Such depictions are not to be regarded as fragments, but as complete works of art (compare cat. 14).

The literal meaning of the name Taweret, *the great one*, symbolizes both her enormous size as well as the extent of her powers. She is the ancient Egyptian composite goddess of childbirth. The interpretation of the stela in New York, then, must be understood within this tradition, although its meaning is complex in the extreme. Certain details, such as the fact that Taweret is standing in the shade of an acacia tree, are significant because this tree is associated with ancient Egyptian medical texts intended to alleviate uterine complaints. Consequently, the images and motifs of this stela are imbued with powerful magical and medical overtones. It appears to have been dedicated by an elite woman named Khonsu, who served in the clergy of Theban Amun, in hopes of either a safe delivery or the wellbeing of her neonate.

The theme of the group under discussion may very well be intended to harness the powers of both Taweret and Amun for the benefit of its owner. Objects featuring the head of the ram of Amun in certain contexts from later periods of Egypt's history demonstrably function as cult objects in sanatoria associated with curative powers. The curative powers of Taweret, specified in the stela of New York, might then be combined with those assigned to Amun to reinforce the desired cure of the individual who dedicated this group.

Published: Anonymous, "La porte du rêve," 2007, p. 43.

References: New York, Metropolitan Museum of Art 47.105.4: Hayes, *Scepter II*, 1959, pp. 384–86, with fig. 242.

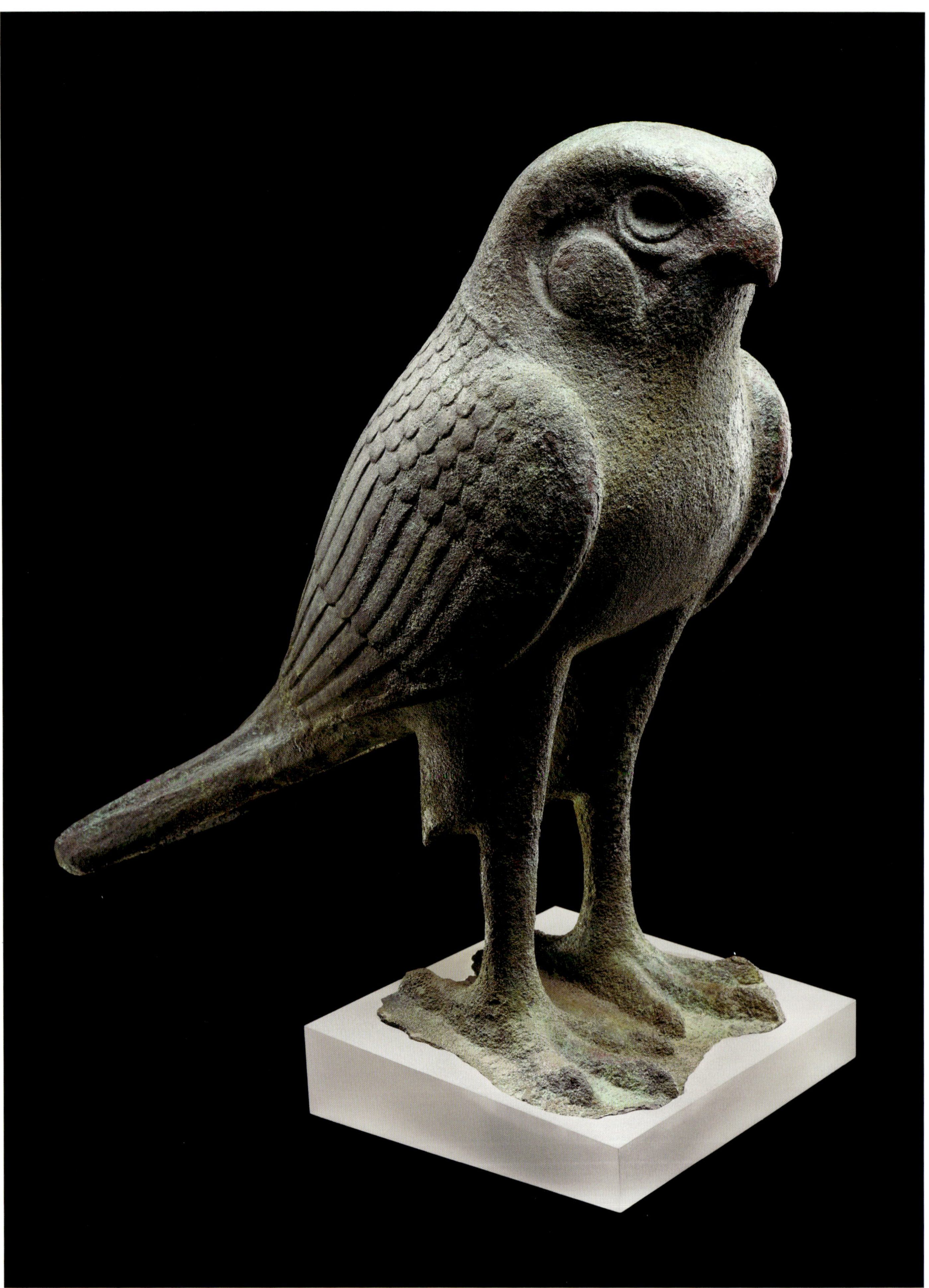

82.

The God Horus as a Falcon

Dynasty XXI–XXV, 1080–655 BC
Bronze, originally with inlaid eyes
Height 18 in.
Inv. no. EG-187

This statue is modeled in broad planes with linear detail reserved for the definition of its feather patterns. It originally stood on an integral plinth, a small portion of which still remains attached to the bottom of its talons. Its eyes were originally inlaid. On the basis of its scale and certain other indicators, one can suggest a dating for this statuette into the Third Intermediate Period, when such large-scale, cast-bronze images were routinely created.

The polyvalence inherent in ancient Egyptian images regards the falcon as a hypostasis of several gods, among whom are Horus, Re-horakhty, and Montu. Without an accompanying inscription or other independent data, an exact identification is moot.

Nevertheless, for the sake of argument, one may tentatively suggest this raptor is a depiction of the falcon-god Horus (compare cat. 55).

The ancient Egyptians observed the falcon to be the highest-flying bird in their environment, and thus associated it with Horus, the sky god par excellence. His nature also embodied concepts of royal power and kingship. Young pharaohs might be styled as

the young falcon who is in its nest

whereas pharaohs after their coronation might likewise be regarded as

the falcon who takes his place within the palace.

Within such a polyvalent, theological framework, the pharaoh is The Living Horus, identified with the dutiful son who avenged the death of his father, Osiris, in a duel that injured his left eye.

One episode of that duel was the appropriation of the particular markings of the falcon's eyes for mathematical notation used by the ancient Egyptians for calculating measures of wheat and dimensions of land. Each of those distinctive feather patterns became a hieroglyph for a specific fraction, based on a system of halving values (fig. 29). The symbols and their accompanying values are shown here and represent the left eye of Horus, injured and torn apart by his uncle Seth (compare cat. 61). Thoth restored his eye, but the sum of the parts equaled 63/64. The missing 1/64 required to make the eye whole was presumably supplied magically by Thoth. This appropriation speaks volumes about just how integrated each element of this polyvalent system of philosophical discourse was, and how those disparate elements were harmoniously introduced into a system in which the tangible and concrete, so essential for the furthering of the plot, were reapplied in a seemingly very different context with new meanings, the significance of which exactly paralleled the theme of the plot from which they were taken. This concept was furthered because the waning and waxing of the moon might also be regarded as analogous to the injured eye restored to health, and the sum of the fractions magically almost equaling one.

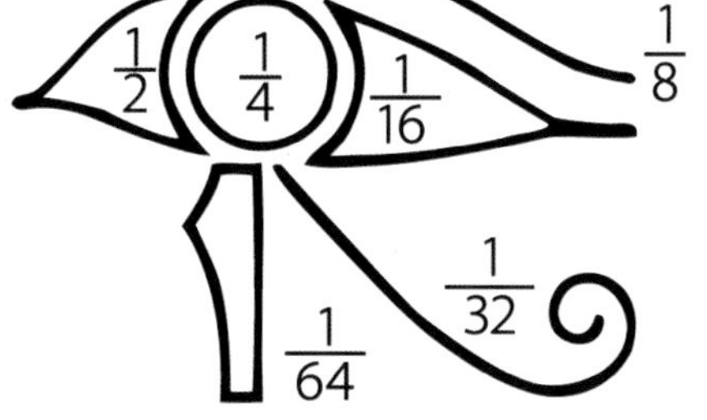

Figure 29
Detail of the fractions made from the eye of a falcon, an illustration from Sir Alan Gardiner, Egyptian Grammar, 3rd edition, Oxford/London, 1969, page 197

Published: Chappaz and Chamay, *Reflets du divin*, 2001, pp. 22–23, no. 3; Künzi et al., *Les trésors*, n.d., fig. 163, pp. 108–9.

References: Gardiner, *Egyptian Grammar*, 1969, p. 197.

83.

Statuette of a Ram

Dynasty XXV–XXX, 745–342 BC
Bronze
Length 4 ⅜ in.
Inv. no. EG-19

The ram is depicted in a striding pose upon a thin, rectangular plinth, the underside of which exhibits two tangs, square in cross section, which were intended for inserting this object into a larger base as part of a group composition that may have included the figure of a worshipper. The status of the ram as a divine being is conveyed by the broad collar around its neck, its three strands ornamented with stylized floral motifs, and by the striated nemes-headdress, which is a variation of that occasionally worn by pharaohs as comparison with the famous gold mask of Tutankhamun reveals.

The ram, called a ba in ancient Egyptian, which is a homonym for the noun meaning "an elemental power," was venerated because of its fecund nature. Due to the polyvalence inherent in the hieroglyphs, which was shared with objects in the real world, the ram came to represent any number of powerful cosmic generators whose fecundity initiated creation. These creator gods included Amun, Heryshef, Khnum, and a deity known simply as "The Ram [*Ba*] of the Delta City of Mendes."

Zoologically speaking, there were two species of ram known to the ancient Egyptians: *Ovis longipes palaeoaegyptiaca* and *Ovis platyura aegyptiaca*. The latter was introduced at a later date and differed in its appearance from the first, exhibiting a lighter build, a fat tail, and horns that curved in a C-shape around the side and bottom of the ear. This bronze statuette adheres to these physical characteristics, and can unequivocally be identified as a hypostasis of the god Amun, habitually represented as that species with such C-shaped horns (compare cat. 79).

Alexander the Great (compare cat. 15) gained possession of Egypt in the late fourth century BC by entering the country without a battle and accepting the surrender of the Persian satrap, or governor. Although he stayed in Egypt for less than a year, he purposefully traveled to the remote Oasis of Siwa in the Western Desert in order to consult the oracle of Amun. While the details of that consultation are debated, Alexander was afterward regarded as the son of that deity, a filial relationship commemorated on a series of posthumously issued silver coins, on which he is depicted with the C-shaped form of the horn of this ram curling around his own ear.

A break at the top of the nemes-headdress in this statuette indicates the presence of a now-lost attribute that is suggested to have been either a uraeus, the sacred cobra, or a sun disk. Images of this same species of ram line both sides of the dromei, or sacred ways, linking the temples of Karnak to those of Luxor in Thebes. Although shown recumbent and not striding, they represent the god Amun wearing a sun disk fronted by a uraeus. It is perhaps the preferable form for this now-missing attribute.

The design tenets that governed the creation of this cast bronze statuette are identical to those that dictated the processes for sculpting in stone, namely, the basic shape of the three-dimensional image is modeled in broad planes with details added as linear adjuncts. These tenets are clearly exhibited here in the modeling of the body and head of the ram and in the ornamentation of its coat, broad collar, headdress, and details of the eyes, nose, and mouth. The modeling and detail are consummate and can better be appreciated by observing the details of the head and the way in which the genitalia of the ram are not only formed but positioned.

The dating of the ram to the Late Period is suggested by comparison with other representations of this animal.

Published: Chappaz and Chamay, *Reflets du divin*, 2001, p. 32, no. 13; Zürich, Archäologische Sammlung der Universität Zürich L 970: Ägyptologischen Seminar, Basel, *Sethos* 1991, p. 38, color pl. 8 (right).

References: Osborn and Osbornova, *Mammals*, 1998, pp. 192–94, with fig. 13-221 (for the species, *Ovis platyura aegyptiaca*); London, British Museum EA63772: Shaw and Nicholson, *Dictionary*, 1995, p. 181.

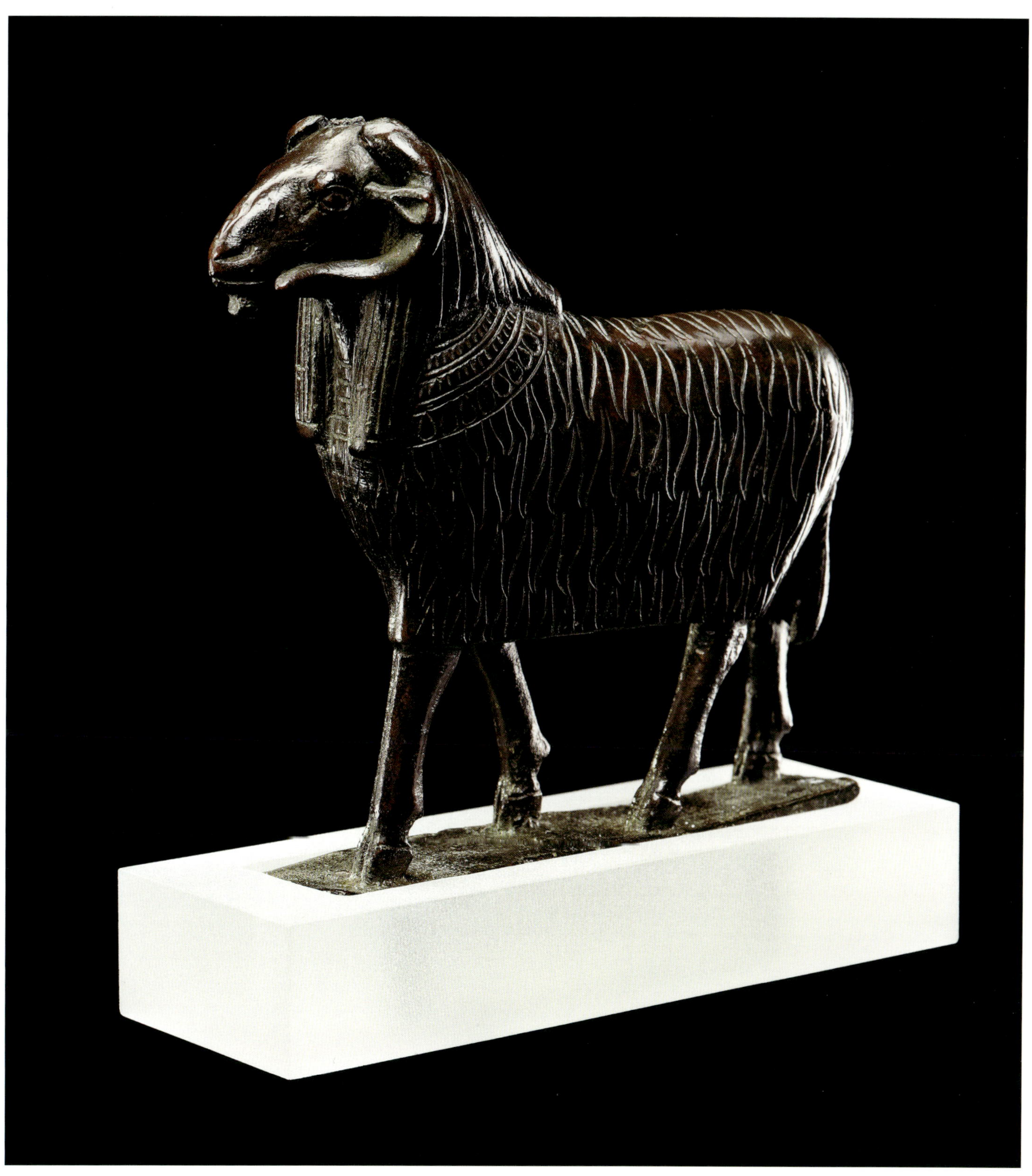

84.

A Statuette of a Striding Hippopotamus

Dynasty XXVI, 664–525 BC
Gilded limestone
Length 3 ¾ in.
Inv. no. EG-191

One of the most endearing characteristics of ancient Egyptian sculpture is its ability to capture the essence of the animal depicted by relying on the subtle merging of plastically conceived planes without recourse to overbearing details. This statuette of a hippopotamus is created in exactly this way. The abstraction inherent in its design conveys this mammal's weight as it lumbers forward in a measured stride on an integral plinth.

The Egyptian lexicon contains several nouns by which this pachyderm was anciently known. The most common were *deb* and *khab*, the latter forming the root of the word meaning, "the bull of the marshland." The hippopotamus might also be called *dns*, "the exceedingly heavy one." Because the hippopotamus might react spontaneously in nature and unexpectedly charge, the Egyptian word meaning "to be impetuous" was often written with the hieroglyph in the form of the head of a hippopotamus.

As a result, the hippopotamus was often regarded as a malevolent beast in ancient Egyptian religion, but the polyvalent nature of ancient Egyptian philosophical discourse allowed for it to acquire positive, benevolent characteristics as well. The benevolent aspect of the hippopotamus was incorporated into the mythology of the goddess Hedjet, "The White (female) Hippopotamus." Her cult was celebrated as early as the Old Kingdom and was particularly popular at Thebes during the New Kingdom. The cult was revived during the Saite Period of Dynasty XXVI.

It is this aspect of the hippopotamus that is celebrated in this statuette. The choice of material, white limestone, clearly indicates that it is a representation of the benevolent goddess Hedjet. The presence of gilding does not negate this identification but rather reinforces it, because gold symbolized the flesh of the deities. The gilding, therefore, implies the divine nature of the animal depicted.

In scale, material, and design this statuette finds its closest parallels in a second, excavated by the German archaeological mission on the Greek island of Samos in the sanctuary of the Greek goddess Hera and presently housed in the museum at Vathy. The archaeological context of this Samian example suggests it is contemporary in date with the Egyptian XXVIth or Saite Dynasty, an era marked by ever-increasing contacts between Greeks and Egyptians.

One can, therefore, suggest that the Samian hippopotamus was dedicated in the sanctuary of Hera as a votive offering by either an Egyptian visiting the island or by a Greek returning home after a trip to Egypt. The white hippopotamus, associated with benevolent characteristics in ancient Egypt, would be an immediately suitable offering for the Greek goddess Hera. This limestone statuette may, therefore, be dated to Dynasty XXVI on the basis of the Samian parallel and would appear to represent the benevolent, white hippopotamus goddess, Hedjet.

Published: For this statuette and its parallel, Vathy, Samos, Archaeological Museum inv.nr. V 1084, see Bianchi, "Hippopotamus," in press; Künzi et al., *Les trésors*, n.d., fig. 166, pp. 114–15.

References: Vernus and Yoyotte, *Bestiaire*, 2005, p. 249.

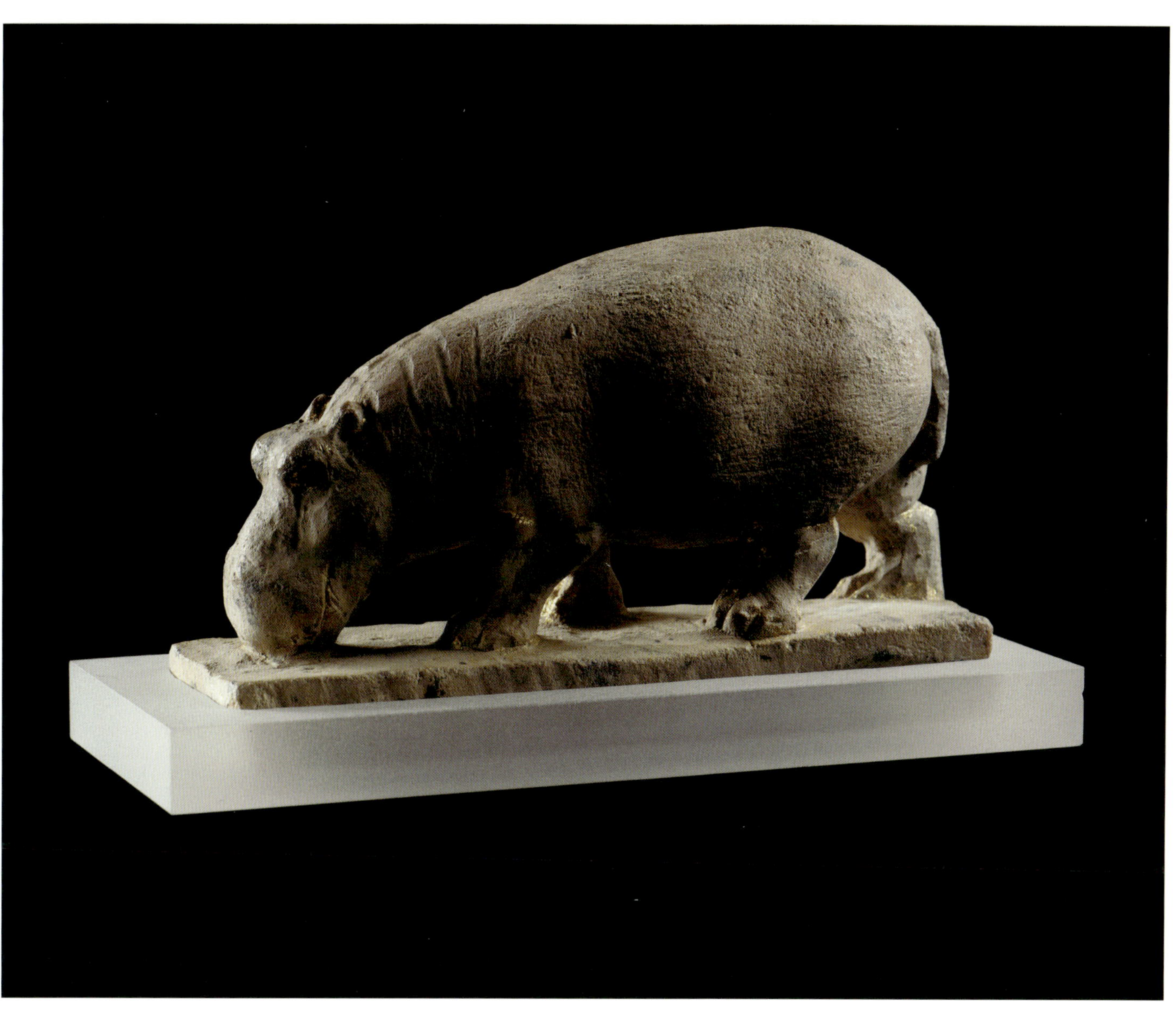

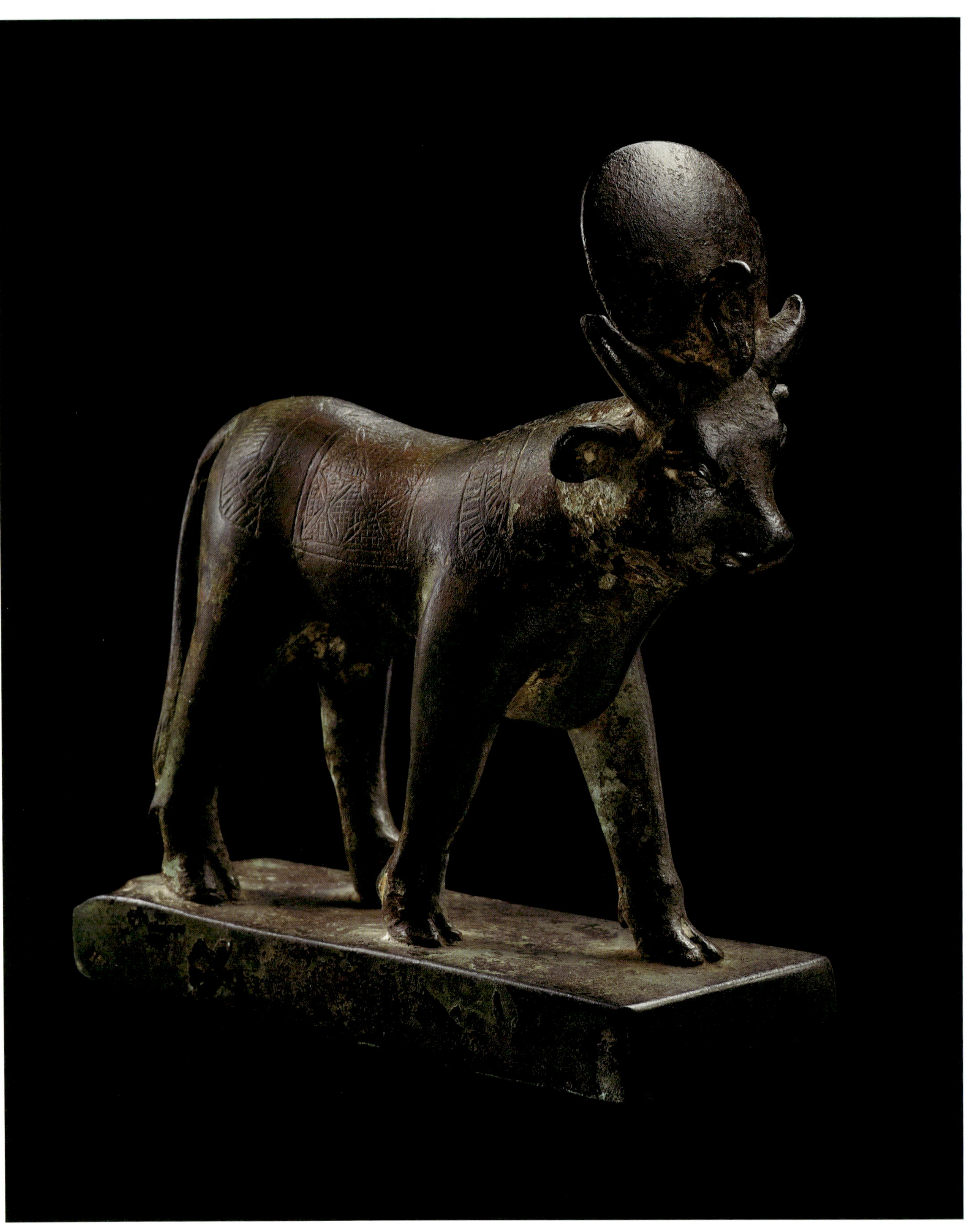

85.

A Large Statuette of the Apis Bull

Dynasty XXVI, 664–525 BC
Bronze with black-and-white stone inlays
Length 6 ⅜ in.
Inv. no. EG-371

This unusually large, cast-bronze statuette of a bull depicts the animal striding forward on a rectangular, integral base. Its proper right eye still retains its original inlays in the form of a white-and-black stone. The muscular forms of its body are modeled in broad planes with incised details so conforming in their general design to the physical characteristics of the Apis Bull that the identification of this statuette as a depiction of that sacred animal is assured. Those characteristics include a diamond-shaped blaze on the forehead, an image of a vulture on the back, and double hairs on its tail. This statuette exhibits additional incised motifs, including both a winged scarab and a tasseled blanket, the crosshatching ornamentation of which suggests an embroidered fabric (compare cat. 73), and a broad collar. His head is adorned with a sun disk fronted by a uraeus.

The Apis Bull was a hypostasis of the creator god of Memphis, and was often regarded as that god's herald. Such bronze statuettes are suggested to have been votive offerings deposited in sanctuaries by pilgrims either asking for prayers to be fulfilled or in thanksgiving for prayers having been answered (compare cat. 31).

Because of the generic nature of ancient Egyptian representations of animals, which seem to remain constant in their design over long periods of time, the dating of bronze statuettes in general and of bronze images of animals in particular is exceedingly difficult, especially when they are not provided with an accompanying inscription (compare cat. 79). On occasion, however, one can identify two statuettes that appear to be virtual clones of one another, although differing in scale. Such is the case of this bull and a bronze example in the Ashmolean Museum in Oxford. Although approximately only half as large as the one under discussion, the Ashmolean Apis Bull exhibits features so correspondingly close in each of its details, especially in the strict correspondence and congruence of all of the incised motifs, that one can tentatively suggest the two are contemporary and might even have been created in one and the same atelier using what would appear to have been the same pattern book.

The example in Oxford is inscribed for an official who is known from historically documented inscriptions to have exercised his functions for a daughter of pharaoh Psametik I of Dynasty XVVI, which suggests it may have been created in a royal atelier. The correspondences it shares with the example under discussion suggests that the present statuette was likewise created in the same royal atelier.

References: Oxford, The Ashmolean Museum 12879.332: Malek, "Handsome Gift," 1999, pp. 401–10.

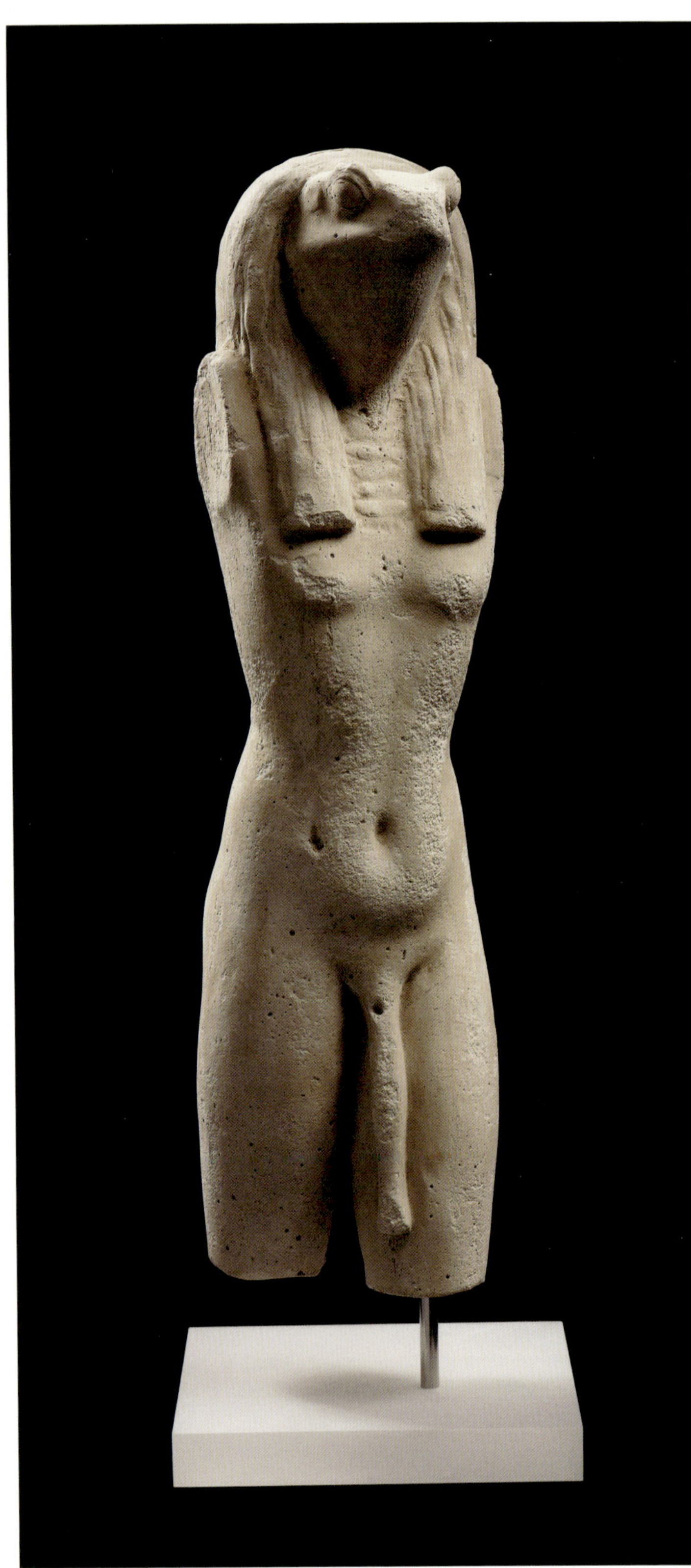

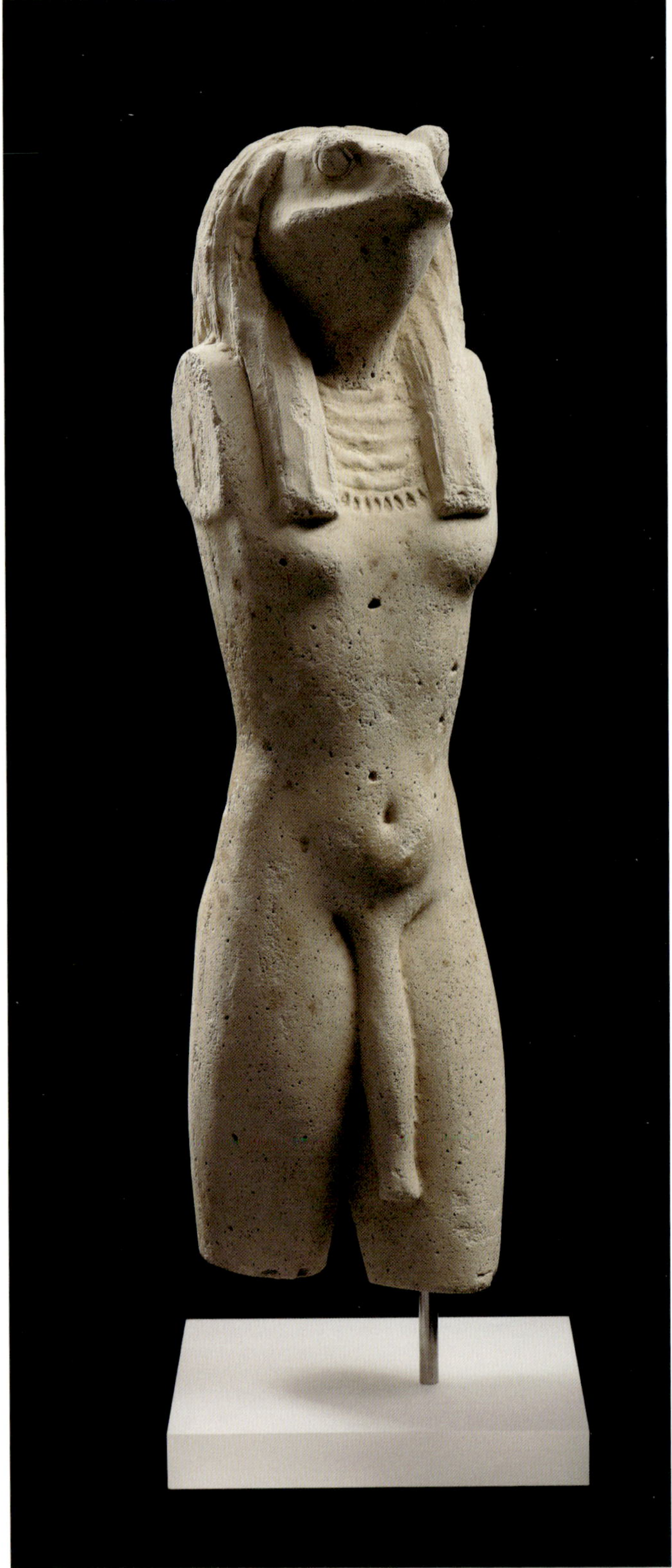

86. and *87.*

Two of the Deities from Hermopolis

Dynasty XXX–Ptolemaic Period, 382–30 BC
Plaster
Height 16 1/16 in. each
Inv. no. EG-288 and EG-289

These two statuettes are virtually identical, designed in accordance with principles that permit both composite beings as well as seemingly incomplete parts of entire images. Each depicts a virtually identical figure with the head of a frog on a human, male torso, preserved from about the level of the knees to the crown of the head. The figures appear to be nude with the exception of a broad collar, and each is wearing a phallus sheath (compare cat. 20). The broad collars consist of four strands of stylized beads, including a row of hollowed-out pendants on the bottom. Whether those cavities were inlaid with secondary materials or filled with a pigmented paste remains moot. Both figures wear striated, tripartite wigs, the relatively narrow lappets of which fall onto the chest and end just above the pectoral muscles. The rear of each wig is finished with a horizontal edge that roughly aligns with the shoulder blades. The modeling of the thighs and torso is done with restraint, but there is a degree of tripartition evident in the chest, which gives prominence to the pectoral muscles. These similarities suggest that the overseers of the institutionally affiliated ateliers in which both of these statuettes were created had recourse to pattern books that enabled them to create virtual copies of the same image (compare cat. 85).

The heads of these two statuettes are identically modeled and intact. They are characterized by a long, somewhat fleshy throat that projects at an angle from the torso, a snub snout that is short and prominent, and globular eyeballs that protrude significantly from their ringed lids. The design of these heads is in keeping with tenets of ancient Egyptian art for representations of animals. As such they capture the essence of the frog more convincingly than any modern biological textbook illustration would.

The arms and legs below the knees have neither been damaged nor intentionally broken off. Their completed state is indicated by the clean, intentionally smoothed surfaces of the truncated legs and arms (compare cat. 79). Within the repertoire of known objects of this type, these two objects appear to be unique. There are no comparable examples exhibiting the head of a frog on a human male torso created in plaster. The modeling of the torsos in tripartition has parallels with other examples, but these are headless.

Modern commentators often describe these works as "unfinished" and refer to them as "trial pieces," that is, models suggested to have been used in sculptural ateliers to instruct apprentices in the art of sculpting. These so-called models were created in both plaster and limestone, only rarely in harder stones. The use of plaster demonstrates it was just as important an artistic medium as stone, and was used from the time of the Old Kingdom.

A minority of scholars rejects the view of these objects as models and argues in favor of their identification as votive objects deposited in sanctuaries by pious pilgrims to secure the benefactions of the deities to whom they are offered. We endorse this minority view. Furthermore, the so-called unfinished state of these two frog deities is intentional, so that the Western definitions of finished/unfinished are inapplicable. The ancient Egyptians accepted such works into the repertoire of their sculptural oeuvre. The so-called Reserve Heads of the Old Kingdom are a case in point. These, like the frog-headed deities under discussion, were intentionally created as completed works of art and functioned in cultic contexts. To date, no one has suggested that these Reserve Heads served as sculptors' models. The frog-headed deities are to be regarded within this ancient Egyptian context, in which a seemingly unfinished part was anciently regarded as complete and functioned in cultic contexts (compare cat. 14).

The identity of this pair of frog-headed composite figures may be suggested by examining a train of four virtually identical figures on a naos, or shrine, reconstructed from fragments, some of which are in the British Museum and one of which is in the collections of the Fondation Gandur pour l'Art (EG-171, not in this exhibition). There one finds depictions in relief of four frog-headed deities with arms and legs, on the feet of which are jackal-headed sandals. Each wears a phallus sheath, secured by a belt, of a somewhat different design, but such minor differences are only to be expected given the differences of the media (compare cat. 9). These figures are identified as Hehm, Kek, Naw, and Amun, who is sometimes replaced by Gereh. These are the four principal gods of the Ogdoad, or college of eight gods, associated with the site of Hermopolis (Ashmunein) who are often paired with their female counterparts, traditionally depicted as goddesses with the heads of serpents. The presence of the phallus sheath reinforces their seminal role as creator gods. Although there are no accompanying inscriptions on the two statuettes under discussion to provide confirmation of this identification, the multiple images of the same frog-headed deity strongly incline one to accept their identification as two of the four gods of the Ogdoad of Hermopolis.

Their dating is suggested not only by comparison with the figures on the naos but also by the treatment of their torsos in tripartition.

Published: Anonymous, "La porte du rêve," 2007, p. 41.

References: Bianchi, "Ex-votos of Dynasty XXVI," 1979, pp. 15ff; Bianchi, "Two Ex-votos," 1981, pp. 31ff; Hastings, *Animal Necropolis*, 1997, pp. 60 and 62; Tomoum, *Sculptors' Models*, 2005.

88.

An Amulet of Pataikos

Dynasty XXVI–Ptolemaic Period, 664–30 BC
Faience
Height 1 ⅝ in.
Inv. no. EG-188

The nude bandy-legged deity stands on an integral plinth with his fisted hands resting at his waist. The features of the face of his disproportionately large head are well executed and include eyes, with articulated upper lids, set into relatively deep sockets under a natural brow, a short nose, and a wide mouth, the lips of which are drawn into a faint smile. An incised line around the top of his head suggests his hair is closely cropped (compare cat. 17).

Often described as dwarves and habitually adduced as taxonomic examples of that physical condition, exacting research now concludes that these images are artifices, designed by the elite by modifying characteristics of short-limbed individuals. The resulting representations are not, therefore, to be understood as examples of naturalism.

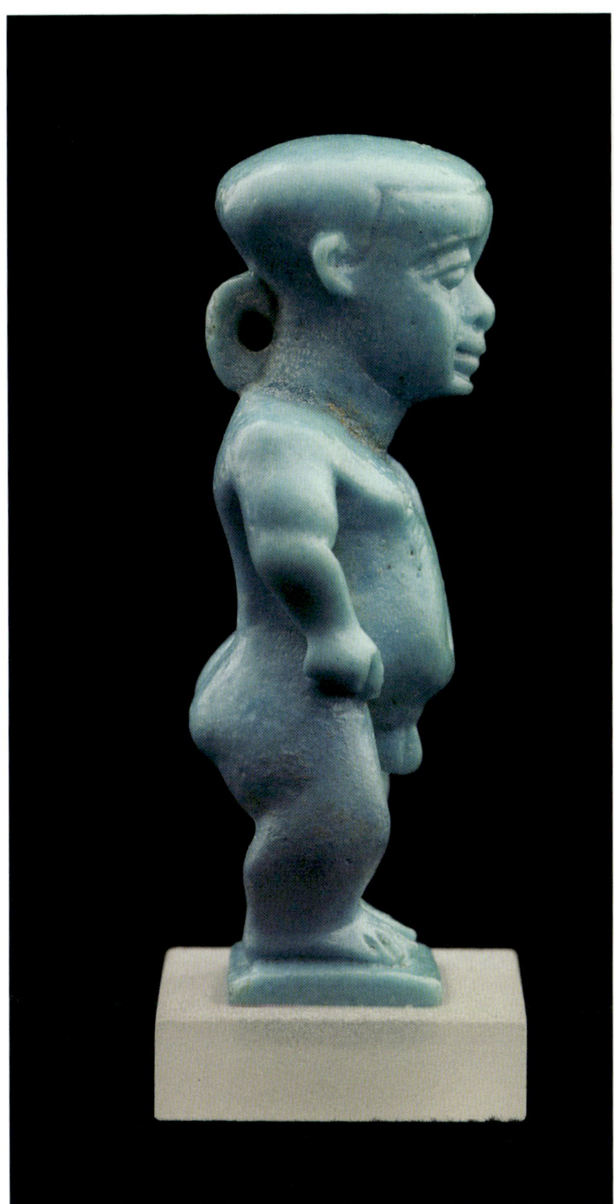
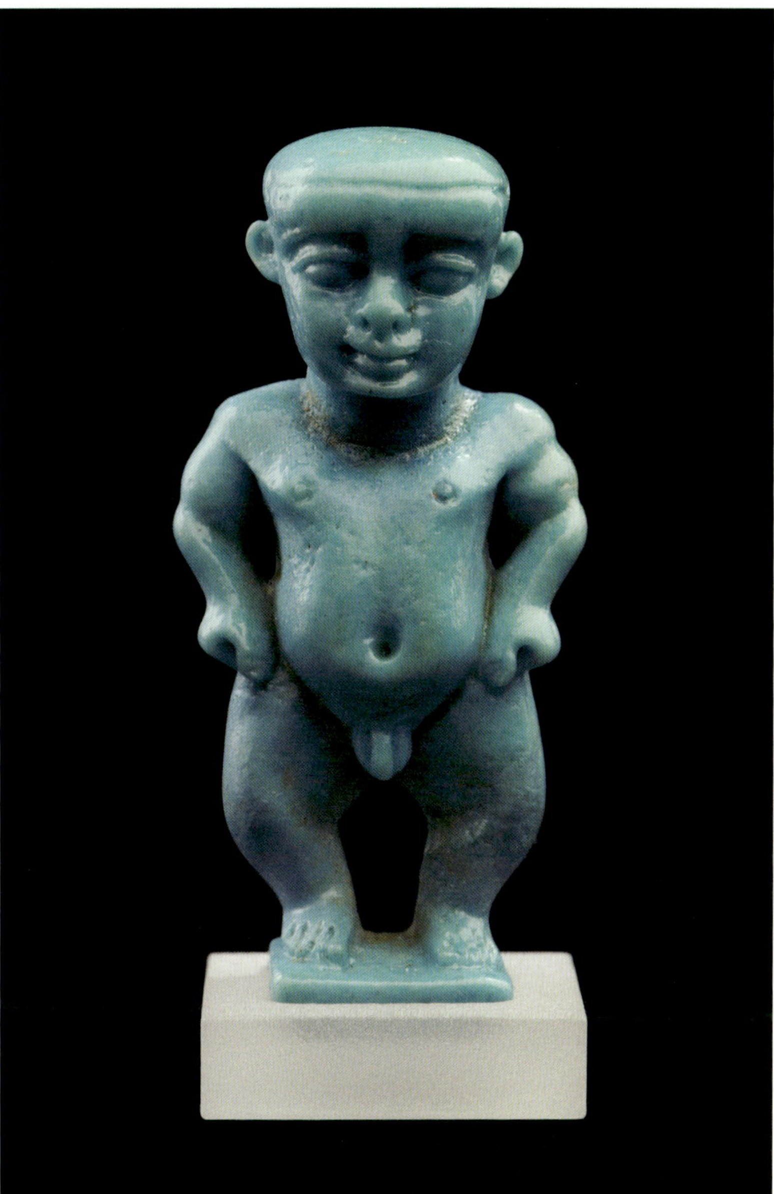

Although not inscribed, this amulet depicts Pataikos, who is associated with Ptah, the creator god of Memphis and patron of craftsmen. Pataikos was often connected with metalworks, particularly with jewelers. Short-limbed individuals and those challenged with walking are universally associated with smithing. One thinks of Hephaistos, the lame blacksmith in Greek mythology, and of both Rumpelstiltskin and the dwarves populating the Nibelungen. The association requires further examination.

The dating of this figure is suggested by parallels.

Published: Chappaz and Chamay, *Reflets du divin*, 2001, p. 40, no. 26.

References: Dasen, *Dwarfs*, 1993.

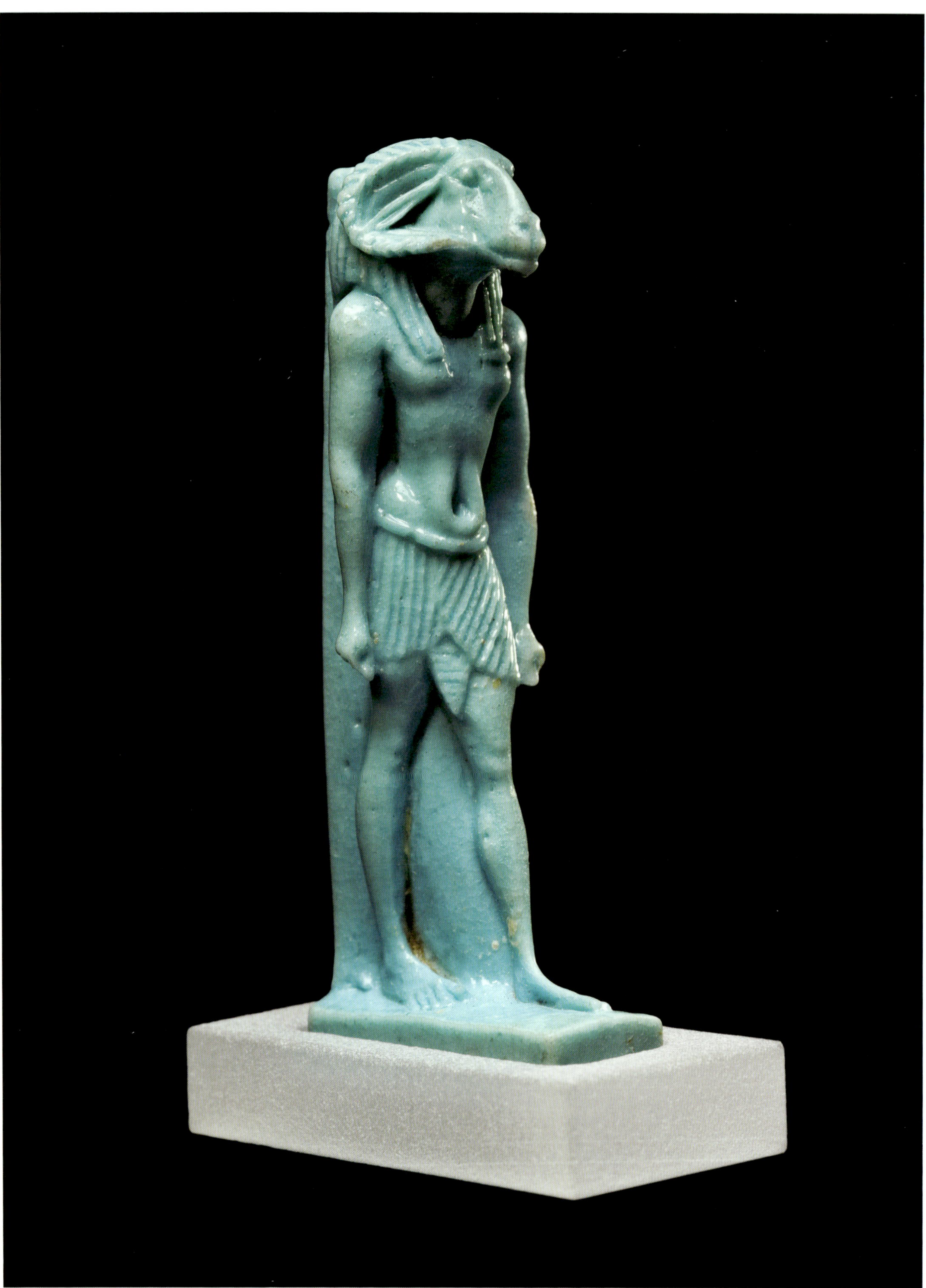

89.

Amulet of a Ram-Headed Diety

Dynasty XXVI–Ptolemaic Period, 664–30 BC
Faience
Height 1 ½ in.
Inv. no. EG-165

Whenever one thinks of ancient Egyptian art, images of monumentality, such as the Great Pyramids of Giza and the Sphinx, immediately spring to mind. But the ancient Egyptians were also capable of creating astonishing works in miniature that belie their size. The principles governing the design of hieroglyphs were in general universally applied to the design of all works of art created in the institutionally affiliated craft ateliers of ancient Egypt. Such a universal application made almost no exception with regard to either medium or scale. Consequently, the design of small amulets, such as this of a composited deity with a ram's head seamlessly joined to a human male body, adheres to the tenets utilized for those of much larger objects.

The ram-headed deity strides forward with his left leg advanced on an integral rectangular plinth, his back abutting an integral back pillar, pierced horizontally just above the level of the elbows for suspension. He is barefoot and bare-chested, wearing only a striated, tripartite wig and pleated kilt secured to the waist with a plain belt. His arms are pressed tightly against his body, with their fisted hands resting on his thighs. Because of the size and material of the amulet, the forearms have been cut free from the matrix, but the negative space between the legs has been retained.

Although not inscribed, the characteristic C-shaped form of the horns that curve around and under the ears is specific to the species and identifies this amulet as a representation of the god Amun (compare cat. 79). The glistening characteristic of faience was associated with the sun, and its green color resonates with associations of the floral kingdom. Consequently, both the material and its color further reinforce the powers of Amun, one of the ancient Egyptian pantheon's most powerful solar deities, who was regarded as a cosmic creator.

The bipartite design of the male torso, with its characteristic disregard for articulating the rib cage; the pinched, wasp waist; the deeply inset, teardrop shape of the navel; and the kilt riding down on the hips, follows stylistic conventions commonly encountered in the sculpture repertoire of the Late Period (compare cat. 69), which suggests the dating of this amulet.

Published: Chappaz and Chamay, *Reflets du divin*, 2001, p. 33, no. 15; Lessing and Vernus, *Dieux*, 1996.

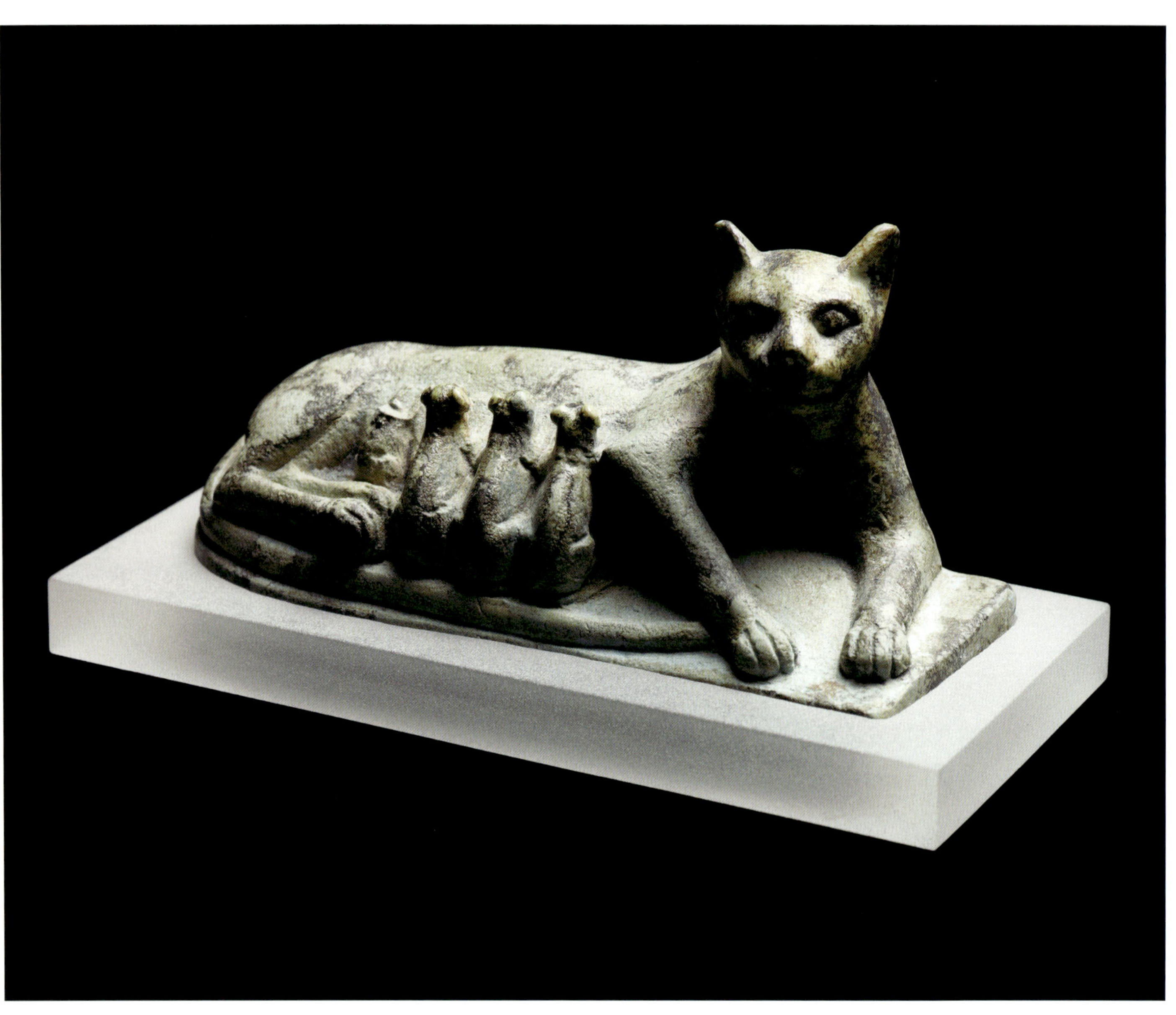

90.

A Queen Nursing Four Kittens

Dynasty XXVI–Ptolemaic Period, 664–30 BC
Faience
Length 3 ⅛ in.
Inv. no. EG-143

The queen, a designation for a female cat, is depicted lying on her left side on a thin, rectangular integral plinth, with her head turned toward the front as she nurses four kittens, the head of one now missing. Similar statuettes, some in bronze, depict a queen in this same pose with exactly four kittens. The frequency with which this group of five is represented suggests that the ancient Egyptians attached a specific meaning to the composition, but the absence of accompanying inscriptions renders an interpretation difficult.

There exist other group compositions featuring five felines, four of smaller scale than the fifth, all on the same integral pedestal, that identify the larger figure as Bastet in their accompanying inscriptions. This would suggest that all of these compositions were anciently connected with either the character of Bastet or one of her mythological associations. In accordance with ancient Egyptian iconographic conventions, smaller figures placed at the feet of deities connected with protection serve as emissary genii, forming a symbolic advance guard, deployed to clear the path of evil. Bastet's role as a guardian of order during the passage from the old to the new year would be in keeping with this association. Perhaps the kittens in such compositions allude to the function of those emissary genii.

The dating of this statuette is suggested by parallels. The grayish color of its faience is doubtless to be attributed to deterioration caused by the environment in which the group composition was placed.

Published: Chappaz and Chamay, *Reflets du divin*, 2001, p. 115, no. 106.

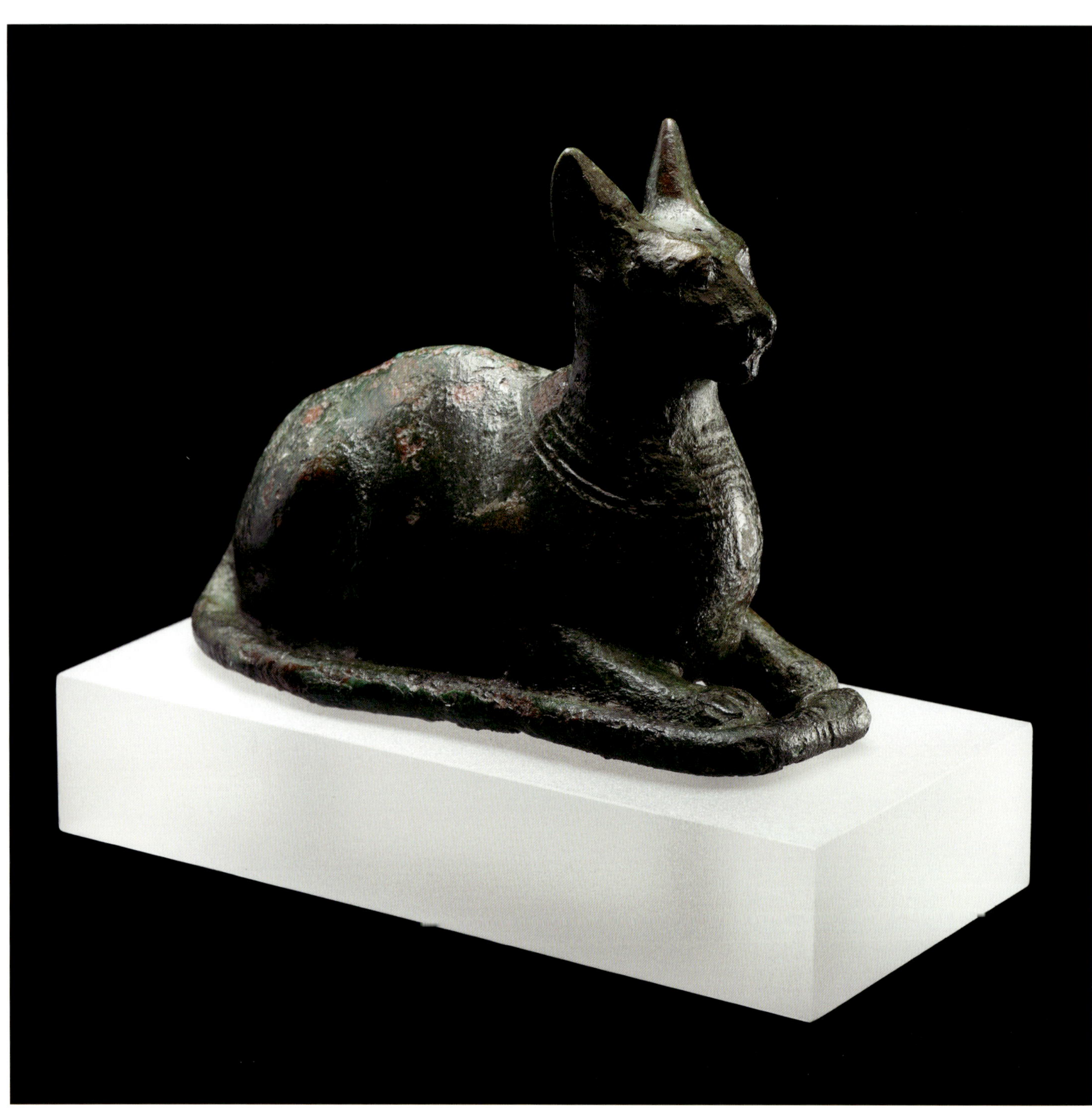

91.

A Statuette of a Pregnant Queen

Dynasty XXVI–Ptolemaic Period, 664–30 BC
Bronze
Length 3 ⅛ in.
Inv. no. EG-101

This statuette represents a queen, or female cat, on the ground, her back legs tucked up under her body, her front legs extended in a pose that suggests that the feline is either about to stand or is in the act of reclining. Her tail, although held close to the body and wrapped around its right side closely following its contours, as design principles dictate, is disproportionately long and extends around her entire body until its tip reaches her extended left paw. Such long tails are not uncommon in depictions of cats, and are encountered on representations of other, contemporary bronze statuettes of the same animal. This length recalls the extraordinarily long tails on cats featured in scenes of fishing and fowling in the marshes decorating tombs of the New Kingdom.

The animal is modeled in broad planes with incision used for the details of the head, particularly the eyes and the broad collar, which consists of six strands of stylized beads designed in groups of two. The reliance on modeling in broad planes contributes to the meaning of this statuette (compare cat. 77), which suggests that she is pregnant.

In its present state, the statuette is divorced from any plinth to which it might originally have been attached and is not inscribed, with the result that its interpretation is moot. In general, the cat was regarded as a symbol of both sexuality and fecundity, because of its legendary propensity to reproduce. The queen was often associated with the moon. One lunar legend maintains that the she would give birth to a series of kittens, one on day one, two on day two, and so on until the last litter of seven would be birthed on the seventh day. The cumulative total of these kittens equaled twenty-eight, the number of days in a lunar month. The subject of a birthing queen was also anciently associated with the goddess Bastet in her sanctuary at Bubastis, where the goddess might be invoked by mothers in labor to assure the successful delivery of their children. The depiction of pregnancy may also allude to the medicinal properties attributed to queens, either pregnant or birthing females. Her placenta and fur were used in various prescriptions used for fumigations. The placenta was an important ingredient in a lotion that prevented hair from turning gray, although the particulars of its dosage and applications were not recorded. Her fur, when mixed with the milk of lactating women, was considered a burn remedy, if applied accompanied by the recitation of a mandated spell.

The ancient Egyptian noun for cat is ***miu***, suggested to be the onomatopoeic equivalent of the English "meow." The noun served as well as a personal name commonly translated as "Kitty." The dating of this statuette is suggested by parallels.

Published: Chappaz and Chamay, *Reflets du divin*, 2001, p. 114, no. 105.

References: Málek, *Cat*, 1993, pp. 27, 57, 73–74, *passim*.

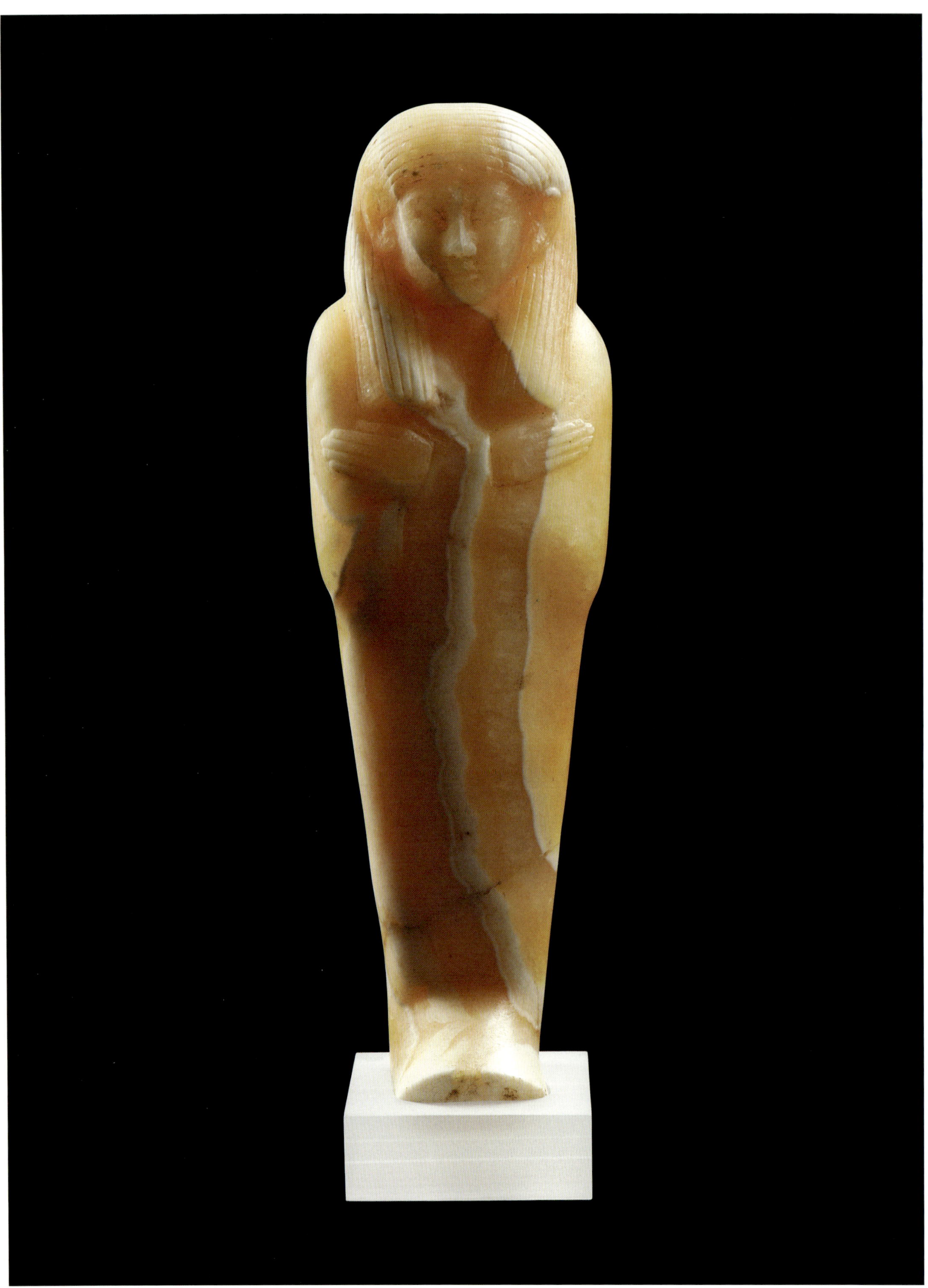

92.

A Shabti, or Funerary Statue

Dynasty XVIII, 1554–1305 BC
Alabaster
Height 8 1/16 in.
Inv. no. EG-70

Statuettes such as these are termed shabtis and despite popular opinion are not to be regarded as slaves or servants of their owners. They were not created to wait hand and foot upon the deceased in the hereafter. That interpretation is based in part, perhaps, on Johann Wolfgang von Goethe's poem, *Der Zauberlehrling* (*The Sorcerer's Apprentice*, 1797). In point of fact, their function was entirely different.

Funerary figures such as this were placed into the tombs of both elite members and pharaohs of ancient Egyptian society, but their function evolved over time. With their first appearance during the course of the Middle Kingdom, the shabtis were both guarantors for the deceased to receive the royal offering formula and avatars who performed specific tasks in the hereafter on behalf of the deceased. Those tasks, anciently regarded as onerous, were specified in Spell 6 of *The Book of the Dead*. During the course of the New Kingdom, one often finds an additional stipulation that the task imposed in the hereafter was obligatory and had to be performed by the shabti. During the course of the Third Intermediate Period, the shabtis were specifically designated as "responders" to emphasize their obligation to answer the roll call for work on behalf of the deceased. One shabti was ideally expected to work just one day a year. It is also during this period that the shabtis were believed to become animated with the rays of the sun and, so animated, enabled the deceased, both male and female, to become Osiris-like.

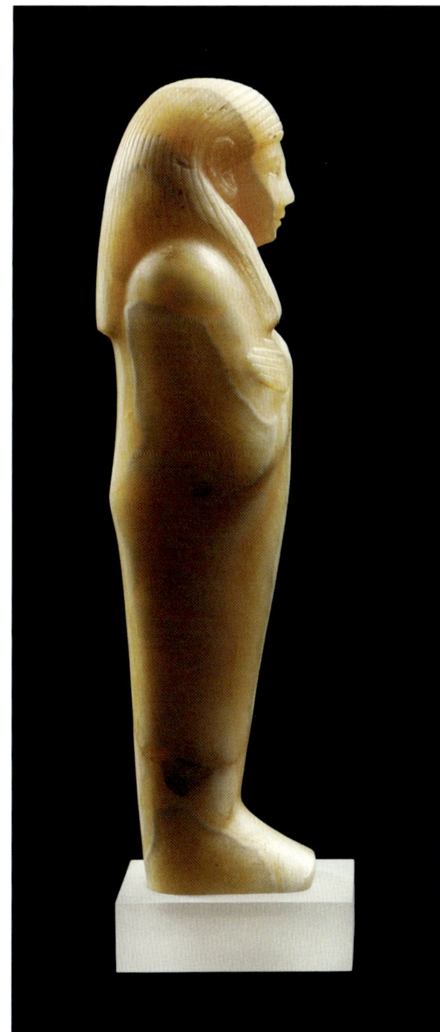

It was during the Third Intermediate Period as well that the canonical number of shabtis became fixed at 401, a total that represents one shabti for each of the 365 days of the ancient Egyptian year and the thirty-six overseers whose task was to ensure that each shabti did in fact work the required one-day annual shift. Three texts from this period clearly demonstrate that sets of 401 shabtis were commissioned either by or on behalf of the deceased for an agreed price, although the exact cost is not always stated. One of these texts also stipulates how the shabtis were animated. A ritualist, assuredly the overseer of the craftsmen in the workshop in which the shabtis were created, was obliged to recite a specific spell in a designated sacred place in the presence of several deities. This ceremony had to be witnessed by a scribe. Then, and only then, after the performance of this actualizing ritual, could the shabtis be placed into the service of the deceased.

Because the practice of placing these shabtis in tombs was so continuous and long-lived, beginning in the Middle Kingdom and only disappearing during the course of the Ptolemaic Period, scholars have been able to trace their stylistic development with a view toward establishing a fairly secure relative chronology for the entire series.

Accordingly, this uninscribed example, clearly a shabti to judge from its size and mummiform design, dates to Dynasty XVIII. Its face, dominated by idealizing features, is framed by a striated, tripartite wig, indicated by incision. The rest of the figure, modeled in broad planes, is otherwise unadorned and only exhibits the hands protruding from beneath its imagined mummy bandages. The use of alabaster connotes permanence and purity, qualities that further the funerary function to which this shabti was put.

Published: Chappaz and Chamay, *Reflets du divin*, 2001, p. 86, no. 71.

References: Schneider, *Shabtis*, 1977, part I.

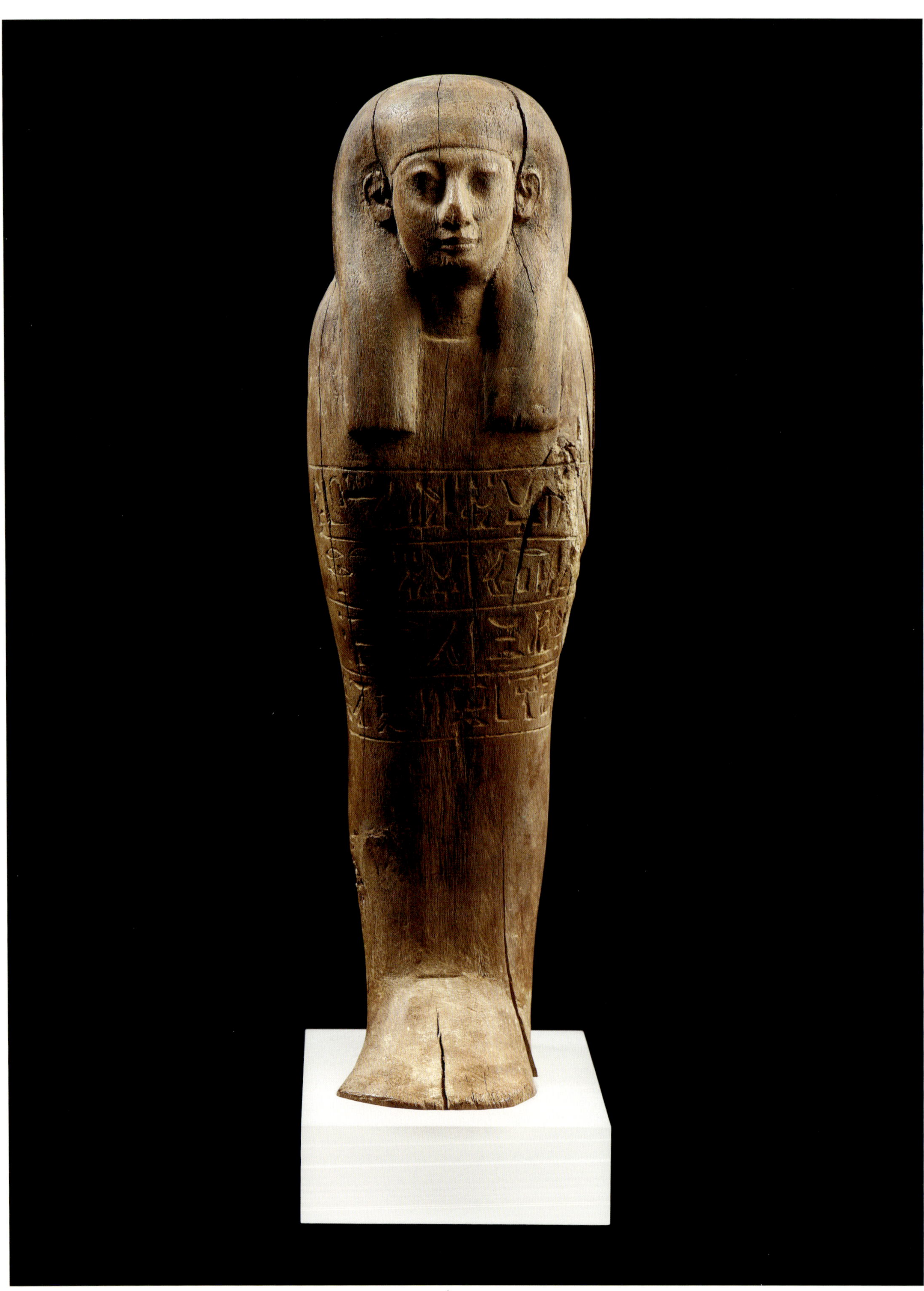

93.

A Shabti of Aa-wepwawet

Early Dynasty XVIII, 1554–1403 BC
Wood, polychromy, gesso, and linen
Height 10 in.
Inv. no. EG-316

Shabtis are a specific type of object created for both the pharaoh and members of the elite in order to symbolically fulfill obligatory but onerous agricultural tasks in the hereafter. This particular example is sculpted from a single piece of wood. In keeping with the ancient Egyptian practice of utilizing every available piece of this material because of its scarcity, the imperfections of the wood employed for this work of art were anciently and intentionally covered with linen, which was coated with gesso to create the illusion of a perfect surface. Such a technical practice was introduced during the Old Kingdom and became very common during the course of the Middle Kingdom, as an examination of any number of wooden statues from that period reveals.

The design of this shabti is based on models created during the Middle Kingdom but exhibits stylistic innovations characteristic of those created during the early part of Dynasty XVIII. These include the specific design of the head and neck, which rise up from the shoulders and imbue the entire figure with an elegant contour. The contours suggest that the figure is entirely wrapped in linen mummy bandages that intentionally link Aa-wepwawet with the god Osiris (compare cat. 67). These bandages leave only the upper part of the neck in the front above the chest and the head and ears exposed. A striated, tripartite wig covers the head with its lappets falling over each shoulder onto the upper chest. This wig is associated with deities and was often worn by the deceased as a symbol of their resurrection and subsequent transformation into a glorified spirit. It has been suggested that shabtis such as this were placed in miniature anthropoid sarcophagi on which spells from either *The Pyramid Texts* or *The Book of the Dead* were inscribed. The role of the shabti as an avatar of the deceased was thus further reinforced.

The inscription in four lines of carefully designed hieroglyphs may be translated as

> *The illuminated one [named] Aa-wepwawet, says: Hail to you, O shabti. If Aa-wepwawet is drafted into the corvee for duties in the god's domain in order to perform all of the work which needs to be done there, namely, the transporting by boat of sand from the west to the east, you shall say, "I shall perform the labor on his behalf. I am here!"*

The name of the owner, Aa-wepwawet, is composed of two elements, the second of which, Wepwawet, is the name of a god, generally depicted as a jackal, who is "the one who opens up the way." This deity enabled the deceased to find his way along the paths leading to the hereafter. The name of the owner of this shabti may be translated as

> *The god who opens up the way [for the deceased] is great.*

Stylistically speaking, this consummately sculpted shabti ranks as an excellent example of early New Kingdom sculpture. The contours of the face are somewhat cordiform, or heart-shaped, with idealizing features dominated by large, almond-shaped eyes, their pupils painted black. The nose features wide wings springing from a narrow bridge, and the horizontally aligned lips are relatively wide and fleshy. These characteristics suggest a dating of this figure into the early part of Dynasty XVIII, in the period before the establishment of the Tuthmoside style of Hatshepsut and Tuthmosis III.

94.

A Shabti of Ray

Dynasty XVII, 1400–1305 BC
Alabaster with traces of blue paste inlays
Height 7 ¼ in.
Inv. no. EG-261

This shabti depicts an elite male named Ray, mummiform, with his arms protruding from beneath his mummy bandages and folded across his upper chest, with their fisted hands holding hoes and seed baskets. His face, characterized by idealizing features, is framed by a striated wig that leaves the ears free, beneath the lappets of which are the floral-formed strands of a broad collar. The design of the hands with their agricultural instruments and the presence of a broad collar beneath the wig find their closest parallels in examples dated to late Dynasty XVIII, to which this example is likewise assigned.

The alabaster imbues the figure with qualities of permanence and purity; the color of the inlays connotes resurrection and rebirth. The exceptional quality of the sculpting is at variance with its inscription, the individual signs of which are less carefully designed and often incorrectly composed. Nevertheless, the inscription, a variation of the standard shabti formula, may be rendered as follows:

> *Hail to you, the illuminated deceased, identified as Osiris, who is the director of the twin granaries, named Ray, true of voice. He says, O Ye shabtis, if one details you to perform any work which is done in the realm of the dead, such as that done by individuals who are, alas, subjected to this type of unpleasantness, in order to cultivate the fields, to irrigate the steep banks, to transport sand from the west to the east or from the east to the west, here I am, you shall say...[on behalf of?] the deceased, identified as Osiris, the director of the double granaries named Ray, true of voice.*

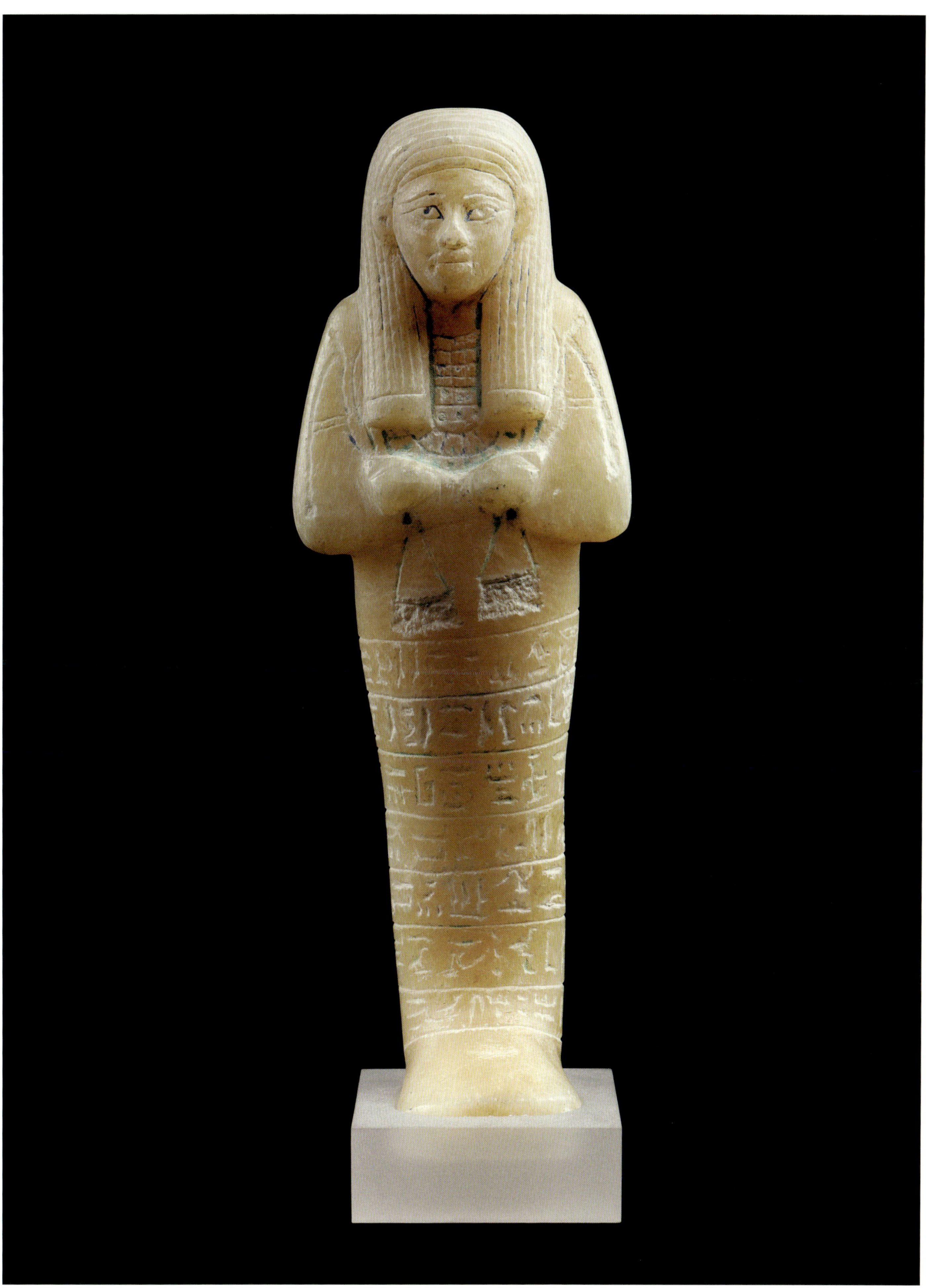

95.

A Shabti of Pharaoh Rameses IX

Dynasty XX, reign of Pharaoh Rameses IX, 1137–1119 BC
Wood
Height 12 ⅛ in.
Inv. no. EG-317

The tomb of Rameses IX in the Valley of the Kings (KV 6) was first studied in modern times by Eduard de Villiers du Terrage and Prosper Jollois, engineers in the employ of Napoleon during his famed expedition to Egypt. In keeping with the practice at the time, they, together with their contemporaries, brought the objects they had found, including the shabtis, back to Europe as souvenirs of their journey. One assumes that the present shabti was once in just such an early collection. It then entered the Dutch collection of Dr. Janette Walen, formed between 1910 and 1940, and was passed on by descent to his son, Dr. F. Janette Walen. Four additional shabtis from this same tomb, likewise inscribed for Rameses IX, were purchased by the British Museum in 1821, not long after the end of the French mission to Egypt. These are at present the only known shabtis inscribed for Rameses IX.

This shabti of Rameses IX is depicted as if wrapped in the mummy bandages of Osiris with its feet covered. The arms are exposed and folded over the chest; the fisted hands hold agricultural implements incised into the surface of the figure. The left hand holds a hoe with a smaller blade, the right a hoe with a broader blade as well as a cord thrown over the shoulder from which is suspended a rectangular sack. The sack, resting on the back and ornamented with a reticulated pattern, was intended to hold either grain or sand.

The king wears an incised broad collar consisting of eight strands of beads, the third from the bottom decorated with radiating strokes doubtless intended to represent floral elements. His other accessories included the nemes-headdress, which is both striated and separated from the forehead by a broad horizontal band. It is gathered up at the back along the upper spine into a tightly twisted, plaited roll. The nemes-headdress is fronted by a uraeus, or royal cobra, the coils of which align with the headband.

The design of the face of Rameses IX on this shabti is cordiform and dominated by almond-shaped eyes, a nose with a thin bridge, and wide wings, beneath which is a horizontally aligned, wide mouth with thin lips. In profile view, the chin projects gently into space. The ears, relatively large in keeping with ancient Egyptian artistic tenets, are exposed, with their lobes nicked.

The choice of wood for the creation of shabtis during the Ramesside Period may perhaps be attributed to Sety I, the first significant pharaoh of the period, whose craftsmen were responsible for the execution of some of the most aesthetically accomplished art created during the entire period. Some of his shabtis were made in wood, and these may have served as the inspiration and point of departure for the craftsmen in the ateliers of Rameses IX.

The front of this shabti is inscribed with nine lines of shallowly incised hieroglyphs, containing one of the longer known versions of the shabti spell. Some of the elements are noteworthy because they are generally not found in inscriptions on shabtis for the elite but are reserved almost exclusively for inscriptions on shabtis of pharaohs.

> *The illuminated one, the Osiris, this pharaoh Neferkare-Setepenre [literally, Perfect is the ka or spirit or the sun god Re, the one chosen by Re], the justified, he says, "O, these shabtis, if one summons [me], if one drafts [me] the Osiris, the son of Re Rameses, Khaemwaset-Mereramun [literally, Rameses,*

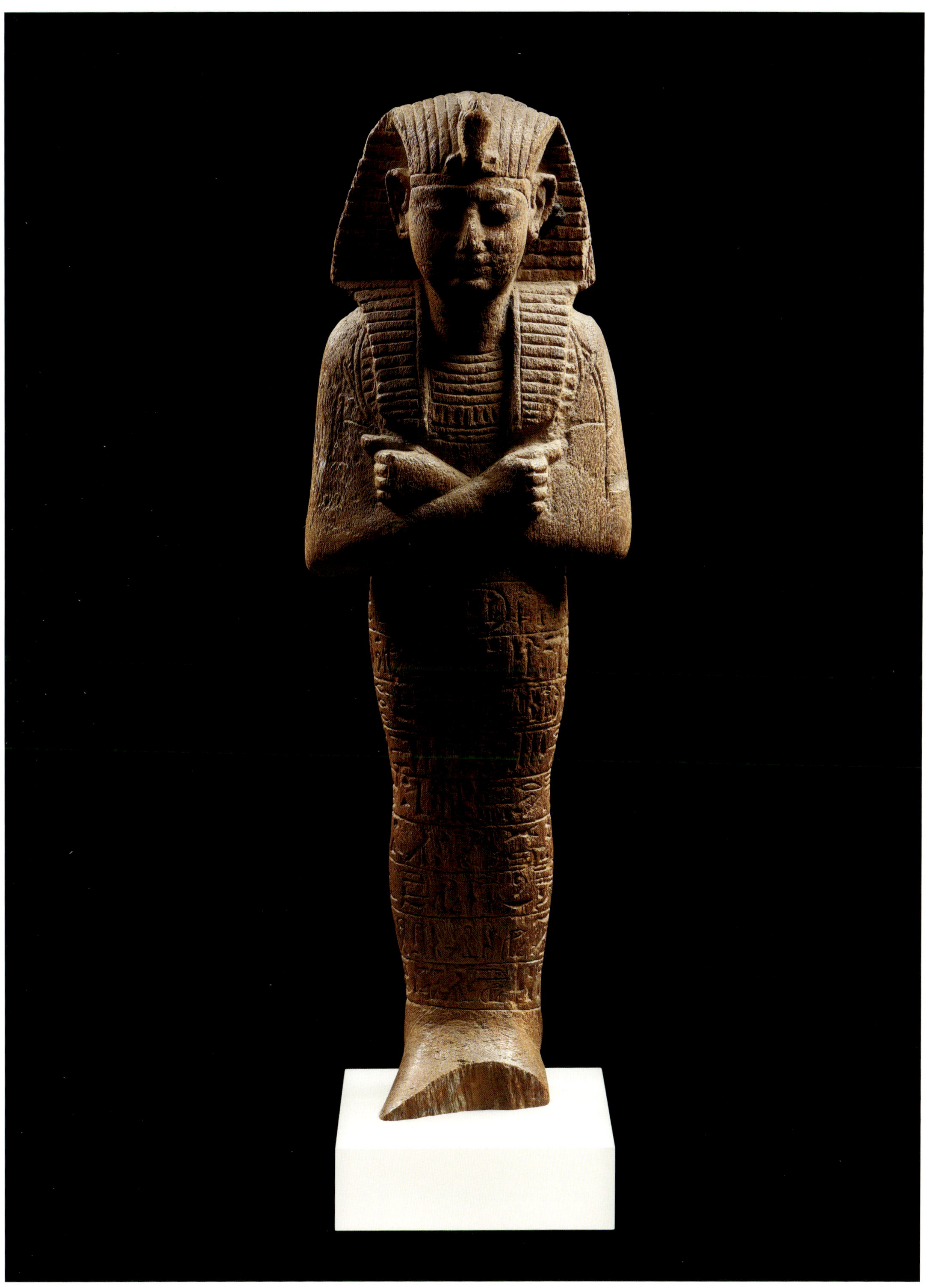

appearing in glory in Thebes, the one beloved of the god Amun], the justified, to do all of the work which needs to be done in the god's domain, to make the fields arable for planting, to irrigate the land along the river banks, to transport by vessel the sand from the east to the west or from the west to the east; if anyone is looking for [him] at any time whatsoever, [you, O shabtis, shall say], "I shall perform all of those tasks; here I am," you shall say there. Now indeed, obstacles are implanted herewith—as a man at his duties.

Published: Andrews and van Dirk, *Objects*, 2006, pp. 152–56, no. 2.43.

96.

Shabti of Hor-iret-iaah

Dynasty XXVI, 664–525 BC
Faience
Height 6 7/8 in.
Inv. no. EG-97

This figure is designed as if enveloped in mummy bandages and is modeled in broad planes with attention to the configuration of the legs. His face is framed by a large, unadorned wig, whose wide lappets recall the design of his massive false beard. Each of his fisted hands holds a hoe.

These shabtis were found within a tomb at Saqqara. In keeping with funerary practices of the period, the total number included figures of overseers, although these were identically designed. The inscription is a third version of Spell 6 of *The Book of the Dead*, which may be freely rendered as:

> *Hail to you, the illuminated deceased, identified with the god Osiris, the director of the antechamber, named Hor-iret-iaah. He says, O this shabti, if one details the deceased director of the antechamber named Hor-iret-iaah, true of voice, to peform any work that is done in the realm of the dead or any other unpleasant duties imposed upon him, as is done by an individual laboring under such assignments, you will say, here I am. You will then be detailed to work at any given time to cultivate the fields, to irrigate the riverbanks, or to transport sand from the west to the east or from the east to the west. Here I am to perform such duties, you shall say.*

Published: Chappaz and Chamay, *Reflets du divin*, 2001, p. 88, no. 73a.

References: Aubert and Aubert, *Statuettes égyptiennes*, 1974, pp. 217, 220–23, and 280.

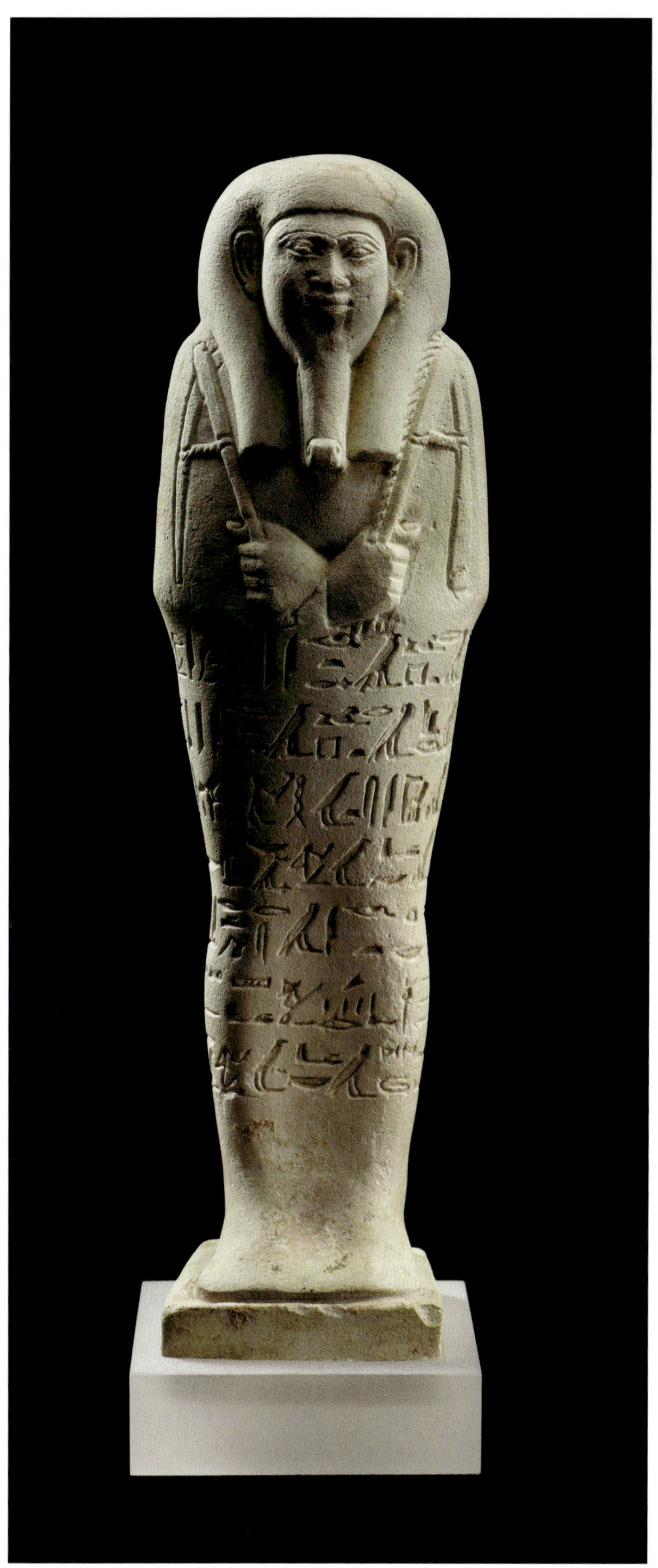

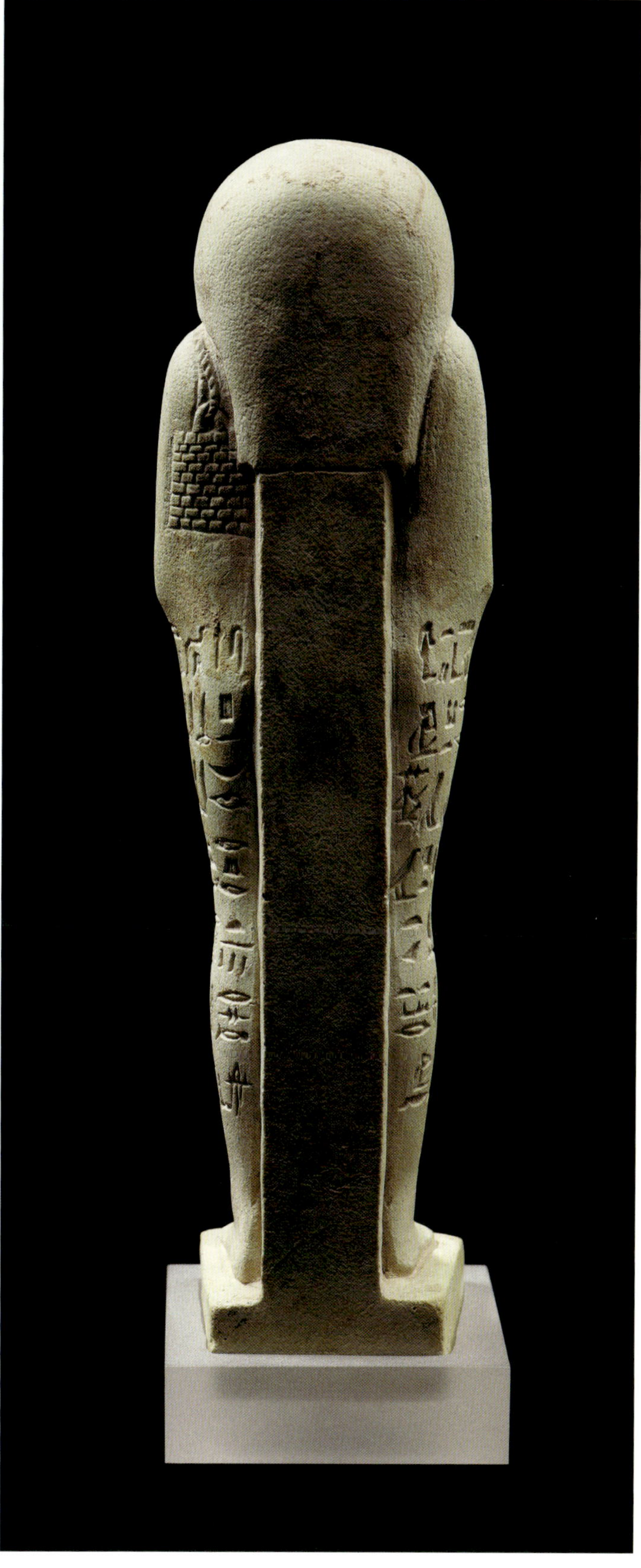

97.

Shabti of Tcha-en-hebu

Dynasty XXVI, time of Pharaoh Amasis, 570–526 BC
Faience
Height 7 ⅛ in.
Inv. no. EG-92

This shabti is modeled in broad planes and cast in a mold together with its integral base. Ten lines of hieroglyphs identify its owner as Tcha-en-hebu, who served as the overseer of the royal fleet under Pharaoh Amasis. His tomb was discovered at Saqqara in 1900. It yielded 401 shabtis that were deposited within the tomb in two groups of 203 and 198. The total includes one shabti for every day of the Egyptian year, with the remainder, exhibiting the same design, to serve as foremen. The carefully sculpted hieroglyphs of this shabti contain the expected formula of Spell 6 of *The Book of the Dead* (compare cat. 96).

The use of faience imbues the shabti with solar characteristics, its greenish blue color with those of the floral kingdom. Both combine to reinforce the wish that such figures could become animated in the hereafter to serve as surrogates for the deceased. This reinforcing by medium and color is stressed by Tcha-en-hebu's introductory epithet designating this shabti as "the one who is caused to be illuminated," which links text and material with the same solar elements.

Published: Chappaz and Chamay, *Reflets du divin*, 2001, p. 88, no. 73b.

References: Aubert and Aubert, *Statuettes égyptiennes*, 1974, pp. 227–28;
Menu, "Les ouchebtis," 2011, pp. 39–49.

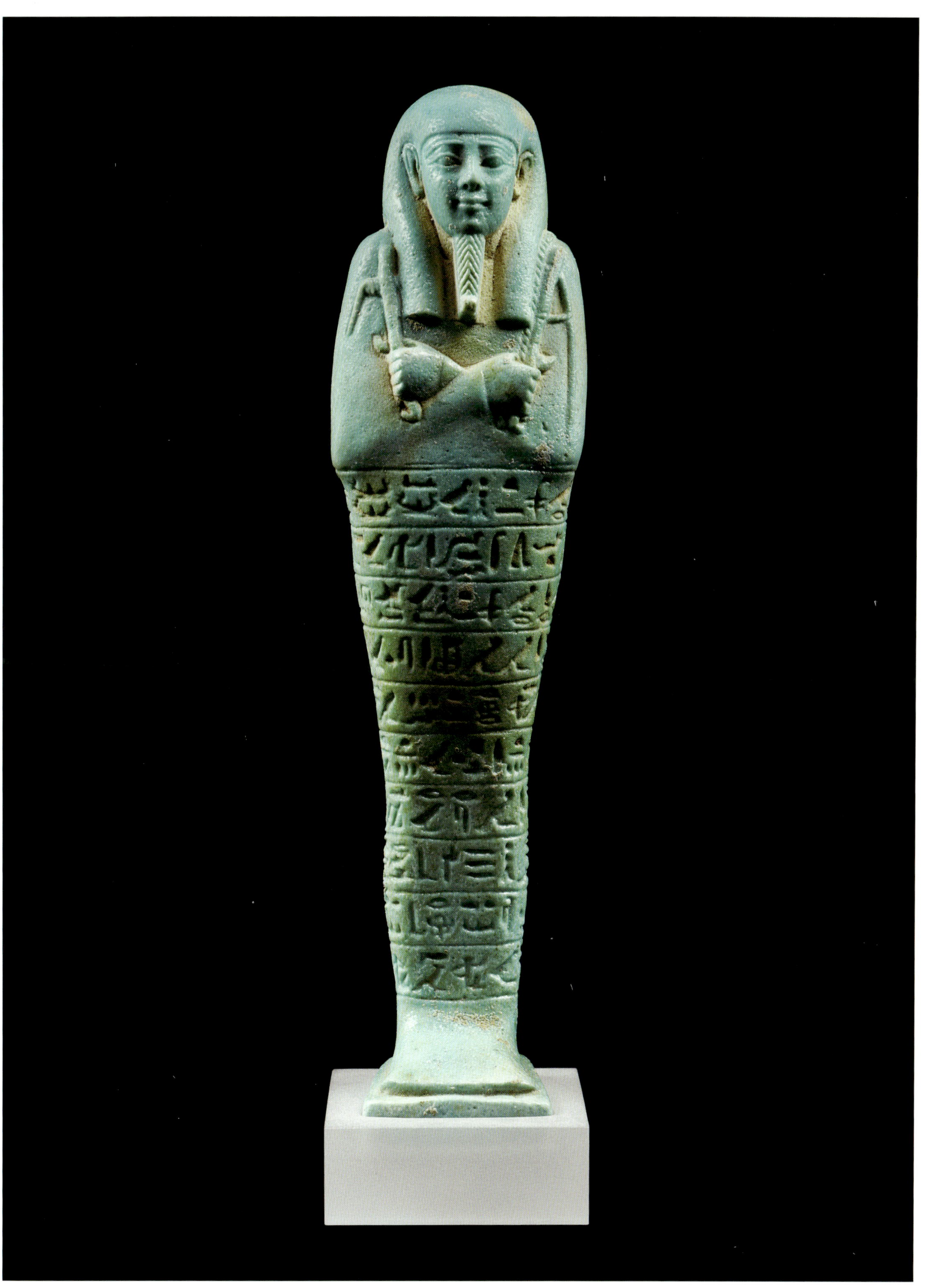

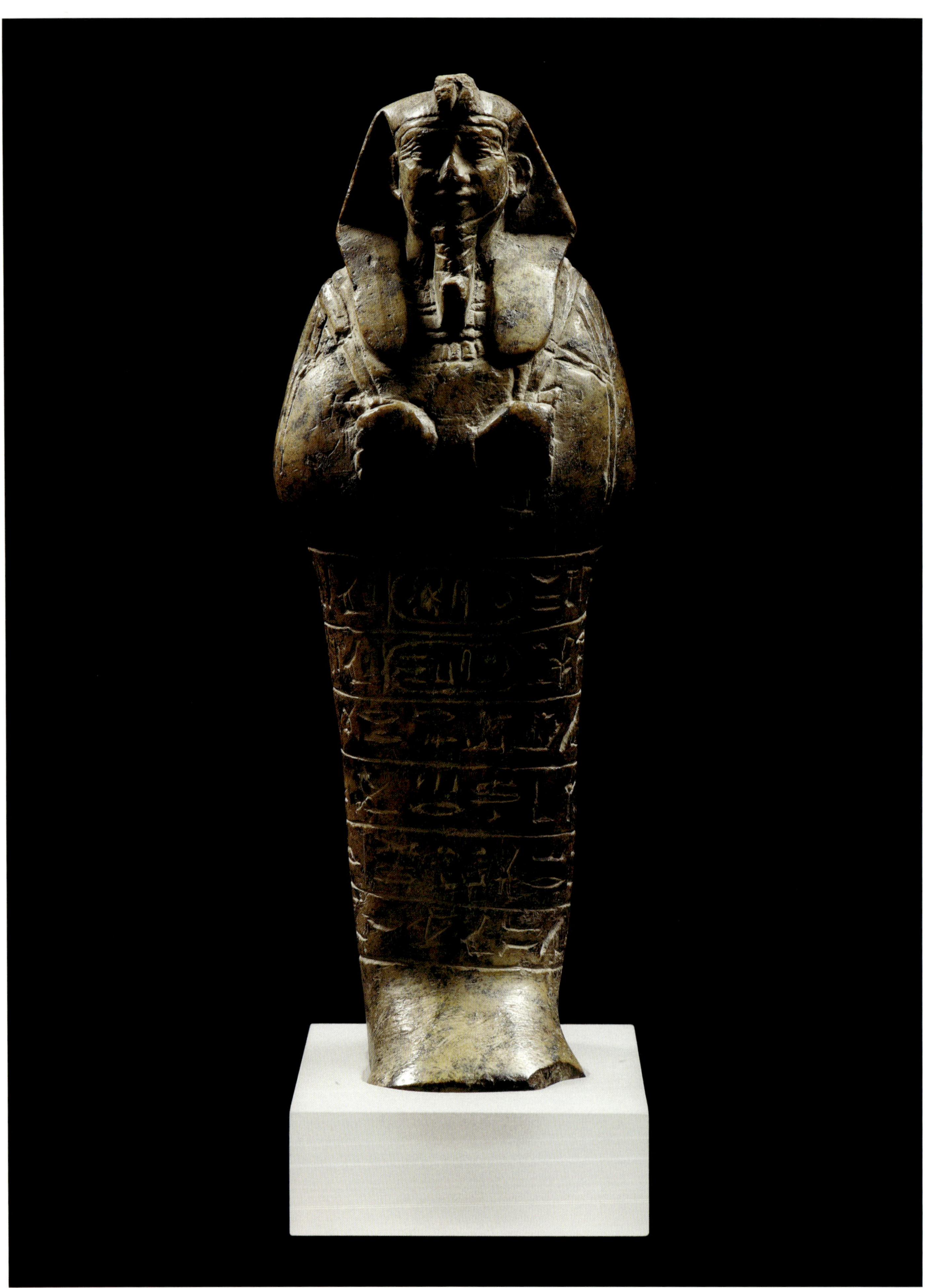

98.

A Shabti of the Nubian Pharaoh Senkamanisken

Napatan Period, reign of Pharaoh Senkamanisken, 643–623 BC
Serpentine
Height 6 5/8 in.
Inv. no. EG-324

The Kushite pharaohs of Napata adopted many features of Egypt's culture, particularly aspects of its funerary practices, including the creation of funerary figurines termed shabtis. Those belonging to Senkamanisken, the present example included, were found within his pyramid in the royal Nubian cemetery at Nuri, located near the Fourth Cataract of the Nile River, during the excavations of the Museum of Fine Arts, Boston, and Harvard University joint mission led by George Andrew Reisner in 1927, the results of which were posthumously published in 1955. He found most of these shabtis on the floor of that pyramid's burial chamber, scattered all about as the result of activities of ancient tomb robbers. They had apparently overlooked two smaller groups of shabtis anciently arranged at the time of the pharaoh's burial, standing shoulder to shoulder against the burial chamber's walls. After completing his excavation, Reisner inventoried 1,277 shabtis of Senkamanisken, of which 410 were sculpted from serpentine. The violation of the tomb, as found by Reisner, precludes drawing conclusions about the total number of such figures originally interred with this king.

The serpentine shabtis of this pharaoh represent the pharaoh mummiform with only his hands protruding from his bandages, holding agricultural tools. He is shown wearing a plain nemes-headdress, fronted by the double uraeus (compare cat. 68), one of the royal insignia of the Kushites, and a thick, plaited false beard.

These were inscribed with Spell 6 of *The Book of the Dead*, and may be translated as

> *The illuminated one, the lord of the Two Lands, the pharaoh Senkamanisken, true of voice, he says, Hail, shabti, if anyone summons the Osiris, pharaoh Senkamanisken, true of voice, in order to perform any work which is required in the necropolis, to cultivate the fields, to irrigate the canals, to carry sand from the East to the West, and vice versa, "Here I am," you shall say.*

Many of these serpentine shabtis, this present one included, are also inscribed on the soles of the feet with enigmatic symbols that have yet to be satisfactorily explained.

The shabtis of Senkamanisken are so similar in style and material to shabtis created for elite members of Egyptian society living at Thebes during Dynasty XXV and XXVI that one suggests that these shabtis were created in Egypt and exported to Napata for inclusion in this pharaoh's pyramid. Many members of the Theban aristocracy continued to maintain their close ties with the Kushites, despite the latter's withdrawal from Egypt.

References: Dunham, *Royal Cemeteries*, 1955, pp. 41–47.

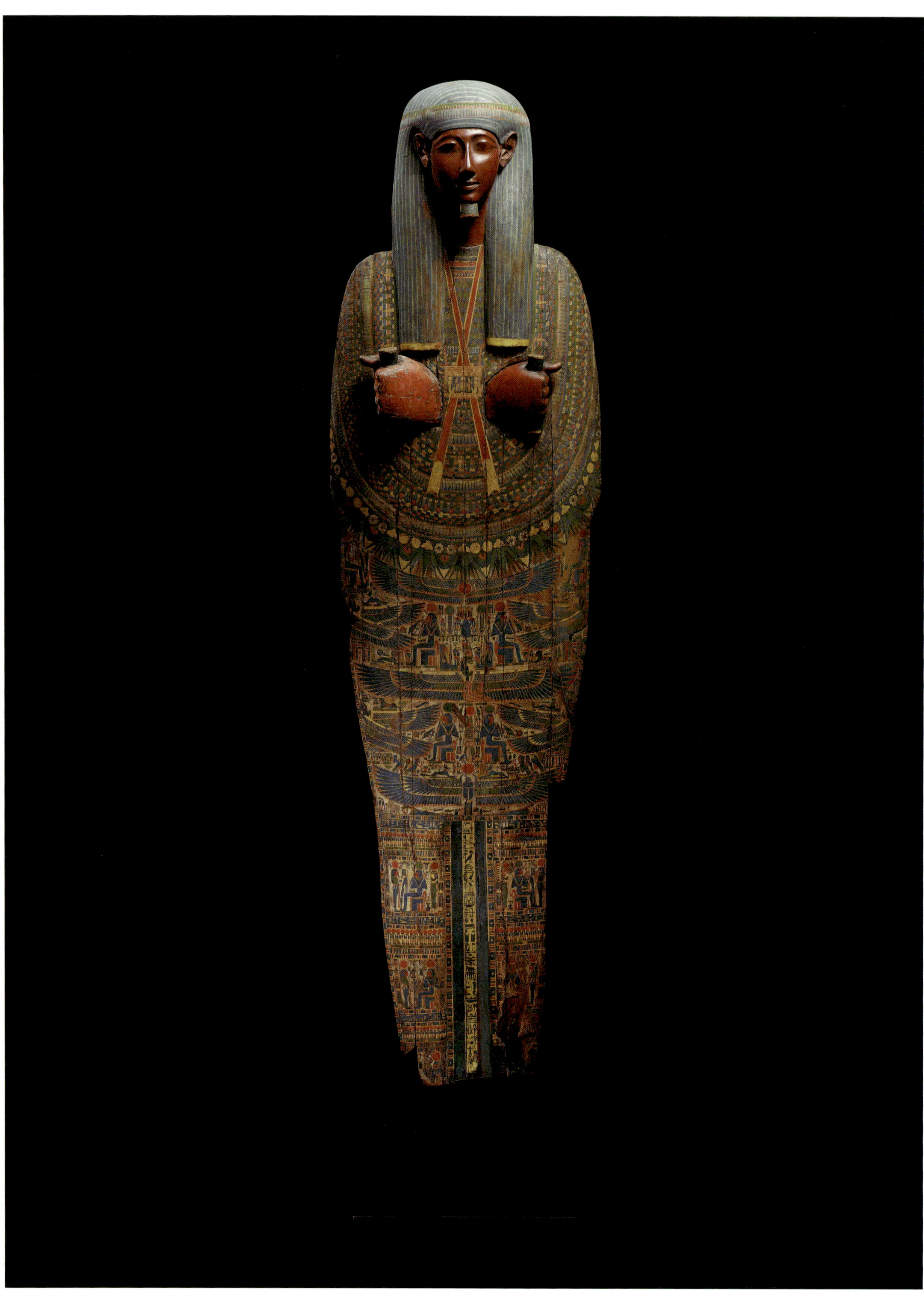

99.

Lid from an Anthropoid Sarcophagus

Dynasty XXI–XXII, 1080–720 BC
Wood, gessoed and painted
Height 62 in.
Inv. no. EG-364

This object is designed as an anthropoid, or human-shaped, lid of a sarcophagus. Its two important motifs are a large broad collar, over which is painted a pair of red bands in imitation of mummy-braces, a phrase adopted from the British English word for "suspenders." Actual leather suspenders were introduced along with other innovations in funerary practice at the end of the New Kingdom, at which time these real suspenders were placed across the linen mummy bandages in which the body was wrapped. Here, the suspenders, painted red and outlined in yellow, in conjunction with a very large broad collar that extends almost to the navel, are the two salient characteristics of sarcophagus lids designated Type V, to which this example can be confidently assigned. These Type V lids were introduced at the end of Dynasty XXI and continued to be manufactured into Dynasty XXII through the reign of Pharaoh Osorkon I. This dating is suggested by the names of high priests at Thebes impressed on leather suspenders that can be correlated with the actual burial of certain pharaohs. A third and fourth characteristic of lids of Type V are the hands, which are the only part of the arms that are designed three-dimensionally and occasionally hold attributes, as here, and the *horror vacui*—almost every inch of the lid's surface is covered with densely packed decorative elements.

According to one inventory, lids of Type V account for eighteen percent of the entire production of so-called yellow-type coffins, thereby ranking them as the second most frequently encountered type. There is a great deal of scholarly discussion with regard to the technique by which this characteristic yellow color was achieved. The academic consensus now suggests that either of two possibilities is correct. One possibility is that the yellow may be an unintentional result of the oxygenation process of the varnish coating of the painted surface of the lid. The other is that the yellow may have been the actual color of choice, intentionally painted on the object.

The cordiform-shaped head of this example exhibits a rich, coffee-colored patina, with the ears and false beard, in the form of a goatee, separately made and attached. The straps intended to secure the false beard in place were originally inlaid, but the inlay is now missing. The physiognomic features of the face are designed in an idealizing idiom that recalls models current during the early Ramesside Period. Certain details have been emphasized by the addition of black paint, particularly the eyes and their brows. The head is framed by a relatively long tripartite wig, now greenish blue and ornamented with thin yellow stripes, its lappets ending in a single, horizontal yellow band. The wig is held in place by a fillet ornamented with floral motifs.

There is an extremely large broad collar, ornamented with several registers of floral motifs as well and terminating in a carefully designed pattern of alternating lotus flowers and rosettes. The three-dimensional, separately crafted hands each holding a so-called emblematic staff, which here are clearly not the stylized versions of a papyrus scroll found in other examples, protrude from the broad collar, between which is depicted a pectoral, placed between them and just below the intersection of the X-pattern created by the crossed braces. The pectoral is in the form of a shrine crowned by a cavetto cornice that features two seated deities crowned with sun disks facing into the composition as if in adoration of a cartouche inscribed in hieroglyphs Djeser-ka-re, the prenomen of the pharaoh Amenhotep I.

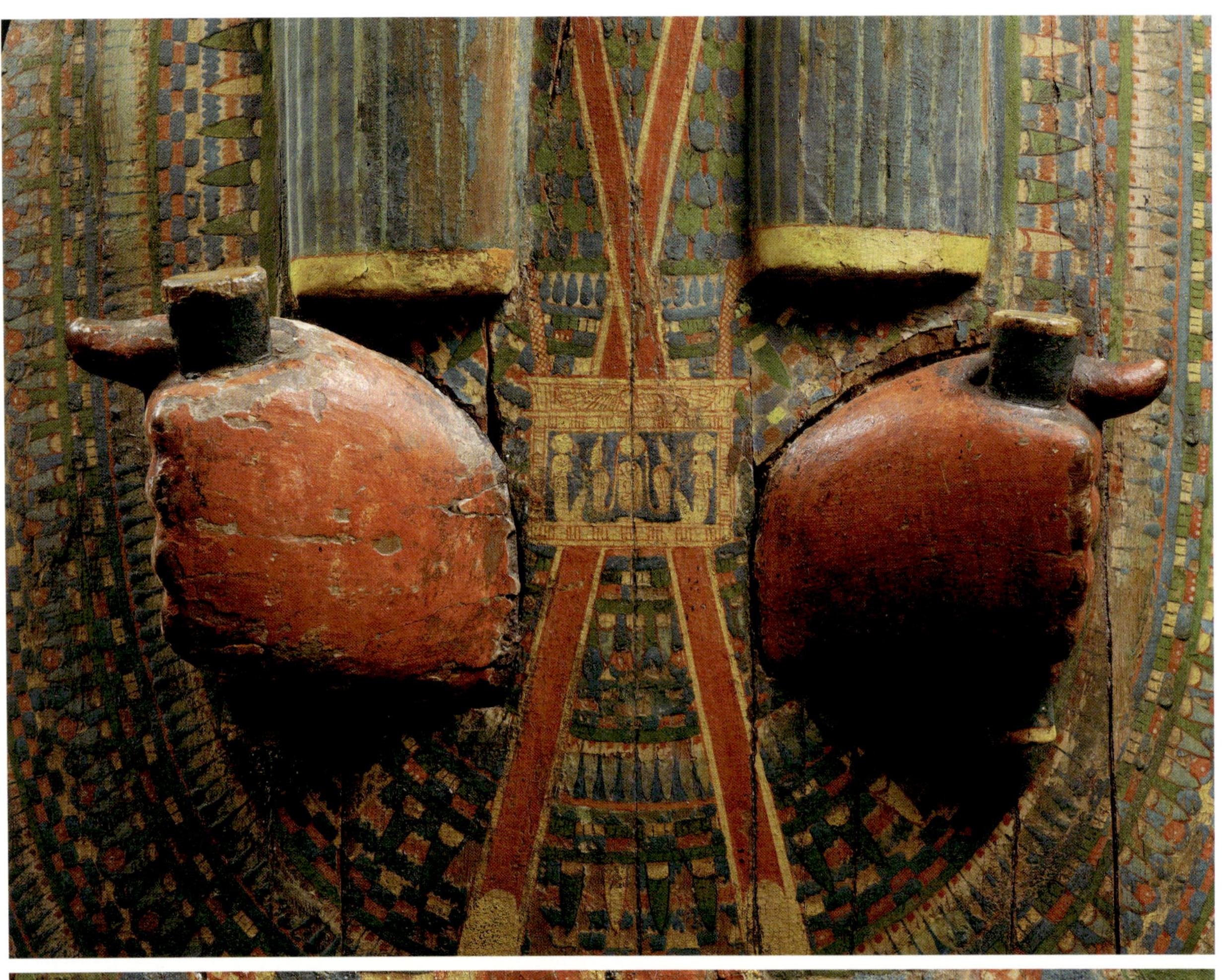

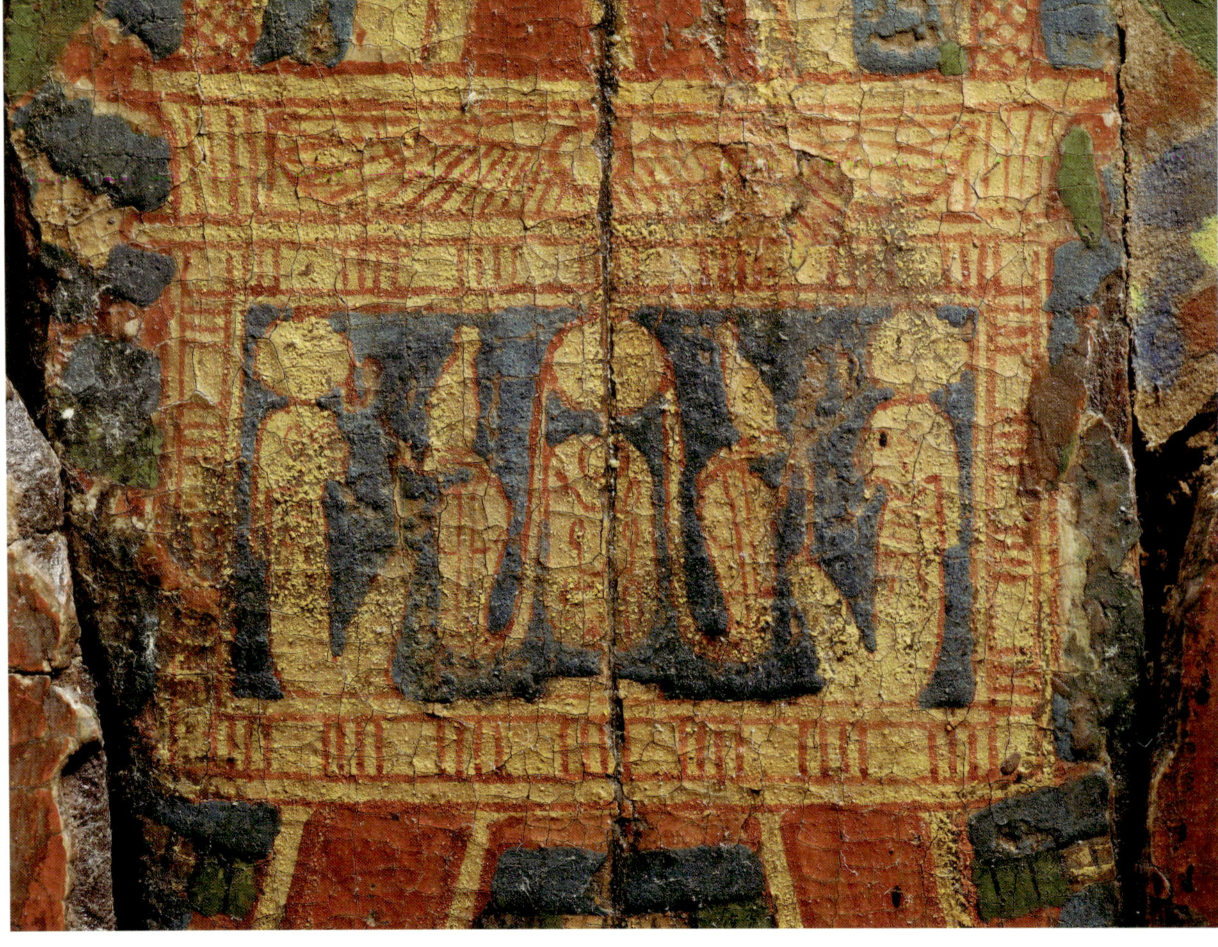

That cartouche is symbolically protected by two large uraei, or cobras, each wearing a White Crown. Amenhotep I, the second pharaoh of Dynasty XVIII, and his mother Ahmose-Nefertari were anciently regarded as the joint founders of the craftsmen village at Deir el-Medineh, whose inhabitants were responsible for the decoration and furnishings of the royal tombs in the Valley of the Kings. Although the location of his tomb remains to be discovered, his cult, among the first to be established for any pharaoh, was long-lived. He became the patron of all subsequent workmen laboring on the royal tombs and creating their furnishings. The commemoration of that pharaoh on this sarcophagus lid created during late Dynasty XXI to early Dynasty XXII clearly demonstrates the longevity of his cult.

The lid is designed as a series of horizontal registers, which may be described from top to bottom as follows:

Register 1

A winged sun disk frames the top of the scene. In each corner, to the right and left, is a depiction of a deity seated upon a throne resting on a neb-sign. Each is crowned by a sun disk, holds a crook and flail, and is depicted mummiform, with braces crossed over the chest. A recumbent jackal fills the space below the wings of a goddess, beneath the lower wing is a human-headed sphinx. The field between these goddess contains two enthroned, mummiform gods, likewise crowned with sun disks and holding a crook and flail. Between them is a single scarab in the center, flanked below left and right by a seated figure, mummiform as well with similar braces and bearded, with an ointment cone on his head. In front of each is a vessel with a falcon-headed lid.

Register 2

This register is framed at the top by a seated winged sun goddess facing right, whose crown, consisting of two ostrich feathers fronted by a sun disk, separates the two falcon-lidded jars in Register 1. Winged goddesses again frame the left and right sides, with a single human-headed sphinx in the field above the upper wing. A vulture with an ankh-sign in front and a *shen*-sign behind fills the space between their wings while a falcon, *ba*-bird, and recumbent jackal fill the space beneath. Two deities, similar to those in Register 1 and likewise composed back-to-back, are separated by a depiction of the Abydos-fetish topped by a sun disk.

Registers 4–6

These registers are divided into two panels, each by a band of vertical hieroglyphs running down the center of the lid. The first register is framed at the top by a winged scarab pushing a sun disk, the field beneath his wings on either side filled by a figure reclining on the ground with his hands raised in adoration. Immediately below to the left and right are the first hieroglyphs encountered on the object. These contain a series of traditional formulae, among which one finds

> *The one revered under Osiris, foremost of the Westerners...*
>
> *The one revered under Isis, the great, the divine mother...*
>
> *A gift which pharaoh bestows upon the gods Ra-Horakhty, Atum...*

Although the name of the owner of this particular lid is not preserved, one can speculate that he served in the priesthood of the god Amun at Thebes during the Third Intermediate Period.

References: Niwinski, 21st *Dynasty Coffins*, 1988.

100.

A Sarcophagus for a Shrew

Dynasty XXX–the early Ptolemaic Period, 380–250/200 BC
Wood, gessoed and painted
Length 12 ½ in.
Inv. no. EG-370

The sarcophagus is trapezodial, narrower at the back than at the front. It is constructed from six worked planks of wood (species not identified), which have been doweled together in keeping with ancient Egyptian traditions of fine joinery. The pegs fastening together the four sides as well as the bottom are still in place, and of the four used to secure the lid, two remain, now protruding (compare cat. 101). The lid is intact. It is interesting to note that the box was assembled by a carpenter and then gessoed before the paint was applied, because the snouts and tails of the shrews in this area are painted on the thin edges of both side boards.

The principal decoration consists of rows of shrews on red ground lines. Each is represented in characteristic profile view with the eyes in front view. The top is additionally adorned with a coiling serpent, only barely visible. The front of the sarcophagus contains the same red ground line divisions, a coiled snake, facing right, at the top, and three shrews in each register, the center one of each group intentionally (apparently) taller than the ones behind and in front.

The shrew is called *amamu* in ancient Egyptian, which some would translate as "glutton." It is not a very large animal and exhibits short, dense fur that is dark gray to brown in color. Shrews are nocturnal, a characteristic upon which ancient Egyptian theologians focused, and nest by hiding under vegetation, stones, or in burrows. Their appearance may be mistaken for that of the ichneumon, and this similarity caused the ancient Egyptians to assimilate the one with the other in some episodes of their mythology.

The nocturnal shrew was associated with the night, darkness, and blindness, and was therefore an appropriate guide for the deceased as they made their journey by night toward resurrection. The "Blind Horus" was believed to have appeared as a shrew when the evil god Seth blinded him in the struggle to avenge Osiris. In this connection, the shrew was also sacred to the goddess Wadjet (compare cat. 72), who was personified as the cobra/uraeus. Taking this form, she helped Horus escape from Seth at another point during their struggle. It is interesting to note that this "protective" function of the shrew may also be indebted to the observation that cats in general avoid killing shrews and, if they do kill one, do not eat it. This natural characteristic imbued the shrew with aspects of both sacredness and invincibility.

And yet there was another dimension to the shrew, and this doubtless developed from its physical resemblance to the ichneumon. As a result, Egyptian theologians maintained that the shrew could be transformed into that creature. The process is described as follows: the blind shrew, who acted as a guide for the deceased during the nocturnal journey, was transformed at dawn, just as the deceased was resurrected, into an ichneumon symbolizing the rising sun in his form as Atum, who was simultaneously regarded as the "Seeing Horus," who regained his vision. At dusk, the ichneumon was transformed into a tiny shrew, and that shrew came to symbolize the cycle of renewal itself. During the Late Period, the shrew was regarded as an incarnation of the god Osiris and could be associated with the number seven. There is even evidence to suggest that amulets in the form of a shrew were utilized as healing charms against such afflictions as boils.

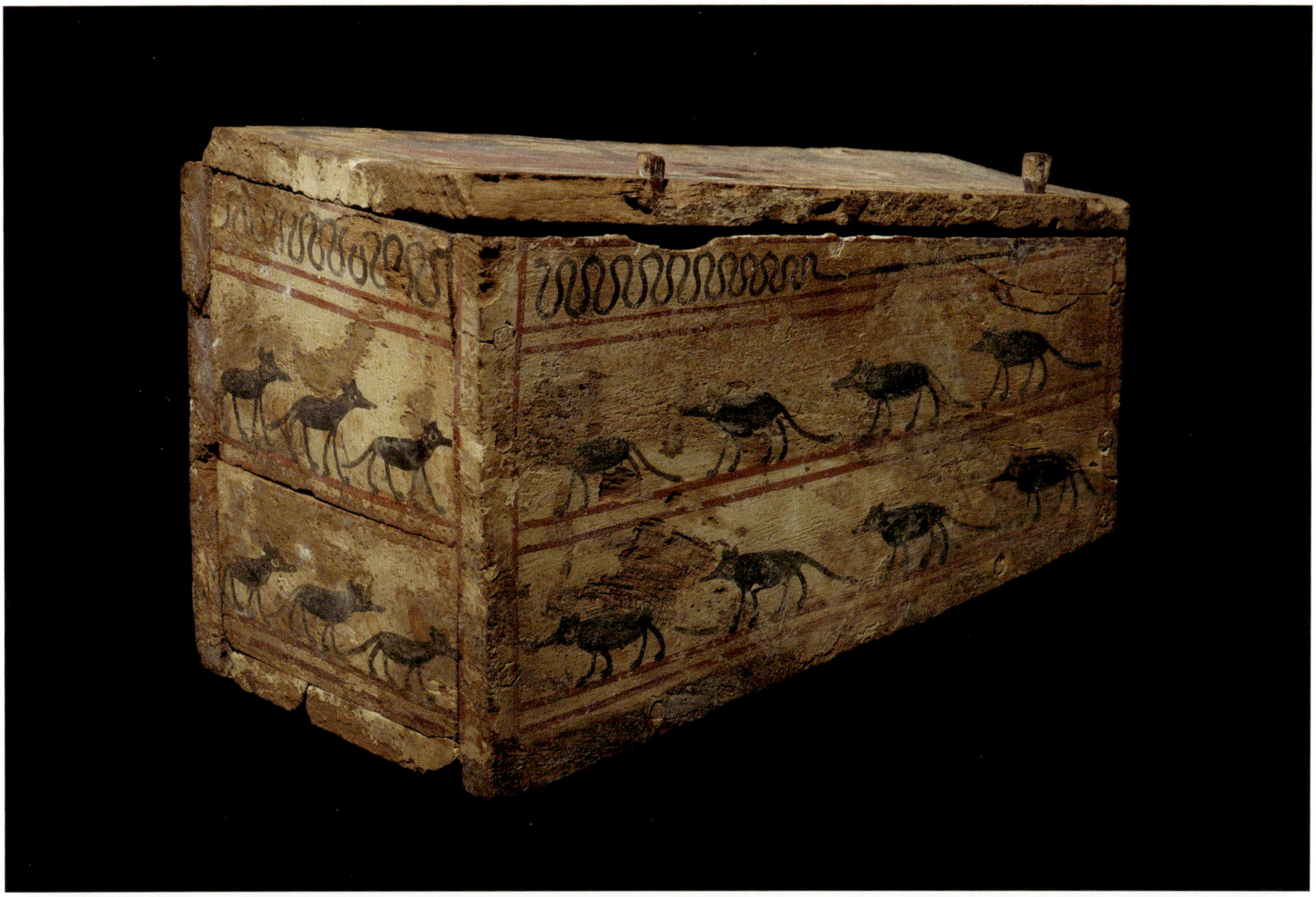

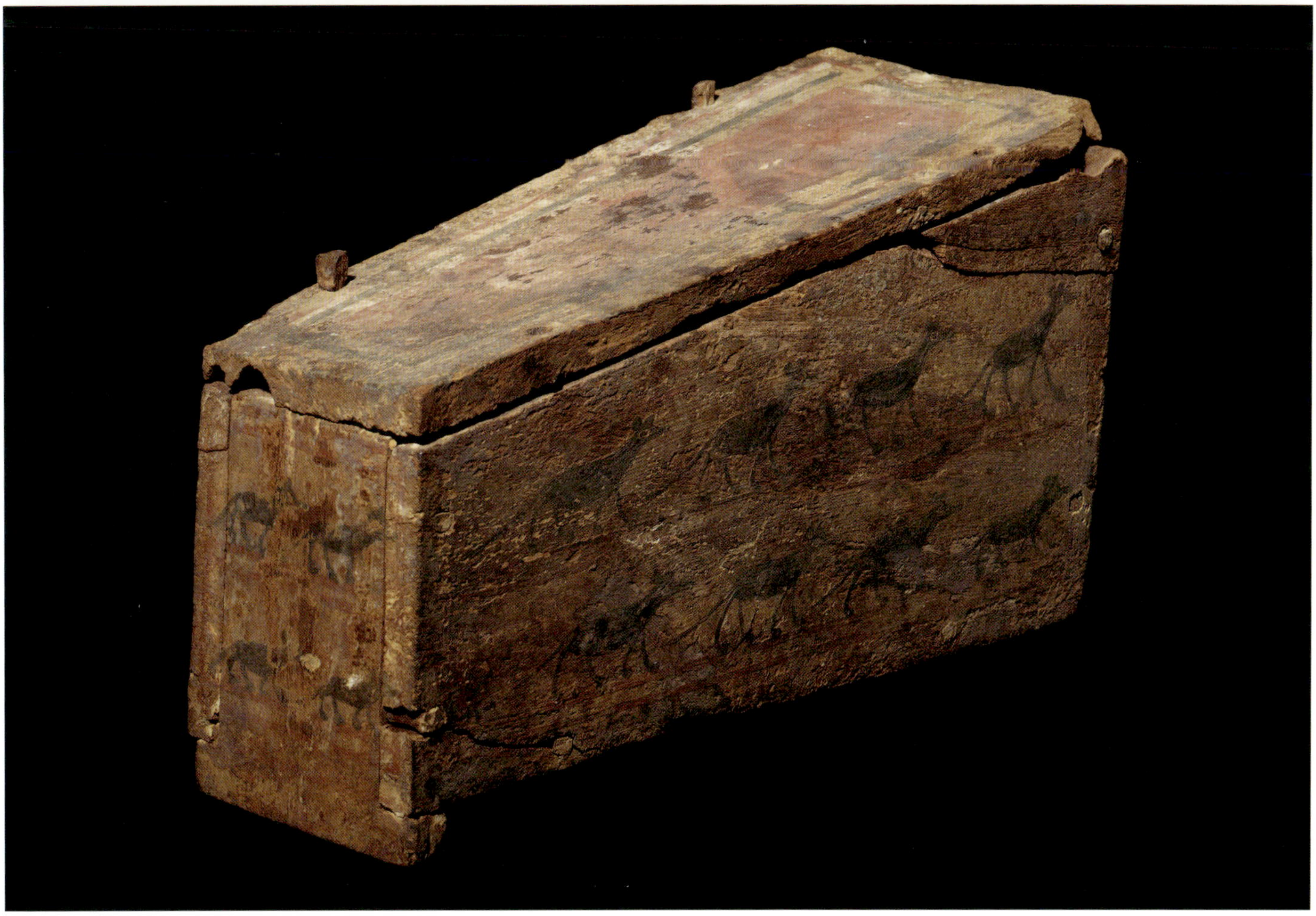

The mummification of animals during the course of the Late Period was big business, and archaeologists have uncovered extensive farms on which animals of almost every imaginable species were raised. The processes involved have been described in minute detail. The mummified animals were often placed into pottery jars, less often into wooden sarcophagi, and sold to pilgrims visiting religious sanctuaries, who would dedicate them to the deities of the land accompanied by the recitation of requisite prayers. Extensive cemeteries of animal mummies are currently attested at both Saqqara and Tuna el-Gebel. Parallels from those cemeteries suggest the dating for this example.

References: Brunner-Traut, "Spitzmaus," 1965, pp. 123–63; Osborn and Osbornova, *Mammals*, 1998, p. 27.

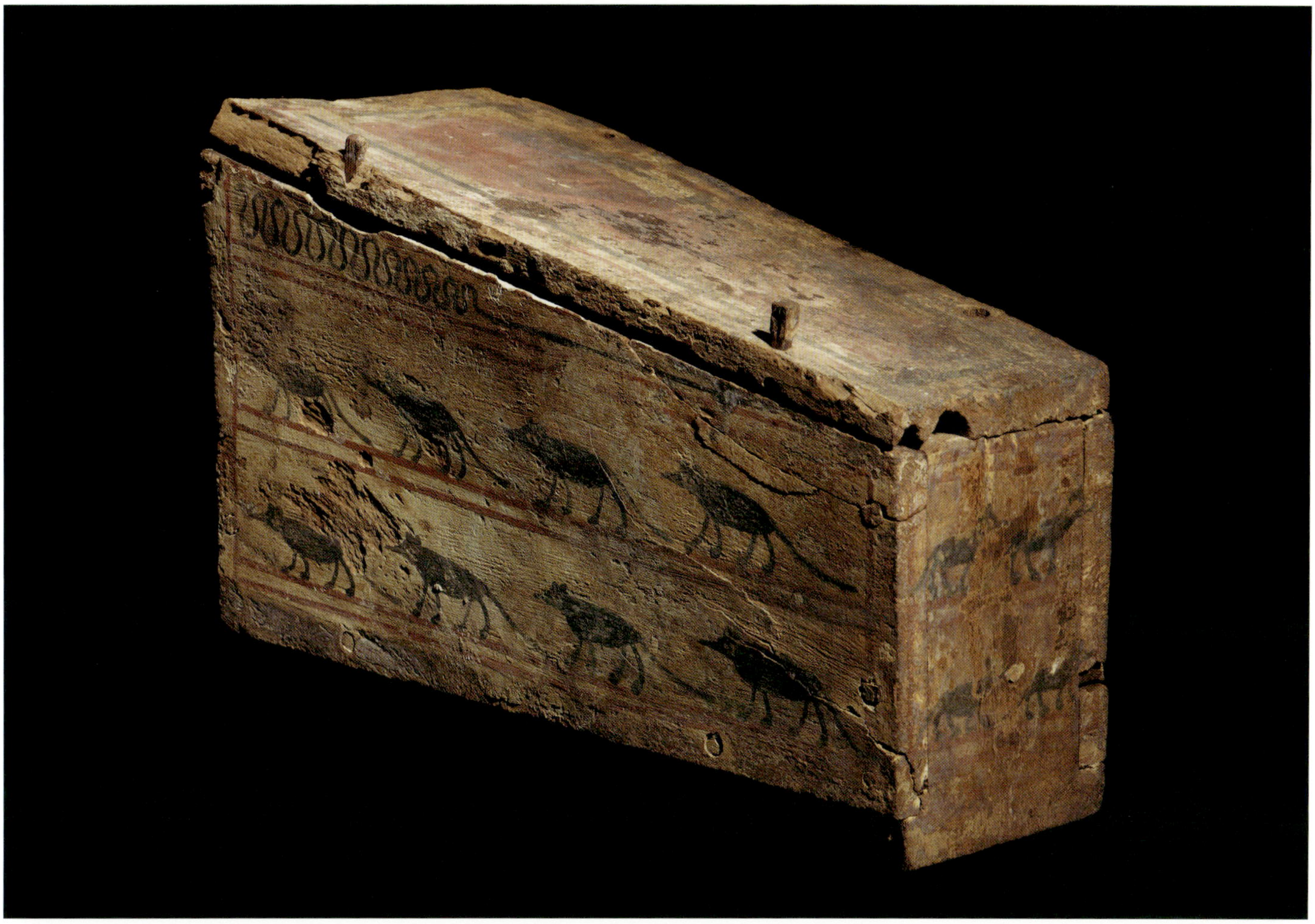

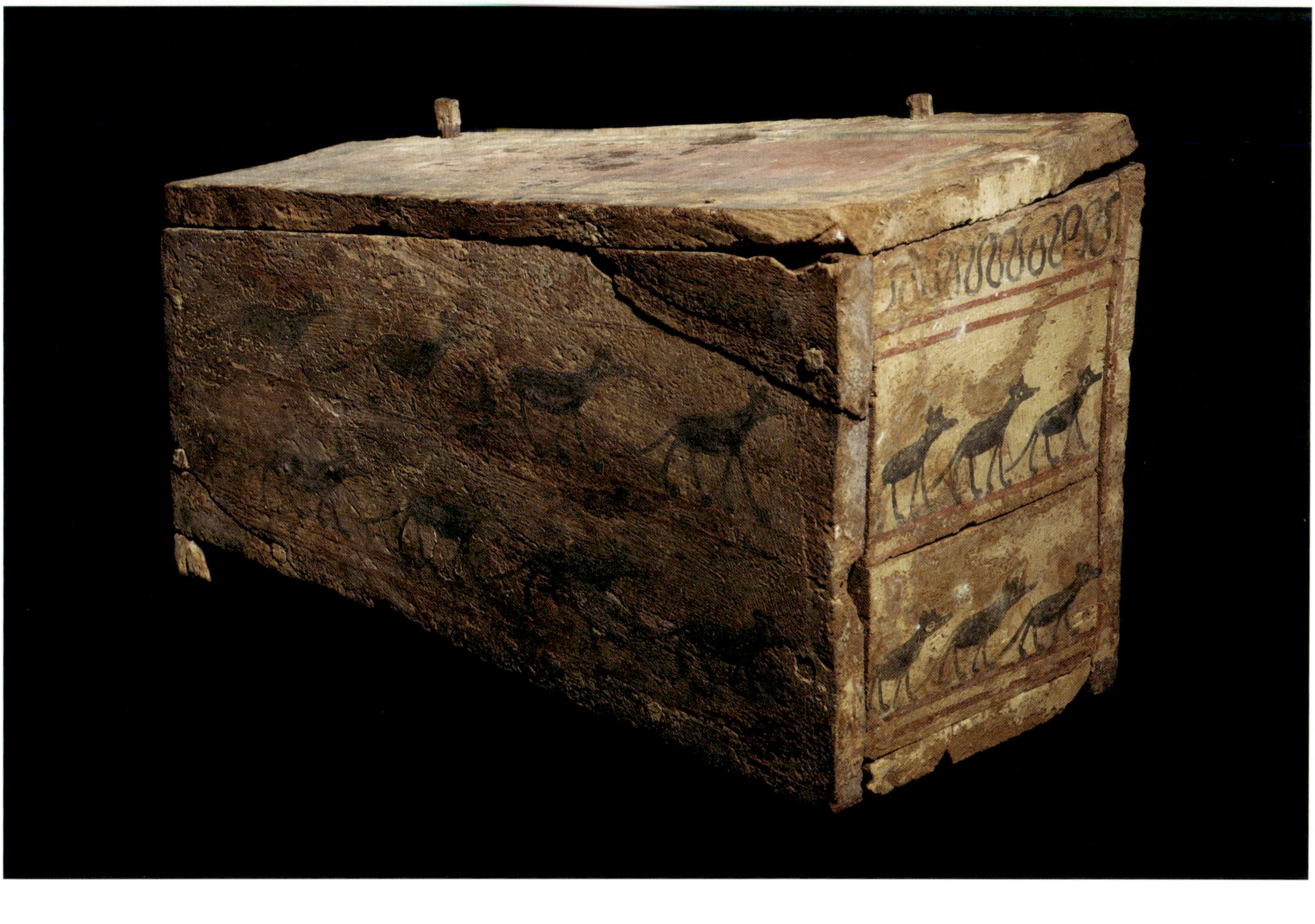

101.

Lid of an Anthropiod Sarcophagus Inscribed for Hor-em-akhet

Dynasty XXI–XXV, 1080–655 BC
Wood with inlays of white stone (alabaster or limestone) and blue glass
Height 80 ½ in.
Inv. no. EG-315

The body of the lid is modeled in broad, restrained planes with little attention to anatomical detail so that the focus is almost exclusively on the head. The head is framed by an exceptionally large and thick wig of echeloned curls, which end in long lappets extending to mid-chest. The ears are exposed behind the lappets, the ends of which are ornamented with four inward-facing uraei, or sacred cobras, each crowned with a solar disk. This elaborate wig is held in place by a thick wreath of stylized floral motifs with vulture wings visible behind the ears.

The head is dominated by an idealized face, the top of the forehead of which is partially concealed by the floral wreath. Secondary materials have been used to ornament the eyes, which are inlayed with a white material (alabaster or limestone?). Their eyelids and cosmetic lines exhibit blue glass inlays secured in place by plaster, the same material being used to create the eyebrows. The nose exhibits a thin bridge, its nostrils drilled. The small mouth features downturned corners.

The lid is inscribed in hieroglyphs, painted black, which provisionally yield the following translation:

Recitation by the Osiris Hor-em-akhet, born of Aset-akhbit"

> *"...Your mother Nut has spread over her name of Shepet. Your face is not constricted (?). Heaven...(?) in you (?) in (?) her name Nut (?)... the god, you cannot in your name of god, who pulls Re (?). One gives (?), one places it on the way (?), that you may enter celebrating (?)... of your, every one (?) to (?)...Possessor of strength (?)...One gives..."*

The dating of this lid has been a matter of speculation because of its unique design. As a result, scholars have suggested that this lid was created in a foreign, perhaps Phoenician, workshop in imitation of Egyptian models, whereas others suggest a dating into the Roman Imperial Period. The signs and content of its inscription as well as its owner's name suggest a pharaonic Egyptian workshop, as does the technique, which relies both upon the inlays of the face and the addition to the end of each lappet of the wig of a separately made panel, decorated with a train of uraei with sun disks on their heads. These panels have been affixed to the wig by an elaborate system of dowels (compare cat. 100).

The dating of this object to Dynasty XXI–XXV is provided by a close parallel in London that features a small head framed by a seemingly disproportionately large wig, inlaid eyes, and three columns of hieroglyphs on down the front. Taken together, this pair suggests that the repertoire of styles for sarcophagi of this period was varied (compare cat. 99).

The appearance of the body of a vulture over the wig is exceptional (compare cat. 62) for an object inscribed for a male (compare cat. 53). Here, it is regarded as affording the deceased protection inasmuch as the inscriptions refer to Nut, the goddess of the sky. She is often described as embracing the deceased and depicted as a female figure with wings attached to each of her arms (compare cat. 74). The appearance of the vulture

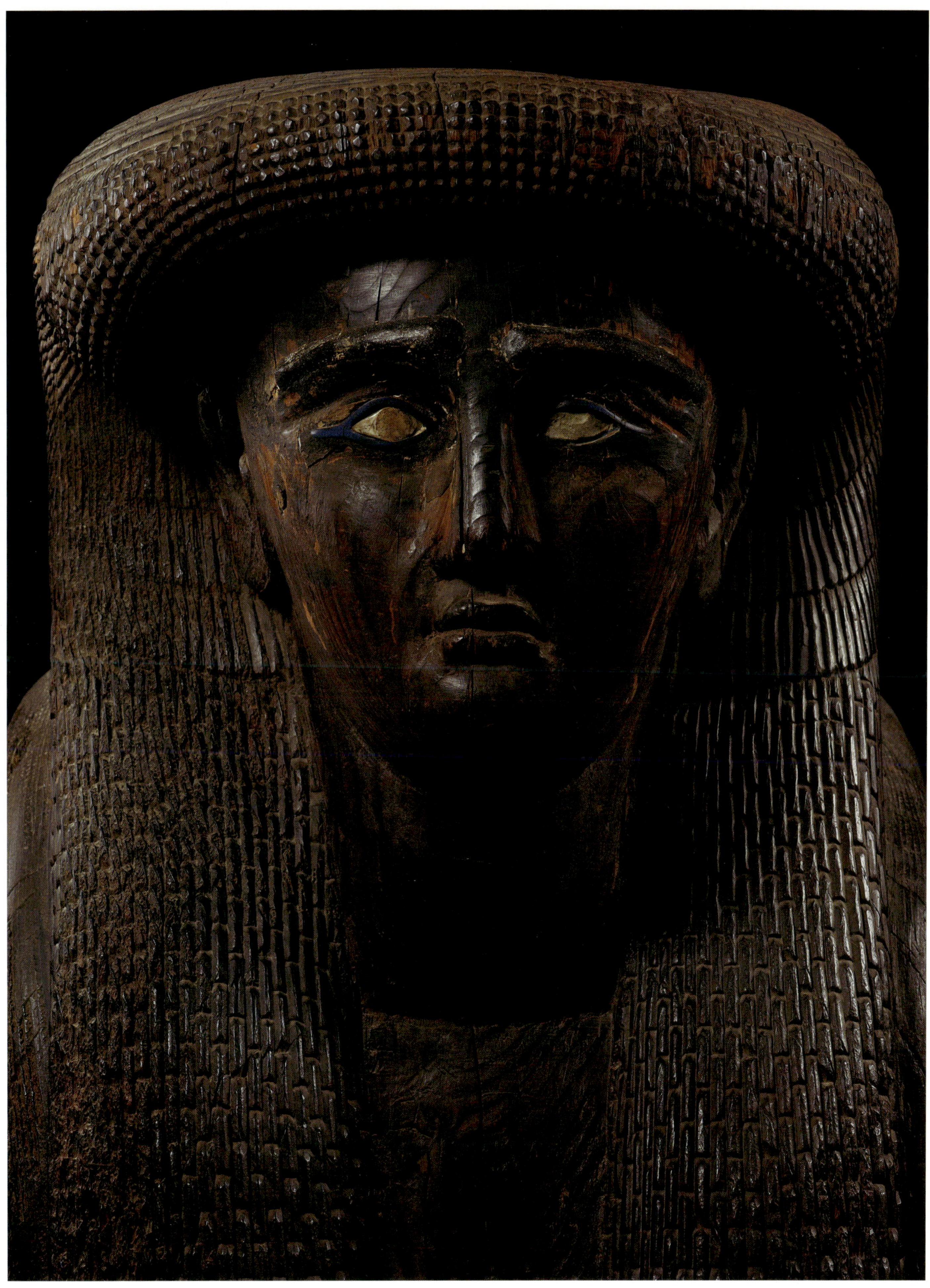

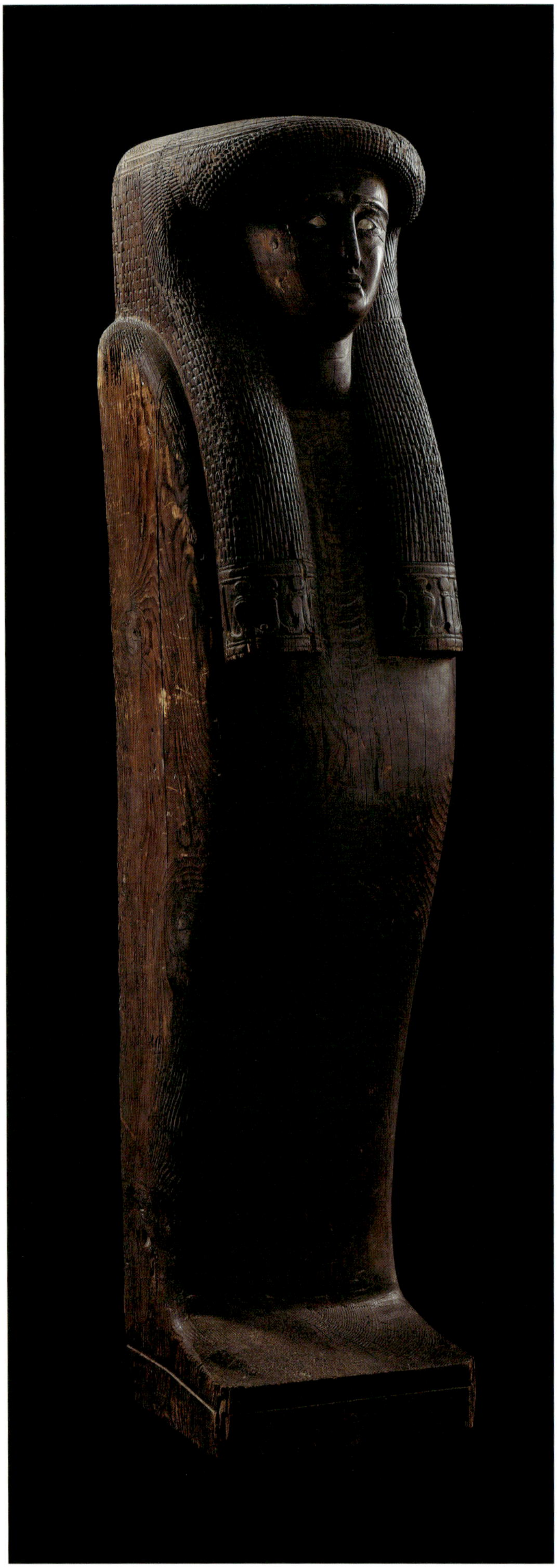

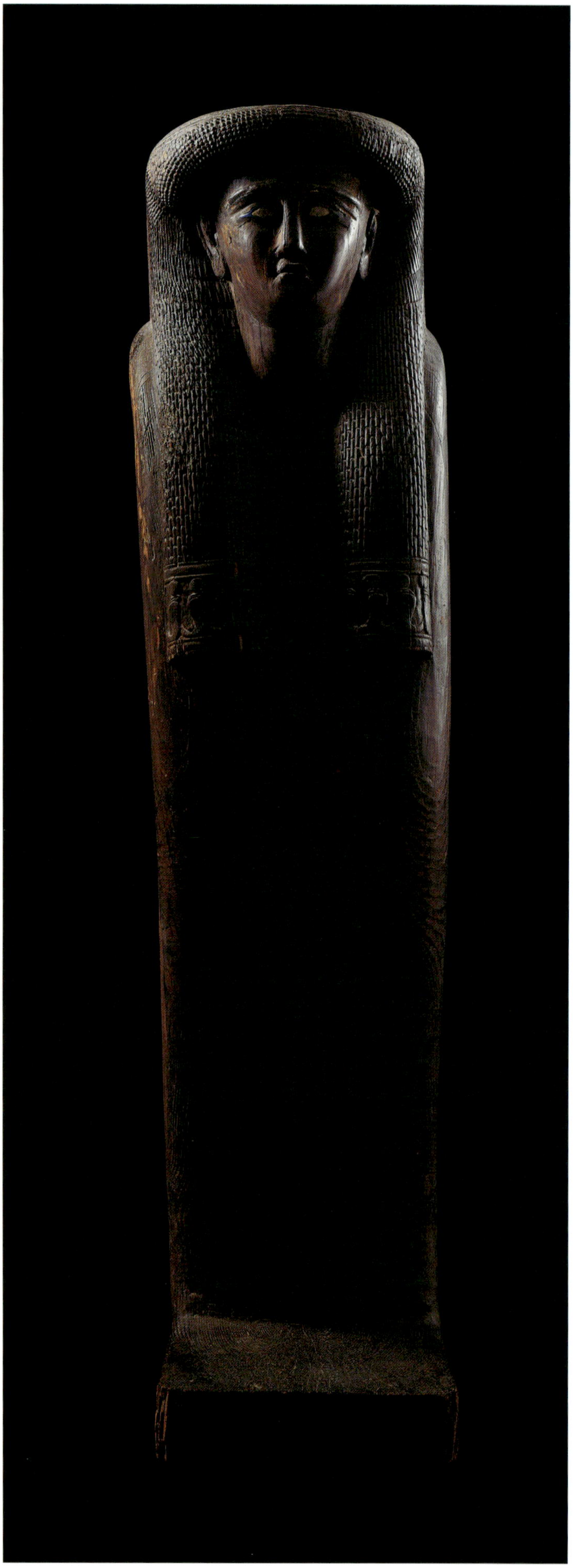

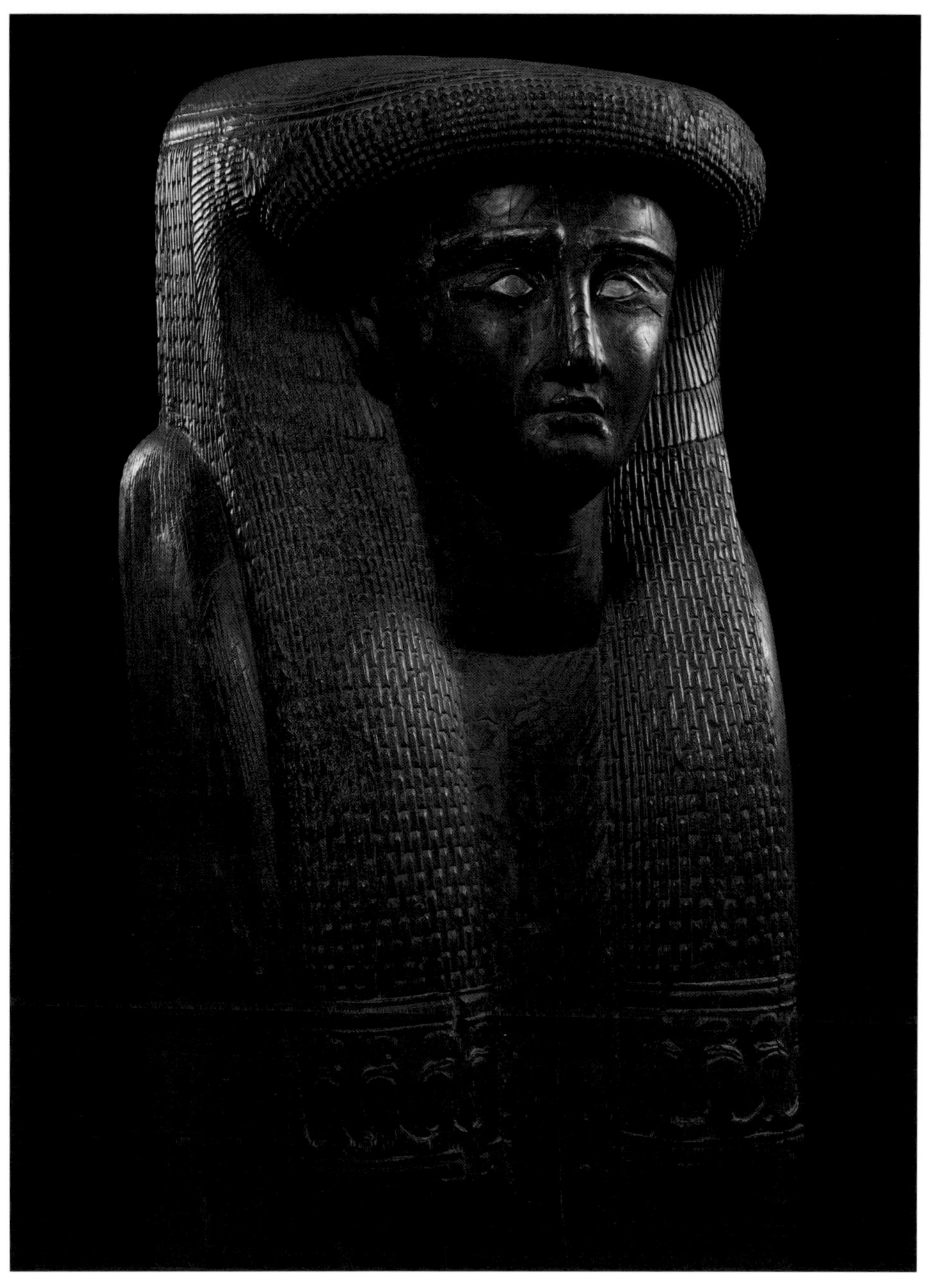

headdress is, therefore, consistent with the mention of that goddess and suggests that the design of both the decorative elements of the lid and its inscription were predetermined as a complementary ensemble. The train of uraei reinforce this protective nature of the decorative scheme.

The inlaid eyes allude to the solar and lunar eyes of the god Horus, which in funerary contexts provide protection as well, but they are also associated with a number of deities who afford the deceased the ability to see clearly during both night and day.

Works Cited in the Catalogue

A

Ägyptologischen Seminar, Basel, *Sethos,*1991
Ägyptologischen Seminar, Basel. *Sethos—ein Pharaonengrab.* Basel, 1991.

Altenmüller, *Die Apotropaia*, 1965
Altenmüller, H[artwig]. *Die Apotropaia und die Götter Mittelägyptens* I–II. Rottweil, 1965.

Andrews, *Amulets*, 1994
Andrews, Carol. *Amulets of Ancient Egypt.* Austin, 1994.

Andrews, *Mummies*, 1984
Andrews, Carol. *Egyptian Mummies.* London, 1984.

Andrews and Dirk, *Objects*, 2006
Andrews, Carol A. R., and Jacobus van Dijk, eds. *Objects for Eternity.* Mainz, 2006.

Anonymous, "La porte du rêve," 2007
Anonymous. "La porte du rêve. Antiquités égyptiennes dans l'intimité des collectionneurs." *ARTPASSIONS* 10 (October 2007).

Anonymous, "Les ivoires de Beersheba," 1995
Anonymous, "Les ivoires de Beersheba." *Les Dossiers Archéologie*, no. 203 (May 1995).

ARCE, *60th Annual Meeting*, 2009
ARCE. *The 60th Annual Meeting of the American Research Center in Egypt. April 24–26, 2009. The Adolphus Hotel, Dallas, Texas.* San Antonio, 2009.

Aston, *Stone Vessels*, 1994
Aston, B.G. *Ancient Egyptian Stone Vessels.* Heidelberg, 1994.

Aubert and Aubert, *Bronzes et or*, 2001
Aubert, Jacques-F., and Liliane Aubert, *Bronzes et or Egyptiens.* Paris, 2001.

Aubert and Aubert, *Statuettes égyptiennes*, 1974
Aubert, Jacques-F., and Liliane Aubert, *Statuettes égyptiennes. Chaouabtis—Ouchebtis.* Paris, 1974.

Aufrère, "Evolution des idées," 1998
Aufrère, Sydney H. "Evolution des idées concernant l'emploi des couleurs dans le mobilier et les scènes funéraires en Egypte jusqu'à l'époque tardive." In *La couleur dans la peinture et l'émaillage l'Egypte ancienne*, ed. Sylvie Colinart et Michel Menu. Bari, 1998.

B

Baines, "Ankh-sign," 1975
Baines, John R. "Ankh-sign, Belt, and Penis Sheath." *Studien zur Altägyptischen Kultur* 3 (1975), pp. 1–24.

Baumgartel, *Cultures*, 1955–60
Baumgartel, E. J. *The Cultures of Prehistoric Egypt.* London, 1955–60.

Begelsbacher-Fischer, *Untersuchungen zur Götterwelt*, 1981
Begelsbacher-Fischer, Barbara L. *Untersuchungen zur Götterwelt des Alten Reiches. Im Spiegel der Privatgräber der IV. Und V. Dynastie.* Freiburg, 1981.

Bénédite, *Miroirs*, 1907
Bénédite, G. *Miroirs.* Cairo, 1907

Berlandini, "Amenhotep III," 1993
Berlandini, Jocelyne. "Amenhotep III et le concept de Heh," *Bulletin. Société d'Egyptologie Genève* 17 (1993), pp. 11– 28.

Berman, *Catalogue*, 1999
Berman, L. M. *Catalogue of Egyptian Art. The Cleveland Museum of Art.* Cleveland, 1999.

Bianchi, *Cleopatra's Egypt*, 1988
Bianchi, Robert Steven. *Cleopatra's Egypt. Age of the Ptolemies.* Brooklyn, 1988.

Bianchi, "Egyptian Metal Statuary," 1990
Bianchi, Robert Steven. "Egyptian Metal Statuary of the Third Intermediate Period (circa 1070–656 BC) from its Egyptian Antecedents to its Samian Examples." In *Small Bronze Sculpture from the Ancient World: Papers Delivered at a Symposium Organized by the Department of Antiquities and Antiquities Conservation and Held at the J. Paul Getty Museum, March 16–19, 1989.* Malibu, 1990, pp. 61ff.

Bianchi, "Elite Image," 1992
Bianchi, Robert Steven. "An Elite Image." In *Chief of Seers: Egyptian Studies in Memory of Cyril Aldred*, ed. E. Goring, et al. London, 1992, pp. 34–48.

Bianchi, "Ex-Votos of Dynasty XXVI," 1979
Bianchi, Robert Steven. "Ex-Votos of Dynasty XXVI." *Mitteilungen des Deutschen Archäologischen Instituts Abteilung Kairo* 35 (1979), 15ff.

Bianchi, "Hippopotamus," in press
Bianchi, Robert Steven. "A Hippopotamus for Hera." *Bulletin of the Egyptological Seminar.* In press.

Bianchi, "Images of Cleopatra," 2001
Bianchi, Robert Steven. "Images of Cleopatra VII Reconsidered." In *Cleopatra Reassessed*, ed. Susan Walker and Sally-Ann Ashton. The British Museum Occasional Paper 103. London, 2001, pp. 22, n. 58.

Bianchi, "Reflections," 1985
Bianchi, Robert Steven. "Reflections of the Sky's Eyes." *SOURCE—Notes in the History of Art* 4 (1985), 10ff.

Bianchi, "Stones," 2007
Bianchi, Robert Steven. "The Stones of Egypt and Nubia." In *The Archaeology and Art of Ancient Egypt. Essays in Honor of David B. O'Connor* I, ed. Zahi A. Hawaas and Janet Richards. Annales du Service des Antiquités de l'Egypte Cahier 36. Cairo, 2007.

Bianchi, "Two Ex-votos," 1981
Bianchi, Robert Steven. "Two Ex-votos from the Sebennytic Group." *Society for the Study of Egyptian Antiquities Journal* 11 (1981), 31ff.

Bietak, "Zur Herjunft des Seth," 1990
Bietak, M. "Zur Herjunft des Seth von Avaris." *Aegypten und Levant* 1 (1990), pp. 9–16.

Bourriau, "Amphora," 1982
Bourriau, Janine D. "Amphora." In *Egypt's Golden Age. The Art of Living in the New Kingdom, 1558–1085 BC*. Exh. cat. Museum of Fine Arts. Boston, 1982, p. 127, no. 114.

Bourriau, "Pitcher," 1982
Bourriau, Janine D. "Pitcher." In *Egypt's Golden Age. The Art of Living in the New Kingdom, 1558–1085 BC*. Exh. cat. Museum of Fine Arts. Boston, 1982, p. 129, no. 118.

Bovot, *Chaouabtis*, 2003
Bovot, J. -L. *Chaouabtis. Des travailleurs pharaoniques pour l'éternité*. Paris, 2003.

Brunner-Traut, "Spitzmaus," 1965
Brunner-Traut, E. "Spitzmaus und Ichneumon als Tiere des Sonnengottes. "*Nachrichten der Akademie der Wissenschaften in Göttingen I. Philologisch-historische Klasse*. Göttingen Vorträge 7 (1965), pp. 123–63.

Bulté, "Cuillères d'offrandes," 2008
Bulté, Jeanne. "Cuillères d'offrandes en faïence et en pierre. Messagères du bien être—et de prospérité." *Revue Egyptologie* 59 (2008).

Burlington Fine Arts Club, *Catalogue* 1922
Burlington Fine Arts Club. *Catalogue of an Exhibition of Ancient Egyptian Art*. London, 1922.

C

Chappaz, *Akhénaton et Nefértiti*, 2008
Chappaz, Jean-Luc, ed. *Akhénaton et Nefértiti. Soleil et ombres des pharaons*. Geneva, 2008.

Chappaz, "Une stèle," 2005–7
Chappaz, Jean-Luc. "Une stèle de donation de Ramsès III." *Bulletin. Société d'Egyptologie Genève* 27 (2005–7), pp. 5–19.

Chappaz and Chamay, *Reflets du divin*, 2001
Chappaz, Jean-Luc, and Jacques Chamay, *Reflets du divin*. Geneva, 2001.

Coche, "Une nouvelle statue," 1970
Coche, C. "Une nouvelle statue de la déssee léontocéphale Ouadjet wp t3wy." *Revue d'Egyptologie* 22 (1970), pp. 51–62.

Cooney, "Persian Influence," 1965
Cooney, John D. "Persian Influence in Late Egyptian Art." *The Journal of the American Research Center in Egypt* 4 (1965), pp. 39–63.

Cour-Marty, "Les Textes," 1994
Cour-Marty, Marguerite-Annie. "Les Textes des Pyramides," In *Hommages à Jean Leclant I Etudes pharaoniques*, ed. Catherine Berge, G. Clerc, and Nicholas Grimal. Cairo, 1994, pp. 123–39.

D

Daressy, "L'animal séthien," 1920
Daressy, G[eorges]. "L'animal séthien à tête d'âne," *Annales du Service des Antiquités de l'Egypte* 20 (1920), pp. 165ff.

Daressy, "Nouvelle forme," 1908
Daressy, Georges. "Une nouvelle forme d'Amon," *Annales du Service des Antiquités de l'Egypte* 9 (1908), pp. 64ff.

Dasen, *Dwarfs*, 1993
Dasen, Véronique. *Dwarfs in Ancient Egypt and Greece*. Oxford/New York, 1993.

D'Avennes, *Atlas*, 1868–78/1991
D'Avennes, E. Prisse. *Atlas de l'Art Egyptien*. Paris, 1868–78; reprinted by Zeitouna, Cairo, 1991.

Dettmer, ...den Sinn für das Schöne erwecken, 1998
Dettmer, Hans-Georg...*den Sinn für das Schöne erwecken...Führer durch das Kestner-Museum Hannover*. Hannover, 1998

Dunand et al., *Des animaux*, 2005
Dunand, Françoise, and Roger Lichtenberg, with the collaboration of Alain Charron. *Des animaux et des hommes. Une symbiose égyptienne*. Paris, 2005.

Dunham, *Royal Cemeteries*, 1955
Dunham, Dows. *The Royal Cemeteries of Kush II Nuri*. Boston, 1955.

Dunham, *Naga el-Der*, 1937
Dunham, D[ows]. *Naga el-Der stelae of the First Intermediate Period*. London, 1937.

DuQuesne, "Seth," 1998
DuQuesne, T. "Seth and the Jackals." In *Egyptian Religion. The Last Thousand Years. Part I. Studies Dedicated to the Memory of Jan Quaegebeur*, ed. W. Clarysse, et al. Leuven, 1998, pp. 613–28.

E

Eggebrecht, *Ägyptens Aufstieg*, 1987
Eggebrecht, Arne, ed. *Ägyptens Aufstieg zur Weltmacht*. Mainz am Rhein, 1987.

el-Din Mokhtar, *Ihnâsya El-Medina*, 1983
el-Din Mokhtar, Mohamed Gamal. *Ihnâsya El-Medina (Herakleopolis Magna). Its Importance and Its Role in Pharaonic History*. Cairo, 1983.

F

Faulkner, *Book of the Dead*, 1994
Faulkner, Raymond. *The Egyptian Book of the Dead. The Book of Going Forth by Day*. Intro. and commentary by Ogden Goelet; preface by Carol Andrews. San Francisco, 1994.

Fazzini, *Iconography*, 1988
Fazzini, R[ichard] A. *Iconography of Religions. Section XVI. Egypt. Fascicle Ten. Egypt. Dynasty XXII–XXV* (Leiden, 1988).

Fazzini, *Images*, 1975
Fazzini, Richard [A.]. *Images for Eternity*. San Francisco/Brooklyn, 1975.

Frechkop, "L'orycterope," 1946
Frechkop, S. "L'orycterope ne serait-il pas le prototype de l'incarnation de Seth-Typhon?" *Chronique de l'Egypte* 21 (1946), pp. 91ff.

G

Gamer-Wallert, *Ägyptische und ägyptisierende Funde*, 1978
Gamer-Wallert, I. *Ägyptische und ägyptisierende Funde von der Iberischen Halbinsel*. Wiesbaden, 1978.

Gardiner, *Egyptian Grammar*, 1969
Gardiner, Alan Henderson. *Egyptian Grammar*. Oxford/London, 1969.

Gasse, "Une stèle d'Horus, 2005
Gasse, Anne. "Une stèle d'Horus sur les crocodiles à propos du 'Texte C.'" *Revue d'Egyptologie* 55 (2005), pp. 23–37.

Germond, "Bestiaire," 2002–3
Germond, Philippe. "En marge du bestiaire: un drôle de canard..." *Bulletin. Société d'Egyptologie Genève* 25 (2002–3), pp. 75–94.

Günther and Wellauer, *Ägyptische Steingefässe*, 1988
Günther, Peter, and Rudolph Wellauer. *Ägyptische Steingefässe der Sammlung Rudolph Schmidt, Solothurn*. Zurich, 1988.

H

Hawass, *Valley*, 2000
Hawaas, Zahi. *Valley of the Golden Mummies*. New York, 2000.

Hayes, *Scepter* I, 1953
Hayes, William C. *The Scepter of Egypt* I. Greenwich, Conn., 1953.

Hayes, *Scepter* II, 1959
Hayes, William C. *The Scepter of Egypt* II. Greenwich, Conn., 1959.

Hendrickx, "Iconography," 1997
Hendrickx, Stan. "The Iconography of the Predynastic and Early Dynastic Period," and cat. 75. in Elizabeth Anne Hastings, *The Sculpture from the Sacred Animal Necropolis at North Saqqara, 1964–76*. London, 1997.

Hill, L., "Their Heads to Keep," 1999
Hill, Lana. "Their Heads to Keep: The Iconography of Ancient Egyptian Headdresses." In ARCE, *60th Annual Meeting*. 2009, p. 53.

Hill, *Gift for the Gods*, 2007
Hill, Marsha, ed. *Gift for the Gods*. New York/New Haven/London, 2007.

Hill, *Royal Bronze Statuary*, 2004
Hill, Marsha. *Royal Bronze Statuary from Ancient Egypt with Special Attention to the Kneeling Pose*. Leiden/Boston, 2004.

Hill and Wilkinson, *Egyptian Wall Paintings*, 1983
Hill, Marsha, and Charles K. Wilkinson, *Egyptian Wall Paintings. The Metropolitan Museum of Art's Collection of Facsimiles*. New York, 1983.

Husson, *Miroir*, 1977
Constance Husson, *L'offrande du miroir dans les temples égyptiens de l'époque gréco-romaine*. Lyon, 1977.

I

ING Belgique et Fonds, *Sphinx*, 2006
ING Belgique et Fonds Mercator, Bruxelles. *Sphinx, Les guardiens de l'Egypte*. Brussels, 2006.

J

Jorgensen, *Catalogue III*, 1998
Jorgensen, Mogens. *Catalogue III. Egypt II (1159–1080 BC)*. Copenhagen, 1998.

K

Keimer, "Die falschlich," 1950
Keimer, L. "Die falschlich als Okapi gedeuten altägyptischen Darstellungen des Gottes Seth." *Acta Topica* 7 (1950), pp. 110–12.

Koenig, *Magie*, 1994
Koenig, I. *Magie et Magiciens dans l'Egypte ancienne*. Paris, 1994.

Koura, 7-*Heiligen*, 1999
Koura, B. Die, *7-Heiligen Öle" und andere Öl- und Fettnamen*. Aachen, 1999.

Kuhlmann, *Das Ammoneion*, 1988
Kuhlmann, Klaus P. *Das Ammoneion*. Mainz, 1988.

Kuhlmann and Schenel, *Das Grab des Ibi*, 1983
Kuhlmann, K[laus P.], and W. Schenel. *Das Grab des Ibi. Theben Nr. 36*. Vol. I, plates. Mainz, 1983.

Künzi et al., *Les trésors*, 2007
Künzi, Frédéric, with Simone Cauvin, Francis Barria, and Artef Abdel Shari. *Les trésors des pharaons*. Geneva, 2007.

L

Lacovara and Trope, *Collector's Eye*, 2001
Lacovara, P. and B. T. Trope, eds. *The Collector's Eye. Masterpieces of Egyptian Art from the Thalassic Collection, Ltd*. Atlanta, 2001.

Leahy and Mathieson, "Tomb of Nyankhnesut," 2001
Leahy, A., and I. Mathieson. "The Tomb of Nyankhnesut (Re)discovered." *The Journal of Egyptian Archaeology* 87 (2001), pp. 33–42, pls. IV–V.

Lembke, "Die Sphinxallee," 1998
Lembke, Katja. "Die Sphinxallee von Saqqara und ihre Werkstatt." *Mitteilungen des Deutschen Archäologischen Instituts Abteilung Kairo* 54 (1998), pp. 267–73.

Lessing and Vernus, *Dieux*, 1996
Lessing, E. and P. Vernus. *Dieux de l'Egypte*. Paris, 1996.

Lucas, *Materials*, 1989
Lucas, A. *Ancient Egyptian Materials and Industries*. 4th edition, rev. and enlarged by J. R. Harris. London, 1989.

M

Mahmoud, "Preliminary Report," 2002
Mahmoud, K. "Preliminary Report on the Tomb of Nyankhnesut at Saqqara: 1st Season of Excavation." *Göttinger Miszellen* 186 (2002), pp. 75–88.

Málek, *Cat*, 1993
Málek, Jaromir. *The Cat in Ancient Egypt*. London, 1993.

Málek, "Handsome Gift," 1999
Málek, J[aromir]. "A Handsome Gift for the Apis." *ISIMU* 2 (1999), pp. 401–10.

Málek, "Provenance," 1980
Málek, J[aromir]."The Provenance of Several Tomb-reliefs of the Old Kingdom." *Studien zur altägyptischen Kultur* 8 (1980), pp. 201–6.

Malek et al., *Topographical Bibliography*, 1999
Málek, Jaromir, Diana Magee, and Elizabeth Miles. *Topographical Bibliography of Ancient Egyptian Hieroglyphic Texts, Reliefs, and Paintings* VIII. Oxford, 1999.

Manniche, *Lost Tombs*, 1988
Manniche, L[ise]. *Lost Tombs. A Study of Certain Eighteenth Dynasty Monuments in the Theban Necropolis* (London 1988), pp. 9–11, Lepsius Tomb AG.

Manniche, *Sacred Luxuries*, 1999
Manniche, Lise. *Sacred Luxuries. Fragrance, Aromatherapy, and Cosmetics in Ancient Egypt*. Ithaca, 1999.

Martin, *Tomb of Horemheb*, 1989
Martin, G. T. *The Memphite Tomb of Horemheb, Commander-in-chief of Tutankhamun. Reliefs, Inscriptions, and Commentary*. London 1989.

McDonald, "Tall Tails," 2000
McDonald, A. "Tall Tails." In *Current Research in Egyptology*, eds. A. McDonald and C. Riggs. Oxford, 2000, pp. 75–81.

Meeks, "Le nom du dieu Bes," 1992
Meeks, Dimitri. "Le nom du dieu Bes et ses implications mythologiques." In *The Intellectual Heritage of Egypt*, ed. Ulrich Luft. Studia Aegyptiaca 14. Budapest, 14ff.

Menu, "Les ouchebtis," 2011
Menu, Bernadette. "Les ouchebtis de Neskhons, entre droit et croyances." *Egypte Nilotique et Méditerranéenne* 4 (2011), pp. 39–49.

MMA, *Age of the Pyramids*, 1999
Metropolitan Museum of Art. *Egyptian Art in the Age of the Pyramids*. New York, 1999.

Moret, *Rituel*, 1902
Moret, Alexandre. *Le rituel du culte divin journalier en Egypte*. Paris, 1902.

Morigi Govi et al., *Il sense*, 1990
Morigi Govi, Cristina, Silvo Curto, and Sergio Pernigotti. *Il sense dell'arte nell'antico Egitto*. Milan 1990.

N

Naville, *Ahnas el Medineh*, 1894
Naville, Edouard. *Ahnas el Medineh (Heracleopolis Magna)*. London, 1894.

Naville, *Season's Work*, 1891
Naville, Edouard. *The Season's Work at Ahnas and Beni Hasan. Special Extra Report*. London, 1891.

Needler, *Predynastic*, 1984
Needler, Winifred. *Predynastic and Archaic Egypt in The Brooklyn Museum*. Brooklyn, 1984.

Nenna et al., "Mobilier," 2003
Nenna, M.-D., et al. "Le mobilier non céramique et les terres cuites. Secteur 5 de la fouille du pont de Gabbari" In *Nécropolis* 2, 2, ed. J.-Y. Empereur and M.-D. Nenna. Cairo, 2003.

Newberry, *Funerary Statuettes*, 1930, 1937, and 1957
Newberry, Percy Edward. *Funerary Statuettes and Model Sarcophagi* I–III. Cairo, 1930, 1937, and 1957.

Newberry, "Pig," 1928
Newberry, P[ercy Edward]. "The Pig and the Cult of the Animal of Seth." *The Journal of Egyptian Archaeology* 14 (1928), pp. 211ff

Niwinski, *21st Dynasty Coffins*, 1988
Niwinski, Andrzej. *21st Dynasty Coffins from Thebes. Chronological and Typologcal Studies*. Mainz, 1988.

O

Osborn and Osbornova, *Mammals*, 1998
Osborn, Dale J., and Jana Osbornova. *The Mammals of Ancient Egypt*. Warminster, 1998.

P

Patch, *Reflections of Greatness*, 1990
Patch, Diana Craig. *Reflections of Greatness. Ancient Egypt at the Carnegie Museum of Natural History*. Pittsburgh, 1990.

Perrot, "Statuettes en ivoire," 1959
Perrot, Jean. "Statuettes en ivoire et autres objets en ivoire et en os provenant des gisements préhistoriques de la région de Béershéba." *Syria* 36, fasc. 1-2 (1959), pp. 8–13, with plates II–III.

Petrie, *Naqada and Ballas*, 1896
Flinders Petrie, W. M. *Naqada and Ballas*. London, 1896.

Posener, *Première Domination*, 1936
Posener,G. *La Première Domination Perse en Egypte. Recueil d'Inscriptions hiéroglyphiques*. Cairo, 1936.

Q

R

Redford, *Akhenaten*, 1984
Redford, Donald B. *Akhenaten. The Heretic King*. Princeton, 1984.

Reeves and Wilkinson, *Valley of the Kings*, 1996
Reeves, Nicholas, and R. Wilkinson. *The Complete Valley of the Kings*. London, 1996.

Roehrig, *Hatshepsut*, 2005
Roehrig, Catharine H., ed. *Hatshepsut, from Queen to Pharaoh*. New Haven, 2005.

Romano, "Bes-Image," 1980
Romano, James R. "The Origin of the Bes-Image." *The Bulletin of the Egyptological Seminar* 2 (1980), pp. 39–56.

S

Sauneron, *Le papyrus magique*, 1970
Sauneron, Serge. *Le papyrus magique illustré de Brooklyn*. Brooklyn, 1970.

Schneider, *Shabtis*, 1977
Schneider, Hans D. *Shabtis*, Part I–III (Leiden, 1977).

Schorsch, "Metal Statuary," 2007
Schorsch, Deborah. "The Manufacturing of Metal Statuary: 'Seeing the Workshops of the Temple.'" In *Gift for the Gods*, ed. Marsha Hill (New York, 2007), pp. 188–99.

Schorsch, "Seth," 2009
Schorsch, Deborah. "Seth, 'Figure of Mystery.'" *The 60th Annual Meeting of the American Research Center in Egypt. April 24–26, 2009. The Adolphus Hotel, Dallas, Texas* (San Antonio, 2009), pages 102–3.

Schoske, *Schönheit*, 1990
Schoske, S. *Schönheit. Abglanz der Göttlichkeit*. Munich, 1990.

Schulz, *Die Entwicklung*, 1992
Schulz, Regine. *Die Entwicklung und Bedeutung des kuboiden Statuentypus I and II*. Hildesheimer ägyptologische Beiträge 33. Hildesheim, 1992.

Schwentzel, *Images d'Alexandre*, 1999
Schwentzel, Chr.-G. *Images d'Alexandre et des Ptolémées*. Paris, 1999.

Shaw and Nicholson, *Dictionary*, 1995
Shaw, Ian, and Paul Nicholson. *British Museum Dictionary of Ancient Egypt*. London, 1995.

Strudwick, "12. Oil Tablet," 1988
Strudwick, N. "12. Oil Tablet." In *Mummies and Magic. The Funerary Arts of Ancient Egypt*. Exh. cat. Museum of Fine Arts. Boston, 1988, pp. 81–82.

T

Taylor, *Journey*, 2010
Taylor, John H., ed. *Journey through the Afterlife. Ancient Egyptian Book of the Dead*. London, 2010.

Teeter, *Before the Pyramids*, 2011
Teeter, Emily, ed. *Before the Pyramids. The Origins of Egyptian Civilization*. Chicago, 2011.

Tiradritti, *Harwa*, 1999
Tiradritti, F. *Il cammino di Harwa. L'uomo di fronte al mistero: L'Egitto*. Milan 1999.

Tomoum, *Sculptors' Models*, 2005
Nadja Samir Tomoum, *The Sculptors' Models of the Late and Ptolemaic Periods*. Trans. Brenda Siller. Cairo, 2005.

Traunecker, "Amenophis IV et Nefertiti," 1986
Traunecker, Claude. "Amenophis IV et Nefertiti. Le couple royal d'après les talattes du IXe pylone de Karnak." *Bulletin. Société d'Egyptologie Genève* 107 (1986), p. 34.

Traunecker, Coptos. *Hommes et dieux*, 1992
Traunecker, Claude. Coptos. *Hommes et dieux sur le parvis de Geb. Orientalia Louvaniensia* Analecta 43. Leuven, 1992.

U

Ucko, "Ivory Figures," 1865
Ucko, Peter J. "Anthropomorphic Ivory Figures from Egypt." *The Journal of the Royal Anthropological Institute of Great Britain and Ireland* 95, pt. 2 (July–December 1865), pp. 214–39.

Ucko, "The Predynastic Cemetery," 1967
Ucko, P[eter] J. "The Predynastic Cemetery N 7000 at Naga-ed-Der." *Chronique d'Egypte* 42/83 (1967), pp. 345–453.

V

Vandier, *Manuel*, 1952
Vandier, Jacques. *Manuel d'archéologie égyptienne. I. La préhistoire*. Paris, 1952.

Vanider, "Ouadjet," 1967
Vanider, Jacques. "Ouadjet et l'Horus léontocéphale de Bouto," *Fondation Piot. Monuments et Mémoire*. Paris, 1967, pp. 7–75.

Vernus and Yoyotte, *Bestaire*, 2005
Vernus, Pascal, and Jean Yoyotte, *Bestaire des Pharaons*. Paris. 2005.

te Velde, *Seth*, 1967
te Velde, Hermann. *Seth. God of Confusion*. Leiden, 1967.

van Dijk, *Objects*, 2006
van Dijk, Jacobus. *Objects for Eternity*. Mainz, 2006.

W

Wiese and Brodbeck, *Golden Beyond*, 2000
Wiese, A., and A. Brodbeck. *The Golden Beyond: Tutankhamun. Tomb Treasures from the Valley of the Kings*. Basel, 2000.

Williams, *New-York Historical Society*, 1924
Williams, C. R. *The New-York Historical Society. Catalogue of Egyptian Antiquities, Numbers 1–160. Gold and Silver Jewelry and Related Objects*. New York, 1924.

Winter, "Alexander der Grosse," 2005
Winter, Erich. "Alexander der Grosse als Pharao in ägyptischen Tempeln." In *Ägypten - Griechenland - Rom: Abwehr und Berührung*, ed. Herbert Beck, Peter C. Bol, and Maraike Bückling. Frankfurt, 2005, pp. 204–15.

X / Y

Z

Ziegler, "Les arts du métal," 1987
Ziegler, Christiane. "Les arts du métal." In *Tanis. L'or des pharaons*. Ministère des Affaires Etrangères/Association Française d'Action Artistique, Paris, 1987, pp. 85–101.

Ziegler, *Naissance de l'écriture*, 1996
Ziegler, C[hristiane]. *Naissance de l'écriture. Cunéiformes et hiéroglyphs*. Paris, 1982.

Ziegler, "Jalons," 1996
Ziegler, C[hristiane]. "Jalons pour une histoire de l'art égyptien: La statuaire du metal au Musée du Louvre." *Revue du Louvre* 1-1996, pp. 26–38.

Checklist of the Exhibition

1. *An Architectural False Door*
Dynasty VI, 2290–2155 BC
Painted limestone
Height 43 ½ in.
Inv. no. EG-254

2. *A Procession of Bearers of Funerary Offerings*
(suggested to have come from the Tomb of Ny-ankh-nesut)
Late Dynasty V or early Dynasty VI, 2450–2155 BC
Three painted limestone panels
Lengths: 37 ¼ in.; 20 ⅞ in.; 18 ½ in.
Inv. no. EG-125

3. *A Procession of Bearers of Funerary Offerings*
(suggested to have come from the Tomb of Ny-ankh-nesut)
Late Dynasty V or early Dynasty VI, 2450–2155 BC
Painted limestone
Length: 17 in.
Inv. no. EG-337

4. *Stela of Nefer-tchebau and His Wife, Ibi*
Dynasty X, 2134–2040 BC
Painted limestone
Height 32 ½ in.
Inv. no. EG-359

5. *Two Registers from an Elite Tomb*
Dynasty XI, 2134–1991 BC
Painted limestone
Height 18 ⅛ in.
Inv. no. EG-352

6. *Two Registers from an Elite Tomb*
Dynasty XII, 1991–1785 BC
Painted limestone
Height 22 ¾ in.
Inv. no. EG-351

7. *A Relief from the Tomb of Djuhty-nefer*
Dynasty XVIII, 1554–1305 BC
Limestone
Length 35 ⅞ in.
Inv. no. EG-196

8. *A Procession of Offering Bearers from an Elite Tomb*
Dynasty XVIII, 1554–1305 BC
Limestone
Length 29 ½ in.
Inv. no. EG-21

9. *A Relief from the Tomb of Nefer-hotep*
Late Dynasty XVIII, 1403–1305 BC
Painted limestone
Length 22 ⅛ in.
Inv. no. EG-271

10. *Offerings to the Aton*
Dynasty XVIII, The Amarna Period, Reign of Pharaoh Akhenaten, 1365–1349 BC
Limestone
Length 21 in.
Inv. no. EG-322

11. *A Round-Topped Funerary Stela Inscribed for Neheh*
Late Dynasty XVIII, 1554–1305 BC
Limestone
Height 36 ½ in.
Inv. no. EG-360

12. *A Round-Topped Funerary Stela*
Late Dynasty XVIII to early Dynasty XIX, 1350–1250 BC
Limestone
Height 21 ⅞ in.
Inv. no. EG-186

13. *A Stela Commemorating a Land Grant for the Maintenance of a Cult Statue in the Name of Pharaoh Rameses III*
Dynasty XX, Reign of Pharaoh Rameses III, 1193–1162 BC
Limestone
Height 32 ⅝ in.
Inv. no. EG-224

14. *A Relief Depicting a Pharaoh*
Dynasty XXX, 380–342 BC
Limestone
Height 6 ¼ in.
Inv. no. EG-366

15. *Fragment of a Temple Relief with the Names and Titles of Alexander the Great*
Macedonian Period, 323–305 BC
Painted limestone
Length 27 ½ in.
Inv. no. EG-162

16. *A Situla, or Ritual Pail*
Dynasty XXVI–XXX, 664–342 BC
Bronze
Height with handle extended 9 ⅜ in.
Inv. no. EG-232

17. *A Cippus, or Magical Stela, Representing Horus on the Crocodiles*
Early Ptolemaic Period, 305–200 BC
Crystalline alabaster
Height 7 in.
Inv. no. EG-77

18. *An Offering Table*
Ptolemaic Period, 305–30 BC
Granodiorite
Length 16 ⅛ in.
Inv. no. EG-17

19. *A Statuette of a Woman*
Predynastic Period, about 4000–3200 BC
Ivory
Height 7 ⅞ in.
Inv. no. EG-174

20. *A Statuette of a Male Figure*
Predynastic Period, 4000–3200 BC
Ivory
Height 9 5/16 in.
Inv. no. EG-175

21. *A Statuette of a Baker*
Dynasty VI, 2290–2155 BC
Painted limestone
Height 11 ⅝ in.
Inv. no. EG-343

22. *A Statuette of an Enthroned Member of the Elite*
Dynasty XII, 1991–1785 BC
Serpentine with traces of red polychromy
Height 10 in.
Inv. no. EG-252

23. *A Bust of an Elite Official*
Dynasty XII, 1991–1785 BC
Granodiorite
Height 10 ½ in.
Inv. no. EG-185

24. *A Bust of an Elite Male Member of Society*
Dynasty XXVI, 664–525 BC
Crystalline limestone, possibly marble
Height 9 ½ in.
Inv. no. EG-30

25. *A Statue of an Elite Member of Egyptian Society*
Dynasty XII, 1991–1785 BC
Basalt
Height 9 ½ in.
Inv. no. EG-29

26. *Mahu Presenting a Sun Stela*
Dynasty XVIII, Reign of Pharaoh Amenhotep II, 1439–1413 BC
Painted sandstone
Height 16 ½ in.
Inv. no. EG-44

27. *A Portrait of an Official*
Dynasty XVIII, 1554–1305 BC
Granodiorite
Height 10 ⅝ in.
Inv. no. EG-5

28. *The Pharaoh Rameses II, called Rameses The Great*
Dynasty XIX, Reign of Pharaoh Rameses II, 1290–1224 BC
Red granite
Height 28 ¼ in.
Inv. no. EG-133

29. *A Life-Sized Bust of a Nursing Woman*
Dynasty XXV–XXVI, 745–525 BC
Red granite
Height 22 ⅜ in.
Inv. no. EG-9

30. *A Sphinx*
Ptolemaic Period, 305–30 BC
Limestone with traces of red pigment
Length 26 ¾ in.
Inv. no. EG-126

31. *Statue of an Apis Bull*
Ptolemaic Period, 305–30 BC
Granodiorite
Length 22 ⅞ in.
Inv. no. EG-32

32. *A Colossal Royal Head*
Ptolemaic Period, 305–30 BC
Limestone with traces of red and blue polychromy and gilding
Height 15 ¾ in.
Inv. no. EG-355

33. *A Neo-Memphite Relief with Offering Bearers and Their Vases*
Dynasty XXV–XXVI, 745–525 BC
Limestone
Length 43 ½ in.
Inv. no. EG-291

34. *A Model Table*
Dynasty V–VI, 2450–2155 BC
Banded alabaster
Diameter 11 ⅞ in.
Inv. no. EG-222

35. *A Piriform Vessel*
Dynasty VI, 2290–2155 BC
Alabaster
Height 5 ¼ in.
Inv. no. EG-250

36. *Vase Inscribed for a Pharaoh Sesostris, with Lid*
Dynasty XII, 1991–1785 BC
Limestone
Height 3 3/16 in.
Inv. no. EG-168

37. *A Canaanite-Shaped Amphora Inscribed for Pharaoh Amenhotep II*
Dynasty XVIII, Reign of Pharaoh Amenhoep II, 1439–1413 BC
Alabaster with blue-paste pigment
Height 10 ¾ in.
Inv. no. EG-353

38. *A Jug*
Dynasty XVIII, 1554–1305 BC
Alabaster
Height 5 ¾ in.
Inv. no. EG-290

39. *A Pitcher*
Dynasty XVIII, 1554–1305 BC
Alabaster
Height 8 ½ in.
Inv. no. EG-311

40. *An Amphora*
Dynasty XVIII, 1554–1305 BC
Alabaster
Height 5 ¾ in.
Inv. no. EG-314

41. *A Miniature Thistle Vase*
Dynasty XVIII, 1554–1305 BC
Alabaster
Height 1 ¾ in.
Inv. no EG-373

42. *A Palette for the Seven Sacred Oils*
Dynasty V, 2450–2290 BC
Alabaster
Length 6 ¾ in.
Inv. no. EG-334

43. *A Cosmetic Spoon*
Dynasty XVIII, 1554-1305 BC
Alabaster
Length 9 ⅝ in.
Inv. no. EG-6

44. *A So-called Cosmetic Spoon in the Form of a Trussed Goose*
Dynasty XXV, 745–655 BC
Unglazed steatite (possibly indurate limestone)
Length 5 ⅝ in.
Inv. no. EG-345

45. *A Vase Inscribed with the Name of Rameses II*
Dynasty XIX, Reign of Pharaoh Rameses II, 1290–1224 BC
Alabaster, encaustic, and gilded
Height 8 ⅞ in.
Inv. no. EG-7

46. *An Amphora*
Dynasty XIX, 1305–1196 BC
Alabaster, encaustic, and wood
Height 16 ¼ in.
Inv. no. EG-323

47. *An Inscribed Vase*
Dynasty XIX–XX, 1305–1080 BC
Painted alabaster
Height 14 3/16 in.
Inv. no. EG-127

48. *A Stone Vessel*
Dynasty XIX–XX, 1305–1080 BC
Alabaster
Height 2 in.
Inv. EG-277

49. *A Vase with Duck-Headed Handles*
Dynasty XVIII–XX, 1554–1080 BC
Alabaster
Height 3 ¾ in.
Inv. no. EG-307

50. *An Inscribed Vase*
Dynasty XXI–XXV, 1080–655 BC
Alabaster
Height 19 in.
Inv. no. EG-308

51. *A Vase Inscribed for Darius I*
Dynasty XXVII, First Persian Period, Regnal Year 33 of King Darius I, 489 BC
Banded alabaster
Height 12 ⅛ in.
Inv. no. EG-356

52. *An Alabastron*
Ptolemaic Period, 305–30 BC
Alabaster
Height 9 ⅞ in.
Inv. no. EG-199

53. *A Scene of the Weighing the Heart from the So-called Book of the Dead*
Ptolemaic Period, 305–30 BC
Papyrus and black ink
Length 44 in.
Inv. no. EG-157

54. *A Necklace with Fifteen Amulets*
Dynasty XXVI–XXX, 664–342 BC
Lapis lazuli and gold
Length as modernly strung 13 ¾ in.
Inv. no. EG-285

55. *Part of a Funerary Broad Collar with Falcon-Headed Terminals*
Ptolemaic Period, 305–30 BC
Gold with inlays of semiprecious stones and glass paste
Length 17 ⅜ in.
Inv. no. EG-184

56. *An Amulet in the Form of a Duck Inscribed for Princess Neferu-re*
Dynasty XVIII, Time of Pharaoh Hatshepsut, 1490–1470 BC
Green chrysoprase (a form of chalcedony)
Length 13/16 in.
Inv. no. EG-166

57. *A Female Figure Lying on a Bed*
Dynasty XVIII–XX, 1554–1080 BC
Painted limestone
Length 6 ¼ in.
Inv. no. EG-303

58. *A Mirror*
Dynasty XVIII, 1554–1305 BC
Bronze
Height 8 1/16 in.
Inv. no. EG-401

59. *A "Pillow" from a Headrest*
Dynasty XVIII, 1550–1305 BC
Possibly cedar
Length 6 ¼ in.
Inv. no EG-206

60. *A Statuette of a Striding Elite Male*
Dynasty VII–XI, 2155–1991 BC
Copper-based alloy
Height 7 ⅜ in.
Inv. no. EG-246

61. *A Statuette of the God Seth*
Dynasty XIX, 1305–1196 BC
Gilded bronze
Height 6 ¾ in.
Inv. no. EG-251

62. *A Statuette of a Priestess*
Dynasty XXI–XXV, 1080–655 BC
Bronze inlaid with glass paste colored blue, red, and black
Height 11 5/8 in.
Inv. no. EG-179

63. *A Bes-Image Serving as a Finial for a Staff*
Dynasty XXI–XXV, 1080--BC
Bronze
Height 8 3/4 in.
Inv. no. EG-23

64. *An Amulet in the Form of a Scorpion*
Dynasty XXVI–Ptolemaic Period, 664–30 BC
Gold
Length 15/16 in.
Inv. no. EG-112

65. Statuette of Isis as a Scorpion Serving as the Finial for a Staff
Dynasty XXI–XXV, 1080–655 BC
Bronze
Height 4 3/8 in.
Inv. no. EG-205

66. *A Palm-Leaf Capital with a Finial in the Form of a Baboon*
Dynasty XXI–XXV, 1080–655 BC
Bronze
Height 6 5/8 in.
Inv. no EG-404

67. *A Statuette of Osiris Enthroned*
Dynasty XXI–XXV, 1080–656 BC
Bronze, originally lavishly inlaid
Height 10 1/2 in.
Inv. no. EG-301

68. *A Statuette of a Child God*
Dynasty XXV, 745–655 BC
Bronze and gold
Height 7 in.
Inv. no. EG-361

69. *A Statuette of a Kneeling Pharaoh in a White Crown*
Dynasty XXVI, 664–525 BC
Bronze
Height 6 1/2 in.
Inv. No. EG-12

70. *A Statuette Inscribed for a Pharaoh Named Psametik*
Dynasty XXVI, 664–525 BC
Bronze
Height 6 3/4 in.
Inv. no. EG-358

71. *A Statuette of the God Nefertum*
Dynasty XXVI, 664–525 BC
Bronze
Height 8 1/2 in.
Inv. no. EG-21

72. *A Monumental Image of the Goddess Wadjet Enthroned*
Dynasty XXVI–XXX, 664–BC
Bronze with limestone inlay and polychromy
Height 20 1/2 in.
Inv. no. EG-413

73. *A Statue of the Cat-Headed Goddess Bastet*
Dynasty XXX, 380–342 BC
Bronze and gold
Height 4 in.
Inv. no. EG-95

74. *The State God Amun and His Bas,*
or Multiple Manifestations of His Elemental Powers
Dynasty XXVI–Ptolemaic Period, 664–30 BC
Bronze inlaid with gold
Height 8 3/8 in.
Inv. no. EG-170

75. *A Statuette of a Mother Goddess Nursing Her Divine Son*
Dynasty XXVI–Ptolemaic Period, 664–30 BC
Bronze
Height 15 5/16 in.
Inv. no. EG-128

76. *Statuette of a Cow-Headed Goddess, Identified as Hesat*
Dynasty XXVI–Ptolemaic Period, 664–30 BC
Bronze with gold inlays
Height 11 7/16 in.
Inv. no. EG-31

77. *A Goddess with Her Aniconic Child*
Dynasty XXVI–Ptolemaic Period, 664–30 BC
Bronze
Height 9 5/16 in.
Inv. no. EG-90

78. *A Statuette of a Goose*
Dynasty XVIII, 1554–1305 BC
Gessoed and painted wood with bronze
Length 13 in.
Inv. no. EG-67

79. *A Head of a Ram*
Dynasty XXV–XXVII, 745–404 BC
Wood with black-and-white stone inlays and bronze additions
Length 7 5/8 in.
Inv. no. EG-28

80. *A Bes-Image*
Dynasty XXVI–Ptolemaic Period, 664–30 BC
Wood inlaid with ivory
Height 4 5/8 in.
Inv. no. EG-37

81. *The Goddess Taweret Offering Amun*
Dynasty XVIII–XX, 1554–1080 BC
Graywacke (schist)
Height 6 5/8 in.
Inv. no. EG-293

82. *The God Horus as a Falcon*
Dynasty XXI–XXV, 1080–655 BC
Bronze, originally with inlaid eyes
Height 18 in.
Inv. no. EG-187

83. *Statuette of a Ram*
Dynasty XXV–XXX, 745–342 BC
Bronze
Length 4 3/8 in.
Inv. no. EG-19

84. *A Statuette of a Striding Hippopotamus*
Dynasty XXVI, 664–525 BC
Gilded limestone
Length 3 ¾ in.
Inv. no. EG-191

85. *A Large Statuette of the Apis Bull*
Dynasty XXVI, 664–525 BC
Bronze with white-and-black stone inlays
Length 6 ⅜ in.
Inv. no. EG-371

86. *A Deity from Hermopolis*
Dynasty XXX–Ptolemaic Period, 382–30 BC
Plaster
Height 16 1/16 in.
Inv. no. EG-288

87. *A Deity from Hermopolis*
Dynasty XXX–Ptolemaic Period, 382–30 BC
Plaster
Height 16 1/16 in.
Inv. no. EG-289

88. *An Amulet of Pataikos*
Dynasty XXVI–Ptolemaic Period, 664–30 BC
Faience
Height 1 ⅝ in.
Inv. no. EG-188

89. *Amulet of a Ram-Headed Diety*
Dynasty XXVI–Ptolemaic Period, 664–30 BC
Faience
Height 1 ½ in.
Inv. no. EG-165

90. *A Queen Nursing Four Kittens*
Dynasty XXVI–Ptolemaic Period, 664–30 BC
Faience
Length 3 ⅛ in.
Inv. no. EG-143

91. *A Statuette of a Pregnant Queen*
Dynasty XXVI–Ptolemaic Period, 664–30 BC
Bronze
Length 3 ⅛ in.
Inv. no. EG-101

92. *A Shabti, or Funerary Statue*
Dynasty XVIII, 1554–1305 BC
Alabaster
Height 8 1/16 in.
Inv. no. EG-70

93. *A Shabti of Aa-wepwawet*
Early Dynasty XVIII, 1554–1403 BC
Wood, polychromy, gesso, and linen
Height 10 in.
Inv. no. EG-316

94. *A Shabti of Ray*
Dynasty XVIII, 1400–1305 BC
Alabaster with traces of blue paste inlays
Height 7 ¼ in.
Inv. no. EG-261

95. *A Shabti of Pharaoh Rameses IX*
Dynasty XX, Reign of Pharaoh Rameses IX, 1137–1119 BC
Wood
Height 12 ⅛ in.
Inv. no. EG-317

96. *Shabti of Hor-iret-iaah*
Dynasty XXVI, 664–525 BC
Faience
Height 6 ⅞ in.
Inv. no. EG-97

97. *Shabti of Tcha-en-hebu*
Dynasty XXVI, Time of Pharaoh Amasis, 570–526 BC
Faience
Height 7 ⅛ in.
Inv. no. EG-92

98. *A Shabti of the Nubian Pharaoh Senkamanisken*
Napatan Period, Reign of Pharaoh Senkamanisken, 643–623 BC
Serpentine
Height 6 ⅝ in.
Inv. no. EG-324

99. *Lid from an Anthropoid Sarcophagus*
Dynasty XXI–XXII, 1080–720 BC
Wood, gessoed and painted
Height 62 in.
Inv. no. EG-364

100. *A Sarcophagus for a Shrew*
Dynasty XXX–early Ptolemaic Period, 380–250/200 BC
Wood, gessoed and painted
Length 12 ½ in.
Inv. no. EG-370

101. *Lid of an Anthropiod Sarcophagus Inscribed for Hor-em-akhet*
Dynasty XXI–XXV, 1080–655 BC
Wood with inlays of white stone (alabaster or limestone) and blue glass
Height 80 ½ in.
Inv. no. EG-315

List of Artworks by Fondation Gandur Inventory Number

Inv. no. EG-2	Cat. 8	A Procession of Offering Bearers from an Elite Tomb
Inv. no. EG-5	Cat. 27	A Portrait of an Official
Inv. no. EG-6	Cat. 43	A Cosmetic Spoon
Inv. no. EG-7	Cat. 45	A Vase Inscribed with the Name of Rameses II
Inv. no. EG-9	Cat. 29	A Life-Sized Bust of a Nursing Woman
Inv. no. EG-12	Cat. 69	A Statuette of a Kneeling Pharaoh in a White Crown
Inv. no. EG-17	Cat. 18	An Offering Table
Inv. no. EG-19	Cat. 83	Statuette of a Ram
Inv. no. EG-21	Cat. 71	A Statuette of the God Nefertum
Inv. no. EG-23	Cat. 63	A Bes-Image Serving as a Finial for a Staff
Inv. no. EG-28	Cat. 79	A Head of a Ram
Inv. no. EG-29	Cat. 25	A Statue of an Elite Member of Egyptian Society
Inv. no. EG-30	Cat. 24	A Bust of an Elite Male Member of Society
Inv. no. EG-31	Cat. 76	Statuette of a Cow-Headed Goddess, Identified as Hesat
Inv. no. EG-32	Cat. 31	Statue of an Apis Bull
Inv. no. EG-37	Cat. 80	A Bes-Image
Inv. no. EG-44	Cat. 26	Mahu Presenting a Sun Stela
Inv. no. EG-67	Cat. 78	A Statuette of a Goose
Inv. no. EG-70	Cat. 92	A Shabti, or Funerary Statue
Inv. no. EG-77	Cat. 17	A Cippus, or Magical Stela, Representing Horus on the Crocodiles
Inv. no. EG-90	Cat. 77	A Goddess with Her Aniconic Child
Inv. no. EG-92	Cat. 97	Shabti of Tcha-en-hebu
Inv. no. EG-95	Cat. 73	A Statue of the Cat-Headed Goddess Bastet
Inv. no. EG-97	Cat. 96	Shabti of Hor-iret-iaah
Inv. no. EG-101	Cat. 91	A Statuette of a Pregnant Queen
Inv. no. EG-112	Cat. 64	An Amulet in the Form of a Scorpion
Inv. no. EG-125	Cat. 2	A Procession of Bearers of Funerary Offerings Suggested to Have Come from the Tomb of Ny-ankh-nesut
Inv. no. EG-126	Cat. 30	A Sphinx
Inv. no. EG-127	Cat. 47	An Inscribed Vase
Inv. no. EG-128	Cat. 75	A Statuette of a Mother Goddess Nursing her Divine Son
Inv. no. EG-133	Cat. 28	The Pharaoh Rameses II, called The Great
Inv. no. EG-143	Cat. 90	A Queen Nursing Four Kittens
Inv. no. EG-157	Cat. 53	A Scene of Weighing the Heart from the so-called Book of the Dead
Inv. no. EG-162	Cat. 15	Fragment of a Temple Relief with the Names and Titles of Alexander the Great
Inv. no. EG-165	Cat. 89	Amulet of a Ram-Headed Diety
Inv. no. EG-166	Cat. 56	An Amulet in the Form of a Duck Inscribed for Princess Neferu-re
Inv. no. EG-168	Cat. 36	Vase Inscribed for a Pharaoh Sesostris, with its Lid

Inv. no. EG-170	Cat. 74	The State God Amun and His Bas, or Multiple Manifestations of his Elemental Powers
Inv. no. EG-174	Cat. 19	A Statuette of a Woman
Inv. no. EG-175	Cat. 20	A Statuette of a Male Figure
Inv. no. EG-179	Cat. 62	A Statuette of a Priestess
Inv. no. EG-184	Cat. 55	Part of a Funerary Broad Collar with Falcon-Headed Terminals
Inv. no. EG-185	Cat. 23	A Bust of an Elite Official
Inv. no. EG-186	Cat. 12	A Round-Topped Funerary Stela
Inv. no. EG-187	Cat. 82	The God Horus as a Falcon
Inv. no. EG-188	Cat. 88	An Amulet of Pataikos
Inv. no. EG-191	Cat. 84	A Statuette of a Striding Hippopotamus
Inv. no. EG-196	Cat. 7	A Relief from the Tomb of Djuhty-nefer
Inv. no. EG-199	Cat. 52	An Alabastron
Inv. no. EG-205	Cat. 65	Statuette of Isis as a Scorpion Serving as a Staff's Finial
Inv. no. EG-206	Cat. 59	A "Pillow" from a Headrest
Inv. no. EG-222	Cat. 34	A Model Table
Inv. no. EG-224	Cat. 13	A Stela Commemorating a Land Grant for the Maintenance of a Cult Statue in the Name of Pharaoh Rameses III
Inv. no. EG-232	Cat. 16	A Situla, or Ritual Pail
Inv. no. EG-246	Cat. 60	A Statuette of a Striding Elite Male
Inv. no. EG-250	Cat. 35	A Piriform Vessel
Inv. no. EG-251	Cat. 61	A Statuette of the God Seth
Inv. no. EG-252	Cat. 22	A Statuette of an Enthroned Member of the Elite
Inv. no. EG-254	Cat. 1	An Architectural False Door
Inv. no. EG-261	Cat. 94	A Shabti of Ray
Inv. no. EG-271	Cat. 9	A Relief from the Tomb of Nefer-hotep
Inv. no. EG-277	Cat. 48	A Stone Vessel
Inv. no. EG-285	Cat. 54	A Necklace with Fifteen Amulets
Inv. no. EG-288	Cat. 86	Deity from Hermopolis
Inv. no. EG-289	Cat. 87	Deity from Hermopolis
Inv. no. EG-290	Cat. 38	A Jug
Inv. no. EG-291	Cat. 33	A Neo-Memphite Relief with Offering Bearers and their Vases
Inv. no. EG-293	Cat. 81	The Goddess Taweret Offering Amun
Inv. no. EG-301	Cat. 67	A Statuette of Osiris Enthroned
Inv. no. EG-303	Cat. 57	A Female Figure Lying on a Bed
Inv. no. EG-307	Cat. 49	A Vase with Duck-Headed Handles
Inv. no. EG-308	Cat. 50	An Inscribed Vase
Inv. no. EG-311	Cat. 39	A Pitcher
Inv. no. EG-314	Cat. 40	An Amphora
Inv. no. EG-315	Cat. 101	Lid of an Anthropiod Sarcophagus Inscribed for Hor-em-akhet

Inv. no. EG-316	Cat. 93	A Shabti of Aa-wepwawet
Inv. no. EG-317	Cat. 95	A Shabti of Pharaoh Rameses IX
Inv. no. EG-322	Cat. 10	Offerings to the Aton
Inv. no. EG-323	Cat. 46	An Amphora
Inv. no. EG-324	Cat. 98	A Shabti of the Nubian Pharaoh Senkamanisken
Inv. no. EG-334	Cat. 42	A Palette for the Seven Sacred Oils
Inv. no. EG-337	Cat. 3	Three Painted Limestone Panels
Inv. no. EG-343	Cat. 21	A Statuette of a Baker
Inv. no. EG-345	Cat. 44	A So-called Cosmetic Spoon in the Form of a Trussed Goose
Inv. no. EG-351	Cat. 6	Two Registers from an Elite Tomb
Inv. no. EG-352	Cat. 5	Two Registers from an Elite Tomb
Inv. no. EG-353	Cat. 37	A Canaanite-Shaped Amphora Inscribed for Pharaoh Amenhotep II
Inv. no. EG-355	Cat. 32	A Colossal Royal Head
Inv. no. EG-356	Cat. 51	A Vase Inscribed for Darius I
Inv. no. EG-358	Cat. 70	A Statuette Inscribed for a Pharaoh Named Psametik
Inv. no. EG-359	Cat. 4	Stela of Nefer-tchebau and His Wife, Ibi
Inv. no. EG-360	Cat. 11	A Round-Topped Funerary Stela Inscribed for Neheh
Inv. no. EG-361	Cat. 68	A Statuette of a Child God
Inv. no. EG-364	Cat. 99	Lid from an Anthropoid Sarcophagus
Inv. no. EG-366	Cat. 14	A Relief Depicting a Pharaoh
Inv. no. EG-370	Cat. 100	A Sarcophagus for a Shrew
Inv. no. EG-371	Cat. 85	A Large Statuette of the Apis Bull
Inv. no. EG-373	Cat. 41	A Miniature Thistle Vase
Inv. no. EG-401	Cat. 58	A Mirror
Inv. no. EG-404	Cat. 66	A Palm-Leaf Capital with a Finial in the Form of a Baboon
Inv. no. EG-413	Cat. 72	A Monumental Image of the Goddess Wadjet Enthroned

Index

A

B

C

N

O

P

Q

R

S

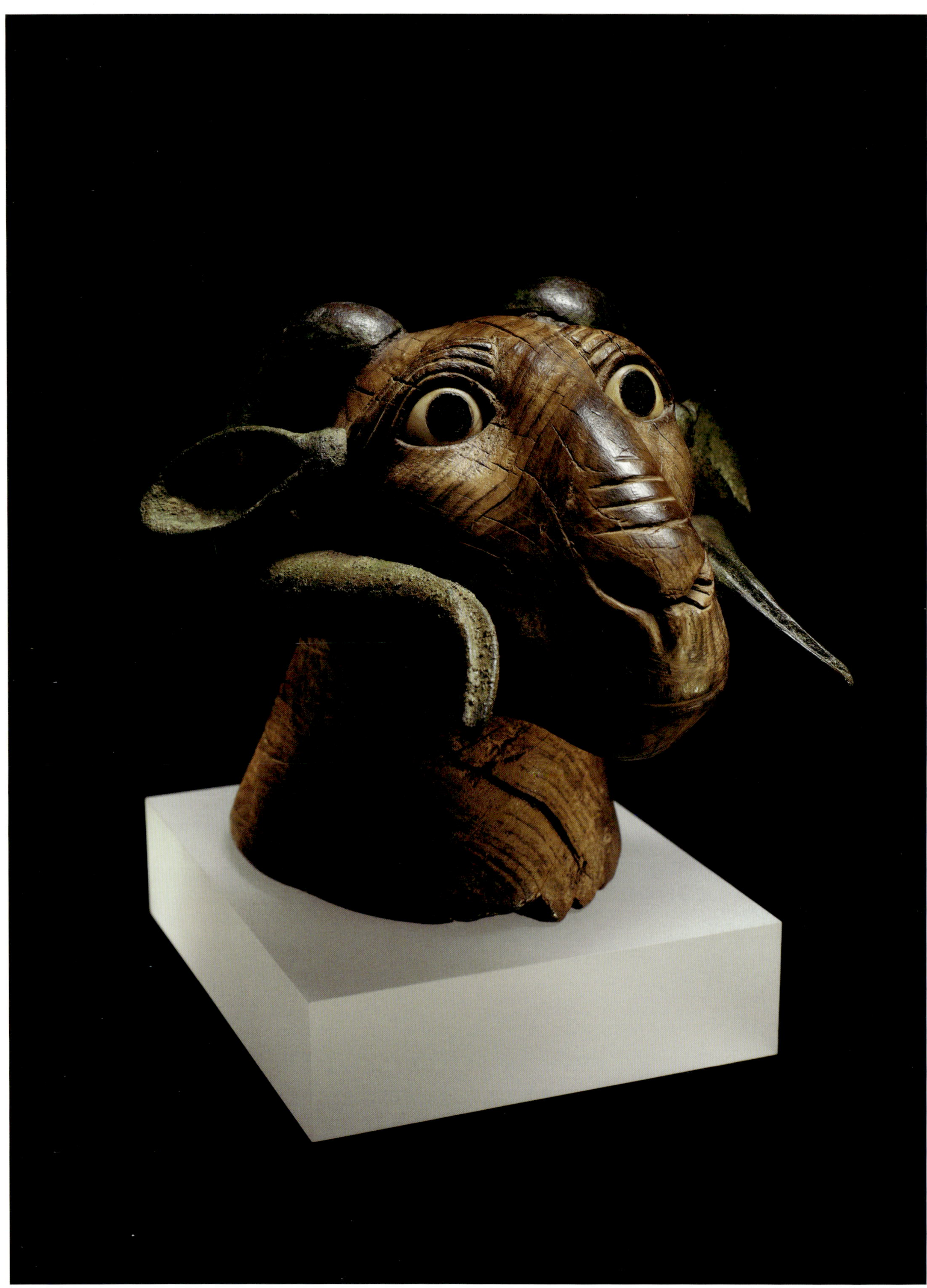

Cat. 79, page 202
A Head of a Ram

T

U

V

W

X

Y

Z

Photography and Illustration Credits

Photographs of all artworks in the exhibition from the Fondation Gandur pour l'Art © Sandra Pointet, with the exception of catalogue no. 38 © Darwin Media, Ltd.

Figures 3, 5, 7, 10, 11, 19–22, 26, and 27, courtesy of ALEA (Archive of Late Egyptian Art), a bibliographic and photographic archive maintained by Robert Steven Bianchi, Holiday, Florida.

Figure 1, p. 15
Egyptian Museum and Papyrus Collection, Berlin;
Bildarchiv Preussischer Kulturbesitz/Art Resource, New York.

Figure 3, p.16
Image supplied and permission by Tadashi Kikugawa.

Figure 4, p. 16
Hieroglyphs drawn by Robert Steven Bianchi.

Figure 6, p. 17
Photograph by Roxanne Sanders Wilson.

Figure 8, p. 21
© Brooklyn Museum of Art.

Figure 9, p. 21
Photograph by Shahrokh Shalchi.

Figure 12, p. 22
Photograph by David Pierce.

Figure 13, p. 23
Image copyright © The Metropolitan Museum of Art.

Figure 14, p. 24
Photograph by Barbara and Jack Mansfield.

Figure 16, p. 28
Photograph by Roxanne Sanders Wilson

Figure 17, p. 28
Courtesy of Thierry Benderitter/Osirisnet.net.

Figure 18, p. 30
© The Brooklyn Museum of Art

Figure 23, p. 36
Courtesy of Thierry Benderitter/Osirisnet.net.

Figure 24, p. 67
The Egypt Exploration Society, London.

Figure 25, p. 82
Line drawing by Julia Jarrett.

Figure 28, p. 207
Image copyright © The Metropolitan Museum of Art.